Attention: Selection, Awareness, a

Donald Broadbent (© Dr Nik Chmiel)

Attention: Selection, Awareness, and Control

A Tribute to Donald Broadbent

Edited by

ALAN BADDELEY
Director,
MRC Applied Psychology Unit,
Professor of Cognitive Psychology
and Fellow of Churchill College,
Cambridge

and

LAWRENCE WEISKRANTZ
Professor of Psychology,
University of Oxford
and
Fellow of Magdalen College,
Oxford

CLARENDON PRESS · OXFORD

Oxford University Press, Walton Street, Oxford OX2 6DP
Oxford New York
Athens Auckland Bangkok Bombay
Calcutta Cape Town Dar es Salaam Delhi
Florence Hong Kong Istanbul Karachi
Kuala Lumpur Madras Madrid Melbourne
Mexico City Nairobi Paris Singapore
Taipei Tokyo Toronto
and associated companies in
Berlin Ibadan

Oxford is a trade mark of Oxford University Press

Published in the United States
by Oxford University Press Inc., New York

© Alan Baddeley, Lawrence Weiskrantz, and the contributors listed on pp. ix–x, 1993

First published 1993
First published in paperback 1995

A catalogue record for this book is available from the British Library

Library of Congress Cataloging in Publication Data
Attention : selection, awareness, and control : a tribute to Donald
Broadbent / edited by A. Baddeley and L. Weiskrantz.
Includes bibliographical references and indexes.
1. Attention. 2. Broadbent, Donald E. (Donald Eric)
I. Broadbent, Donald E. (Donald Eric) II. Baddeley, Alan D., 1934–
III. Weiskrantz, Lawrence.
BF321.A84 1993 153.7'33–dc20 93-12363
ISBN 0 19 852374 2

Printed in Great Britain by
Antony Rowe Ltd, Chippenham, Wiltshire

Acknowledgements

Many persons helped to ensure the success of the meeting and to make this book a reality. In particular, Diane Berry and Dylan Jones played a very active, invaluable role in the organization from start to finish. Mrs Jane Brooks helped graciously with the administrative arrangements. The photograph of Donald Broadbent was kindly provided by Nik Chmiel. Financial support from Merck, Sharp, and Dohme, the Oxford Experimental Psychology Fund, and the MRC Applied Psychology Unit, is gratefully acknowledged. The biographical sketch of Donald Broadbent was reprinted (together with up-dating) from the article that appeared in the *American Psychologist*, January 1976, pp. 53–6, to mark the occasion of his receiving an APA Distinguished Scientific Contribution Award for 1975. We are grateful to the American Psychological Association for permission to reproduce it.

1993   A.B.
L.W.

Contents

Contributors

Professor Alan Baddeley, MRC Applied Psychology Unit, 15 Chaucer Road, Cambridge CB2 2EF, UK

Dr Dianne Berry, Department of Psychology, University of Reading, Earley Gate, Whiteknights, Reading RG6 2AL, UK

Dr Paul Burgess, Department of Psychology, University College, London, Gower Street, London WC1E 6BT, UK

Dr John Driver, Department of Experimental Psychology, University of Cambridge, Downing Street, Cambridge CB2 3EB, UK

Dr John Duncan, MRC Applied Psychology Unit, 15 Chaucer Road, Cambridge CB2 2EF, UK

Professor G. Robert J. Hockey, Department of Psychology, University of Hull, Hull HU6 7RX, UK

Professor Larry L. Jacoby, McMaster University, Department of Psychology, 1280 Main Street West, Hamilton, Ontario, Canada L8S 4K1

Professor Dylan Jones, School of Psychology, University of Wales, PO Box 901, Cardiff CF1 3YG, UK

Dr Peter McLeod, Department of Experimental Psychology, University of Oxford, South Parks Road, Oxford OX1 3UD, UK

Professor Neville Moray, University of Illinois at Urbana-Champaign, Department of Mechanical and Industrial Engineering, 140 Mech. Engineering Building, MC-244, 1206 West Green Street, Urbana, Illinois 61801, USA

Dr Michael I. Posner, Institute of Cognitive and Decision Sciences, University of Oregon, Eugene, Oregon 97403, USA

Professor Patrick M. A. Rabbitt, Age and Cognitive Performance Research Centre, University of Manchester, Oxford Road, Manchester M13 9PL, UK

Professor James Reason, Department of Psychology, University of Manchester, Oxford Road, Manchester M13 9PL, UK

William Revelle, Professor and Chair, Department of Psychology, Northwestern University, Evanston, Illinois 60201, USA

Dr Ste-Marie, McMaster University, Department of Psychology, 1280 Main Street West, Hamilton, Ontario, Canada L8S 4K1

Professor Dr Andries F. Sanders, Vrije Universiteit, Faculteit der Psychologie, De Boelelaan 1111, 1081 HV Amsterdam, The Netherlands

Dr L. Henry Shaffer, Department of Psychology, Washington Singer Laboratories, University of Exeter, Exeter EX4 4QG, UK

Professor Tim Shallice, Department of Psychology, University College, London, Gower Street, London WC1E 6BT, UK

Dr Andrew Smith, Director, Health Psychology Research Unit, School of Psychology, University of Wales College of Cardiff, PO Box 901, Cardiff CF1 3YG, UK

Dr John D. Teasdale, MRC Applied Psychology Unit, 15 Chaucer Road, Cambridge CB2 2EF, UK

Dr Jeffrey P. Toth, McMaster University, Department of Psychology, 1280 Main Street West, Hamilton, Ontario, Canada L8S 4K1

Dr Anne Treisman, Department of Psychology, University of California, Berkeley, California 94720, USA

Professor Endel Tulving, Tanebaum Chair in Cognitive Neuroscience, Rotman Research Institute of Baycrest Centre, Toronto, Ontario, Canada M6A 2E1

Professor Lawrence Weiskrantz, Department of Experimental Psychology, University of Oxford, South Parks Road, Oxford OX1 3UD, UK

Donald Broadbent

D onald Broadbent was born on 6 May 1926 in Birmingham, England. He normally identifies himself as Welsh, however, partly on the grounds of ancestry and partly because his home was in Wales throughout adolescence. Originally he was interested in the natural sciences, and therefore when he entered the Royal Air Force (RAF) in 1944 he took the route that involved taking a compressed short course in engineering, largely aeronautical, at Pembroke College, Cambridge. He had already become somewhat unhappy at the prospects for research in physical science, feeling that the frontier of knowledge lay rather remote from undergraduate work and only very few could reach it.

The time spent out of academic life drew to Broadbent's attention a number of practical problems in personnel selection and equipment design, and he gradually learned that a scientific approach to these problems was not only possible but was being actively pursued. His flying training was carried out in the United States. There he found that the subject of psychology, then unheard of by most young people in Britain, was quite widely studied on the other side of the Atlantic. Therefore, when peace made many pilots redundant for flying duties, he entered the personnel selection branch of the RAF, and worked for a time in their Vocational Advice Service. On returning to Cambridge he declared himself firmly as intending to study psychology. His superiors in Pembroke were surprised and properly cautious, because they had every reason to suspect letters announcing such an intention mailed from the Western Desert. But they yielded, and from 1947 to 1949 he read experimental psychology in the department of Professor Sir Frederick Bartlett at Cambridge. By sheer accident, this was a highly suitable place; the department was well established, with an orientation firmly toward the natural sciences rather than philosophy, and a strong applied slant. The major influence was Bartlett, but there was a strong attachment to the then-novel 'cybernetic' ideas of K. J. W. Craik, who had died before Broadbent entered the department, but who left manuscripts outlining the aim of understanding human nature in terms of control systems. The department was in a ferment of excitement applying these ideas to practical problems and to general psychological theory.

When Broadbent got his bachelor's degree in 1949 he had intended to seek a job in industry, but the nearest thing available was a post with the Royal Navy studying the possible effects of noise on performance. This job was originally intended to be at one of the naval laboratories. Administratively, however, the pay came through the Applied Psychology Unit of the Medical Research Council (MRC), which was based in Bartlett's department and of which Craik had been the first director. When the naval laboratory originally intended for this work discovered that it would involve very loud noises disturbing to all within earshot, the job simply stayed in Cambridge, and so did Broadbent. From an employment point of view the rest of his career is easy: he worked in the Applied Psychology Unit for 25 years, until 1974.

Between 1949 and 1958 Broadbent worked on two main lines, chiefly for the Royal Navy. One of these was the problem of noise. Many excellent studies had shown that effects of noise could not be found on psychological tests of the kind then current, and indeed such studies continue until the present day. The aim of the new project, therefore, was to see whether effects would appear on tasks that had little in common with traditional psychological tests: for example, would noise affect the vigilance tasks invented by N. H. Mackworth in 1943 to tackle an RAF problem? The tests finally chosen did show effects. But they were deliberately long and monotonous, and needed to be used over and over again. Consequently, Broadbent was also employed on problems arising from gunnery and air-traffic control systems, in which many channels of speech communication were delivered to the same listener. This problem had the merit of allowing short and quick experiment, so that it could be pursued during intervals in the slow plod of building up data on the effects of noise.

The work on communication systems drew attention to the fact, then neglected by psychologists, that most people spend their lives surrounded by numerous stimuli, and yet cannot react or report discriminatively to most of them. The new language of information and control was highly appropriate to building models of systems that show 'attention' in this way, and predictions from these models were also useful in fresh practical situations. For example, the studies of noise also showed disruption of attention. Taking the two principles that a selective device is located early in the nervous system and that it is preceded by a temporary buffer store, Broadbent proceeded enthusiastically to apply these principles widely throughout psychology. In 1958 he published *Perception and communication* as an attempt to show the virtue of the approach to psychology through information-processing.

In the same year (1958) Mackworth emigrated to North America, leaving the Applied Psychology Unit without a director. When Bartlett retired in 1952 the Unit had moved from the University of Cambridge to separate premises in the same city. There were few other places where engineering psychologists could work, and Broadbent had no tenure: he was therefore highly relieved when offered the directorship, even though this meant the administrative work of running what was at the time one of the largest psychological laboratories in Europe. In considerable compensation, he acquired as a research assistant M. H. P. Gregory, who was later to become his wife.

Scientifically, the next step was to deal with two problems that arose in about 1960. First, it turned out that the stimulus most likely to receive attention was often determined by content or meaning, and not merely by simple physical characteristics. This suggested paradoxically that the content of the stimulus was analysed before the decision to do so was reached. On the other hand, the effects of noise and other stresses could not be treated merely as distraction (for example, because effects of noise were linked specifically with doing the wrong thing rather than with failing to do anything at all). These difficulties forced a view of the perceptual system that was less determinate and more comparable to a statistical decision. The degree of bias in favour of some percepts rather than others could be used to explain the sensitivity to events with particular meanings, and the occurrence of commissive errors in noise could be interpreted as a general change in bias resulting from arousal. On the other hand, concentration on a particular source of stimulation appeared as a change in the evidence used for statistical decision. This new synthesis appeared as *Decision and stress* in 1971, and the bulk of this book revealed the extent to which work on these problems had expanded since *Perception and communication* was written.

Throughout this time, a good deal of effort was going into a 'front-office' role of defending applied psychology in general and the Unit in particular, in a culture that was still (outside the MRC) somewhat hostile. Apart from a number of committees for the Royal Navy and the RAF, Broadbent served on the Biological Research Board of the Medical Research Council, on the Social Science Research Council, as Recorder and later President of the Psychology Section of the British Association for the Advancement of Science, as President of the British Psychological Society and of the Experimental Psychology Society, and as a Council member of the Ergonomics Research Society. He was also Chairman of the Scientific Committee of St Dunstan's (the organization for blinded British veterans) and a Member of the Scientific Consultative Group of the BBC. Initially these efforts were merely a holding operation, and by 1966 the number of scientists in the Unit was only just over half the number it contained when Broadbent first joined it. In the mid-1960s, however, there was a sudden explosion of interest in psychology in British universities, combined with a well-deserved recognition of the achievements of Broadbent's colleagues at the Applied Psychology Unit. Several of them became professors elsewhere, and one, Alan Baddeley, returned to the directorship of the Unit in 1974. Broadbent himself, never having obtained a Ph.D., submitted his papers to Cambridge University for a Doctorate of Science in 1965 and was successful. In 1968 he became a Fellow of the Royal Society, and in 1971 a Foreign Associate of the US National Academy of Sciences. He has given the Pillsbury Lecture (Cornell), the Fitts Lectures (Michigan), the Myers Lecture (British Psychological Society), and the William James Lectures (Harvard). He is also a Fellow of the Human Factors Society and of the Acoustical Society of America.

In 1974 he and his wife left the Applied Psychology Unit, to concentrate more vigorously on their own personal research interests. The MRC provided salaries and rented laboratory space for them from the University of Oxford. In the same year Broadbent became a Fellow of Wolfson College, Oxford, and he also received a CBE. In 1975 he received the Distinguished Scientific Contribution Award from the American Psychological Association, and in 1978 the Distinguished Foreign Colleague Award from the Human Factors Society.

In Oxford, Broadbent continued his research on noise, working with Dylan Jones and Andrew Smith. He and his wife also started three new lines of research, which were carried through until their retirement. The first was to look at cognitive strategies in relation to work. This research developed into a long programme of studies which investigated the effects of stress in industry, particularly whether differences in medical symptoms could be found as a result of different jobs. Initially, cross-sectional studies were carried out with car-factory workers and electricity workers, but more recently longitudinal studies have been conducted with supermarket employees and volunteers from General Practice.

The second line of work involved an extensive series of laboratory studies on attention and memory. Working with Susan Gathercole, Peter FitzGerald, and Tony Gillie, the primary aim was to provide a better account of strategic differences in attention and memory. The final major line of research that Broadbent and his wife started was to look at the control of long-range behaviour and relate this to cognitive strategies. Initially, this involved watching people play business games at Henley Management College, but this soon developed into a long series of laboratory studies on implicit and explicit learning in the control of complex systems. Much of this work was done in collaboration with Dianne Berry.

Whilst extending his research interests, Broadbent continued to sit on a number of national committees. During the 1980s he chaired the SERC Image Interpretation committee and the Joint Research Council Committee on Cognitive Science/Human–Computer Interaction. He also chaired the Advisory Committee on the Safety of Nuclear Installations Study Group on Operator–Plant Interface. He has received Honorary Doctorates from the University of Southampton, the University of York, the University of Loughborough, the City University, the Free University of Brussels, Cranfield University, the University of Wales, the University of Leuven, and the University of Dundee.

In Memoriam

Donald Broadbent died suddenly on April 10, 1993. This deeply saddening event took place as this book was about to go into production. The authors all spoke at the meeting, and wrote, with his active participation in mind, and we do not wish to change that image in any way. His death was tragic, but his influence will long continue to be alive.

April 1993   A.B.
                                                             L.W.

I. Perception: selection and attention

Introduction

Peter McLeod

Why do some events come to be reported, remembered or to control action, while others do not? Donald Broadbent's most famous contribution to the solution of this question appeared in *Perception and communication*. He proposed that a peripheral selective filter would allow stimuli with a particular physical characteristic to gain an advantage in processing over those which did not possess it. Two of the papers in this section discuss how selection by physical characteristic might be performed. In Treisman's model of visual search it is achieved by inhibition from feature maps of locations on the 'master-map' of stimulus information which do not contain the target feature. McLeod and Driver examine one particular form of filtering, the selection of stimuli which share a common movement characteristic. They suggest that the ability to filter by movement arises, not because of the action of a physical entity, the filter, but as a result of the fact that moving stimuli are represented much better than stationary ones in cortical areas such as MT.

In *Decision and stress* Broadbent added two further selective mechanisms, pigeon-holing and categorization. These accounted for selection by the biasing of central mechanisms towards one outcome rather than another. A number of the papers discuss situations where such effects can be seen in operation. Treisman shows that expected objects can receive preferential treatment in visual search. She models this observation by allowing object files (the source of information about likely objects) to bias the master-map of stimulus information in the same way that feature maps bias the master-map to permit filtering. Duncan reports that two decisions about one object can be made as easily as one, while two decisions about two different objects produce a performance decrement compared to either decision alone. This suggests a bias of the information-processing system towards the processing of objects. One question raised by this conclusion is the nature of the process which can unify the different sources of information about an object given that these will be distributed across a range of physically independent extrastriate regions. Jones shows the influence of another central bias—the auditory system's predisposition for parsing auditory streams as if they were speech. An irrelevant auditory input will interfere with a concurrent visual short-term memory task if it has temporal characteristics which result in its being segmented into speech-like objects, even if it is not speech.

In *The Maltese Cross* Broadbent emphasized that the relation between central and peripheral information-processing structures was one of reciprocal interaction rather than a serial flow of information from input to output. Duncan suggests that this reciprocity can be seen in the relation between selection and current goal; the current goal influences what the filter will be set to select, but the input might also result in a change of goal. He looks for a common mechanism responsible for goal-setting in a variety of different contexts with data from patients with frontal-lobe damage, dual-task performance in normals, and studies of general intelligence. The *Maltese Cross* model also emphasizes the importance of subjective strategies in information-processing. This point is developed in Sanders' paper, which shows that the timing of saccadic eye-movements and the length of the fixations between them are under strategic control.

ONE

The perception of features and objects

Anne Treisman

Selective attention was one of Donald Broadbent's earliest interests. He emphasized its implications for our view of the brain as an active, information-processing system rather than a passive 'switch-board' (Broadbent 1958). His approach was to start with general questions, excluding as broad a range of possible models as possible with each set of experiments, and so narrowing down to a functional flow-chart of the operations underlying performance. This general view of our goal, as well as his more specific ideas on attention, has inspired and guided my research since I was a graduate student. It still seems to me to be the best strategy for experimental psychologists, and the most likely to lead to testable mappings on to possible neural systems in the brain. In recent years, I have tried to apply it in exploring the visual perception of features and objects and the role of attention in creating the integrated and organized representations that we consciously experience.

Some years ago I summarized a set of findings from experiments on visual search, texture segregation, and the perception of brief, masked displays (Treisman and Gelade 1980). The results seemed to fit coherently together: search for feature-defined targets is parallel, but search for a conjunction of features seems to require attention. Texture segregation is easy when based on simple features, but difficult or impossible when the boundaries are defined only by conjunctions. Cueing attention in advance helps us to identify a conjunction much more than it helps with any of its features. When attention is overloaded, illusory conjunctions are formed, and so on. These findings fit nicely together to support what I labelled feature-integration theory, summarized in the framework shown in Fig. 1.1 (Treisman 1988). The claims were that simple features are registered in parallel across the visual field, in a number of specialized subsystems. Information from the resulting feature maps is localized and recombined to specify objects through the use of focused attention, scanning serially through a master-map of locations and giving access to the features currently occupying the attended location. These are then integrated to form a representation of the object in that location.

But of course simple stories never stay that way. We can either complicate and stretch them to fit new discoveries, or we can scrap

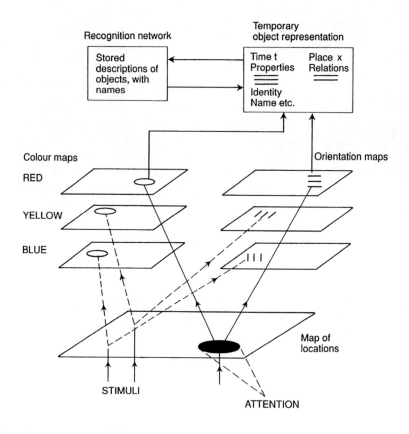

FIG. 1.1. Framework proposed to account for the role of selective attention in feature integration. (Reprinted from Treisman (1988). Copyright 1988 by Lawrence Erlbaum Associates.)

them. People usually start with the first alternative before moving to the second, and I am no exception. In this paper, I will select a few of the more interesting developments and see whether I can update this picture so that it will accommodate them without bursting at the seams. I will try to group the new findings and ideas under five main headings, as follows: (1) What *are* features anyway?; (2) Divided attention vs. inattention vs. pre-attention; (3) The coding of locations and conjunctions; (4) Object files and object selection; and (5) Selection for action.

FEATURES

So what *are* features anyway? Back in 1980, they were the colours, orientations, and shapes on my ink-drawn tachistoscope cards. That saved me some difficult decisions about whether they are the features of the 2D image as coded by retinal receptors, or the features of real-world, three-dimensional objects. I have always insisted that this is an empirical question to be answered by converging operations designed to diagnose the functional features in the visual dictionary. Functional features are defined, in terms of the theory, as properties for which we have evolved or acquired separate sets of detectors responding in parallel across the visual scene. The detectors need not be individual neurones; they could be groups or hierarchies of cells so long as they respond directly to their particular properties without attentional control and without (much) crosstalk from other functional detectors.

Among the behavioural diagnostics I suggested were pop-out in search, the ability to mediate texture segregation, and the possibility of recombination in illusory conjunctions. For the features I tried out, these operations did converge quite well. But many questions remained open. I will briefly describe some recent findings and their implications.

The first concerned the coding of separable features *within* dimensions—for example different colours or different orientations. When I drew my picture of the mind, I put in three feature maps for each dimension, mainly because drawing fifty was beyond my artistic abilities. But I now like the idea that the visual system uses 'coarse coding' (Hinton 1981), representing different values on each dimension by ratios of activity in just a few separate populations of detectors (for example, red, green, blue, and yellow; or vertical, horizontal, and left and right diagonal). If this is correct, it suggests that attention should be needed not only to integrate features *across* dimensions (for example, colour with orientation) but also to integrate them *within* dimensions (blue and red to make purple; vertical and diagonal to make a more steeply tilted orientation). I should then predict serial search for these new within-dimension conjunctions, and the risk of illusory conjunctions when focused attention is prevented. Figure 1.2(a) shows a display I used both in a search task and to test for illusory conjunctions when it was flashed briefly and masked (Treisman 1991). The target is a purple bar tilted 27° left among pink vertical bars and blue bars tilted 63° left. In both cases, I compared performance with a target with standard values (blue vertical among purple and turquoise tilted bars, with similarity relations matched: Fig. 1.2(b)). The standard target

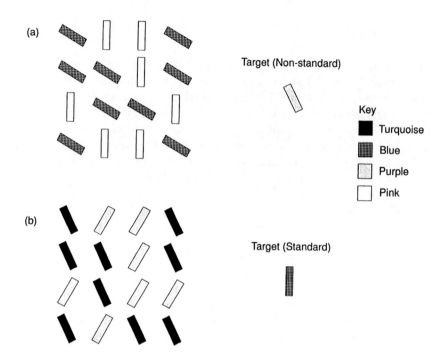

FIG. 1.2. Examples of displays used to test search for targets defined either (a) by 'non-standard' colours and orientations, which may be coded as conjunctions of coarsely coded features within the dimensions of colour and orientation, or (b) by 'standard' colours and orientations, which may have their own specialized feature maps.

should be less dependent on conjoining two coarse-coded values. In fact, the non-standard 'conjunction' target gave much steeper search functions (Fig. 1.3) and far more illusory conjunctions than the standard targets (26 per cent compared to 6 per cent). So maybe the few discrete examples of feature maps in my figure are not, after all, a caricature, but a serious proposal.

The second discovery was made in a study with Cavanagh and Arguin (Cavanagh *et al.* 1990). Our results seem to require a feature hierarchy as well as parallel feature modules. We distinguished surface-defining features from shape-defining features. Shape is characterized by the spatial layout of discontinuities in any one or more surface features. For example, we can create a horizontal bar (Fig. 1.4) whose boundaries are defined by changes in brightness, colour, stereoscopic depth, texture, or direction of motion. We showed that simple *shape-*

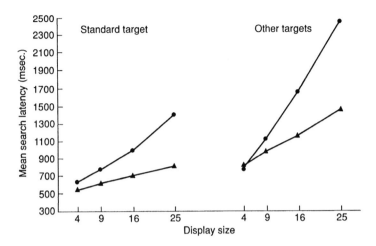

FIG. 1.3. Search latencies in search for a 'standard' target or for 'non-standard' targets.

defining features like orientation and size could be detected in parallel within at least five different *surface*-defining media—luminance, colour, relative motion, texture, and stereoscopic depth. The displays contained bars differing in orientation or dots differing in size, where the elements were defined by discontinuities in each of these five media. When the differences in size or orientation were sufficiently

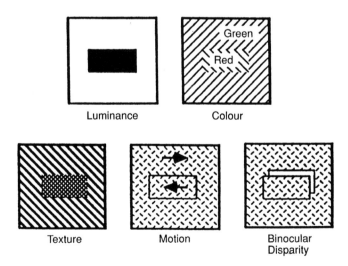

FIG. 1.4. Rectangles defined by discontinuities in various surface-defining media.

discriminable, they gave flat search functions in every case. Interestingly, we found that some of the same coding principles apply within all these media: in particular each showed a search asymmetry between the standard feature (vertical) and the deviating feature (tilted). Luminance and colour are first-order features defining points whose spatial, temporal, or interocular relations in turn can define second-order discontinuities. Thus we have a hierarchy of possible shape-defining media, with features of shape coded either separately within each, or perhaps in some subsequent pooled representation.

Finding constraints on perception is as important as finding capacities. My students and I have recently found examples of media which do *not* create directly detectable features. Kathy O'Connell and I defined orientations by the virtual lines connecting pairs of dots (Fig. 1.5).

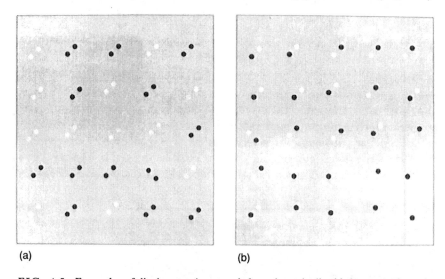

(a)   (b)

FIG. 1.5. Examples of displays testing search for a dot pair tilted left among dot pairs tilted right, where the direction of contrast within pairs is (a) the same, and (b) different. (Note that the grey shown here is lighter than the one actually used, which was about equally different from the white and the black dots.)

When both dots in a pair share the same direction of contrast (both dark on a light background or the reverse, as in the display on the left), a unique orientation pops out of a display just as it does for lines, bars, or edges. However, if each dot pair consists of one black and one white dot on an intermediary grey background (as in the display on the right of Figure 1.5), search is slow and apparently serial (O'Connell and Treisman, submitted).

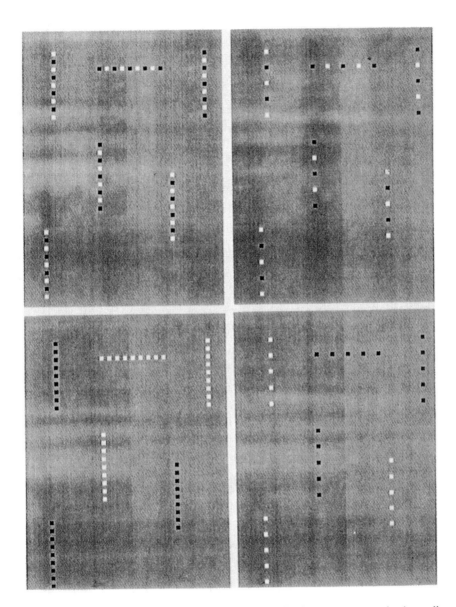

FIG. 1.6. Displays testing search for a vertically oscillating target among horizontally oscillating targets, where the stimuli in each set either share the same direction of contrast or alternate in contrast. The figure shows all the dots simultaneously, but in the actual displays they were presented sequentially, giving an impression of motion. The upper displays show short-range motion and the lower displays show long-range motion.

Similarly, we can create apparent motion by presenting dots success-ively in different locations. If the spatial and temporal separations are small enough to activate the short-range motion system, a vertically oscillating set of dots will pop out of a horizontally oscillating back-ground (Ivry and Cohen 1990). However, Todd Horowitz and I showed that if successive dots within an oscillating sequence alternate in contrast relative to a grey background, so that if one is black the next is white and vice versa (Fig. 1.6, right-hand displays), again search becomes serial rather than parallel. We found that detecting *long*-range motion, when the dots are separated by at least three dot-widths, requires attention whether the dots share the same direction of contrast or whether they alternate in direction of contrast across successive locations.

Putting these studies together, it seems that there may be two separate luminance media, (darker and lighter contrast), each support-ing parallel processing. When elements defined in separate media must be combined to generate either apparent motion or the orientation of a virtual line, we have a conjunction problem, and focused attention is required.

The third set of feature findings are the recent discoveries of three-dimensional properties that also pop out. Enns (1990; Enns and Rensink 1990) used geometric stimuli suggesting cubes that differed either in their three-dimensional orientation or in the apparent direc-tion of illumination (Fig. 1.7, right-hand display). Although from the

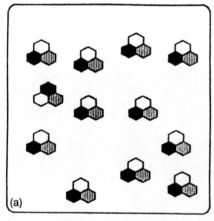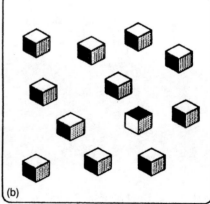

FIG. 1.7. Displays used by Enns and Rensink to demonstrate pop-out in search for targets defined by the direction of lighting (b), but not for target patterns of matched complexity that cannot be interpreted as three-dimensional figures (a). (From Enns and Rensink 1992.)

point of view of the retinal image, these are relatively complex conjunctions of lines and luminance, the unique cube could be detected in parallel, whereas the corresponding target in the flat display on the left in Fig. 1.7 could not. Similarly, Ramachandran (1988) showed good parallel segregation based on differences in shape from shading, with a group of convex eggs standing out clearly from a background of egg-shaped hollows. Only the spatial pattern of shading defined the target.

This research suggests that the features that determine grouping and pop-out are features that specify three-dimensional objects in the real world rather than features of the retinal image. Certainly, the location map in my model must represent real-world locations rather than retinal ones, since subjects make eye and head movements in scanning displays. Broadbent and Broadbent (1990) have also shown that viewing distance has little effect on the interference from flanking distractors, suggesting that attention operates on real rather than retinal separation. The visual system seems from the earliest stages to be bent on representing the real world around us, detecting the particular combinations and correlations of physical dimensions that specify object properties, such as convexity, transparency, and occlusion, as well as surface colour, depth, and motion. Some may be directly sensed: for example, Lehky and Sejnowski (1988) suggest that simple cells in VI are actually specialized to sense shape from shading rather than line or bar orientations. However, 3D properties can often be *interpreted* only for a particular setting of parameters (for example, light from above, a tilted surface, forward motion of the observer). So some combination of information is required before the elementary features yield a veridical description of the scene. Why would these stimuli not count as conjunctions requiring focused attention?

DIVIDED ATTENTION VS. PREATTENTION VS. INATTENTION

A possible solution depends on a distinction between divided attention and preattention. In my earlier papers, I followed Neisser (1967) in attributing feature pop-out and texture segregation to '*pre*attentive processing'. However, in applying the distinction to explain performance, I now prefer to contrast *divided* attention with focused attention (Treisman and Gormican 1988). Preattentive processing cannot directly affect responses or experience; it is an inferred stage of early vision, which I attribute to the separate feature modules. Before any conscious visual experience is possible, some form of attention is required, since information from the different feature maps must be combined. We can never be aware of a free-floating orientation, colour, or shape. What varies across tasks is how broadly or narrowly focused the attention window is. Thus I assume a dichotomy between preattentive and attentive processing levels, and a continuum between divided and focused attention, as the size of the attention window narrows down or spreads wide. Texture segregation, visual pop-out, and detection of global alignment and shape (see, for example, Donnelly *et al.* 1991) are done with a broad setting of the attention window, integrating feature maps at a global level. Accurate localization and conjoining of features for individual objects require narrowly focused attention. Note, however, that, when the distractors are homogeneous and arranged in a regular array like a circle or a grid, even a conjunction target is sometimes detectable as a break in alignment or a gap in the global shape or texture.

When we set the parameters for interpreting a particular three-dimensional scene (or a 2D representation of 3D objects, as in Ramachandran's and Enns and Rensink's experiments), the setting is normally a global one, applied to the scene as a whole. Divided attention allows an overall assessment of global features like illumination, surface orientation, or optic flow. Ramachandran showed that the visual system adopts a unique setting to specify the source of light (the normal assumption being light from above). This implies that brightly-lit surfaces are facing upwards, and any discrepant surface in an otherwise homogeneous array of elements can be interpreted as a concavity. A prediction is that 3D features would no longer pop out in a heterogeneous array to which no global interpretation can apply. Epstein and Babler (in press) have in fact shown that with heterogeneous arrays of real 3D objects, attention is needed to see real shape by combining projected shape and slant in depth, even though separately both projected shape and slant are detected in parallel.

The distinction between preattention and divided attention is also relevant in interpreting the results of texture-segregation experiments. I claimed in an early paper that segregation occurs preattentively within separate modules (Treisman 1982). Callaghan (1984) showed, however, that there may be interference in judging one kind of boundary when another varies orthogonally. The reason, I believe, is that we cannot consciously access the representations created within any individual feature module, so preattentive segregation is not directly reflected in phenomenal segregation. If separate boundaries are defined within the dimensions of colour and orientation, they will be combined with divided attention to form a global representation of the display, and we will normally see both. In Fig. 1.8, we clearly see four subdivisions created by two different boundaries, even though at the pre-

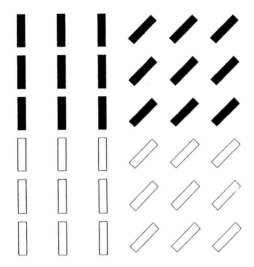

FIG. 1.8. Example of a display in which we see two boundaries, one defined by colour and one defined by orientation.

attentive level the two boundaries could still be quite independently registered. What we *cannot* do is see global boundaries that are defined by separate conjunctions of local elements, for example blue Vs and red Os among blue Os and red Vs (Treisman and Gelade 1980). We cannot simultaneously *focus* attention on each local element and *divide* attention to see the global boundaries defined by the local conjunctions.

In addition to preattention and divided attention, a third fate may lie in store for sensory stimuli: they may be *un*attended when attention is narrowly focused elsewhere. In this case, even global feature boundaries should no longer be available, if they emerge only when attention is divided over the scene. For the same reason, pop-out might no longer occur for a unique feature embedded among contrasting distractors. Some recent findings by Rock and his colleagues (Rock *et al.* 1992; Rock and Mack, in press) are consistent with the predictions. They asked what information is available about truly *un*attended stimuli. Their subjects focused attention on the lines of a plus to judge their relative length. When on the fourth trial an unexpected stimulus showed up in one quadrant, on the very first trial on which it appeared, about one-quarter of the subjects were completely blind to it. The majority, however, could report its presence, the quadrant it appeared in, and its colour, but not its shape, even when the alternatives were simple and highly discriminable; nor could they segregate textures by orientation or group elements by any *Gestalt* principles of organization. The results contrast with those obtained with divided attention in some of the predicted respects.

To recap on features, preattention, and divided attention. The new ideas I have outlined are the hypothesis of coarse coding within dimensions; a hierarchical ordering of surface-defining media, each supporting a similar coding of features of shape; separate representations for figures defined by darker and by lighter contrast, with focused attention required to combine across representations; the idea that feature-coding remains parallel and global up to the level that defines surfaces in a three- (or perhaps 2½-) dimensional world; and finally a distinction between *pre*attention (inaccessible to awareness and to the control of behaviour), *in*attention (that reflects whatever results of preattentive processing can still be retrieved once attention is redirected), and *divided* attention (that integrates the preattentive, feature-defined boundaries and allows conscious access to global properties of the display).

CODING OF FEATURE LOCATIONS AND CONJUNCTIONS

Next I will update the ideas I put forward on the coding of feature locations and conjunctions. In my early papers I reported strong attentional constraints on the localization of features and on the coding of conjunctions. I have not altogether changed my mind, but again new findings have led me to elaborate my account.

I will start with feature localization. Gelade and I reported that feature targets could be identified substantially better than chance even when they were wrongly localized, whereas identification of conjunction targets was at chance (Treisman and Gelade 1980). Johnston and Pashler (1990) correctly pointed out a possible guessing artefact in our experiment: since only two targets were used, subjects might sensibly guess the less discriminable of the two on trials when they did not see the more discriminable. As a result accuracy would be above chance on identification, but the subject would obviously have no information about location. Johnston and Pashler repeated our experiment with better-matched features and more discriminable locations and found little or no evidence that feature identities were available independently of their locations. Note, however, that their criterion for accurate localization was very crude; in effect, they counted the location correct if the subject placed the target in the correct half of the display. My theory would allow this degree of accuracy if subjects simply focused attention in advance on either, randomly selected, half of the display. They could then locate the side that contained the target feature by noting whether it was within or outside the window of attention.

I ran another version of the same experiment, using twelve possible feature targets instead of two, to minimize the guessing artefact (Fig. 1.9). I found identification that was substantially above chance (0.35, where chance was 0.08) when subjects made adjacent location errors, and slightly but significantly above chance (0.15) when they picked some more distant location. They were also well above chance in locating the target feature when they got its identity wrong (0.39, where chance was 0.125), but only when the distractors were homogeneous. Perhaps subjects can detect a discontinuity in the location map without knowing *what* defined it, as well as detecting the presence of a unique feature without always knowing *where* it was. There does seem to be a dissociation between what and where, even if it is less extreme than Gelade and I initially believed.

Do these results mean that features are preattentively bound to coarsely defined locations, as suggested by Cohen and Ivry (1989)? Or could it be the case that, without attention, features are truly 'free-floating', but subjects can rapidly zoom attention in on the approximate area before the sensory information is lost? 'Free-floating' was a term I used in my early papers, which has since caused me some regrets! When I used the expression, I was referring to information that we can consciously access, not to the information implicitly available in the preattentive code. As is implied by the term 'feature maps', I assumed that feature locations are implicitly coded, but suggested that they are accessed, or made explicit, only through focused attention. The more narrowly focused, the more precise the localization will be for features within the attention window. To test the attentional versus the coarse-feature localization accounts, it would be interesting to compare conditions where attention is initially divided across the display with a condition where attention is narrowly focused elsewhere, on the stimuli for a primary task presented to one side or other of the display. We are currently trying to run such a condition.

Next let us look at the coding of conjunctions. Quite a few studies now have shown fast or parallel search for conjunction targets (see for example Duncan and Humphreys 1989; Humphreys *et al.* 1989; McLeod *et al.* 1988; Nakayama and Silverman 1986; Steinman 1987; Treisman 1988; Treisman and Sato 1990; Wolfe *et al.* 1989). These studies fall into two separate categories, which I believe should be distinguished because they deal with two different kinds of conjunctions: (1) spatially integral conjunctions of properties like colour and orientation, for example a bar that is red and vertical; (2) spatial arrangements

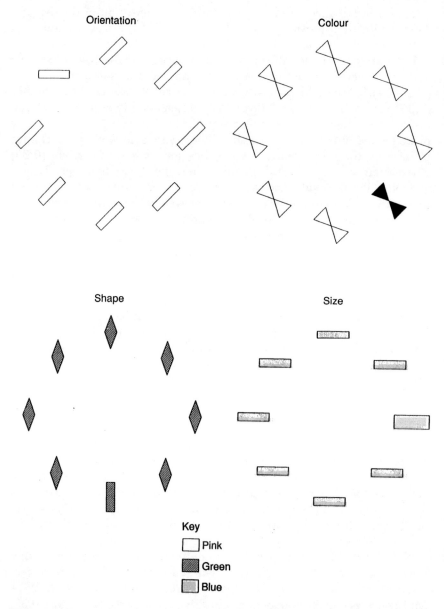

FIG. 1.9. Examples of displays used to test the dependency between identification and localization of feature targets. There were twelve possible targets (diamond, rectangle, hourglass; pink, blue, green; small, medium, large; vertical, tilted, horizontal), shown against a homogeneous set of randomly selected distractors differing in only one feature from the target. Subjects were asked to identify and localize the odd one out.

of parts of shapes, for example T among Ls, each comprising a vertical and a horizontal line but in different relative locations.

I will discuss first the results with conjunctions of properties. Experiments showing parallel processing have in common the use of highly discriminable properties to define the conjunctions. Nakayama, Wolfe *et al.*, and I all suggested similar accounts—that separate grouping by highly distinctive features might allow selective access to their intersection. For example, if we can selectively shut out anything that is coloured green and also anything that is vertically oriented, a red horizontal target will emerge from a background of green horizontal and red vertical distractors without any need to conjoin its features.

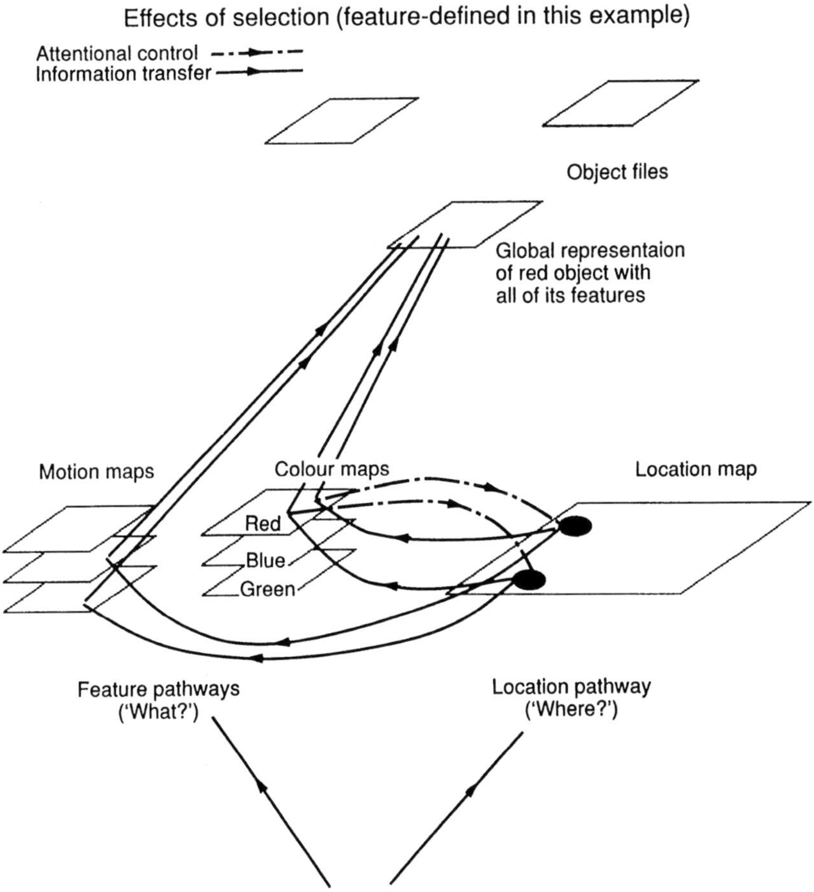

FIG. 1.10. Figure illustrating the idea that attention might select locations containing particular features, by inhibitory (or excitatory) links from particular feature maps to the master-map of locations.

Within my framework, I suggested that the mechanism for achieving this may be through inhibitory connections from the feature maps to the master-map of locations (Fig. 1.10). Notice that the same inhibitory feature control could also play a role in enhancing figures against ground—a more generally useful task, if one wants to supply evolutionary motivation.

In conjunction search, the *efficient* use of this strategy depends on prior information about either the features of the target (inhibit anything that is *neither* red *nor* horizontal) or the features of the distractors (inhibit anything that *is* green or vertical). When all we have is information about distractor *conjunctions*, this strategy should fail. Sato and I gave subjects two sessions of practice at shutting out two predefined conjunction distractors, for example, large pink right-diagonal distractors and small green left-diagonal distractors. We found that, despite learning these two fixed distractor types, our subjects were unable to achieve pop-out for the six targets defined by other conjunctions of the same simple features. In another experiment, we compared separate measures of grouping salience and of search rates, using the same conjunction displays. Subjects both matched the global shape of the boundaries dividing one set of distractors from the other (Fig. 1.11), and searched for a conjunction target. The correlation

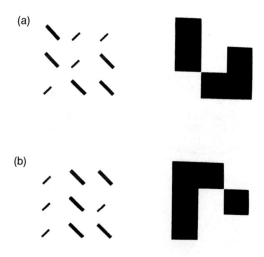

FIG. 1.11. Examples of displays used to test the correlation between a same–different matching task (comparing a solid figure with the outline of cells containing one set of distractors) and the search rate for conjunction targets defined in the same displays (from Treisman and Sato 1990, p. 463).

between the two tasks across six different conjunction targets was 0.92, supporting the idea that segregation mediates conjunction pop-out for known targets.

What about conjunctions of parts? Unlike integral dimensions, two parts of the same object cannot share exactly the same location. Feature-controlled inhibition of locations may therefore be ineffective, and a different account may be needed for cases where these conjunctions seem to pop out (see for example Humphreys *et al.* 1989). I have two different suggestions, each of which may play a role in explaining performance. I will give one now and save one for later, after I have laid a little more groundwork.

The first point to note is that what counts as a separable part is an empirical question, not something that can be decided *a priori*. Conjunctions of parts often give rise to new emergent features, which may themselves be directly detectable. One example is the closure generated when three lines form a triangle rather than an arrow (Pomerantz *et al.* 1977; Treisman and Paterson 1984). Parallel detection of conjunctions with emergent features is not a problem for my theory, except that it makes it hard to disprove. We can argue that if search looks parallel, an emergent feature must be present, and if an emergent feature is present, search will be parallel. The way out of this circularity is to find converging evidence for 'featurehood' of the particular property in question. For example, Paterson and I showed that closure could give texture segregation and migrate to generate illusory conjunctions with other features, as well as mediating parallel search. Unless other tests for featurehood have been tried and failed, I think it is difficult to prove that conjunctions as such are detected in parallel.

Let me recap the main developments in the localizing and conjoining story. I think I still want to hold on to my basic premiss, claiming that when other strategies are ruled out, focused attention *is* required both to locate and to conjoin. However, I and others have proposed a second form of attentional selection, controlled not by an externally directed window of attention but by inhibition from one or more separable feature maps. This allows selection of a subset of elements that are spatially intermingled with others rather than grouped in a single spatial window. Coarse coding of features may explain why conjunction pop-out depends on highly discriminable features. If inhibition is controlled by separate feature maps, it may only be possible to select between stimuli that have non-overlapping representations.

The new model also differs from my earlier ones in showing parallel access to the shared location map and to the feature maps, making it consistent with the notion of separate parallel pathways coding 'what' and 'where' (first proposed by Schneider (1969) in relation to cortical vs. midbrain systems, and more recently by Ungerleider and Mishkin (1982) in relation to separate dorsal and ventral cortical pathways). Having drawn both sequential orders in different papers, one with the feature modules preceding the location map and one in which they followed it, I now suggest a two-way interaction, allowing either direction of control. When we are given location information in advance (for instance a spatial cue to where the target will appear), we use the attention window to restrict which features we select. When we have advance information about the relevant features, we use inhibitory control from the appropriate feature maps. When we have neither, we choose an appropriate scale for the attention window and scan serially through locations.

One additional point on the nature of attentional control: throughout this discussion, I have used the notion of inhibitory control and the analogy of a window of attention rather than a spotlight (Treisman and Sato 1990). On this view, the problem for perception is one of suppressing all *but* the correct picture of the scene, not one of building up a single correct picture. This idea resembles the filtering model of attention that Broadbent originally proposed in the 1950s, and it echoes William James' idea (1890) that attention is like a sculptor carving one statue selected from the many latent within a single block of stone. Within the feature-integration domain, the implication is that, without attentional control, *all* possible conjunctions of the features currently present would be formed rather than *none* of them. The choice of this interpretation is at present somewhat arbitrary, but it fits at least with the most relevant piece of physiological evidence—the finding by Moran and Desimone (1985) that attention narrows the receptive field of cells receiving the critical stimuli. Other physiological instantiations are of course possible, for example the recent proposal by Eckhorn *et al.* (1988) that feature-binding depends on synchronized oscillations in the visual cortex. If firing rates can be synchronized only for one set of units at a time, for example, and the synchronized units control further processing, the effect would be equivalent to gating all other activity at whatever level this bottleneck occurs.

OBJECT FILES AND OBJECT SELECTION

So far I have proposed two attentional strategies provided by the interaction between feature modules and the location map. We may need a third. In the past few years, a debate has been brewing between location-based and object-based theories of attention. I have been firmly on both sides since 1983, when, together with Kahneman and

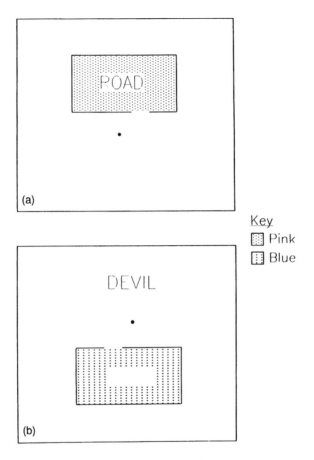

FIG. 1.12. Examples of displays used to test the effect of perceptual objects on the ease of dividing attention between reading a word and locating a gap in a rectangle. The distances from fixation are matched in the two displays, but subjects were faster to read the word and more accurate in locating the gap in (a) than in (b).

Burkell, I described attentional effects that could not be attributed to spatial selection and that seemed to reflect the selection of perceptual objects. We gave subjects a divided-attention task (Fig. 1.12)—to read a word as quickly as possible and to locate the gap in a rectangular frame (Treisman *et al.* 1983). We found that they did better when the frame surrounded the word than when the word was outside the frame, even though the spatial separation of the gap and the word was exactly the same in both cases. It seems that attending to the word made subjects select the whole perceptual object. This included the frame when it was around the word, but not when it was separate (cf. a similar experiment by Duncan 1984).

Our idea was that information about any particular object in the field is collected within an episodic representation which includes all its current arbitrary properties, as they appear in its present location at the present time. We used the analogy of an object file that specifies the current state of a particular object and updates it if necessary when the object moves or changes. When attention is focused on a single element in the display, the object file represents that single element. When attention is divided more broadly, the object file creates a global representation with the emergent features that characterize the overall structure of the elements as a group.

An experiment by Pylyshyn and Storm (1988) gives perhaps the most dramatic evidence of object-based selection (although Pylyshyn himself offers a different account). Their task would, in our terms, depend on object files in their purest form. Imagine eight identical white dots on a screen. Four randomly selected dots flash for a second, telling you that you are responsible for those and that you should ignore the others. Then all eight start to move in random directions quite fast, their pathways intermingling. After a few seconds, one of the eight dots flashes again and you must say whether it was one of your dots or not. The only thing that distinguishes your four dots from the others is their past history of movement through space and time. Yet subjects can do the task—not perfectly, but well above chance.

How could this task be explained within my perceptual framework? Pylyshyn argued that spatial attention could not be used because it is generally assumed to be unitary, like a single window or spotlight. The dots were moving too fast and too unpredictably to allow a switching account in which the attention window repeatedly cycles from one dot to the next. However, Meg Wilson and I have shown that attention *is* needed to track the dots accurately. When we gave subjects a concurrent task of monitoring the colour and texture of a border around the moving dots, they did much worse on both tasks.

The second attention mechanism I proposed—control from one or more feature maps—would be ruled out because the target dots are identical in all their features to the non-targets. That leaves a third possible selection mechanism—control from one or more object files, since these are the structures that individuate objects and maintain their identity through change and motion. Perhaps attention can be controlled through object files acting back on to the master-map (Fig. 1.13) to select constantly changing locations together with the features they contain (Treisman 1992; see also Humphreys et al. 1992, for similar ideas).

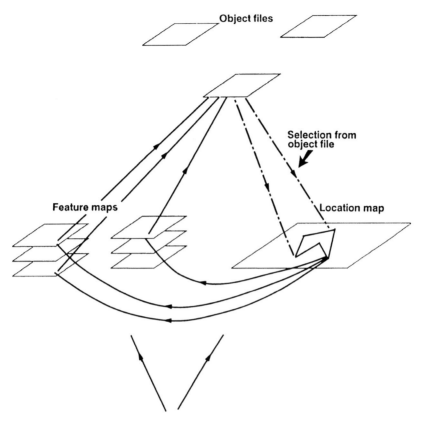

FIG. 1.13. Figure illustrating the idea that attention could select the locations currently containing a particular object, through links between a currently active object file and the master-map of locations.

There is some evidence that a single global object file may be used in this task, rather than a separate one for each target dot. When one does the task, one has the impression that one is watching the vertices of a single polygon deforming in time. Yantis (1992) showed that dot trajectories that collapse the polygon tend also to destroy the ability to track the relevant dots. When the target dots flash at the beginning of a trial, subjects may set up an object file containing the global shape implied by virtual lines joining the positions of the target dots. They also select those dot locations in the master-map by downward control from the object file. When the dots start to move, subjects update the deforming shape that the dots define for as long as they can maintain the object file. If the global shape collapses when dot trajectories cross, they may lose the representation, and as a result lose track of some or all the target dots. (Yantis offers a similar account in somewhat different language.)

The idea that an object file can exert attentional control may also help to explain certain cases of conjunction pop-out. Earlier in this paper, I deferred a suggestion about the coding of conjunctions of parts, to which I will now return. It applies only to within-object conjunctions that share the same parts in different spatial arrangements (for example Ts among inverted Ts) and not to between-object conjunctions, which recombine parts from two separate objects. Within-object conjunctions are often tested with homogeneous distractors, whereas displays testing between-object conjunctions must contain at least two different distractor types. There may be something special about the coding of identical elements. Duncan and Humphreys (1989) attribute

Time 1

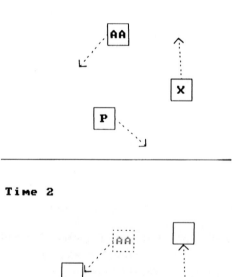

Time 2

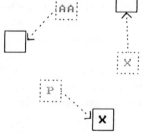

FIG. 1.14. Examples of displays used to test the role of attention in creating object files. The pair of identical letters represent a single letter flashed on and off to attract attention. Between time 1 and time 2 the frames moved empty to their new locations.

the advantage of homogeneous displays to the strength of grouping by similarity. But for conjunction displays this presupposes that all stimuli are identified automatically, and that attention limits arise only post-perceptually (as Duncan and Humphreys indeed believe).

If one thinks, as I do, that there are also perceptual limits, the conjunction homogeneity effect needs some other explanation. Perhaps we can use object-based selection in another way, as follows. Suppose that initially a single random element in a homogeneous conjunction display is identified with focused attention, setting up an object file for its parts and their spatial relations. This token is then used as a template to suppress matching objects across the whole display in parallel, allowing detection of any single discrepant object against the homogeneous background. Because attention is needed to maintain an object file, spatially parallel suppression is possible only for one template at a time. If the distractors are not identical (for example if a set of distractor Ts are presented in varied orientations) a unique item no longer pops out. Nor does a between-object conjunction, because its distractors are necessarily of two different kinds.

To summarize so far: object perception and attention, as I interpret them, depend on a three-way interaction—between the feature maps, the location map, and a current object file. Different tasks lead to different control strategies, picking one of these subsystems to select information from the other two. Notice that for object-based selection we necessarily have an attentional cycle. I have claimed that attention is needed to set up an object file, but that once set up, the object can maintain attention to the location or locations that it currently occupies.

THE ROLE OF ATTENTION IN SETTING UP OBJECT FILES

What evidence do we actually have that attention is needed to set up an object file, beyond the evidence about conjoining features? Kahneman and I looked at this question in the context of a priming paradigm with moving objects. We tried several different experiments, of which I will describe two. In the first, we manipulated attention with a peripheral cue that is likely to call attention (Fig. 1.14). We presented three frames, then exposed a letter briefly in each, flashing one of the three letters off and on again, in order to attract attention to it. The frames then moved empty to three new locations. Finally a single letter appeared in one of the three frames, and the subject named it as quickly as possible. The letter sometimes matched one of the earlier three and sometimes did not. The question was whether the priming benefit would be 'object-specific', and, if so, whether this would be the case only for the attended (double-flashed) letter, as it should be if attention is required to integrate the letter with its frame. This is indeed what we found. When the final letter matched the flashed letter, priming was much stronger if the final letter appeared in the same frame as the prime. When it matched one of the two *un*attended letters, significant priming did occur, but it was no longer object-specific.

In the second experiment, we presented only one preview letter in one of the three frames, and now found almost no object-specificity. Why not? Our suggestion is that, with no competing letters present, there is no need to focus attention down to the letter in its local frame. Instead, attention is divided over the display as a whole. The three frames are entered into a global object file which rotates and expands, and the single letter moves freely within that global object. It is always identified, since there are no competing letters, and it is always re-trieved and matched to the target, whether it is in the same frame or a different one. The phenomenology here is that the initial letter seems to skip from its early frame to the final one if it appears in a different frame in the final display.

To test this rather *ad hoc* account, we tried anchoring the target letter to its own frame by presenting neutral stimuli (asterisks) in each of the other two frames of the first display (Fig. 1.15). This should lead subjects to focus attention and to individuate the single letter within its own particular frame, which in turn should increase the tendency to match within rather than across frames. Sure enough, the anchoring asterisks had the predicted effect. The preview benefit was now twice as large when the target letter appeared in the same frame rather than a different frame. Thus the pattern of results is consistent with the idea that attention is involved in establishing object files and integrating information within them.

OBJECT FILES AND THE CONTROL OF ACTION

So far I have not said much about the age-old debate on early vs. late selection (which began about the time I first became a graduate student). Would the three selection strategies—location-based, feature-based, and object-based selection—count as early or late selection? I think all three constitute possible early-selection mechanisms, but the level of selection will depend on whether the perceptual load is high or low, and in particular whether it poses a conjunction problem. My belief is that early selection occurs only when the perceptual load would otherwise create interference within the perceptual analysers. Some years ago,

Time 1

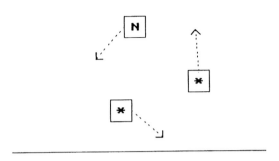

Time 2

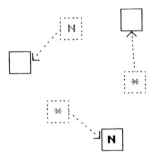

FIG. 1.15. Example of displays used to test the effect of asterisks in the first field in inducing object specificity of priming.

I suggested that the nervous system may be 'forced to use whatever discriminative systems it has available, *unless* these are already fully occupied . . . so that we tend to use our perceptual capacity to the full on whatever sense data reach the receptors' (Treisman 1969, p. 296). Recently Nilli Lavie (in preparation) has confirmed in several different experiments that interference from irrelevant distractors in an Eriksen task varies inversely with the load imposed by processing the target.

Perceptual overload is, however, not the only reason for attentional selection. In most situations we must also select what to respond to and how to respond. Early-selectionists have always been early-plus-late selectionists. The elegant findings reported by Rizzolatti and Berti (1990) have shown how attention and perception are tailored to the type of overt behaviour they are supporting. When the perceptual load is low, and especially when conflicting responses are evoked, selection for action will be the only form of selection, and it may well show different properties from those of early selection.

A clear example of late selection is the negative priming paradigm devised, under another name, by Greenwald (1972) and further explored by Neill (1977) and by Tipper and his colleagues (for example Allport *et al.* 1985; Tipper 1985; Tipper and Driver 1988). Typically only two letters or pictures are presented and a naming response is required, where the naming response would normally be equally strongly evoked by the relevant and by the irrelevant item. In this paradigm the single unattended letter or picture is clearly identified on at least some proportion of trials, since it becomes harder to select on the following trial. Neumann and De Schepper (1991), however, found a steep reduction in negative priming as the number of irrelevant letters increased from one to two or three, consistent with a switch to early selection when the load is increased.

De Schepper and I used overlapped nonsense shapes (like those used by Rock and Gutman 1981), to test whether inhibition in negative priming tasks is attached to temporary object files, created on the fly, or whether it is better thought of as affecting nodes in a permanent

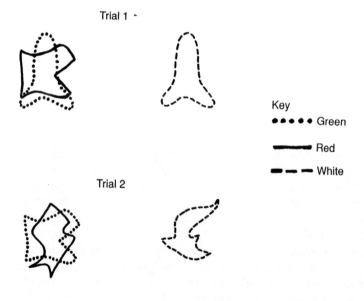

FIG. 1.16. Example of displays used to test the role of object tokens in the negative priming paradigm. Subjects were slower to decide whether the green shape in the second display matched the white shape when it also matched the unattended red shape on the preceding trial. This was the case even on the very first pair of trials in which a new shape was presented.

recognition network of object types. We asked subjects to make a same–different judgement comparing the green shape in an overlapped pair with a single white one to the right, ignoring the red shape in the overlapped pair (Fig. 1.16). We found that negative priming was actually strongest on the very first trial on which a new shape was presented. Since the subjects had never seen that shape before, they must have created a new object file for the irrelevant as well as for the relevant shape, and the inhibition must have been attached to the representation within that object file, irrespective of whether the response was the same as that on the previous trial or different from it. The inhibition therefore depends neither on the existence of a pre-established identity or label, nor on a shared response.

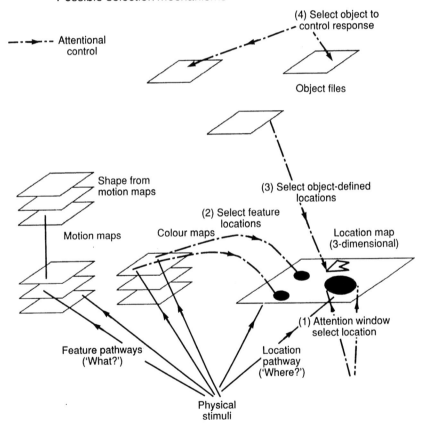

FIG. 1.17. Figure illustrating the four different forms of attentional selection, mediated by interactions between the location map, the feature maps, an object file, and a late-selection stage determining which object file should control the response.

So, to complete my revised picture of the perceptual system, I now add a late-selection stage to the other three forms of attentional selection (Fig. 1.17). In tasks like the negative priming paradigm, the suggestion is that attention determines which identified object file should currently control the choice of response. When the perceptual load is low, it may be the only form of attentional selection. However, when the load is high, I still believe in early selection, just as I did many years ago when I first read *Perception and communication* (Broadbent 1958). It is a tribute to Donald that the questions he raised then are still exciting debate, exploration, and new discoveries as we celebrate his *Festschrift* today.

ACKNOWLEDGEMENTS

This research was supported by US Air Force Office of Scientific Research and Office of Naval Research, Grant number 90-0370. The manuscript is submitted for publication with the understanding that the US Government is authorized to reproduce and distribute reprints for government purposes, notwithstanding any copyright notation thereon. Preparation of this chapter was also supported by the Russell Sage Foundation.

I am grateful to Daniel Kahneman and Beena Khurana for helpful comments and to Marcia Grabowecky, Ephram Cohen, and Beena Khurana for help in preparing the figures.

REFERENCES

Allport, D. A., Tipper, S. P., and Chmiel, N. R. J. (1985). Perceptual integration and postcategorical filtering. In *Attention and performance XI* (ed. M. Posner and O. S. M. Marin), pp. 107–32. Lawrence Erlbaum, Hillsdale, NJ.

Broadbent, D. E. (1958) *Perception and communication*. Pergamon Press, Oxford.

Broadbent, D. E. and Broadbent, M. H. P. (1990). Human attention: the exclusion of distracting information as a function of real and apparent separation of relevant and irrelevant events. *Proceedings of the Royal Society, London, Series B*, **242**, 11–16.

Callaghan, T. C. (1984) Dimensional interaction of hue and brightness in preattentive field segregation. *Perception and Psychophysics*, **36**, 25–34.

Cavanagh, P., Arguin, M., and Treisman, A. (1990). Effect of surface medium on visual search for orientation and size features. *Journal of Experimental Psychology: Human Perception and Performance*, **16**, 479–91.

Cohen, A. and Ivry, R. (1989). Illusory conjunctions inside and outside the focus of attention. *Journal of Experimental Psychology: Human Perception and Performance*, **15**, 650–63.

Donnelly, N., Humphreys, G. W., and Riddoch, M. J. (1991). Parallel computation of primitive shape descriptions. *Journal of Experimental Psychology: Human Perception and Performance*, **17**, 561–70.

Duncan, J. (1984). Selective attention and the organization of visual information. *Journal of Experimental Psychology: General*, **113**, 501–17.

Duncan, J. and Humphreys, G. (1989). Visual search and stimulus similarity. *Psychological Review*, **96**, 433–58.

Eckhorn, R., Bauer, R., Jordan, W., Brosch, M., Kruse, W., Munk, M., and Reitboeck, H. J. (1988). Coherent oscillations: a mechanism of feature linking in the visual cortex? *Biological Cybernetics*, **60**, 121–30.

Enns, J. T. (1990). Three dimensional features that pop out in visual search. In *Visual search* (ed. D. Brogan), pp. 37–45. Taylor and Francis, London.

Enns, J. T. and Rensink, R. A. (1990). Influence of scene-based properties on visual search. *Science*, **247**, 721–3.

Enns, J. T. and Rensink, R. A. (1992). *Visual search II*. Taylor and Francis, London.

Epstein, W. and Babler, T. Searching for shape in 3D space. *Perception and Psychophysics*. (In press.)

Greenwald, A. G. (1972). Evidence of both perceptual filtering and response suppression for rejected messagees in selective attention. *Journal of Experimental Psychology*, **94**, 58–67.

Hinton, G. E. (1981). Shape representation in parallel systems. In *Proceedings, 7th International Joint Conference on Artificial Intelligence*, pp. 1088–96. Vancouver, BC, Canada.

Humphreys, G. W., Quinlan, P. T., and Riddoch, M. J. (1989). Grouping processes in visual search: effects of single- and combined-feature targets. *Journal of Experimental Psychology: Human Perception and Performance*, **118**, 258–79.

Humphreys, G. W., Riddoch, J., and Muller, H. (1992). Where, what and why: on the interaction between ventral object vision and dorsal space vision in humans. (In preparation.)

Ivry, R. B. and Cohen, A. (1990). Dissociation of short- and long-range apparent motion in visual search. *Journal of Experimental Psychology: Human Perception and Performance*, **16**, 317–31.

James, W. (1890). *The Principles of psychology*. Dover, New York.

Johnston, J. C. and Pashler, H. (1990). Close binding of identity and location in visual feature perception. *Journal of Experimental Psychology: Human Perception and Performance*, **16**, 843–56.

Lavie, N. Perceptual load as a necessary condition for early attentional selection. (In preparation.)

Lehky, S. R. and Sejnowski, T. J. (1988). Network model of shape-from-shading: neural function arises from both receptive and projective fields. *Nature*, **333**, 452–4.

McLeod, P., Driver, J., and Crisp, J. (1988). Visual search for a conjunction of movement and form is parallel. *Nature* (London), **332**, 154–5.

Moran, J. and Desimone, R. (1985). Selective attention gates visual processing in the extrastriate cortex. *Science*, **229**, 782–4.

Nakayama, K. and Silverman, G. H. (1986). Serial and parallel encoding of visual feature conjunctions. *Investigative Ophthalmology and Visual Science*, **27** (Suppl. 182).

Neill, W. T. (1977). Inhibitory and facilitatory processes in selective attention. *Journal of Experimental Psychology: Human Perception and Performance*, **3**, 444–50.

Neisser, U. (1967). *Cognitive psychology*. Appleton Century Crofts, New York.

Neumann, E. and DeSchepper, B. G. (1992). An inhibition-based fan effect: evidence for an active suppression mechanism in selective attention. *Canadian Journal of Psychology*, **46**, 1–40.

Pomerantz, J., Sager, L., and Stoever, R. G. (1977). Perception of wholes and their component parts: some configural superiority effects. *Journal of Experimental Psychology: Human Perception and Performance*, **3**, 422–35.

Pylyshyn, Z. W. and Storm, R. W. (1988). Tracking multiple independent targets: evidence for a parallel tracking mechanism. *Spatial Vision*, **3**, 179–97.

Ramachandran, V. S. (1988). Perceiving shape from shading. *Scientific American*, **259**, 76–83.

Rizzolatti, G. and Berti, A. (1990). Neglect as a neural representation deficit. *Revue Neurologique*, **146**, 626–34.

Rock, I. and Gutman, D. (1981). The effect of inattention on form perception. *Journal of Experimental Psychology: Human Perception and Performance*, **7**, 275–85.

Rock, I. and Mack, A. Attention and perceptual organization. In *Cognitive approaches to human perception* (ed. S. Ballesteros). Lawrence Erlbaum, Hillsdale, NJ. (In press.)

Rock, I., Linnett, C. M., and Grant, P. (1992). Perception without attention: Results of a new method. *Cognitive Psychology*, **24**, 502–34.

Schneider, G. E. (1969). Two visual systems. *Science*, **163**, 895–902.

Steinman, S. B. (1987). Serial and parallel search in pattern vision. *Perception*, **16**, 389–98.

Tipper, S. P. (1985). The negative priming effect: inhibitory effect of ignored primes. *Quarterly Journal of Experimental Psychology*, **37A**, 571–90.

Tipper, S. P. and Driver, J. (1988). Negative priming between pictures and words in a selective attention task: evidence for semantic processing of ignored stimuli. *Memory and Cognition*, **16**, 64–70.

Treisman, A. (1969). Strategies and models of selective attention. *Psychological Review*, **76**, 282–99.

Treisman, A. (1982). Perceptual grouping and attention in visual search for features and for objects. *Journal of Experimental Psychology: Human Perception and Performance*, **8**, 194–214.

Treisman, A. (1988). Features and objects: the fourteenth Bartlett memorial lecture. *Quarterly Journal of Experimental Psychology*, **40A**, 201–37.

Treisman, A. (1991) Search, similarity, and integration of features between and within dimensions. *Journal of Experimental Psychology: Human Perception and Performance*, **17**, 652–76.

Treisman, A. (1992). Representing visual objects. In *Attention and performance, XIV* (ed. D. Meyer and S. Kornblum), pp. 163–75. Lawrence Erlbaum, Hillsdale, NJ.

Treisman, A. and Gelade, G. (1980). A feature-integration theory of attention. *Cognitive Psychology*, **12**, 97–136.

Treisman, A. and Gormican, S. (1988). Feature analysis in early vision: evidence from search asymmetries. *Psychological Review*, **95**, 15–48.

Treisman, A. and Paterson, R. (1984). Emergent features, attention, and object perception. *Journal of Experimental Psychology: Human Perception and Performance*, **12**, 3–17.

Treisman, A. and Sato, S. (1990). Conjunction search revisited. *Journal of Experimental Psychology: Human Perception and Performance*, **16**, 459–78.

Treisman, A., Kahneman, D., and Burkell, J. (1983). Perceptual objects and the cost of filtering. *Perception and Psychophysics*, **33**, 527–32.

Ungerleider, L. G. and Mishkin, M. (1982). Two cortical visual systems. In *Analysis of visual behavior* (ed. D. J. Ingle, M. A. Goodale, and R. J. W. Mansfield), pp. 549–86. MIT Press, Cambridge, Mass.

Wolfe, J. M., Cave, K. R., and Franzel, S. L. (1989). Guided search: an alternative to the feature integration model for visual search. *Journal of Experimental Psychology: Human Perception and Performance*, **15**, 419–33.

Yantis, S. (1992). Multielement visual tracking: attention and perceptual organization. *Cognitive Psychology*, **24**, 295–340.

TWO

On the output of a visual fixation

Andries F. Sanders

D onald Broadbent's work is not quoted in this paper. The dynamics of visual fixations and eye-movements happened to be one of the few subjects in human information-processing which remained somewhat at the periphery of his research interest. One cannot do everything in a lifetime. Yet the notions and ideas in this area rely very much on more general models about human information-processing that he defined in the 1950s and 1960s. In addition he aroused my interest in Experimental Psychology when I spent some months at the Applied Psychology Unit in 1957–8 as a young and thoroughly inexperienced researcher. Thus I feel that, if something is relevant in what follows in the coming pages, it is deeply influenced by Donald's thinking and general approach.

The control of fixations and saccades. Visual information-processing, then, is characterized by a continuous alternation of fixations and saccadic eye-movements. It has been well established that intake of information occurs almost exclusively during fixations, since the threshold for vision is quite high during saccades (see for example Matin 1974). This phenomenon of saccadic suppression is a very general one, and observed at successions of small saccades during reading as well as at a single large saccadic shift between widely separated fixation points (Houtmans and Sanders 1983). For example, changing the text during saccades usually remains undetected, thus constituting the basis of saccade-contingent presentation techniques in the analysis of reading (see for example Rayner and Pollatsek 1987). The fact that intake of information is limited to periods of fixation raises various issues about the output of a fixation and about the integration of information across fixations (Rayner and Pollatsek 1989; Carr 1986).

The results of eye-movement recordings, both in reading and in free search, show clearly that there is little uncertainty or hesitation when to end a fixation—and, hence, when to start a saccade—and where to land for the next fixation. The duration of fixations and the size and direction of the connecting saccades appear to guarantee efficient processing. With respect to the question which factors determine when to leave and where to land there are two main opposite views, one in terms of internal, and the other in terms of external control.

The internal-control theory assumes that the duration of a fixation and the position of the next saccade are independent of direct externally present information, and are top-down controlled by the brain. A certain fixation duration and a size and direction of the saccades are set, and thus determined by internal strategies. For example, in free search the saccades might be controlled by a certain strategy, like searching horizontally or in concentric circles. External stimuli are supposed to have only an indirect effect on control. Thus if subjects know that more complex material has to be read, they may set either a longer fixation duration, or a smaller saccade, or both (Salthouse and Ellis 1980). Internal control further suggests that, when suddenly confronted with a more complex signal, subjects temporarily lose control, followed by a change in the setting of fixation duration or saccade length. A consequence of internal control is that, apart from random variation, fixation duration should be constant for a given level of complexity of the visual material. In his deadline model, Ollman (1977) has outlined a comparable internal control notion with respect to choice-reaction processes.

In contrast, external control assumes that a saccade is triggered in a bottom-up fashion, by the completion of processes relating to the fixated signal and to the programming of the movement (see for example McConkie 1979). In the same way the size and the direction of a saccade are determined by peripheral information obtained during the preceding fixation. The most promising and informative point is selected for a more detailed inspection. In support of external control, the eyes do not land at random positions during reading but somewhere in the middle of a word. Again, the duration of the fixations is more variable and more related to the complexity of the material than would be predicted by exclusive internal control (Rayner and Pollatsek 1987). In addition, the duration of a fixation is affected when a fixated word is suddenly changed. It should be noted that there are also views which assume a contribution of both external and internal control. For example, Engel (1976) suggested that, in free search, subjects obtain information about everything that is present in a 'conspicuity' area around their fixation point. If a target or a promising candidate for a target happens to be within this area, the eyes will jump there at the next fixation, suggesting external control, since the saccade is elicited by an outward stimulus. However, in the absence of a promising candidate, the next fixation is either randomly or systematically determined by internal control and not by guidance from external stimulation.

Processing during a saccade? A major issue is whether information acquired during a certain fixation can be elaborated during the subsequent saccade to the next fixation. If processing during a saccade is possible, there is less reason to suppose that the jump is triggered by the completion of certain processes. The reason is simply that processing continues irrespective of whether the eyes fixate or move. However, if processing during a saccade is not possible the visual material acquired during a fixation needs processing until it reaches a code that can survive the saccade. It is suggested that the end-product of certain processing stages provides suitable codes in this respect. Some processes, relating to currently fixated material, might be postponed until the next fixation, so that a fixation may be engaged with (a) further processing of earlier fixated signals, (b) acquiring currently fixated signals, and (c) obtaining hypotheses about future signals in an attempt at establishing an integrated picture of the environment.

Despite its relevance, the issue of processing during saccades has received little attention. There is a theoretical paper by Russo (1978) in which it is assumed that signal-processing and saccadic activity occur in parallel for the mere reason that saccades are a prototype of automatic activity, so that nothing seems to preclude the continuation of signal-processing. In contrast there are notions with at least the implicit assumption that processing cannot continue during a saccade. A well-known example is Just and Carpenter's (1978) proposal to use gaze duration—defined as the sum of the fixations devoted to an object—as an index of processing. Although for all practical purposes the inclusion of saccadic times may only slightly affect gaze duration the proposal still represents an implicit theoretical stand on the issue.

The functional visual field. The present paper aims at investigating the issues of the output of a fixation and processing during saccades by way of the paradigm of the functional visual field (Sanders 1963, 1970a). In an experimental trial of the standard version of this paradigm two signals are simultaneously presented at eye-level, and separated by a large (45° or even 100°) binocular visual angle. At the start of a trial subjects fixate the position at which the left signal (SL) will be presented. Inspection of SL is followed by a single large saccade—eventually completed by a head movement—to the location of the right signal (SR). A trial ends with some joint response to both signals, usually a same-different response. Measurement of the horizontal eye-movement by a standard electro-oculographic technique enables separate estimates of the time elapsing between the presentation of the signals and the start of the saccade (TL); the time to complete the saccade (TM); and, finally, the time between the arrival of the eyes at SR and the completion of the response (TR) to be made. The rationale underlying this paradigm is simply to find out how manipulations of SL and SR may affect these three dependent variables, and the extent to which the dependent variables represent adequate time measures of the ongoing processes.

Earlier research with this paradigm was largely concerned with effects of angular separation between SL and SR. The general tenet of the results was that it is useful to distinguish three areas in the functional visual field, characterized by differences in the efficiency of processing, namely: an area in which SL and SR can be processed by mere peripheral viewing (stationary field); an area in which eye-movements are needed (eye field); and, finally, an area in which combined eye–head movements are needed (head field). In the head field successive separate percepts would be needed for processing SL and SR; in the eye field a hypothesis about SR would be obtained during fixation of SL; while in the stationary field SL and SR would be processed as a chunk in a single percept. More recent work (for example Houtmans and Sanders 1984; Sanders and Houtmans 1985a) extended the earlier findings and updated the theoretical framework. They also suggested that questions about the output of a fixation and about processing during a saccade might be profitably approached by means of the paradigm (Sanders and Houtmans 1984).

Measuring TL and TR. A first prerequisite for this endeavour is that the transitions from TL to TM and from TM and TR can be reliably measured and that they represent meaningful entities. Similar methodological questions are sometimes discussed with respect to the measurement of traditional choice-reaction time (Pachella 1974; Pieters 1985), but seem particularly relevant when introducing a new type of time measure. As to measurement, the transition from TL to TM is usually sufficiently abrupt—owing to the negligible inertia of the eyes—to establish its point of occurrence by way of a relatively simple automatic algorithm with an accuracy of about 10 msec. The same can be said with respect to TM and TR provided that subjects are trained to carry out a rapid and single saccade. With respect to the meaningfulness of the measures there is the general problem whether processing can start immediately at the start of a fixation or whether there is an initial refractory period. There is an additional problem in the case of a combined eye–head movement. When the eyes catch SR and signal the head to stop, the slower head needs some time to carry out this instruction. Consequently the eyes must carry out a compensatory movement so as to keep SR fixated. The question may then be raised whether TR should be measured from the end of the fixation, or from the end of the compensatory movement.

These preliminaries were addressed by Sanders and Reitsma (1982) and by Houtmans and Sanders (1983). Sanders and Reitsma changed the standard paradigm in that SL merely served as a trigger to start the saccade, while SR required an overt choice-reaction. There was a control condition without a saccade in which SR was the only signal, requiring the same choice-reaction as in the experimental condition. SR was preceded by an auditory warning that occurred either 1 sec. or 300 msec. before the presentation of SR in two separate blocks of trials. The results showed that TR, measured from the end of the saccade, was about as long as the choice-reaction time in the control condition with the 300-msec. warning interval. This suggests (a) that processing can start immediately at the start of a fixation without a refractory period; (b) that a compensatory eye-movement does not preclude processing; and (c) that the speed of processing at TR equals that of the best-prepared responses in choice-reactions.

These conclusions were supported by Houtmans and Sanders (1983), who used the standard paradigm at an angular separation of either 45° or 100°, but varied stimulus onset asynchrony (SOA) of SL and SR. SL was always presented first, while SR was randomly presented at various intervals, so that it might appear either during TL, or during TM, or even after the end of the saccade, in which cases TR was obviously measured from the onset of SR, instead of from the start of the fixation. During the interval there was a small fixation light at the position at which SR would be presented. The results showed the usual finding that at the eye field separation of 45° TR was shorter than at the head field separation of 100°, but only when SOA was so small that SR still appeared during TL. When SR was presented during TM or at a still larger SOA, TR was about as long in the eye field as in the head field. This result supports the notion about the eye field that subjects obtain a hypothesis about SR during fixation of SL. In addition, in the head field SOA had no significant effect on TR, which is in line with the interpretation that SL and SR require separate percepts. This result also confirms the hypothesis that processing SR can start immediately upon fixation of SR and that processing SR is not hampered by a compensatory eye-movement.

Perceptual processing during TL. Is TL affected by manipulations of SL? If central processing of SL can continue during TM, the effects on TL should be minor, since TM offers ample opportunities, i.e. about 100 msec. at 45°, and about 200 msec. at 100°. In contrast, if processing during TM is prohibited, the full effect of a manipulation should be reflected in TL, or eventually in TR, when the completion of a process is not strictly bound to the actual fixation of SL or its location. In one study, Sanders and Houtmans (1985*b*) used digit symbols as signals. They varied the signal quality of SL between blocks—intact vs. degraded—while SR was always intact. In a control condition SL was presented as a single signal, requiring a traditional choice-reaction

(CRT). The results showed that the effects of signal quality on TL were about as large as on CRT in the control condition. Sanders and Houtmans concluded from these data that the saccade is not started before the perceptual analysis of SL has been completed.

In a second experiment Sanders and Houtmans (1985*b*) varied the presentation time of SL (75, 180, and 500 msec.). The rationale was that, if SL is continuously available during TL, processing might profit from its presence, which in turn could explain full perceptual processing during TL. Yet the results did not support this possibility, in that TL proved remarkably insensitive to the presentation-time of SL. Again, the effect of signal quality was fully reflected in TL. Subjects appear to complete perceptual processing during TL irrespective of the presence or absence of SL.

Which processing stages could be involved in perceptual processing? The results of additive factors analyses of choice-reaction times suggest at least three stages, i.e. *preprocessing*, affected by signal contrast; *feature analysis*, affected by signal quality; and *identification*, affected by mental rotation (see Sanders 1980, 1990 for a detailed discussion). It might be noted in passing that the distinction between a featural analysis and a subsequent integrative identification of a signal is in line with recent models on the interrelations between perception and visual attention (for example Treisman 1988).

To test the hypothesis that perceptual processing, as implied by all three stages, is completed during the fixation, van Duren (1993) investigated the deduction that the joint effects of signal quality and mental rotation should be reflected in TL. SL consisted again of digit symbols that could be upright or 90° rotated in separate blocks. The task was to decide whether SL was in a normal or a mirrored position, and to respond by pressing an appropriate response key. SR consisted of one out of two letters indicating whether the response should be actually carried out or should be withheld. As control conditions van Duren introduced a new technique: SL was presented as a single stimulus, which should be responded to with a saccade to the right when the digit was in the normal position, while the saccade should be withheld when the digit was mirrored, or vice versa. The results showed equally large effects on TL of signal quality and of mental rotation in the experimental and in the control conditions. Furthermore, the effects of signal quality and mental rotation on TL were additive, which is consistent with the results of the additive-factors studies. Van Duren concluded from these data that perceptual analysis during TL includes processes of identification, as well as of feature analysis.

The effect of task context on TL. This last study raised the question to what extent perceptual processing during TL depends on the nature of the task. As has been mentioned, the usual task in studies on the functional visual field has always consisted of a same–different response with respect to SL and SR. If the saccade is merely triggered in a bottom-up fashion by the completion of a certain processing stage relating to SL, then the nature of the ultimate response should have little effect on TL. Alternatively, there could be top-down effects, controlling the extent of processing SL during TL. In that case the depth of processing during TL should depend on what is required during TR.

To address this issue van Duren and Sanders (1992) compared the effects of four different tasks on TL in a between-subjects analysis of covariance design. One task was the traditional same–different task, while in another task SR consisted of a go–no-go signal with respect to the response to TL. (This condition has already been outlined in the discussion of the last study.) In still another task subjects calculated the sum of the digits presented as SL and SR, and responded by indicating an even or uneven outcome. In a final task SR indicated the response-mapping of the digits presented as SL. The rationale behind these tasks was that they might allow various levels of processing during TL. In the same–different task a physical code of SL seems the minimal basis for comparison with SR, while determination of the sum of SL and SR always requires a semantic code of SL during SR. The depth of the code of SL in the response-mapping condition may be in between the just-mentioned tasks. The three conditions have in common the feature that, since essential information is absent, response-determination cannot occur during TL. This aspect of the situation is different in the go–no-go condition, since the final response is known during TL, although it is not clear whether it should be actually carried out.

The results showed no systematic effects of task condition on TL. Again, the size of the effect of signal quality on TL was unaffected by the nature of the task at TR. Thus, the results suggest that processing SL during TL is bottom-up in the sense that, irrespective of the context of the task, the saccade is triggered by the outcome of a certain processing stage relating to SL. Specifically, the results of van Duren suggest that identification is completed during TL, while response-choice is postponed until fixation of SR.

The suggestion that a constant level of identification of SL is achieved during TL is irrespective of the demands of the final response is supported by some results of Hansen and Sanders (1988), who carried out an experiment on physical versus name identity-matching by means of the functional visual field. In this study, SL and SR consisted of letters that were characterized by either pure physical identity, pure name identity, or mixed physical and name identity in separate blocks of trials. In the pure conditions, the alternative identity did not occur. For instance, in the pure name-identity condition, there were no trials in which the letters had also physical identity. The results showed that the type of identity-match did not affect TL. Instead the full effect of physical versus name identity-matching (Posner 1978) occurred during TR. This result supports the bottom-up view that TL is always analysed up to and including the name-code, irrespective of the demands at TR. The effect of physical vs. name identity on matching-time arises during the comparison of SL and SR, and appears not to affect the depth of processing during TL.

Yet the general conclusion that task context does not affect TL may well be premature, since, contrary to the above-discussed results, Sanders and Houtmans (1985a) found an effect of context on TL. They used either digit symbols (4,5) or columns of 4 or 5 dots as SL and SR in a standard same–different task. TL proved to be considerably less in the case of dots–dots than of dots–digit. There was a similar, but much smaller effect in the case of digit–digit versus digit–dots, suggesting that the level of analysis during TL depended on the forthcoming comparison during SR. The finding that the effect occurred in particular when SL consisted of dots could imply that the physical code of dots—perhaps line length?—and the code of the number of dots (4,5) are sufficiently distinct to enable separate outcomes of a perceptual analysis. By contrast, the physical shape and the meaning of a digit might have become so intrinsically related that their outcome cannot be top-down controlled. The issue deserves further consideration.

Encoding SL under time-stress. So far, the results suggest that the perceptual analysis of SL *must* be completed in advance of the saccade. The question is whether exceptions can be found to this rule, and, if so, whether perceptual processing can proceed during a saccade on those occasions. A first study on this question was carried out by Sanders and Houtmans (1985b, exp. 3), who tried to force subjects to leave SL before the completion of perceptual processing. A tone was presented 100 msec. in advance of SL, and subjects were instructed to respond to the tone by initiating the saccade to SR. Observing this instruction means that SL is briefly viewed 'in the course of initiating the saccade', but obviously without the opportunity of a full perceptual analysis.

The results showed that observing this instruction was hard indeed. The results of four subjects had to be discarded altogether for the simple reason that they kept fixating SL until perceptual processing had been completed. This conclusion was based on the finding that their TL in the experimental condition was about equally as long as in the control condition in which the tone was omitted. The results of four other subjects could be analysed, since they observed the instruction at least at a certain proportion of trials, while on other trials TL was longer but always shorter than in the control condition without a tone. Observing the instruction was concluded from comparison with a control condition in which SL was omitted, so that a pure reaction-time to the tone was measured. The results of the experiment showed clearly that, when SL was left too early, TR was prolonged proportionally, so that there was no evidence for further processing during the saccade. In the case of 'same' trials TR was less prolonged than in the case of 'different' trials, resulting in a considerably larger fast same effect (Farrell 1985). This supports the deduction that further processing of SL takes place during TR, and suggests a facilitation when joint processing of SL and SR during TR leads to the same result. Finally, with an eye field angular separation between SL and SR, the results showed that too early a start of the saccade eliminated the usual advantage of the eye field at TR, suggesting that, under those conditions, no peripheral hypothesis is obtained about SR.

Thus the Sanders and Houtmans study shows that, perhaps under extreme conditions, SL can be left before completion of perceptual processing, and yet a code can still be established that can be used as a starting-point for further perceptual processing of SL during TR. The issue was further investigated in some experiments by Sanders and Rath (1991), who were principally interested in the issue of speed–accuracy trade-off during perceptual processing. If subjects can be made to leave SL at some early stage, one may wonder whether they are capable of setting a continuous criterion along the lines of optional stopping with respect to the amount of information acquired before initiating the saccde (see for example Vickers and Packer 1980). The alternative is that the initiation of the saccade must rely on some discrete partial outcome (see for example Meyer et al. 1988). The optional stopping notion seems more in line with continuous-flow conceptions of processing information, while the discrete codes hypothesis is more consistent with linear stage models (Coles et al. 1985; Sanders 1990).

Sanders and Rath presented SR for a brief period, which forced subjects to leave SL early so as to avoid missing SR. If subjects can set a fine-grained optional stopping criterion, they should be capable of detecting both signals. Alternatively, if completion of perceptual processing of SL is a prerequisite for initiating the eye-movement, SR would be certainly missed. At first sight the results suggested the latter alternative: subjects proved either to anticipate the arrival of SL so as not to miss SR, or to react to SL and miss SR, which led to two distinct distributions. The only trials at which both signals were detected concerned anticipations in which the eyes happened to leave SL some 20 to

80 msec. after the presentation of SL. Thus the data seemed to support a 'fast guess' strategy (Yellott 1971), consisting of a mixture of anticipations and fully analysed SL at the moment of starting the saccade.

The problem with this conclusion was that at those trials at which subjects reacted to SL, TL was significantly less than TL in a control condition without time-pressure. This led to the conclusion that, when under time-stress, subjects may refrain from a full perceptual analysis of SL, and start the saccade upon completion of an earlier stage of processing. Sanders and Rath suggested that this might be the preprocessing stage, as derived from the application of the additive-factors logic to choice-reactions (Sanders 1990).

One consequence of this hypothesis is that, when under time-stress, the duration of TL should be insensitive to the complexity of SL. This hypothesis was verified in two further studies which had mental rotation of SL as an additional variable. Indeed, the results showed that, when under time-stress, TL was unaffected by mental rotation, while it was sensitive in a low-speed control condition. The results also confirmed that an early start of the saccade results in a proportionally longer TR, which is a further disproof of perceptual processing during the saccade.

The nature of the perceptual code at TL. Taking the results together, the evidence consistently shows evidence for full perceptual processing of SL during TL with the exception of what happens in conditions of speed-stress, in which the outcome of preprocessing seems to trigger the saccade. Yet this conclusion faces one possible snag. The problem is that Sanders and Houtmans (1985b) also found a small but consistent effect of the signal quality of SL on TR. This could be taken to imply that a degraded SL still takes some processing time during TR, which is clearly at odds with the hypothesis that the perceptual analysis of SL is completed during TL. The issue was studied in depth by Hansen and Sanders (1988), who proposed various possible explanations for the effect. Indeed, one explanation is that perceptual processing is not fully completed at SL, and is even less so when SL is degraded. This explanation predicts that the effect of signal quality of SL on TR occurs irrespective of the quality of SR.

One alternative is in terms of redundancy. This explanation stresses the similarity between SL and SR. When SL and SR are both intact, they have more common features than when SL is degraded and SR is intact. Again, when SL and SR are both degraded, they have more common features than when SL is intact and SR is degraded. This means that the effect of signal quality of SL on TR should depend on the quality of SR: a degraded SL would fare better with a degraded

SR, while an intact SL would fare better with an intact SR. The results of Hansen and Sanders favoured the redundancy hypothesis: a degraded SL prolonged TR when SR was intact, while a degraded SL reduced TR when SR was degraded relative to the appropriate control conditions.

Hansen and Sanders interpreted this result as evidence for the hypothesis that the code of SL, which is stored for subsequent comparison with SR, consists of all features of SL, both relevant and irrelevant. This can explain the fact that a degraded SL can be more easily compared with a degraded SR than with an intact SR, while an intact SL is more easily compared with an intact SR.

Feature comparison versus process priming. Thus Hansen and Sanders assumed that the after-effect of SL on TR is due to comparing individual features of SL and SR. The more features overlap—both relevant and irrelevant—the more efficient the comparison. This position has been recently debated by Los, who argued that the assumption that facilitation occurs as there are more identical individual features of SL and SR only applies to the case of identical degradation patterns of SL and SR. Yet Hansen and Sanders had intentionally used a variety of degradation patterns so as to avoid stimulus-specific effects. Los carried out an experiment in which SL was a go–no-go signal with respect to the saccade to SR, while SR required a two-choice reaction. At the same time SL and SR consisted of different digit sets. He varied the signal quality of both SL and SR, and obtained results that were similar to those of Hansen and Sanders (1988): a degraded SL facilitated a response to a degraded SR, and inhibited a response to an intact SR, while an intact SL facilitated a response to an intact SR and inhibited a response to a degraded SR. The fact that these findings were obtained in a situation in which SL and SR consisted of different signal sets, and in which the task avoided any element of comparison, suggested that the effect might be due to perceptual priming, but of a more abstract pathway rather than of a specific perceptual pattern. Processing a degraded signal has been argued to require a more complex perceptual pathway than processing an intact signal (see for example van Duren and Sanders 1988). Hence a degraded SL might activate the more complex pathway, thus facilitating processing of a degraded SR. Again, an intact SL would activate the more simple pathway that cannot be used for a degraded SR. It is evident that the discussed alternatives resemble the theoretical alternatives in the explanation of the fast same effect in same–different judgements (Farrell 1985).

Postperceptual processing and fixation duration. The conclusion remains, therefore, that perceptual processing is normally completed during SL and that perceptual processing during the saccade is prohibited. An obvious next question is whether higher-order postperceptual processes are also bound to fixations, or whether they can continue in parallel with a saccade. This question was first addressed by Boer and van der Weygert (1988), who asked subjects to categorize SL as target or non-target, and varied target-set size (2–4 items). SR showed the mapping rule for the target–non-target response on two response keys for that particular trial. (In fact Boer and van der Weygert were the first to deviate from the standard same–different task with respect to SL and SR, which inspired van Duren and Sanders (1992) to a more systematic study of the effects of type of task.)

Boer and van der Weygert found a small effect of set size on both TL and TR, but the sum of these effects was considerably smaller than the effect of set size in a standard memory-search control condition. They concluded that postperceptual processes (a) are not bound to fixation of the underlying signal, and (b) can be carried out in parallel with the saccade. This last conclusion met the difficulty that about half the effect of set size, as observed in the control condition, was still present at TL and TR, despite the fact that the saccade lasted sufficiently long to account for the full effect of set size in the case of parallel processing. This led Boer and van der Weygert to assume a reduced processing efficiency during the saccade due to sharing a limited capacity. This assumption is unsatisfactory for the simple reason that it is hard to imagine that a saccadic shift, as a prototype of an automatic process, is capacity-consuming.

Recently, van Duren (in preparation) has proposed an alternative interpretation of the results of Boer and van der Weygert. She argued that, instead of parallel processing during the saccade, the results could as well indicate parallel categorization of SL and encoding of SR. This might be especially conceivable, since the outcome of encoding SR was directly relevant to the overt response to SL. Van Duren carried out an experiment in which one group of subjects had the response-mapping condition of Boer and van der Weygert, while another group had a double classification task, in which both SL and SR had their own consistent and mutually exclusive target set. Subjects responded 'same' when both SL and SR were either targets or non-targets, and 'different' otherwise. As in the Boer and van der Weygert study, the main variable was the target set size of SL.

The results were consistent with the first conclusion of Boer and van der Weygert, namely that categorization of SL is not bound to TL. The results deviated from their second conclusion, because the full effect of set size—derived from the control condition—recurred in the fixation latencies, about equally divided over TL and TR. In the double categorization task the effect of the set size of TL was considerably larger than expected from the control condition. Van Duren suggested that her deviant results might be due to less practised subjects than in the Boer and van der Weygert experiment. Indeed, the level of practice is likely to be highly relevant, since parallel activity is supposed to develop with practice (see for example Schneider *et al.* 1984).

Van Duren (in preparation) repeated her study, therefore, with more practised subjects and with another important addition, namely instructions about the location at which SL should be categorized. Separate groups of subjects received the instruction of either completing categorization during TL, or not categorizing at all during TL. The results in the response-mapping condition were now consistent with those of Boer and van der Weygert, in that about half of the effect of set size did not recur in the fixation times. Instructional set did not change this result: if instructed to categorize during TL, half of the set-size effect occurred during TL and nothing during TR. When instructed to refrain from categorizing during TL, there was no effect of set size during TL, but half of the effect occurred during TR.

Unfortunately this result can be explained by partial parallel processing during the saccade as well as by parallel processing during encoding SR. In either case one would expect that subjects do not obey the instruction to complete categorization during TL. Instead they would utilize the free processing space in parallel with either the saccade or with encoding SR. However, in the double categorization task, subjects obeyed the instruction: the full effect of set size was either present or absent during TL, depending on how they had been instructed. This difference between the response-mapping and the double categorization task is at odds with the notion of parallel categorization and saccadic activity, since the hypothesis would not expect an effect of the nature of the processes during TR. The results were consistent with van Duren's assumption of interference or facilitation during TR of processes concerned with SL. In both her experiments the double classification condition showed considerable interference during TR.

One explanation for the interference in the double-classification condition could be memory load: the target set size for SL amounted to either two or four items, while the set size for SR was always two items, making a total memory load of either four or six items. A load of six items might be too much near span, and therefore produce interference during TR. This assumption expects less interference when subjects complete categorization of SL during TL than when categorization of both items is done during TR. In fact the results showed the reverse picture: without categorization during TL, TR took about as long as with categorization during TL. The conclusion emerges that double categorization is most easily done as one integrated activity, instead of as two separate activities.

Summary and prospects. Together, the results of this research suggest four broad conclusions. First, there is no evidence for perceptual and categorical processing during a saccade. Second, perceptual processing is usually completed during the fixation of the signal. The exception is when subjects suffer from time-stress, in which case the saccade may be triggered by the result of preprocessing. This result is more in line with linear-stage than with continuous-flow models of information-processing. Third, the level of perceptual analysis during TL seems to be largely independent of the total task context, and therefore is bottom-up determined. Yet there are exceptions to this rule that should be more carefully studied. Fourth, postperceptual processes are not bound to the fixation of the particular signal from which they emerge, although they still seem to occur during fixations. The moment of their occurrence is under strategic control. It should be added that, so far, categorization has been the only postperceptual activity that has been systematically studied.

The evidence that perceptual activity is fully reflected in TL has interesting consequences, since this feature renders TL a prime candidate for Wundt's D-reaction, i.e. a reaction that measures discrimination without response-choice. Early efforts in this direction failed in view of a lack of control over whether subjects had really completed discrimination before responding (Berger 1886). In fact TL might be profitably used as a tool for deciding between a perceptual or a decisional locus of variables affecting CRT. For example, de Jong and Sanders (1986) varied the relative signal frequency of SL and failed to find any effect on TL, suggesting that the locus of relative signal frequency is not perceptual (see also Sanders 1970*b*). In fact, the paradigm offers a promising avenue for studying a range of other issues in the literature, among which are same–different judgements (Farrell 1985), identity-matching (Posner 1978), speed–accuracy trade-off (Meyer *et al.* 1988), and continuous-flow versus discrete-stage processing (Miller 1988).

The completion of perceptual activity during TL and the lack of evidence for processing during saccades is clearly more consistent with external control than with internal control of fixation duration. It should be noted, though, that some crucial experiments are still lacking. Since almost all studies varied conditions between blocks of trials, an internal-control model might still hold that fixation duration is internally set in accordance with the expected complexity of the signals. This means that studies on blocked versus mixed presentation are urgently needed.

It is intriguing to speculate about the question of why central processing and saccadic activity cannot occur in parallel. The least that may be said is that a simple capacity-sharing model fails to account for the results. Instead one might think along the lines that the instruction to start a saccade blocks further processing of the signal in favour of storing a completed code. If this were valid, the obvious question that arises is whether the failure to observe processing during a saccade is limited to the present set of conditions, all characterized by a single long saccade, or whether it represents a more general phenomenon.

In other words, there remains the question to what extent the results of the paradigm can be generalized. This applies to single choice-reaction processes—are the perceptual processes during TL identical to perceptual processes during a traditional choice-reaction?—as well as to more complex activities like search and reading. In contrast to the rapid alternation of fixations and saccades that those activities involve, in this case there are only two fixations connected by an unusually large saccade, and this is a considerable difference. At the same time, however, there are conceivable variations to fill the gap. For example, fixation of SL might be preceded by an initial saccade. Comparison of results from small and simple paradigms with those from somewhat more complex ones are at the basis of the back-to-back research strategy proposed by Gopher and Sanders (1984), which still seems to remain promising for progress in our trade.

REFERENCES

Berger, G. O. (1886). Über den Einfluss der Reizstärke auf die Dauer einfacher psychischer Vorgänge mit besonderer Rücksicht auf Lichtreize. *Philosophische Studien*, 3, 38–93.

Boer, L. C. and van der Weygert, E. C. M. (1988). Eye movements and stages of processing (1988). *Acta Psychologica*, 67, 3–17.

Carr, T. H. (1986). Perceiving visual language. In *Handbook of perception and human performance* (ed. K. R. Boff, L. Kaufman, and J. P. Thomas), Ch. 29. Wiley, New York.

Coles, M. G. H., Gratton, G., Bashore, T. R., Eriksen, C. W., and Donchin, E. (1985). A psychophysiological investigation of the continuous flow model of human information processing. *Journal of Experimental Psychology: Human Perception and Performance*, 11, 529–53.

de Jong, F. and Sanders, A. F. (1986). Relative signal frequency imbalance does not affect encoding in choice reactions. *Acta Psychologica*, 62, 211–23.

Engel, F. L. (1976). Visual conspicuity as an external determinant of eye movements and selective attention. Unpublished thesis, T. H., Eindhoven.

Farrell, B. (1985). Same–different judgments: a review of current controversies in perceptual comparisons. *Psychological Bulletin*, 98, 419–56.

Gopher, D. and Sanders, A. F. (1984). S-Oh-R: Oh stages! Oh resources! In *Cognition and motor behaviour* (ed. W. Prinz and A. F. Sanders), pp. 231–53. Springer, Heidelberg.

Hansen, W. and Sanders, A. F. (1988). On the output of encoding during stimulus fixation. *Acta Psychologica*, **69**, 95–107.

Houtmans, M. J. M. and Sanders, A. F. (1983). Is information acquisition during large saccades possible? *Bulletin of the Psychonomic Society*, **21**, 127–30.

Houtmans, M. J. M. and Sanders, A. F. (1984). Perception of signals presented in the periphery of the visual field. *Acta Psychologica*, **55**, 143–55.

Just, M. A. and Carpenter, P. (1978). Inference process during reading: reflections from eye fixations. In *Eye movements and the higher psychological functions* (ed. J. W. Senders, D. F. Fisher, and R. A. Monty), pp. 157–75. Erlbaum, Hillsdale, NJ.

McConkie, G. W. (1979). On the role and control of eye movements in reading. In *Processing of visible language* (ed. P. A. Kolers, M. E. Wrolstad, and H. Bouma), pp. 37–48. Plenum, New York.

Matin, E. (1974). Saccadic suppression: a review and an analysis. *Psychological Bulletin*, **81**, 899–917.

Meyer, D. E., Irwin, D. E., Osman, A. M., and Kounios, J. (1988). The dynamics of cognition and action: mental processes inferred from speed–accuracy decomposition. *Psychological Review*, **95**, 183–237.

Miller, J. O. (1988). Discrete and continuous models of human information processing: theoretical distinctions and empirical results. *Acta Psychologica*, **67**, 191–257.

Ollman, R. T. (1977). Choice reaction time and the problem of distinguishing task effects from strategy effects. In *Attention and performance*, Vol. 6, (ed. S. Dornic), pp. 99–113. Erlbaum, Hillsdale, NJ.

Pachella, R. G. (1974). The interpretation of reaction time in information processing research. In *Human information processing* (ed. B. Kantowitz), pp. 41–82. Erlbaum, Hillsdale, NJ.

Pieters, J. P. M. (1985). Reaction time analysis of simple mental tasks: a general approach. *Acta Psychologica*, **59**, 227–69.

Posner, M. I. (1978). *Chronometric explorations of mind*. Erlbaum, Hillsdale, NJ.

Rayner, K. and Pollatsek, A. (1987). Eye movements in reading: a tutorial review. In *Attention and performance*, Vol. 12, (ed. M. Coltheart), pp. 327–67. Erlbaum, Hillsdale, NJ.

Rayner, K. and Pollatsek, A. (1989). *The psychology of reading*. Prentice-Hall, Hillsdale, NJ.

Russo, J. E. (1978). Adaptation of cognitive processes to the eye movement system. In *Eye movements and the higher psychological functions* (ed. J. W. Senders, D. F. Fisher, and R. A. Monty), pp. 89–112. Erlbaum, Hillsdale, NJ.

Salthouse, T. A. and Ellis, C. L. (1980). Determinants of eye fixation duration. *American Journal of Psychology*, **93**, 207–34.

Sanders, A. F. (1963). *The selective process in the functional visual field*. van Gorcum, Assen, Netherlands.

Sanders, A. F. (1970a). Some aspects of the selective process in the functional visual field. *Ergonomics*, **13**, 101–17.

Sanders, A. F. (1970b). Some variables affecting the relation between relative stimulus frequency and choice reaction time. *Acta Psychologica*, **33**, 45–55.

Sanders, A. F. (1980). Stage analysis of reaction processes. In *Tutorials in motor behavior* (ed. G. E. Stelmach and J. Requin), pp. 331–54. North Holland, Amsterdam.

Sanders, A. F. (1990). Issues and trends in the debate on discrete vs continuous processing of information. *Acta Psychologica*, **74**, 123–67.

Sanders, A. F. and Houtmans, M. J. M. (1984). The functional visual field revisited. In *Limits of perception* (ed. A. J. van Doorn, W. A. van der Grind, and J. J. Koenderink), pp. 359–79. V.N.U. Science Press, Utrecht.

Sanders, A. F. and Houtmans, M. J. M. (1985*a*). Perceptual processing modes in the functional visual field. *Acta Psychologica*, **58**, 251–61.

Sanders, A. F. and Houtmans, M. J. M. (1985*b*). There is no central stimulus encoding during saccadic eye shifts: a case against general parallel processing notions. *Acta Psychologica*, **60**, 323–38.

Sanders, A. F. and Rath, A. (1991). Perceptual processing and speed–accuracy trade-off. *Acta Psychologica*, **77**, 275–91.

Sanders, A. F. and Reitsma, W. D. (1982). The effect of sleep-loss on processing information in the functional visual field. *Acta Psychologica*, **51**, 149–62.

Schneider, W., Dumais, S. T., and Shiffrin, R. M. (1984). Automatic and controlled processing and attention. In *Varieties of attention* (ed. R. Parasuraman and D. R. Davies), pp. 1–27. Academic Press, New York.

Treisman, A. M. (1988). Features and objects: the fourteenth Bartlett memorial lecture. *The Quarterly Journal of Experimental Psychology*, **40A**, 201–37.

van Duren, L. T. (1993). Central stimulus processing during saccadic eye movements. In *Perception and cognition: advances in eye-movements research* (ed. G. D'Ydewalle and J. van Rensbergen). North Holland, Amsterdam.

van Duren, L. and Sanders, A. F. (1988). On the robustness of the additive factors stage structure in blocked and mixed choice reaction designs. *Acta Psychologica*, **69**, 83–94.

van Duren, L. and Sanders, A. F. (1992). The output code of a visual fixation. *Bulletin of the Psychonomic Society*, **30**, 305–8.

Vickers, D. and Packer, J. (1980). Effects of alternating set for speed and accuracy on response time, accuracy and confidence in a unidimensional task. *Acta Psychologica*, **50**, 179–97.

Yellot, J. L. (1971). Correction for fast guessing and the speed–accuracy trade-off in choice reaction time. *Journal of Mathematical Psychology*, **8**, 155–99.

THREE

Selection of input and goal in the control of behaviour

John Duncan

INTRODUCTION

Without Broadbent's *Decision and stress* (1971) my life would have been occupied by entirely different concerns. Given this book in my first summer as an undergraduate, I read it on my father's farm. Sometimes the book was propped open on the steering-wheel of a tractor in the corner of a cornfield; in general reading was interspersed with the kind of practical activity that was Broadbent's inspiration. Very much as outlined by Lorenz (1966), my experience was a kind of intellectual imprinting, arising from two characteristics in particular. First was the discovery of a psychology in which theoretical principles developed naturally from the observations they purported to explain. Second was breadth: using relatively few postulates, there was an integrated attempt to address a broad range of the phenomena of everyday behaviour. In my view, these characteristics are at the root of the importance that filter theory—extended in *Decision and stress* from *Perception and communication* (1958)—still retains today. Indeed, some of its basic principles remain central to the research I shall summarize here.

A glance at any ordinary, complex visual scene makes attentional limitations immediately apparent. At any given time we can take up and use only a small amount of the total available information. Such limitations imply *selectivity*: the experience is that we 'pay attention' to some things at the expense of the remainder. These two considerations—limitation and selectivity—were at the core of filter theory. To capture limitations, Broadbent (1958) proposed a 'limited-capacity system' through which inputs must pass to acquire control over behaviour. At any given time, this system was able to transmit only a small fraction of the available sensory information. To capture selectivity, the limited-capacity system was preceded by a 'filter' accepting some inputs and rejecting others.

Of course, such a filter cannot behave randomly. The information that is selected must be that which is relevant to current behaviour.

One issue, therefore, is *how the filter is controlled* by current behavioural concerns.

Leading on from this thought is another. It would doubtless be a mistake to think of selection as entirely a matter of *input*. Human behaviour is intrinsically goal-directed, by which we mean roughly the following (Miller *et al.* 1960): in stimulus–response or S–R systems the unit of behavioural analysis is the S–R pair, while in goal-directed systems the unit of analysis is a triple—current state, goal or desired state, and actions chosen to diminish the difference between the two. Just as evidently as we use at any given time only a small proportion of the available visual input, so also do we select only a small set of goals and actions. 'Selection' is a matter of selecting whole triples—goal state, relevant information concerning the current state/environment, and actions—for control of behaviour.

At first it might be tempting to see input selection as in some sense secondary to goal selection. In a typical experiment, for example, a person might be told to select only red letters from a visual array; in this case the operations of selecting red are dependent upon the goal established by prior instruction. Outside the laboratory, however, it is always true that new events can arise to overturn current concerns. If one turns into a field intending to plough but finds sheep streaming in through a gap in the fence, this new environmental input for the moment overturns the entire pre-existing goal structure. Thus input selection and goal selection must be addressed together.

So much for the functional background; in this chapter, too, one of my major goals will be to relate functional models to primate visual neurophysiology. Though much of our information here comes from the macaque, there is good reason to suppose that similar conclusions apply to the human brain. Beyond striate cortex, visual information in the macaque is distributed to a network of more than 20 separate brain areas. These are specialized for different purposes; in particular, there is at least partial specialization for processing different visual attributes. Examples include area MT in the temporal lobe, specialized for analysis of visual motion (Zeki 1978); and Ungerleider and Mishkin's (1982) broad division of the system into dorsal and ventral 'streams', the former leading from striate cortex into the parietal lobe, and concerned with analysis of spatial relations; the latter leading from striate to inferotemporal cortex, and dealing with object recognition. Within this cortical network there is widespread 'attentional modulation' of the visual response, i.e. dependence of the response on relevance to behaviour. Most commonly, this has been reported as either enhanced response to a relevant stimulus (for example, in parietal cortex: see Bushnell *et al.* 1981), or inhibited response to an irrelevant stimulus (for example, areas V4 and IT in the ventral stream: see Moran and Desimone 1985). One of my questions will be how such modulations at the level of the single cell relate to what we know at the level of behaviour.

The chapter has three sections. The first deals with input selection in the usual constrained experimental setting, where the goal structure is rather fixed. I consider the nature of Broadbent's (1958) 'limited-capacity system'—in particular its relation to visual attributes and objects—and control over the selective filter. The second, brief section deals with unilateral neglect, and the issue of competition within perceptual–motor systems. The last section deals with the relationship between input and goal selection, and discusses recent work on frontal lobe function, 'general intelligence' or Spearman's g, and dual task interference.

INPUT SELECTION WITH CONSTRAINED GOAL STRUCTURE

Limited-capacity system

I begin with Broadbent's (1958) limited-capacity system, and hence the difficulties that can arise when two or more visual discriminations are required simultaneously. What sort of limit do these difficulties imply? There are two hypotheses in particular that are relevant here: originally considered by Treisman (1969), they are now given additional point by knowledge of cortical specialization.

According to the first hypothesis, the visual system might be divided into a number of special-purpose 'analysers', each dealing with a particular visual attribute. For example, there might be one analyser for colour, another for motion, another for location and so on. Treisman's (1969) suggestion was that simultaneous visual discriminations might be much easier when they involve different analysers than when they must compete for the same one. As we have seen, the neurophysiological evidence for parallel analysers is now rather strong. Treisman's (1969) hypothesis amounts to the suggestion that these separate cortical systems might be functionally as well as anatomically parallel.

Over the past several years, I have run quite a number of experiments testing the analyser view. In all cases the basic method has been the same. A pair of objects is briefly presented and followed by a 'backward masking' pattern. The subject must identify one attribute of each object, making a two-alternative forced-choice response for each. For half the subjects the two simultaneous discriminations concern the same dimension (hence analyser); for example, the relevant attribute for both objects might be orientation. For the remaining subjects two different discriminations are required; thus orientation might be relevant for one object, but location for the other. The question is simply: are two simultaneous discriminations performed better when they concern different visual attributes?

Attributes that have been used include location, orientation, size, spatial frequency, shape, colour, brightness, texture, and motion. Various hypotheses concerning the nature of 'analysers' have been addressed, including the neurophysiological hypothesis that distinct cortical areas might be distinct analysers, and the possibility of separate analysers for contour and surface characteristics. With only one exception, the results have always been the same. As compared with control conditions, there is a substantial drop in accuracy when two simultaneous discriminations—one per object—are required. This drop is precisely the same whether the two discriminations concern the same or different attributes.

The exception should be noted: when a colour judgment is paired with a judgment of either size or motion, the usual drop in accuracy— as compared to a single-discrimination control—is eliminated for the colour judgement *only*. This unexplained exception apart, the evidence seems clearly to rule out the analyser hypothesis. There is no suggestion that anatomically parallel visual areas are parallel also in function.

The second of Treisman's (1969) hypotheses was that it may be wrong to think of the limited-capacity system in terms of elementary attributes or discriminations. The key factor may not be the nature or number of discriminations, but the number of *objects* to be dealt with (see also Neisser 1967, and Treisman's more recent developments of feature-integration theory, for example, in this volume). Functionally, this would suggest that early *Gestalt* grouping operations organize visual input into discrete packages or chunks ('objects'), and that the limited-capacity system makes available whole packages or object descriptions, with all their associated attributes, for control of behaviour. Neurophysiologically this is an even more interesting hypothesis. Given analysis of an object's separate attributes in at least partially separate cortical areas, the implication would be some kind of *co-ordination* of attentional modulations. Thus 'attention' to an object description might be a state developing in concert across multiple extrastriate regions.

Again the test of this view is straightforward; using the same displays as before, subjects are asked to make two simultaneous discriminations concerning *the same* object. In initial experiments using this method, I found that simultaneous discriminations concerning the same object showed absolutely no interference: performance was no better when only a single discrimination was required (Duncan 1984). Subsequently this result has been confirmed in experiments using all the elementary attributes listed earlier, this time without exceptions. To demonstrate such results the simple method of simultaneous two-alternative forced-choice discriminations has several advantages, avoiding the need for complex post-cues indicating which judgement to report (Vogels *et al.* 1988), and the performance loss that is statistically inevitable whenever multiple decisions are combined in a single response (Duncan 1980*a*; and see for example Corbetta *et al.* 1990).

Such results lend strong support to the view that the action of the limited-capacity system is to make available whole object descriptions for the control of behaviour. Along the same lines, others have shown that selection of multiple elements from a display is facilitated by perceived grouping between them (for example, Fryklund 1975; Kahneman and Henik 1977). As we have said, the corresponding neurophysiological hypothesis must be that 'attention' to an object involves co-ordinated changes across multiple extrastriate areas.

Control of the filter

I turn now to control of the filter, and in particular selection of *that information that is relevant to behaviour.* Many of the relevant experiments have used some variant of visual search (Neisser 1963). In this task, the subject must decide whether some pre-specified target (for example, a red element, a letter X) is present in a multi-element array. In many tasks, the experience is that the target 'pops out' of the array, or that attention is drawn directly to it (see for example, Egeth *et al.* 1972). In terms of filter theory this suggests an obvious interpretation: the filter is able to reject non-targets, selecting only the target for access to the limited-capacity system. In support of this view, the finding is often that target-detection time is independent or all but independent of the number of non-targets. The same can be found for accuracy of target-detection when stimulus exposures are brief; and in this case there is the additional finding that two simultaneous *targets* show strong inter-ference (Duncan 1980*b*, 1985; cf. the earlier auditory experiments of Moray *et al.* 1976; Sorkin *et al.* 1973). This is exactly the result we should expect if the filter passes targets but not non-targets to the limited-capacity system.

Of course, there are also many tasks in which time to detect a target is *not* independent of the number of non-targets (Neisser 1963; Treisman and Gelade 1980). An obvious interpretation is that the filter in these cases is imperfect: non-targets are not always excluded from the limited-capacity system, producing the same kind of difficulty (though at reduced magnitude) as we see with simultaneous targets (Duncan 1980b, 1985). On this interpretation, search experiments can be used to investigate the efficiency of selection, or the conditions affecting control of the filter.

A great deal of research using this method may be summarized as follows. First, many different visual attributes can serve as the basis for efficient selection. Thus target-detection can be independent of the number of non-targets with targets defined by colour, orientation, size, shape, etc. (for example, Treisman and Gormican 1988), as well as more complex characteristics such as alphanumeric class (Egeth *et al.* 1972) and various multi-attribute conjunctions (Treisman 1988; Wolfe *et al.* 1989). Second, the efficiency of selection varies continuously across tasks, the slope of the function relating search time to the number of non-targets varying from zero to 100 msec./item or more (see, for example, Duncan 1987). Third, as we might expect, one important factor is similarity between targets and non-targets (Duncan and Humphreys 1989; Neisser 1963). Whatever the particular attribute that distinguishes targets from non-targets, the harmful effect of non-targets increases as they are made more similar to the target. Fourth, non-targets may be rejected more easily, the stronger is the perceived grouping between them (see, for example, Bundesen and Pedersen 1983; Duncan and Humphreys 1989).

Such findings suggest the following account of filtering (Duncan and Humphreys 1989). One way to describe selection is to say that elements in an array must *compete* for access to the limited-capacity system; the problem, accordingly, is to assign high strengths or weights to targets and low weights to non-targets. Given that any sort of stimulus can in principle be relevant to behaviour, this must require matching of each input element to some flexible advance description of the *sort of information currently required*, which we call an attentional template (cf. Naatanen 1985). The closer is match to this template, the higher is the weight assigned. The content of the template must be entirely task-specific; in visual search, the template will specify whatever property distinguishes targets from non-targets, allowing targets to receive the highest weights.

The model accounts for the data as follows. When non-targets are sufficiently unlike targets, they match the template (target description) poorly, and receive negligible weights. Under these circumstances the number of presented non-targets is immaterial. But as target–non-target similarity increases, and with it non-target weight, selection becomes progressively less efficient. To handle the effects of non-target grouping, Duncan and Humphreys (1989) propose a mechanism of weight linkage—the stronger is perceived grouping between two elements, the greater is the tendency to select or reject them together, building into the control system an assumption that strongly grouped elements are likely either all to be relevant or all irrelevant in any given behavioural setting.

This model of the filter again raises neurophysiological issues. How might attentional templates be implemented in the modular primate visual system? One attractive hypothesis is that matching of inputs to templates takes place in different extrastriate regions, depending on the particular content of templates in different tasks. For example, a template specifying target motion might be implemented in a correspondingly specialized area such as MT, while a template specifying that the relevant stimulus should be in a particular location should have quite a different implementation, perhaps in the parietal lobe. Put together with the findings on selection of whole-object descriptions, this hypothesis would have a further interesting entailment. Though selection might be locally *controlled* in different extrastriate regions—depending on the task's particular selection criterion—the *result* would have to be the distributed, co-ordinated change of the selected object's description that we have already hypothesized.

Data in support of this idea concerning templates were obtained in a recent study of the activity of single neurones in cortical area V4 (Haenny *et al.* 1987). An important station in the object-recognition stream, V4 has cells selective for such properties as line orientation, size, and colour (Desimone and Schein 1987). In the experiment of Haenny *et al.* (1987), recordings were made while the monkey performed a target-detection task based on orientation. At the start of each trial, a target orientation (for example, vertical) was specified by touch, the monkey feeling an appropriately oriented grating by hand. There followed a sequence of visually-presented test gratings, which the monkey was to inspect for a match to the target. As expected, V4 neurones often showed marked selectivity for the orientation of visual test gratings. A given neurone, for example, might fire strongly whenever a vertical grating was displayed, no matter whether it was target or non-target. Just as common, however, was selectivity for *target* orientation. In this case the neurone might fire most strongly on trials with a vertical target orientation, no matter what the particular visual input, and in some cases, such selective firing began as the target orientation was first specified and was then sustained throughout the trial. Of course, sustained discharges carrying information about future behaviour are by no means confined to prestriate cortex; such discharges can be seen in premotor cortex (for example, Godschalk *et al.* 1985), prefrontal cortex (for example, Funahashi *et al.* 1989), etc., and it seems entirely likely that data like those of Haenny *et al.* (1987)

give only a partial view of the full implementation of an attentional template. Such data, nevertheless, suggest at least a contribution from sustained activity in an appropriately specialized prestriate region.

A new study of V4

It may be useful to end this section on a cautionary note, with some neurophysiological data gathered recently in collaboration with Earl Miller, Leonardo Chelazzi, Jennifer Hart, and Bob Desimone at the National Institute of Mental Health in Bethesda. Previous studies of extrastriate attentional modulation have rested heavily on some form of *spatial* selection: the monkey knows *where* a relevant stimulus will appear. There are various reasons to suppose, however, that spatial and non-spatial cues may work quite differently. Spatial selection, for example, has been reported to enhance early components of the visual evoked potential, while non-spatial selection produces only a later 'processing negativity' (Hillyard *et al.* 1985). With this in mind, we undertook a study of single-cell responses in area V4 of the macaque during a colour-selection task.

Each trial began with a foveal colour patch indicating to the animal the *target* colour for that trial. Because of our recording site, this pre-cue was typically outside the recorded cell's receptive field. About a second later, there followed a peripheral test display, consisting (in the most relevant case) of two patches within the receptive field. In different versions of the task, the monkey had either to *detect* any patch of the target colour (releasing a lever but maintaining fixation), or make a saccade to it. As in the spatial selection task of Moran and Desimone (1985), therefore, the test display contained two stimuli, one relevant to the animal's task (the target) and the other irrelevant (the non-target).

The results, however, were quite different from those of the earlier study. Across cells there was no reliable tendency for enhancement of responses to the relevant stimulus or inhibition of responses to the irrelevant stimulus, confirming the suspicion that selection based on colour may be quite different from and perhaps later than selection based on space. A second negative result concerned attentional templates: though V4 is a key region in the processing of colour (Zeki 1978), there was no evidence for sustained activity carrying information about target colour from the time of the pre-cue to the time of the test. The study is still in progress, and it would be a mistake to over-interpret such negative results. Nevertheless, they do give us a warning that attempts to link functional models to the underlying neurophysiology are still in their infancy.

Summary

To sum up: on the nature of Broadbent's (1958) 'limited-capacity system', the behavioural data rule out the hypothesis of specialized perceptual analysers, but lend strong support to the object hypothesis. Neurophysiologically, this implies that anatomically parallel cortical systems are not functionally parallel, and that 'selective attention' may be a state developing in concert across the multiple extrastriate areas that deal with a selected object's different attributes. Data on control of the 'selective filter' suggest a process of matching inputs against an attentional template specifying what information is needed in current behaviour. Though there is evidence to support the hypothesis of template activity in an appropriately specialized prestriate region (V4 for orientation), our own negative findings show at least that such activity is not a necessary component of target detection.

UNILATERAL NEGLECT

Though the previous section emphasized selection within the visual system, selection is of course *for* control of behaviour. Relevant in this connection is the phenomenon of unilateral neglect. Very often, damage to one side of the brain can produce a bias against behaviour directed towards the contralateral side of the body or of space, sometimes specific for a particular type of stimulus or a particular effector (Bisiach and Vallar 1988). The lesion can be in many different areas of the brain, including parietal cortex (Bisiach and Vallar 1988; Critchley 1953), premotor cortex (Rizzolatti *et al.* 1985), frontal eye fields (Latto and Cowey 1971), superior colliculus (Latto and Cowey 1971), etc. An important point may be that many of these areas have a clear perceptuo-motor function. In all four of the above areas, for example, neurones have both sensory and motor properties. As one example, Taira *et al.* (1990) describe neurones in the posterior parietal cortex whose response is related to particular types of hand grip, and in some cases, such neurones also respond to the sight of an object suitable for such a grip. This might be described as response to the 'affordance' of the stimulus (Gibson 1979); a similar point can be made for certain neurones in the frontal eye field (Goldberg and Colby 1989).

For present purposes, the key point about unilateral neglect is that we seem again to be dealing with systems in which stimuli *compete*, and in which competition is guided by cues indicating *behavioural relevance*. For example, neglect of a stimulus contralateral to the lesion is often much stronger when a second stimulus is also present in the ipsilateral (unimpaired) field ('extinction'; see Bisiach and Vallar 1988). As for cues to behavioural relevance, neglect may be ameliorated by specific instructions to focus upon the neglected side (Posner *et al.* 1984) or limb (Critchley 1953). It is unclear what relationship exists between this competition in perceptual–motor systems and attentional modulation in more specifically visual areas. Presumably, however, the two some-how work together to enable the visual description of an object for control of behaviour.

GOAL SELECTION

Thus far we have made match to an attentional template the key factor in our account of selection. In competition for the control of behaviour, the selected stimulus is that which best matches some advance speci-fication of relevant or needed information. As I have mentioned, however, such an account can be only partially correct. In a changing world, new events can always arise to overturn current concerns; or in other words, it is not always possible to specify 'relevant' information in advance, since the next segment of behaviour may be something unexpected. A little thought suggests that everyday behaviour has very much this character. For the driver of a car, for example, it might be very hard to predict whether the next input gaining control of beha-viour will be a STOP sign, a friend waving unexpectedly in the street, or a scream from children in the back. People not only select inputs that are relevant to current goals; they also select goals partially on the basis of current inputs.

The problem of goal selection has been addressed mainly in the liter-ature on 'problem-solving', and in this context, many people have pointed out that we need some scheme like that illustrated in Fig. 3.1 (for example, Anderson 1983; Duncker 1945; Hayes-Roth and Hayes-Roth 1979). The current or stimulus state suggests one set of candidate goals (p_1, p_2, etc.), i.e. next-states that could or should be developed from the current one. This is the process we have just described, whereby events in the world suggest possible goals or lines of beha-viour. Equally important, however, is a process of *working backwards* from currently active goal states to suggest *relevant* next-states (r_1, r_2, etc.), i.e. sub-goals that would bring the currently active goal closer. The whole set of alternative candidate goals, both the p and the r next-states, must somehow be weighted by relative importance to the organ-ism, this weighting determining which candidates are actually selected for pursuit.

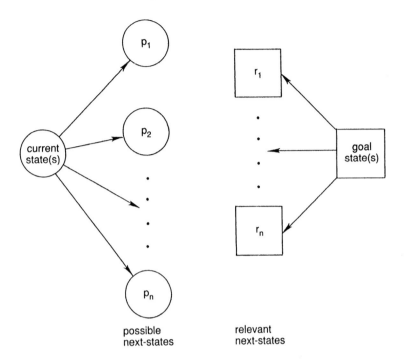

FIG. 3.1. Activation of candidate goals. The current state activates possible next-states, while the goal state activates relevant next-states. Reprinted by permission from Duncan (1990).

Thus the stimulus actually selected for control of behaviour is not simply the best match to a pre-existing specification of what is needed in pursuit of a current goal. The goal itself may change; the selected stimulus is the one most relevant to the selected goal. As was pointed out by Norman (1968), this amounts to selection of the stimulus that in a sense is most 'important'. In the literature, much debate has centred around the complexity of the decision-rule by which selection is controlled. A central topic has been complexity of perceptual classifications; for example, whether selection can only be controlled by simple stimulus features like colour, or also by more complex aspects of shape (Broadbent 1971). A rather separate point has perhaps been underemphasized: though it is conceivable that simple stimulus features (colour, motion, etc.) could often be a strong clue to 'importance', it must still be true that selection is in a sense controlled by 'meaning', involving at least implicit reference to the consequences of several different possible lines of behaviour.

Recently, I have been working on the hypothesis that a central system for goal weighting or selection is reflected in three different phenomena: the effects of frontal lobe damage, individual differences in 'general intelligence' or Spearman's g, and interference between dissimilar, concurrent tasks (Duncan 1990). Classically, the effect of an extensive frontal lesion is widespread disorganization of behaviour; the goal-directed structure so characteristic of normal behaviour—a sequence of actions moving the person from the state he or she or the world is in to the state he or she wishes to attain—is lost or impaired, producing behaviour that is 'fragmented', 'bizarre', or 'irrelevant' (Luria 1966). Importantly, this disorganization can influence many different behavioural domains—perceptual tasks, recall, problem-solving, respect for social conventions, etc.—suggesting impairment in a system of rather widespread importance. By hypothesis, this is a central goal-weighting system. Turning to individual differences, the primary evidence for a factor of 'general intelligence' or g is the phenomenon of widespread positive correlations between even dissimilar tasks; though the correlation may be weak, people doing better on one task will tend also to do better on another. To explain this observation, Spearman (1927) postulated that a general or g factor makes some contribution to a person's score on all manner of different tests; in modern terms one might think of this as an information-processing system making some contribution to the organization of many different tasks, by hypothesis a goal-weighting system. If this interpretation is accepted, it is easy to show which tasks are most strongly correlated with (i.e., are the best measures of) g; these then are the conventional 'intelligence' or IQ tests. Lastly, interference between concurrent tasks depends partly on their similarity, suggesting conflicts within special-purpose processing systems (see, for example, Treisman and Davies 1973). Even when tasks superficially are quite dissimilar, however, some modest interference generally remains (see, for example, McLeod and Posner 1984). Again the hypothesis is that such interference reflects conflicts within a general goal-weighting system. Of course, such ideas have several precedents. For example, dual-task interference has been linked to frontal lobe function by Norman and Shallice (1980), and to Spearman's g by Ackerman (1988).

Several current lines of work support these hypotheses. For example, it is conventionally held that the disorganization of behaviour seen after extensive frontal damage is unrelated to g, since frontal patients sometimes show little evidence of IQ impairment (see, for example, Mettler 1949; Warrington et al. 1986). With Paul Burgess, however, I have recently shown that we must draw a distinction between two quite different kinds of test, which in the normal population may give much the same answer but in the frontal patient may not. The first kind of test is based on obtaining a person's *average* performance on a wide range of separate sub-tests, each of which on its own may be only weakly correlated with g. This is the basis of the most clinically popular tests like the WAIS; as Spearman (1927) showed, it works with any sufficiently diverse set of sub-tests, for much the same reason as averaging several poor estimates of any quantity yields a single much better estimate. An alternative, however, is to find a single test which on its own has a high g correlation. In some ways this is preferable, since now the measurement is based on behaviour which actually seems to make a heavy demand on any 'g' system. Such tests turn out to be those with a substantial element of novel problem-solving, for example matrices or verbal analogies (Marshalek *et al.* 1983). Our current work suggests that, when we select exactly those frontal patients who provide the conventional evidence for preserved IQ, for example those with WAIS IQs of 125 or greater, still we find massive losses in a test based instead on geometrical problem-solving (Cattell's Culture Fair: Institute for Personality and Ability Testing 1959). Even these frontal patients, in other words, show impairment in a task with heavy involvement of a g system.

A second line of research deals with g correlations and dual-task interference (Duncan *et al.*, in press). Imagine any set of diverse tasks. By hypothesis, some will be strongly dependent on the central goal-weighting system, and these should show both high g correlations and substantial interference from a dissimilar, concurrent task. Other tasks will be less dependent, thus showing lower g correlations and weaker dual-task interference. In fact it can be shown that, if the effect of a concurrent task is simply to reduce each person's effective level of g, then, across different tasks, g correlations should be linearly related to dual-task decrements expressed as z-scores. So far this prediction has been tested on only rather a weak data set—12 separate components of driving skill, measured on the road in an instrumented car, all of which showed only the modest g correlations and dual-task decrements that one would expect of a simple, highly-practised activity. Across the 12 skills, nevertheless, profiles of g correlation and dual-task decrement were in good agreement ($r = 0.67$).

There are other lines of evidence that might be mentioned. For example, consistent practice has been argued to reduce frontal impairments (Luria and Tsvetkova 1964), g correlations (Ackerman 1988), and dual-task interference (Schneider and Shiffrin 1977). The decline in many different kinds of performance in old age—in which frontal damage is strongly implicated (Mittenberg *et al* 1989)—may be largely explained by a reduction in g (Rabbitt and Goward, in press). I shall finish, however, with one reason for thinking of all these phenomena in terms of goal selection. One of the most striking aspects of frontal impairment is mismatch between *knowledge* of a task's requirements and actual behaviour; though instructions have been understood, behaviour may suggest no attempt to obey them. For example, patients may make repetitive errors in the Wisconsin card-sorting task while actively stating that these responses are incorrect (Milner 1963). In the same vein, Luria (1966) described patients who had been asked to lift their hand in response to a light; when the light came on, the patient might say, 'I should raise my hand!', yet make no attempt to do so.

Returning to Fig. 3.1, we may say that verbal instructions are one aspect of the environment that normally (at least in the context of an experiment) control goal selection: the task requirements specified in the instructions are expected to become the goals that the subject pursues. When this does not happen in the frontal patient—when behaviour not only fails, but suggests no *attempt* to succeed—we have direct evidence that normal constraints on goal selection are impaired.

Even in frontal patients, such mismatches between knowledge and behaviour have been noted only as an occasional clinical phenomenon. In recent work with Hazel Emslie, Phyllis Williams, and Roger Johnson, however, I have been investigating a task that produces such errors very commonly. The subject sees pairs of letters and digits, briefly presented side-by-side in the centre of a screen. On each trial thirteen such pairs are presented, one after the other, at a rate of 400 msec./pair. There are three task requirements. First, the subject is to repeat out loud any letters, ignoring digits. Second, he/she is to watch for letters only on one side at a time, left or right. An instruction WATCH LEFT or WATCH RIGHT is shown before the trial. Third, a symbol presented between the tenth and eleventh pairs sometimes requires a switch of side. A plus sign means that, for the last part of the trial, the subject should watch the right, while a minus means watch left.

Of 7 frontal patients who have been tested, 5 showed no response whatever to the plus/minus cue over a series of 12 trials, despite always describing correctly what response was required. We do not yet know what aspects of this task make the phenomenon so common; factors under consideration include the number of simultaneously-specified goals or task requirements, and the focus on behaviour immediately after instruction, before even one successful trial. What is significant, however, is that under these conditions the same phenomenon now begins to appear in normal people, and is very closely related to scores on Cattell's Culture Fair test of g. Failures are essentially absent in people above a Cattell IQ of 100, but very common below 85. Again, even people who ignore the plus/minus cue invariably state correctly what *should* be done. If the experimenter points out the errors that are made, furthermore, these errors are quickly eliminated; it is not that the subject is *incapable* of following the instruction, but rather that this instruction on its own is insufficient to guarantee that the goal it specifies will be focused upon. Though these are still preliminary observations, they support the hypothesis of impaired goal selection in both frontal patients and normal people who score poorly on g. Perhaps too they suggest conditions under which this goal-weighting system is stressed sufficiently to produce reliable failures.

CONCLUSION

As we should expect of a psychological term taken from everyday life, the meaning of 'attention' is doubtless imprecise. At least in part, however, we refer by this term to the selection of what I have called whole control triples—active goal, relevant aspect of the stimulus input, and action chosen to bring the goal state closer.

There are aspects of this selection process that seem rather exclusively visual: for example, the grouping or co-ordination process whereby the visual entity selected for control of behaviour is a description of a whole object, with all of its attributes. Similarly there are aspects that seem rather exclusively related to goals—the weighting of alternative goal states on grounds of net benefit to the organism. As I have said, however, selection of whole object descriptions within the visual system, competition between stimuli within perceptual–motor systems, and selection of goals with its contribution from the frontal lobe, must doubtless all be co-ordinated. Our task is to understand how the brain's multiple selection systems combine to produce the integrated acts of 'attention' that we see at the level of behaviour.

ACKNOWLEDGEMENTS

Parts of this research were supported by the Transport and Road Research Laboratory under research contract 9652/32, NATO under grant CRG880085, the US Office of Naval Research under grant N00014-91-J-1347, and the Air Force Office of Scientific Research, Air Force Systems Command, USAF, under grants AFOSR-90-0043 and AFOSR-90-0343. The US Government is authorized to reproduce and distribute reprints for Governmental purposes notwithstanding any copyright notation thereon.

REFERENCES

Ackerman, P. L. (1988). Determinants of individual differences during skill acquisition: cognitive abilities and information processing. *Journal of Experimental Psychology: General*, **117**, 288–318.

Anderson, J. R. (1983). *The architecture of cognition*. Harvard University Press, Cambridge, Mass.

Bisiach, E. and Vallar, G. (1988). Hemineglect in humans. In *Handbook of Neuropsychology*, Vol. 1, (ed. F. Boller and J. Grafman), pp. 195–221. Elsevier, Amsterdam.

Broadbent, D. E. (1958). *Perception and communication*. Pergamon, London.

Broadbent, D. E. (1971). *Decision and stress*. Academic Press, London.

Bundesen, C. and Pedersen, L. F. (1983). Color segregation and visual search. *Perception and Psychophysics*, **33**, 487–93.

Bushnell, M. C., Goldberg, M. E., and Robinson, D. L. (1981). Behavioral enhancement of visual responses in monkey cerebral cortex. Modulation in posterior parietal cortex related to selective visual attention. *Journal of Neurophysiology*, **46**, 755–72.

Corbetta, M., Miezin, F. M., Dobmeyer, S., Shulman, G. L., and Petersen, S. E. (1990). Attentional modulation of neural processing of shape, color, and velocity in humans. *Science*, **248**, 1556–9.

Critchley, M. (1953). *The parietal lobes*. Edward Arnold, London.

Desimone, R. and Schein, S. J. (1987). Visual properties of neurons in area V4 of the macaque: sensitivity to stimulus form. *Journal of Neurophysiology*, **57**, 835–68.

Duncan, J. (1980a). The demonstration of capacity limitation. *Cognitive Psychology*, **12**, 75–96.

Duncan, J. (1980b). The locus of interference in the perception of simultaneous stimuli. *Psychological Review*, **87**, 272–300.

Duncan, J. (1984). Selective attention and the organization of visual information. *Journal of Experimental Psychology: General*, **113**, 501–17.

Duncan, J. (1985). Visual search and visual attention. In *Attention and performance XI*, (ed. M. I. Posner and O. S. M. Marin), pp. 85–104. Erlbaum, Hillsdale, NJ.

Duncan, J. (1987). Attention and reading: wholes and parts in shape recognition. In *Attention and performance XII*, (ed. M. Coltheart), pp. 39–61. Erlbaum, Hillsdale, NJ.

Duncan, J. (1990). Goal weighting and the choice of behaviour in a complex world. *Ergonomics*, **33**, 1265–79.

Duncan, J. and Humphreys, G. W. (1989). Visual search and stimulus similarity. *Psychological Review*, **96**, 433–58.

Duncan, J., Williams, P., Nimmo-Smith, M. I., and Brown, I. The control of skilled behavior: learning, intelligence, and distraction. In *Attention and performance XIV*, (ed. D. Meyer and S. Kornblum). MIT Press, Cambridge, Mass. (In press.)

Duncker, K. (1945). On problem solving. *Psychological Monographs*, **58**, (Whole No. 270, 1–113).

Egeth, H., Jonides, J., and Wall, S. (1972). Parallel processing of multielement displays. *Cognitive Psychology*, **3**, 674–98.

Fryklund, I. (1975). Effects of cued-set spatial arrangement and target–background similarity in the partial-report paradigm. *Perception and Psychophysics*, **17**, 375–86.

Funahashi, S., Bruce, C. J., and Goldman-Rakic, P. S. (1989). Mnemonic coding of visual space in the monkey's dorsolateral prefrontal cortex. *Journal of Neurophysiology*, **61**, 331-49.

Gibson, J. J. (1979). *The ecological approach to visual perception*. Houghton-Mifflin, Boston.

Godschalk, M., Lemon, R. N., Kuypers, H. G. J. M., and Van der Steen, J. (1985). The involvement of monkey premotor cortex neurones in preparation of visually cued arm movements. *Behavioural Brain Research*, **18**, 143-57.

Goldberg, M. E. and Colby, C. L. (1989). The neurophysiology of spatial vision. In *Handbook of Neuropsychology*, Vol. 2, (ed. F. Boller and J. Grafman), pp. 301-15. Elsevier, Amsterdam.

Haenny, P. E., Maunsell, J. H. R., and Schiller, P. H. (1987). State dependent activity in monkey visual cortex: II. Retinal and extraretinal factors in V4. *Experimental Brain Research*, **69**, 245-59.

Hayes-Roth, B., and Hayes-Roth, F. (1979). A cognitive model of planning. *Cognitive Science*, **3**, 275-310.

Hillyard, S. A., Munte, T. F., and Neville, H.J. (1985). Visual–spatial attention, orienting, and brain physiology. In *Attention and performance XI*, (ed. M. I. Posner and O. S. M. Marin), pp. 63-84. Erlbaum, Hillsdale, NJ.

Institute for Personality and Ability Testing (1959). *Measuring intelligence with the Culture Fair Tests*. Institute for Personality and Ability Testing, Champaign, Illinois.

Kahneman, D. and Henik, A. (1977). Effects of visual grouping on immediate recall and selective attention. In *Attention and performance VI*, (ed. S. Dornic), pp. 307-32. Erlbaum, Hillsdale, NJ.

Latto, R. and Cowey, A. (1971). Visual field defects after frontal eye-field lesions in monkeys. *Brain Research*, **30**, 1-24.

Lorenz, K. (1966). *On aggression*. Methuen, London.

Luria, A. R. (1966). *Higher cortical functions in man*. Tavistock, London.

Luria, A. R. and Tsvetkova, L. D. (1964). The programming of constructive ability in local brain injuries. *Neuropsychologia*, **2**, 95-108.

McLeod, P. and Posner, M. I. (1984). Privileged loops from percept to act. In *Attention and performance X*, (ed. H. Bouma and D. G. Bouwhuis), pp. 55-66. Erlbaum, Hillsdale, NJ.

Marshalek, B., Lohman, D. F., and Snow, R. E. (1983). The complexity continuum in the radex and hierarchical models of intelligence. *Intelligence*, **7**, 107-27.

Mettler, F. A. (ed.) (1949). *Selective partial ablation of the frontal cortex: a correlative study of its effects on human psychotic subjects*. Hoeber, New York.

Miller, G. A., Galanter, E., and Pribram, K. H. (1960). *Plans and the structure of behavior*. Holt, Rinehart, and Winston, New York.

Milner, B. (1963). Effects of different brain lesions on card sorting. *Archives of Neurology*, **9**, 90-100.

Mittenberg, W., Seidenberg, M., O'Leary, D. S., and DiGiulio, D. V. (1989). Changes in cerebral functioning associated with normal aging. *Journal of Clinical and Experimental Neuropsychology*, **11**, 918-32.

Moran, J. and Desimone, R. (1985). Selective attention gates visual processing in the extrastriate cortex. *Science*, **229**, 782-4.

Moray, N., Fitter, M., Ostry, D., Favreau, D., and Nagy, V. (1976). Attention to pure tones. *Quarterly Journal of Experimental Psychology*, **28**, 271–83.

Naatanen, R. (1985). Stimulus processing: reflections in event-related potentials, magnetoencephalogram and regional cerebral blood flow. In *Attention and Performance XI*, (ed. M. I. Posner and O. S. M. Marin), pp. 355–73. Erlbaum, Hillsdale, NJ.

Neisser, U. (1963). Decision-time without reaction-time: experiments in visual scanning. *American Journal of Psychology*, **76**, 376–85.

Neisser, U. (1967). *Cognitive psychology*. Appleton-Century-Crofts, New York.

Norman, D. A. (1968). Toward a theory of memory and attention. *Psychological Review*, **75**, 522–36.

Norman, D. A. and Shallice, T. (1980). *Attention to action: Willed and automatic control of behavior* (Report No. 8006). University of California, Center for Human Information Processing, San Diego.

Posner, M. I., Walker, J. A., Friedrich, F., and Rafal, R. D. (1984). Effects of parietal injury on covert orienting of attention. *Journal of Neuroscience*, **4**, 1863–74.

Rabbitt, P. M. A. and Goward, L. Age, intelligence and reaction time. *Quarterly Journal of Experimental Psychology*. (In press.)

Rizzolatti, G., Gentilucci, M., and Matelli, M. (1985). Selective spatial attention: one center, one circuit, or many circuits? In *Attention and performance XI*, (ed. M. I. Posner and O. S. M. Marin), pp. 251–65. Erlbaum, Hillsdale, NJ.

Schneider, W. and Shiffrin, R. M. (1977). Controlled and automatic human information processing: I. Detection, search, and attention. *Psychological Review*, **84**, 1–66.

Sorkin, R. D., Pohlmann, L. D., and Gilliom, J. (1973). Simultaneous two-channel signal detection: III. 630 and 1400 Hz signals. *Journal of the Acoustical Society of America*, **53**, 1045–51.

Spearman, C. (1927). *The abilities of man*. Macmillan, New York.

Taira, M., Mine, S., Georgopoulos, A. P., Murata, A., and Sakata, H. (1990). Parietal cortex neurons of the monkey related to the visual guidance of hand movement. *Experimental Brain Research*, **83**, 29–36.

Treisman, A. M. (1969). Strategies and models of selective attention. *Psychological Review*, **76**, 282–99.

Treisman, A. (1988). Features and objects: the fourteenth Bartlett memorial lecture. *Quarterly Journal of Experimental Psychology*, **40A**, 201–37.

Treisman, A. M. and Davies, A. (1973). Divided attention to ear and eye. In *Attention and performance IV*, (ed. S. Kornblum), pp. 101–17. Academic Press, London.

Treisman, A. and Gelade, G. (1980). A feature integration theory of attention. *Cognitive Psychology*, **12**, 97–136.

Treisman, A. and Gormican, S. (1988). Feature analysis in early vision: evidence from search asymmetries. *Psychological Review*, **95**, 15–48.

Ungerleider, L. G. and Mishkin, M. (1982). Two cortical visual systems. In *Analysis of visual behaviour*, (ed. D. J. Ingle, M. A. Goodale, and R. J. W. Mansfield), pp. 549–86. MIT Press, Cambridge, Mass.

Vogels, R., Eeckhout, H., and Orban, G. A. (1988). The effect of feature uncertainty on spatial discriminations. *Perception*, **17**, 565–77.

Warrington, E. K., James, M., and Maciejewski, C. (1986). The WAIS as a lateralizing and localizing diagnostic instrument: a study of 656 patients with unilateral cerebral lesions. *Neuropsychologia*, **24**, 223–39.

Wolfe, J. M., Cave, K. R., and Franzel, S. L. (1989). Guided search: an alternative to the feature integration model for visual search. *Journal of Experimental Psychology: Human Perception and Performance*, **15**, 419–33.

Zeki, S. M. (1978). Uniformity and diversity of structure and function in rhesus monkey prestriate visual cortex. *Journal of Physiology*, **277**, 273–90.

FOUR

Filtering and physiology in visual search: a convergence of behavioural and neurophysiological measures

Peter McLeod and Jon Driver

INTRODUCTION

In Broadbent's celebrated information-processing model of 1958 a central role was played by the filter, which 'operated by selecting those stimulus events which possessed some common feature . . . passing on all other features of those events to the limited capacity system for analysis' (Broadbent 1971, p. 9). The filter selected among competing inputs and passed on only a subset of these, thus lowering the computational load on a subsequent limited-capacity process.

In this chapter we describe a novel form of visual selectivity—filtering by movement. That is, selecting all those stimuli with a particular movement characteristic from a display of moving and stationary stimuli. We will show that this form of selection has the characteristics of Broadbentian 'filtering'—the stimuli selected for further processing share a common feature, and the non-selected stimuli do not interfere with subsequent processing of the selected stimuli. The accuracy with which Broadbent's original description fits this behaviour, investigated thirty years later, is a testimony to the sharpness of his original insights.

One of the major shifts of emphasis in psychological explanation since 1958 has been the attempt to incorporate increasing knowledge about brain structure into models of cognitive performance. This can be seen in efforts to show that data from brain-damaged patients illuminate models of normal cognitive process (for example Shallice 1988), or that the same conclusions about brain systems can be reached either by studying their physiology or by examining their performance in psychophysical experiments (for example Livingstone and Hubel 1987).

However, it is not clear that studying the physiological mechanisms which underlie psychological processes will always be helpful. As yet we know relatively little about the relationship between brain structure and behaviour. Broadbent (1985) warned about the dangers of confusing levels of explanation when relating physiological and behavioural data. He suggested that the appropriate level of explanation in psychology is computational, and that the physiological implementation of a mechanism may be irrelevant to its analysis at this level.

In this chapter we explore the relation between our behavioural data on filtering by movement and neurophysiological evidence concerning the probable underlying mechanism in the visual system. At a computational level, the behaviour corresponds to Broadbent's description of filtering in 1958. But describing this behaviour as 'filtering' does not explain the fine details of performance. Why can the filter be set to select certain combinations of movement characteristics but not others? Why is it easier to select moving stimuli than stationary stimuli in some displays, but the reverse in others? We shall show that evidence from neuroscience provides solutions to these puzzles, and promotes a somewhat different conception of filtering to that suggested by Broadbent's famous diagram of information-flow in the nervous system. That makes one think of filtering as the consequence of a general-purpose, unitary mechanism—the filter. But the neuroscience data we describe (single-cell recordings from the primate visual system and studies of a patient with a specific deficit for visual motion) suggest that the ability to perform filtering by movement stems from the fact that moving and stationary stimuli are represented in different parts of the visual system. The different properties of these distinct areas offer an explanation for the fine details of the filtering behaviour.

FILTERING BY MOVEMENT

Conjunction search. Our experiments on filtering by movement were based on Anne Treisman's pioneering work, summarized in her chapter in this book. She observed that when a simple feature difference distinguished the target from non-targets in visual search (for example a green target among red non-targets, or a target X among non-target Os), deciding whether or not the target was present seemed to be effortless. Subjectively, attention was immediately drawn to the target. This was confirmed by the behavioural data which showed that the time to detect a target was scarcely affected by the number of non-targets in each display. By contrast, when the target was defined by a conjunction of features (for example a green X among green Os and red Xs) the task became more difficult, and search time increased with the number of non-targets in the display. The subjective experience of searching these conjunction displays again accords with the behavioural data—attention is no longer drawn to the target. Detecting it requires active search. Treisman and Gelade (1980) concluded that visual feature integration requires spatial attention, and their hypothesis continues to shape the field.

Moving conjunction search. We repeated the basic conjunction search experiment, but with the previous colour distinction (red versus green) replaced by a motion distinction (moving versus stationary), so that subjects searched for targets defined by a conjunction of form and movement (McLeod *et al.* 1988). In our first study, the target was an X moving up the screen among randomly interspersed Os moving up the screen and stationary Xs (see Fig. 4.1). In this, as in all the experiments to be described, subjects searched for a target which was present on 50 per cent of trials, responding Yes or No with a button in each hand. On different blocks of trials there were different numbers of non-targets in the display. The result of primary interest is the extent to which detection time increases with the number of non-targets. The search rate obtained by plotting detection time against number of stimuli provides an index of task difficulty.

Even though the target is defined by a conjunction of features, searching for a moving X among stationary Xs and moving Os is effortless. The behavioural data confirm this subjective impression—

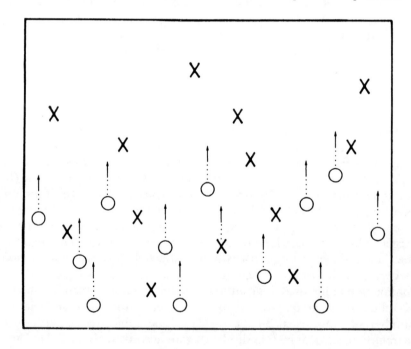

FIG. 4.1. A typical display. The dotted lines indicate moving stimuli. The target is a moving X.

search time is scarcely affected by the number of non-targets. This result, referred to as 'parallel search', is usually found for feature search rather than conjunction search. Introspection suggests one account for this outcome. Phenomenally, the display breaks into two separate groups, one moving up the screen and one stationary. It seems easy to restrict attention to the group moving up the screen, even though the moving and stationary stimuli are spatially intermingled. Once attention has been restricted to the moving items, the task becomes a simple feature search in the moving group for an X among Os, consistent with the parallel search result.*

The initial operation in this hypothesized sequence, the restriction of attention to the moving stimuli and exclusion of the spatially inter-leaved static stimuli, is what we call 'filtering by movement'. This operation fits Broadbent's description of filtering as selection by a common feature, with direction of motion as the critical attribute. Can it also be characterized as filtering in the sense that non-selected items are excluded from further processes? One of the central controversies in the study of attention has been the processing received by unselected items. Broadbent (1982) cited observations that the identities of un-selected items often have little influence on the processing of selected items as crucial evidence in favour of the filtering concept. If filtering is an appropriate description of the selection process involved in our moving search experiments, the non-selected (i.e. stationary) items should have little influence on the processing of the selected (i.e. the moving stimuli). In fact, we were able to demonstrate that the inter-mingled static items can be 'filtered out' during search for a moving target to the extent that their identity has *no* influence on the search process.

Our demonstration involved the task of searching for an R among intermingled Ps and Qs. Previous research using this task in static displays found it to be very difficult, presumably because every feature of the target is shared by one or other of the types of non-target. We showed that the task can be made much easier (search rate drops dra-matically from 58 msec./item to 15 msec./item) by moving the Qs and the target R (if present) up the screen while leaving the Ps stationary (McLeod *et al.* 1988). The filtering account would suggest that this improvement arises because the stationary Ps do not get past a filter

---

* One might, of course, wonder why in Treisman and Gelade's (1980) colour–form conjunction experiments the filter could not be set to select all items with the target colour. This would turn the task into feature search for the target shape among the items with the target colour, so that search time should become independent of the number of distractors. It turns out that parallel search for conjunctions of colour and form can be obtained provided the difference between target and non-target colour is sufficiently vivid (Wolfe *et al.* 1989; Treisman and Sato 1990).

which is set for motion, and hence cannot affect search for the moving R among the moving Qs. On this account, the form of the stationary stimuli should have no impact on the ease of search for the moving R.

We confirmed that this is the case by changing the static Ps to static Qs. If the form of the static non-targets has any influence on search, this manipulation should improve performance for two reasons; the target R now has unique shape features which distinguish it from all the non-targets, and the non-targets are homogeneous in shape, which is known to benefit search (see for example Duncan and Humphreys 1989). However, our manipulation of shape for the static non-targets had no effect whatsoever. Search for a moving R among moving Qs took the same time whether the intermingled stationary stimuli were Ps or Qs. This is an impressive demonstration of the extent to which items that do not possess the selected feature can be prevented from affecting attentional processing.

The fact that the unattended (i.e. static) items in these experiments did not influence attentional processing does not prove that they went completely unprocessed, simply that they were excluded from the search process. Nevertheless, it demonstrates conditions under which a strong prediction of filter theory is found to hold. The experiments show that an operation separating moving and stationary stimuli can take place in the visual system, with the consequence that difficult search tasks (for example for R among Ps and Qs, become easier. We now describe a set of experiments exploring the properties of this operation. To anticipate, we will argue that while filtering provides an appropriate framework for considering the operation, the boundary conditions for efficient filtering by motion can best be understood in relation to the underlying physiology.

(i) Incoherent movement. In the studies described above the motion of the moving stimuli was coherent—they all went in the same direction. Given the well-known power of 'common fate' as a grouping principle, it is perhaps unsurprising that subjects can attend to a subset of items in a display when they all move in a particular direction. What happens if the stimuli move in different directions? Can the filter be set to accept any item which is moving, irrespective of its direction? We tested this in an experiment similar to that first described (search for an X moving up among Os moving up and static Xs), except that individual moving stimuli could move up, down, left, or right at random (McLeod *et al.* 1991). Although responses are slower than when the moving stimuli have a common direction, target detection is still independent of the number of non-targets. It appears that the movement filter can be set to accept any moving item and reject all stationary items.

(ii) Filtering by direction of movement. The tasks described so far all involve separating moving and stationary stimuli. What happens in a display where all the stimuli move, and attention must be directed towards one particular direction of motion? We examined this with displays where the target X (if present) and the non-target O*s* moved in one direction, while the non-target X*s* moved in another (McLeod *et al.* 1991). Search was as easy in this task as when the non-targets were stationary. Thus the filter can be set to select one particular direction of movement and ignore others.

(iii) A limit on the movement filter. We know from these experiments that the filter can be set to accept several different directions of motion, or only a single direction. However, in a further experiment we showed that the task is much harder when subjects have to search both among stimuli moving in one direction and among stationary stimuli, while ignoring stimuli moving in a different direction (McLeod *et al.* 1991). Thus it appears that the movement filter cannot be set to accept one particular direction of moving stimuli *and* stationary stimuli at the same time. This result cannot be attributed to a difficulty in attending to more than one common-fate group, since there is no difficulty in attending to several *moving* common-fate groups simultaneously. Neither can it be attributed to a particular difficulty in attending to static stimuli, as subjects can search in a stationary group and reject the moving with relative ease.

(iv) Asymmetry in movement search. Anne Treisman has recently demonstrated that the phenomenon of asymmetry in visual search is widespread (Treisman and Gormican 1988). Any visual-search task involves the search for a target among distractors. The task can be turned round, with the roles of target and distractor reversed. Despite the apparent logical similarity of these tasks their difficulty is often different. For example, one can search for a vertical line among oblique, or reverse the task and search for an oblique among vertical. The second task turns out to be easier than the first. We found just such an asymmetry in our experiments with movement. We repeated the first experiment with the target now a stationary X. That is, the display contained stationary O*s* and moving X*s* and the target, if present, was a stationary X. Performance was worse. With these stimuli it is harder to search for a target among the stationary stimuli than among the moving.

Why should this be so? Like the limits on which movement features can be searched for simultaneously, outlined in the previous section, we can discover such results by studying behaviour, but get no insight into why they happen.

THE NEURAL SUBSTRATE OF FILTERING
BY MOVEMENT

At this point we turn to neuroscience data on the visual system. We want an explanation for two observations. First, the relative ease of attending to items which move in any direction while ignoring static ones, compared with the difficulty of attending to static stimuli plus one direction of motion while ignoring another direction. And second, the asymmetry which makes it easier to search for moving rather than stationary targets.

Neurophysiological data. The major protection from retina to cortex goes to the striate cortex (area V1). From there information passes by a variety of routes to different cortical areas. One of these routes, through the thick stripes of area 18 to the medial temporal area (MT) appears to be specialized for handling information about stimulus motion (Livingstone and Hubel 1987). Many of the cells in MT show a selective response for stimuli with particular speeds and directions. A comparison of the responses of cells within MT to that of cells within area V1 to moving and stationary slits shows that cells in MT are relatively more sensitive to moving stimuli, and less sensitive to stationary (Albright 1984; Felleman and Kaase 1984). This fits the requirements of a system which could perform as a movement filter. The pathway involving MT may underly the ability to filter by movement by providing a representation of just the moving items, to which attention can then be directed. If this is how filtering by movement is achieved, we can begin to understand why it is relatively easy to attend to all moving items and ignore static items, but relatively difficult to attend to static items and those with a single direction of motion at the same time.

A particularly interesting property of some cells in area MT has been demonstrated by Allman *et al.* (1985). They identified movement cells by showing that they responded to motion in a particular direction within a classical receptive field. They then showed that this response could be attenuated if a large area of background outside the receptive field moved in the same direction as the stimulus within the receptive field. Thus the cells do not just respond to any movement, but specifically to *anomalous* movement, movement which differs from the general movement of the visual field. This would be an essential property for a useful movement filter in the visual system of a moving organism. Once an animal moves there will be optic flow across its retinae, so a movement filter which simply responded to any retinal motion could not distinguish independently moving objects from static objects in the environment. A system representing motion only when it differs from the background motion could get around this problem.

Of course, on the basis of single-cell properties we cannot conclude whether MT acts as a movement filter. The data simply show that cells in this area have appropriate properties.

Neuropsychological data. The idea that one role of the pathway involving MT might be to separate moving and stationary stimuli is supported by visual-search data from a neurological patient, LM. Her case has been described in detail by Zihl (Zihl *et al.* 1983, 1991). Following a venal sinus thrombosis, she suffered bilateral damage to extrastriate areas of the occipital and parietal cortex. The damage includes regions which are thought on the basis of PET scan studies to be the human homologue of monkey MT. LM has preserved vision for stationary stimuli, including normal colour vision, normal acuity and so on, but has a wide range of deficits all related to aspects of moving stimuli (Zihl *et al.* 1983, 1991; Baker *et al.* 1991; Hess *et al.* 1989).* The fact that her complex deficits are all related to various aspects of stimulus motion, while her vision appears normal for stationary stimuli, suggests, in agreement with the single-cell recordings, that there is a specific pathway within the primate visual system for handling motion information.

We tested her ability to perform visual-search tasks like those described earlier, where she was required to detect targets defined by a conjunction of form and motion (for example a moving X among moving Os and stationary Xs). Like ordinary subjects she is capable of detecting feature targets, defined by either unique form or unique movement, across the visual field in parallel. Thus, if she has to detect whether there is a single X in a display of Os, or a single moving X in a display of stationary Xs, her detection time is unaffected by the number of non-targets in the display. Her overall response times to detect the single moving stimulus are slower than normal (she takes about 1 sec. compared to a normal value of about 250 msec.) but there is no effect of increasing the number of non-targets. Thus, she can detect movement (at 1°/sec.) and, like normals, can do so across the visual field in parallel. However, when she has to detect a conjunction of this motion distinction with the form distinction (a moving X among moving Os and static Xs) her search, unlike that of normals, becomes slow and serial. Her detection-time increases to about 160 msec./item

---

* LM is sometimes described as being 'motion blind'. This is not an accurate description since, for example, we have found in unpublished studies that she is capable of correctly describing the events in Johansson displays where form information is only available by interpretation of motion.

(McLeod *et al.* 1989). We demonstrated that her difficulty with this task is caused by an inability to separate moving and stationary stimuli and then exclude the latter from search. The stationary X*s* interfered with her search for the moving X. In other words, one consequence of damage to the suspected human homologue of area MT was that she lacked the ability to filter by movement.*

THE RELATION BETWEEN BEHAVIOURAL AND NEUROPHYSIOLOGICAL DATA

The behavioural data show that people can filter by movement. The neurophysiological evidence shows that a particular cortical area contains cells with properties which could be the basis of a movement filter. The patient data suggests a link between these two lines of evidence, since someone with damage involving the cortical area is unable to produce the behaviour. We can summarize the evidence so far as suggesting that filtering by movement is achieved by a part of the visual system which represents all the moving objects in a display but none of the stationary. The pathway involving area MT is a plausible candidate. In the rest of this paper we shall try to show that our hypothesis about the underlying neural structure can help in understanding the behavioural data on filtering by movement, revealing these data to be orderly and predictable rather than arbitrary.

Predicting behaviour from neurophysiology. The neurophysiological evidence suggests that, rather than viewing filtering by movement as an example of the operation of a general-purpose mechanism within the nervous system, it might be more appropriate to consider it as a specific consequence of the visual system's segregation into distinct pathways. One such pathway represents only moving stimuli, with static stimuli represented elsewhere.

Evidence from neuroscience and psychophysics suggests that representation within the motion pathway differs from representation in the pathways handling stationary stimuli in a number of respects. We designed search-tasks to exploit these differences, using displays of intermingled moving and stationary stimuli, which required, for efficient search, that attention was directed to just the moving or just the static items. If our account of filtering in terms of distinct visual path-

---

* Her search for conjunction targets that did not include motion as a feature (e.g. a conjunction of colour and form) was within the normal range, showing that the damage to her visual system produced a decrement specific to detecting conjunctions involving motion, not to detecting conjunctions in general.

ways is appropriate, search should be easier among the moving items for attributes which are well represented by the moving pathway, and easier among the static items for attributes which are well represented in the part of the system which handles stationary stimuli.

Conjunction search within a moving group (for a moving X among moving Os and static Xs) is easier than a comparable search within a stationary group (for a static X among static Os and moving Xs). This asymmetry suggests that the system used for identifying static conjunction targets is less successful at filtering out moving non-targets than the movement filter is at filtering out static ones. This proposal is consistent with the existing neurophysiological data; while cells in MT are sensitive to moving stimuli but have little response to static stimuli, no cells with a comparable preference for static stimuli over moving stimuli have been found. The proposal is also consistent with psychophysical evidence about different channels in the visual system which analyse moving and stationary stimuli. Tolhurst (1973) found that preadaptation with a moving grating reduced the sensitivity for detecting either a moving or stationary grating. In contrast, preadaptation with a stationary grating affected the sensitivity for a stationary grating but not for a moving one. This result suggests two subsystems in the visual system. One represents moving but not static items, and is responsible for threshold judgements about moving stimuli. This corresponds to our proposed movement filter. Since this subsystem does not respond to static stimuli, thresholds for moving stimuli are unaffected by preadaptation with static stimuli. A second channel or set of channels (which we will call the form subsystem) is responsible for threshold judgements involving static stimuli. However, it has some representation of moving stimuli as well. Hence thresholds for static stimuli can be affected by preadaptation with either moving or stationary stimuli. The crucial point to note here is the asymmetry. The system used for making judgements about moving items effectively filters out stationary stimuli. But the system used for making judgements about stationary stimuli is less effective at filtering out the moving.

Neurophysiological and psychophysical data suggest further differences between the parts of the visual system representing moving or stationary objects, besides their respective abilities to filter out stationary or moving stimuli. Neurones in cortical areas which are specialized for motion processing (such as MT) have less finely-tuned orientation-sensitivity and lower spatial resolution than those in other visual areas (Livingstone and Hubel 1987). Similarly, channels which are shown psychophysically to be especially sensitive to moving stimuli have relatively broad tuning for orientation (Sharpe and Tolhurst 1973) and

TABLE 4.1. The relative abilities of those parts of the visual system specialized for handling moving or stationary stimuli

	Filtering by movement	Representation of form
Movement subsystem	Good	Poor
Form subsystem	Poor	Good

spatial frequency (Livingstone and Hubel 1987; Tolhurst 1973; Breitmeyer and Ganz 1976).

Thus, the overall picture from neurophysiology and psychophysics is that the areas of the visual system which specialize in processing motion are good at filtering out stationary stimuli, but have a relatively poor representation of visual form. In contrast, areas which are specialized for representing the form of stationary stimuli are relatively poor at filtering out moving stimuli, but of course have a good representation of form. These contrasting abilities are summarized in Table 4.1. The crossover of abilities allows us to predict the possibility of an interaction between the fineness of the form-discrimination which separates target and non-target, and the ease of searching for the target in a group of moving versus stationary stimuli. The argument is as follows:

(i) *Search for a moving conjunction target.* This task can be done within the movement filter provided the form-distinction between target and non-targets is one which can be captured by the relatively crude representation of form within this system. Since the movement filter will exclude the static non-targets with the target shape, search will be fast and parallel. However, if the form-distinction between target and non-target is made more subtle, the representation in the movement filter may no longer be adequate for distinguishing target and non-targets among the moving stimuli. The task will then have to be performed by the form sub-system. This represents both moving and stationary items, so it can do the task. But since there will be no possibility of filtering by movement the task will be slow and serial.

(ii) *Search for a static conjunction target.* This task will be carried out by the form subsystem. Since the form subsystem is relatively poor at filtering out the moving non-targets which have the target shape, performance will not be as good as it is with moving targets in the conditions when the motion filter can be used to exclude the static non-targets (i.e. with an easy form-discrimination). However, as the form subsystem has good form-discrimination, it will be able to distinguish target and non-target whether the form-distinction is fine or gross. Thus we should not see a dramatic change in performance as the difficulty of the form-discrimination changes.

In summary: search for a moving conjunction target should be fast and parallel if the form-distinction is relatively easy, but should become slow and serial if the form-distinction is more subtle. If the target is stationary, search will not be as good as search for a moving target if the form-distinction is easy. But the drop in performance as the difficulty of the form-discrimination increases should be less than with a moving target. Thus we predict that there will be an interaction between the difficulty of the form-discrimination, and whether the target is moving or stationary.

This is precisely what we found in an experiment where the required form-judgement was either a relatively crude orientation discrimination (45° versus vertical) or a fine one (9° versus vertical) (Driver and McLeod 1992). Typical displays are shown in Fig. 4.2.

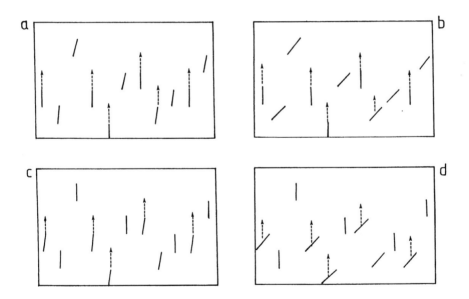

FIG. 4.2. Typical displays. The dashed lines indicate moving stimuli. In the upper panels the target is one of the moving lines. It is distinguished from the moving non-targets either by a small orientation difference (a) or by a large difference (b). In the lower panels the target is stationary. There is either a small (c) or a large (d) orientation difference between target and stationary non-targets.

In the moving conjunction-search tasks, subjects searched for a moving tilted line among moving vertical lines and static tilted lines. Search was parallel (3 msec./item for target detection) in the 45° tilted vs. vertical condition (Fig. 4.2, panel b), but much slower (23 msec./item for target detection) in the 9° conditon (Fig. 4.2, panel a). In the static conjunction tasks, subjects searched for a static tilted line among static vertical lines and moving tilted lines. Performance was worse than the moving task in the 45° case (Fig. 4.2, panel d), but better in the 9° case (Fig. 4.2, panel c). Thus increasing the difficulty of the orientation discrimination had less effect when the target was stationary than when it was moving. This interaction is shown in Table 4.2. It can be seen whether one looks at the search rates given by the slopes of

TABLE 4.2. Search for a target defined by a conjunction of movement and form. The target is either moving or stationary. The form-difference distinguishing target and non-targets is either easy (45° vs. vertical) or difficult (9° vs. vertical). Upper panel shows search rates (msec./item) from trials on which a target was detected; the lower panel shows average search times (msec.) averaged across Yes and No trials and set-sizes of 7, 15, and 25 items.

Note that in both cases there is an interaction. Search for a moving target is easier than for a stationary target provided the form-distinction between target and non-target is easy. But if the form-distinction is difficult, search is easier for a stationary target than for a moving.

Target detection rates (msec./item)

| | | Form discrimination | |
		Difficult	Easy
Target	Moving	23	3
	Stationary	16	11

Decision time (msec.)

| | | Form discrimination | |
		Difficult	Easy
Target	Moving	1223	749
	Stationary	1048	850

the set-size functions (upper panel) or at the overall speed of response (lower panel). This is precisely the interaction between the difficulty of the form-distinction and whether or not the conjunction target is moving or stationary which we predicted on the basis of the established neurophysiological and psychophysical properties of visual subsystems sensitive to moving or to stationary stimuli summarized in Table 4.1.

These data demonstrate that the fine details of filtering by motion are predictable on the basis of neurophysiological and psychophysical evidence about the properties of distinct channels within the visual system. We have established, behaviourally, boundary conditions on filtering by motion. First, although subjects can restrict their attention to just the moving items in order to make a simple form-discrimination, they cannot restrict attention simultaneously to items moving in one direction plus static items. Second, their ability to restrict attention to just the moving items is no help if they have to make a fine form-discrimination within them.

These facts about filtering by motion make sense in the light of the neuroscience data on distinct pathways in the visual system. They would remain arbitrary and unexplained facts for any analysis which made no reference to the underlying neural structures. Filtering by movement may not be a typical example of the relationship between behavioural analyses of cognitive operations and neurophysiological data, because more is known about the neurophysiology of the primate visual system than about most other cognitive systems. However, at least in this case the relationship between behavioural data and neuroscience data does appear to be one of convergence and symbiosis.

REFERENCES

Albright, T. (1984). Direction and orientation selectivity of neurons in visual area MT of the macaque. *Journal of Neurophysiology*, **52**, 1106–30.

Allman, J., Miezin, F., and McGuinness, E. (1985). Direction and velocity specific responses from beyond the classical receptive field in the middle temporal visual area (MT). *Perception*, **14**, 105–26.

Baker, C., Hess, R., and Zihl, J. (1991). Residual motion perception in a 'motion-blind' patient, assessed with limited-lifetime random dot displays. *Journal of Neuroscience*, **11**, 454–61.

Breitmeyer, B. and Ganz, L. (1976). Implications of sustained and transient channels for theories of visual pattern masking, saccadic suppression and information processing. *Psychological Review*, **83**, 1–36.

Broadbent, D. (1958). *Perception and communication*. Pergamon Press, Oxford.

Broadbent, D. (1971). *Decision and stress*. Academic Press, London.

Broadbent, D. (1982). Task combination and selective intake of information. *Acta Psychologica*, **50**, 253–90.

Broadbent, D. (1985). A question of levels: comment on McClelland and Rumelhart. *Journal of Experimental Psychology: General*, **114**, 189–92.

Driver, J. and McLeod, P. (1992). Reversing visual search asymmetries with conjunction search of movement and orientation. *Journal of Experimental Psychology: Human Perception and Performance*, **18**, 22–33.

Duncan, J. and Humphreys, G. (1989). Visual search and stimulus similarity. *Psychological Review*, **96**, 433–58.

Felleman, D. and Kaase, J. (1984). Receptive-field properties of neurons in Middle Temporal Area (MT) of owl monkeys. *Journal of Neurophysiology*, **52**, 488–513,

Hess, R., Baker, C., and Zihl, J. (1989). The 'motion-blind' patient: low level spatial and temporal filters. *The Journal of Neuroscience*, **9**, 1628–40.

Livingstone, M. and Hubel, D. (1987). Psychophysical evidence for separate channels for the perception of form, color, movement and depth. *The Journal of Neuroscience*, **7**, 3416–68.

McLeod, P., Driver, J., and Crisp, J. (1988). Visual search for a conjunction of movement and form is parallel. *Nature*, **332**, 154–5.

McLeod, P., Heywood, C., Driver, J., and Zihl, J. (1989). Selective deficit of visual search in moving displays after extrastriate damage. *Nature*, **339**, 466–7.

McLeod, P., Driver, J., Dienes, Z., and Crisp, J. (1991). Filtering by movement in visual search. *Journal of Experimental Psychology: Human Perception and Performance*, **17**, 55–64.

Shallice, T. (1988). *From neuropsychology to mental structure*. Cambridge University Press.

Sharpe, C. and Tolhurst, D. (1973). The effects of temporal modulation on the orientation channels of the human visual system. *Perception*, **2**, 23–9.

Tolhurst, D. (1973). Separate channels for the analysis of the shape and the movement of a moving visual stimulus. *Journal of Physiology*, **231**, 385–402.

Treisman, A. and Gelade, G. (1980). A feature integration theory of attention. *Cognitive Psychology*, **12**, 97–136.

Treisman, A. and Gormican, S. (1988). Feature analysis in early vision: evidence from search asymmetries. *Psychological Review*, **95**, 15–48.

Treisman, A. and Sato, S. (1990). Conjunction search revisited. *Journal of Experimental Psychology: Human Perception and Performance*, **16**, 459–78.

Wolfe, J., Cave, K., and Franzel, S. (1989). Guided search: an alternative to the feature integration model for visual search. *Journal of Experimental Psychology: Human Perception and Performance*, **15**, 419–33.

Zihl, J., von Cramon, D., and Mai, N. (1983). Selective disturbance of movement vision after bilateral brain damage. *Brain*, **106**, 313–40.

Zihl, J., von Cramon, D., Mai, N., and Schmid, C. (1991). Disturbance of movement vision: further evidence and follow up observations. *Brain*, **114**, 2235–52.

FIVE

Objects, streams, and threads of auditory attention

Dylan Jones

One of Donald Broadbent's longest-standing interests has been in auditory attention. Through the use of the 'split span' technique and subsequent theoretical work he has made a significant contribution to our understanding of the fate of unattended material (Broadbent 1958, 1971). By showing how certain types of unattended material were difficult to apprehend or recall, it was possible for him to pinpoint the level to which they had been processed. The notion of processing at a pre-attentive level was to have a profound influence on our understanding of information-processing in both the auditory and visual modality (see also Broadbent 1983). Alas, the volume of work on auditory attention is now rather small, overwhelmed in these proceedings and elsewhere by research on visual attention. Nevertheless, despite the enormous strides made in the 1960s and 1970s (see, for example, Broadbent 1982 for an overview), there are several issues in auditory attention which remain to be understood. This chapter reports recent research on auditory distraction using visual short-term memory tasks in which the primary manipulation is the nature of background sound. By studying the degree of disruption produced by a range of sounds it has been possible to reveal the degree to which sound is processed pre-attentively and to study the confluence of information from visual and auditory modalities. In addition it is hoped that these studies will suggest ways in which serial short-term recall may be modelled.

This chapter offers some generalizations about the nature of auditory attention which have implications for a range of cognitive functions. The generalizations are embodied in a theory of working memory which uses the analogy of a blackboard on which objects are assembled (known as the Object-Orientated Episodic Record or O-OER model). These objects may be of visual or auditory origin, and a stream of objects is joined in memory by links or pointers. Essentially this chapter is about how these objects are formed and how they are organized into streams.

For the most part, the studies to be described are ones involving focused attention in which the subject is required to undertake a task presented in the visual modality and to ignore events in the auditory modality. The typical experiment is relatively simple: visual lists are presented serially, and written serial recall is required. On some trials sound is also present. An important common feature of the experiments is that subjects are told specifically to ignore what they hear and that they will not be asked to recall any information presented auditorily. The auditory stream is thus referred to as being 'irrelevant'. Early investigations of performance using this paradigm established that if speech is played during a trial then recall is impaired, and by a non-trivial amount, typically of the order of 30 per cent (see Colle and Welsh 1976; Colle 1980).

What are the general characteristics of the sound that determine the degree of disruption? What are the characteristics of the task which augment or diminish the degree of disruption? The answers to these questions can be addressed in terms of seven generalizations about auditory distraction and working memory.

SEVEN EMPIRICAL GENERALIZATIONS

1: Intensity and meaning have no effect

The first significant point is that the effect of speech on serial recall is not much like that of white noise. Indeed, the effect of broad-band noise on serial recall is inconsistent (see Jones 1990 for a review); but other factors also point to the conclusion that speech and noise have qualitatively different effects. Most notably, the effect of irrelevant speech on serial recall is independent of intensity (see Colle 1980), which implies that it is not a consequence of any change in the subject's state of arousal.

Given that intensity is not important, a natural first guess is that the meaning of the speech is important, so that the person's attention is drawn away by the relatively more captivating contents of the auditory channel. As it happens, this guess turns out to be completely wrong, at least for serial recall. A number of studies have shown that speech in a language which the person does not understand leads to disruption (Colle and Welsh 1976; Colle 1980; Salamé and Baddeley, for example 1982); and that the effect is roughly the same as for narrative English for English speakers (Jones et al. 1990). It is worth noting in passing that tasks such as reading show a different pattern of results. They are sensitive to the effects of meaning (Martin et al. 1988; Jones et al. 1990), but the relation of such effects to those found with serial recall awaits further analysis.

The absence of an effect of meaning is particularly interesting since it suggests that supra-segmental factors such as the organization of speech sounds into higher-order groupings may play a minor role, and that some factor operating at the level of the syllable is important. A related result, that reversed speech has effects equivalent to those of normal narrative speech (Jones *et al.* 1990) further confirms the hypothesis that meaning plays a minor role, but also reinforces the suspicion that some process related to the low-level analysis of speech is at work. Moreover, reversed speech does not contain familiar acoustic/phonetic sequences, and suggests that pattern-recognition mechanisms used for *identifying* speech sounds may not play a significant role.

2: Disruption occurs in memory not at encoding

Does the interference occur when the material is being registered or encoded? Or does it happen with codes already registered in memory? If the effect only occurs at encoding it implies that it could occur with any task, provided it is sufficiently attention-demanding. Evidence converges from several experiments to suggest unequivocally that, at least as far as serial recall is concerned, effects at encoding are minimal, and that the effect's locus is in memory. First, effects are largely absent from non-memory tasks; and second, effects are found when the person is only exposed to speech in the period *after* encoding.

Non-memory tasks. A number of unpublished studies show that irrelevant speech has no effect on many non-memory tasks. For instance, the visual serial reaction task (in which the stimuli are non-verbal and the load on memory is very small) is one which is sensitive to continuous white noise (see, for example, Jones 1983) but proves entirely immune to the effects of irrelevant speech. We have also been able to show that irrelevant speech has no effect on speech *production*. In an unpublished study we were able to assess the quality of subjects' speech by using information supplied by computer-based speech-recognition algorithms. Each time an automatic speech-recognizer encounters an utterance it yields a goodness-of-fit measure of its similarity to the speaker's templates against which it is compared (see Frankish *et al.* 1992 for a discussion). In a task in which subjects read postcodes aloud in a simulated parcel-sorting task, we compared goodness-of-fit measures in conditions of silence with those in the presence of irrelevant speech. Even over a prolonged period of work, lasting some forty minutes, there was no sign that the presence of irrelevant speech affected the quality of speech production.

The effect of irrelevant speech on naming of words has been subject to a good deal of research. However, the results are rather inconsistent.

Cowan and Barron (1987) found that the naming of both colour-words (in black ink) and Stroop interference material (colour-words in an incompatible hue) was slowed if subjects also heard colour-words while doing the task. Subjects were required to say aloud either the colour of a string of printed X*s* (which acted as a control condition), or the colour words printed in incongruously coloured ink (the Stroop material). The effects of several types of auditory material were contrasted with silence: spoken colour-words, the English alphabet, the word 'the' repeated continuously, and instrumental music. Only spoken colour-words produced any disruption. This contrasts with the state of affairs with memory tasks, since the effect on the Stroop task is brought about only by auditory material which bears some *semantic* relation to the material which is being read. Cowan (1989) used a slightly different technique in which subjects were required to name the colour of dots, and again only *semantic* interference was found: auditory colour-words slowed naming, but non-colour words did not. However, several other studies have failed to show this cross-modal semantic interference. Five experiments in our laboratory using procedures similar to those just described failed to show the effect (Miles *et al.* 1989; Miles and Jones 1989). Similar studies with comparable procedures undertaken else-where have proved equally negative (Thackray and K. Jones 1971; Thackray *et al.* 1972). On the basis of this evidence it seems fairly safe to conclude that when studied in this way word-naming is relatively immune to disruption from extraneous speech, although later in the chapter it will be argued that in some circumstances cross-modal effects at encoding can occur.

Timing of the exposure. Serial recall tasks involve three phases: an encoding phase; a partially overlapping rehearsal phase; and the re-trieval phase. If irrelevant speech disrupts the initial registration of the visual stimulus, then one should only find the effect if the disrupting material is present at the first of these stages. In two studies we have shown that irrelevant speech produces impairments of equal magnitude at presentation and rehearsal phases (Quayle *et al.* 1988; Miles *et al.* 1991). The effect of irrelevant speech is markedly diminished if the subject also has to undertake an articulatory suppression task. It is important to note that the effect is roughly the same whether the joint action occurs at either presentation or rehearsal stage. This last result is of significance because it distinguishes two possible outcomes. If the disruption were taking place at encoding, irrelevant speech and articu-latory suppression would exert independent and additive effects at input; but during the rehearsal stage of the task only concurrent articu-lation would have an effect (due to inhibition of subvocal rehearsal of target items), whereas irrelevant speech would have no effect. In contrast, if performance results from interference in memory, irrelevant speech and articulatory suppression would have equal effects at both stages of the task. This latter pattern was the one which was in fact observed.

These studies did not deal with effects at the retrieval phase; but the evidence cited above on speech-production, together with a range of other findings, suggests that there is either no effect at retrieval or that, because retrieval contains components of production and memory, the effect will be an extension of the one found during rehearsal. This generalization suggests that we should look more closely at the different functional components of retention as a means of discovering how precisely the interference occurs between extraneous speech and material being rehearsed in memory. Clearly, it is possible that some kinds of operation in memory are not influenced by irrelevant speech, whereas others may show very great sensitivity.

3: Disruption only occurs with serial recall

Are some aspects of memory performance more susceptible to disruption than others? All the studies cited thus far that demonstrate an irrelevant speech effect have involved serial recall, which leads us to question whether other types of recall and memory for non-verbal material are also susceptible. One way we have attempted to tackle this issue is to see if some already-identified memory subsystems are immune to the effect of irrelevant speech. Immunity from disruption would add weight to the suggestion that the effect is not one due to interference at encoding, but rather stems from the functional characteristics of the memory system. For example, Morris and Jones (submitted) used a task involving memory for the position of dots, a task which requires very little verbal mediation. Performance in this task showed no effect of irrelevant speech, but nevertheless was sensitive enough to interference to be adversely affected by a concurrent tracking task. Using a slightly different approach, Morris and Jones (1990a) studied the supposed action of the central executive portion of the working memory system by presenting subjects with lists of unpredictable length and asking them to recall the last four items that they saw. By varying list-length the number of times the set of items under active rehearsal was updated could be manipulated. In these experiments the number of updates was to be varied between zero and six. Although irrelevant speech impaired memory, the effect was roughly the same regardless of the number of updates that had to be made. Control processes deployed to govern *updating* in memory therefore seem to be immune to the effects of irrelevant speech, while the serial recall component remains susceptible to disruption.

Another way to resolve the issue is to contrast two tasks that are roughly equated in terms of attentional demands, and then to manipulate independently the type of information to be retained. In one experiment subjects are shown a list of digits, followed by a probe digit. The subject's task is to report the digit that appears after the probe in the list, a requirement which calls upon the retrieval of order information. Irrelevant speech has its usual deleterious effect on performance of this task. In a variant of this procedure, again a serial list of integers is presented, but this time the subject is required to detect a digit that had been *omitted* from the list. In this case, knowledge of serial order is not a prerequisite of successful recall, and there is no effect of irrelevant speech. These results harmonize well with the finding of Salamé and Baddeley (1990) that free-recall tasks are relatively immune to the disruptive effects of speech. They also suggest that the interference is based on disrupting the order of events, and that order cues from the irrelevant speech may be in conflict with those generated by the process of rehearsal in working memory. Logically, it is entirely possible that such cues also could be present in non-speech sounds.

4: Speech and non-speech are equipotent

Salamé and Baddeley (1982), in a seminal work, suggest a model to account for the 'unattended speech' effect that has two stages: a filter that excludes non-speech sounds and a phonological store in which the 'phonological similarity' between the irrelevant speech stream and the list for recall determines the degree of disruption. Evidence of the second stage of the model is based on an experiment which compared quiet with three types of speech having different degrees of similarity to the to-be-remembered digit list: 'phonologically similar' words (*tun* (one), *gnu* (two), *tee* (three), *sore* (four), etc.); 'phonologically dissimilar' words (*tennis, jelly, tipple*, etc.); and the integers themselves, described as the 'semantically similar' condition. The semantically- and phonologically-similar words gave comparable degrees of disruption, while the effect of phonologically dissimilar words was significantly less, but still appreciably worse than the quiet control (Salamé and Baddeley 1982, Experiment 5). This outcome suggests a mechanism in which the degree of disruption is proportional to the similarity between the auditory memory-codes in the two streams. The 'phonologically dissimilar' words were *longer* than the other two types, but this is probably not a significant confounding feature, since in an earlier experiment Salamé and Baddeley (1982) had shown that long and short words produce roughly the same amount of disruption (see also Salamé and Baddeley 1986).

The notion of the filter employed in the first stage of the model was based on the finding that broad-band noise (either continuous or intermittent) failed to disrupt serial recall (Salamé and Baddeley 1982; Jones et al. 1990). However, there are logical and empirical objections to the notion of a filter. The intended meaning of the term 'phonological similarity' has never been made explicit; but assuming it is intended to encompass attributes such as 'rhyming', then logically disruption could only occur with speech input. However, the pattern of disruption would still give the illusory appearance of a filter mechanism even if all sounds were passed by the filter (Jones et al. 1992). By itself, this logical objection undermines considerably the idea of a filter. It would be further weakened by finding that non-speech sounds produced effects identical in form and size to those of speech.

To test this possibility we used sequences of tones, and found that a random sequence of four tones produced impairments hitherto only produced by speech. Even more striking was the finding that the disruptive effect of four tones was as great as that for a sequence of four syllables. This evidence, coupled with the logical difficulty mentioned above, suggests that the concept of a speech-specific filter is unnecessary, and that many types of sound may cause disruption to memory performance.

These results imply that tones and speech are equipotent: the distinctiveness of a multidimensional stimulus like speech gives it no greater disruptive potency than a simple steady-state tone (*pace* Liberman and Mattingly 1985; Lieberman 1984). That acoustically these two types of material are so different, but give rise to more or less identical effects on performance must confound any account based on the similarity of the visual and auditory material. The results suggest further that some simple analysis of the auditory stream, insensitive to the gross acoustic differences between speech and steady-state tones, serves as the basis for disruption.

5: 'Auditory changing state' is a necessary condition

If speech and non-speech are equipotent, what feature of the sound brings about disruption? In several studies we have been able to demonstrate that if no between-utterance variation occurs in the irrelevant speech-stream, then no disruption ensues. So, for example, if the irrelevant stream is made up of a repeated syllable, or of a continuous vowel-sound (created by digital processing of a sustained 'ah', for example) then no disruption of serial recall occurs. However, if a sequence of *different* syllables is heard (even when the syllables are drawn from a set as small as three), then the usual disruption is found (Jones *et al.* 1992, Experiment 1). Moreover, the effect is the same whether the syllables are heard in a fixed or random order, suggesting that *supra-syllabic* organization or 'top-down' influence is not very important (as is also suggested by the absence of an effect of meaning) and that some factor at the level of the single segmented utterance is at work. These results do not in themselves constitute a case against the disruption in memory's being due to similarities in sound between the stream and the list; but they do suggest that syllable-to-syllable variation in the irrelevant stream is also an important factor, rather than any specific relationship between the heard and seen material.

Not every attribute of the spoken word may serve as the basis for signifying such changing state, however. For example, if the same utterance is repeated but with a different (synthesized) voice with each new utterance, the irrelevant speech effect remains negligible. Similarly, in unpublished studies we have shown that if a repeated utterance changes in loudness from one utterance to the next, the disruptive effect of speech is rather small. This pattern of results suggests that the representation of speech sounds in memory is relatively abstract. Although the representation apparently does not include information about the speaker or about intensity, it has become clear that it does include some information over and above the phonetic features necessary for the discrimination of phonemes. This point may be illustrated by the results of an experiment in which five copies of an utterance are made and then transformed digitally so that they form a series spaced a semitone apart. The use of digital processing techniques ensures that these utterances are phonetically identical in every characteristic except pitch.

Nevertheless, sounds generated by this procedure give rise to a pronounced disruption of serial recall (Jones and Macken, in press). Another example is the case in which disruption occurs when the same utterance is repeated and the interval between utterances is made variable rather than fixed (Jones and Macken, submitted). In these two instances the phonetic characteristics do not vary from utterance to utterance, but the speech nevertheless manages to interfere with serial recall. It is significant that in this case the magnitude of disruption is as large as it is with material which displays very great variation, such as narrative speech. In the two examples just given, every parameter but one was held constant: thus changing state is being conveyed here purely by change in pitch between utterances, or by a change in the interval between utterances. The fact that in both examples the sound-based similarities between the auditory material and the visual list are also constant further suggests that some mechanism in addition to auditory similarity must be at work.

One possibility is that changing state and auditory similarity are two independent modes of disruption. An experiment by Jones and Macken (in press) looked at this possibility. Instead of using words in the irrelevant speech, syllables were used that were either identical to the visual list or were distinctly different. However, it might be argued that this is a contrast of *lexical identity* rather than of *phonological similarity*. Since Salamé and Baddeley (1982) used lexical identity as a condition (their 'semantically similar' condition), and found effects identical to a condition which they called 'phonologically similar', in which non-digit words were used (like 'tun', see above), the objection to lexical identity as a condition must therefore lose much of its force. In the event, our study showed that in relation to controls there was a very large effect of irrelevant speech, but only a small effect in the 'identical syllable' condition.

As operationalized in these studies the notion of 'changing state' has powerful explanatory force, although it can be criticized for being rather all-encompassing, since it lacks the refinement to predict which sounds will show most disruption. One possibility is that changing state only applies to discrete sounds, change being signified by silence-defined boundaries.

6: Auditory events are segregated into streams

In the light of the foregoing the term 'irrelevant speech effect' now appears inappropriate. In its stead we propose the term 'auditory changing state effect'. The evidence already reviewed points to the fact that change was not specified at the supra-syllable level, but it is not yet clear whether change could be specified only in terms of successive utterances or whether the degree of within-utterance change was also important. Evidence is beginning to emerge which points to the fact that only between-utterance variability is important. For example, the fact that successive *steady-state* tones produce effects equivalent to those of a string of syllables (in which the pitch and amplitude are co-varying within each syllable) suggests that within-sound variability has little effect on the degree of disruption (Jones and Macken, in press).

We examined the idea that within-sound variation is less influential than between-sound variation by extending an observation made by Morris *et al.* (1987). They showed that when a passage was either spoken or sung the usual disruption of serial recall occurred, but when the same passage was hummed, the disruption was markedly diminished. One possible reason for the diminished effect is that humming is an extended utterance largely free of cues to segmentation. In turn, this suggested two hypotheses. First, if non-speech stimuli are not clearly segmented into separate entities by silence they will fail to disrupt serial recall. Second, that for strings of speech, silence is not necessary, since recognition processes such as those of categorical perception will act to segment the stream (see also Morris and Jones 1990*b*).

The first hypothesis was put to the test by generating electronically a continuous sound which consisted of slow, random, pitch-glides. The changes in frequency, though not sudden, were continuously varying and clearly discernible. As we predicted, since there was no discontinuity, this form of change was insufficient to bring about disruption of serial recall. However, if the *same* glides were interrupted regularly by silence, disruption did occur. We used this technique to show also that within-sound variation is less important than between-sound variation, in an experiment in which the ratio of sound to silence was either 1:1 or 4:1. Specifically, the silences were always 200 msec. but the length of the sound could either be 200 msec. or 800 msec. Arguably, for each separate sound the variation in stimulation would be greater in the latter case; but in fact both conditions showed very similar effects on serial recall.

The second hypothesis, that speech sounds do not require silence for segmentation, was tested by synthesizing a speech sound which ranged over eight vowel sounds, and was thus *continuously* voiced. Despite being continuous, such sounds did produce an irrelevant speech effect. Moreover, introducing regular silences into the stream between each vowel did not augment the degree of disruption in serial recall (Jones *et al.*, in press). This is just as one might expect if the top-down processes of speech segmentation had already been applied to the continuous utterance.

As a simple generalization, therefore, the auditory stream should be segmentable and the segmented sound must change state from sound to sound if it is to have an effect on serial recall. For non-speech, segment boundaries are usually marked by periods of silence, but for speech the overlearned categories used in speech perception may serve to segment the signal on the basis of feature-extraction, even when it is acoustically continuous. However, alternative interpretations are possible. For example, recent work on the perception of stops and glides in speech suggests that discrimination is based on correlated attributes of the speech signal. Walsh and Diehl (1991) found that the cues used in distinguishing stops from glides in speech are similar to those used in making discriminations in non-speech stimuli. The implication is that those changes of frequency and amplitude which typically occur at the boundaries of a speech sound could also serve as the basis for segmentation of the speech stream. Hence a simple process detecting changes in the natural correlations found in auditory signals rather than a process based on recognizing features of speech could serve as the basis for segmentation. This is further suggested by the fact that reversed speech (which contains unusual, unfamiliar acoustic–phonetic sequences for which the subject is unlikely to have well-developed mechanisms of feature-extraction) is as potent as narrative speech in producing disruption in the irrelevant-speech paradigm.

Regardless of which interpretation is correct, the important point is that the results of these studies may help to account for the inconsistent results found by Salamé and Baddeley (1989) with a variety of musical stimuli which ranged over vocal and instrumental music. The effects could not be anticipated on the basis of the speech/non-speech distinction alone, and the results of our studies suggest that a more useful way in which the outcome could be predicted would be the ease with which the stream can be segmented.

7: Streaming overrides the effect of changing state

Evidence is just beginning to emerge that a simple version of the changing-state hypothesis is inadequate. It appears that superordinate organization of the material into auditory streams may overcome the effect of changing state (see Bregman 1990; Handel 1989). In a recent experiment (Jones and Macken, submitted) we contrasted the effects of two types of stream organization. In both cases the spoken material was the same: a sequence of three syllables was presented in a fixed order. In one condition the syllables were presented monaurally, so that the subject heard just one stream of varied syllables, localized in the middle of the head. We predicted that a single coherent stream would be formed, but one within which the contents were changing and which would hence meet the conditions for changing-state effect. In the other condition the same syllables were presented, but this time arranged so that each was assigned exclusively to one stream. For example 'J' might always appear on the left side, 'U' in the middle of the head, and 'C' on the right side. Subjectively, this arrangement is perceived as three streams, each of which contains a repeated consonant. If changing state were the dominant factor responsible for disrupting serial recall we would expect that both settings would produce roughly equivalent degrees of disruption. In fact, the stereophonic presentation was less disruptive than the monaural presentation, which is what one would expect if streaming had an over-arching influence upon changing state. It seems clear that higher-order organizational factors can diminish the effect of changing state. However, spatial position is not the only basis on which streaming can occur (see Bregman 1990 for a general discussion) and we may therefore expect a range of organizational factors to modulate the changing-state effect. For example, a repeated utterance presented at *regular* intervals does not produce significant degrees of disruption, but when the timing of the repeated utterance is *irregular*, disruption is increased markedly (Jones and Macken, submitted).

A BLACKBOARD MODEL OF MEMORY: THE OBJECT-ORIENTED EPISODIC RECORD MODEL

What are the theoretical implications of the findings? The pattern of results suggests a particular type of model of working memory. This is one based on a blackboard-type formulation which owes much to Anderson's (1983) ACT* model, Kahneman and Triesman's (1984) notion of 'object file', and Marr's (1976) 'object tokens'. We propose that, in addition to a blackboard, there are three main attributes to the model: objects, streams, and threads. We have adopted the apparently paradoxical word 'objects' applied to sound, where 'events' might seem more appropriate. This is intended to highlight the amodal character of the representation and an analogy with visual processing. 'Objects' are activated on the blackboard, and may arise from a variety of sensory channels. Those based on visually-presented words co-exist and are functionally isomorphic with objects from auditory input. Those from a visual source are usually activated via deliberate conscious control. Objects of auditory origin can be formed without conscious control, and separate objects are derived from an auditory stream by relatively simple pre-attentive processes of streaming and object formation. The third attribute, 'threads', is used as a metaphor for the process of rehearsal. Provisionally, we have given the name Object-Oriented Episodic Record (O-OER) to the model.

Object formation. For the auditory modality, this process of object formation is achieved by the process of segmentation. Our studies indicate that non-speech signals must be interspersed with silence in order for the stream to be treated as being segmented; but it may not be safe to conclude that this is the *only* way in which objects may be formed, at least not until the whole range of potential cues to segmentation has been explored within the irrelevant-speech paradigm. In particular, everyday experience of music suggests that an otherwise unbroken signal can nevertheless be perceived as being segmented by sufficiently sharp *changes* in pitch and intensity so as to form 'objects'.

Although it is natural to argue that those detection and classification mechanisms normally associated with categorical perception of speech are responsible for its segmentation, in the present context this point of view is not wholly convincing. Reversed speech, which contains unfamiliar acoustic–phonetic sequences, produces roughly the same degree of disruption as English narrative (Jones *et al.* 1990). This suggests that pattern-recognition mechanisms are not in play, at least not those which are involved in recognizing phonemic categories. Instead, we propose a *correlated attribute hypothesis* that may underpin the segmentation of speech and non-speech sounds (see Jones *et al.*, in press). Within the speech signal, correlated changes in attributes such as pitch and loudness are particularly frequent at the boundaries of utterances, and we argue that it is these characteristics, rather than those of phoneme recognition, that are responsible for segmentation.

Results from a detailed examination of cross-modal priming are interpreted to mean that the notion of object is not exclusive to the auditory domain, and that objects may be formed by a combination of evidence from the auditory and visual modalities. These experiments follow up the work on cross-modal Stroop interference described above, but with very much closer control over the contents and timing of the auditory and visual material. In single trials the latency of colour-naming was measured. After several experiments we found that the degree of interference depended on the precise details of the way in which audition and vision are synchronized. In one set of studies we found that when the patch of colour to be named was always preceded by a visual warning, and the presentation of the sound was not synchronized with the patch, no interference was observed. When the paradigm was changed slightly, then cross-modal effects were found. Specifically, if the visual and auditory signals were phenomenally simultaneous, and if the appearance patch was temporally unpredictable and presented without visual warning, then what was seen was influenced by what was heard. It seems that when the colour patch is an element of the visual stream of information, then the sound is treated as a separate entity. If there is coherence between the auditory and visual stimulus, then the auditory and visual dimensions of the event are perceived as attributes of a single object. We were able to test this hypothesis directly by manipulating coherence in spatial terms. When the voice came from a position close to the screen on which the visual stimulus was presented the effect then was much greater than if it came from behind the subject (Jones and Hapeshi 1991).

Streams. Objects can be organized into streams, and, although each object will exist as a separate entity on the blackboard, perceptual factors will organize and link them. The production rules which govern the organization of such streams are already well documented by the work on auditory streaming (see, for example, Bregman 1990). If the stream contains the repetition of the same item, then no links will be formed. For auditory material, it is proposed that links will be formed automatically by this streaming. For material of visual origin, objects and streams are formed by deliberate rehearsal. The links between items are produced in this case by the act of articulating the list. If, during the presentation of a visual list, the articulation process is otherwise engaged by such activities as articulatory suppression, then the process of laying down the links will not proceed successfully, and serial recall will be correspondingly impaired. Additionally, we speculate that linkages within memory will also help to signify boundaries (such as end-of-list or end-of-rehearsal groups) which act as distinctive markers for retrieval.

Within the model, it is the integrity of the links, not the items, that is time-dependent and therefore limits serial-recall performance. In most models of working memory, once items are encoded, it is assumed that they are shuttled within or between stores. In contrast, within the O-OER model the items themselves are assumed to have relatively prolonged lives, but the time-limited nature of the links governs the fidelity of serial recall.

Threads. Within the O-OER framework, the process of rehearsal is one of retracing the 'episodic trajectory' (Rummelhart 1991) of the original list on the blackboard. That is, it is assumed that the blackboard has a relatively large number of objects upon it and sets of links representing different streams. Successful recall depends upon the navigation of links and objects of the original list. A useful metaphor for the processes underpinning rehearsal of the list is that of a 'thread' which has to be run through each object. Notice that it is not the items themselves that are revivified by rehearsal, but rather the links that bind the objects. Background auditory stimulation also produces objects on the blackboard, both through detection of changing state and through streaming, and sets up competing linkages in memory. The nature of interference, therefore, is due to competing trajectories, those from auditory stimulation acting as a potential source of interference for those laid down by articulation of visual items for serial recall.

The model makes no specific predictions for memory tasks other than those involving serial recall, but is restricted to considering the blackboard layer as one which contains only episodic information. It seems perfectly plausible that once objects are formed on the board other attributes such as meaning may be represented at some layer 'beneath' the blackboard, but again linked to the objects.

In its general characteristics the O-OER model marks a departure from conventional descriptions of auditory processing, particularly as it applies to memory. Unlike Broadbent's Maltese Cross model (Broadbent 1984), and many similar ones within cognitive psychology, it is not modular. Rather it suggests that the essential problem for working memory is keeping track of the links between representations rather than how to revivify the representations themselves. It argues that processing is constrained both by the characteristics of events and by the organizational processes embodied in production systems that bind attributes to make distinct entities or objects. For example, instead of supposing that different processing resources are devoted to the processing of verbal material in each modality (as Morton 1979 has done), the model assumes that there can be commonality of processing, but that this will only become apparent if material in the two modalities is coherent across the spatial or temporal domains. In the temporal domain, synchrony of two continuously varying attributes, such as is found with speech and lip movements, for example, will show this coherence particularly well. This general perspective is distinctly different from the view that performance is governed by the codes imparted by the particular modality of input (see Jones and Morris, in press).

The evidence presented in this chapter may be interpreted as suggesting a number of modifications to current models of working memory. It is hoped that the results of the present series of studies conducted in my laboratory have also informed theory-construction in other areas: in explicating further the processes of attention in memory; by furthering our understanding of the confluence of information from the eye and ear; and in clarifying the debate about the functional distinction between speech and non-speech. This evidence, together with the inchoate O-OER model, is offered in tribute to Donald Broadbent's contribution to our understanding of human behaviour.

ACKNOWLEDGEMENTS

Thanks are due to Hadyn Ellis, Clive Frankish, Bill Macken, Alison Murray, and Philip Tucker for their criticisms of earlier versions of the chapter. Financial support for most of the experimental work reported here has come from the Economic and Social Research Council in the form of project grants.

REFERENCES

Anderson, J. R. (1983). *The architecture of cognition*. Harvard University Press, Cambridge, Mass.

Bregman, A. S. (1990). *Auditory scene analysis*. MIT Press, Cambridge, Mass.

Broadbent, D. E. (1958). *Perception and communication*. Pergamon, Oxford.

Broadbent, D. E. (1971). *Decision and stress*. Academic Press, London.

Broadbent, D. E. (1982). Task combination and selective intake of information. *Acta Psychologica*, **50**, 253–90.

Broadbent, D. E. (1983). Recent advances in understanding performance in noise. In *Proceedings of the Fourth International Congress on Noise as a Public Health Problem* (ed. G. Rossi), pp. 719–38. Edizione Tecniche a Cura del Centro Ricerche e Studio Amplifon, Milan.

Broadbent, D. E. (1984). The Maltese cross: a new simplistic model for memory. *Behavioural and Brain Sciences*, **7**, 53–68.

Colle, H. A. (1980). Auditory encoding in visual short-term recall: effects of noise intensity and spatial locations. *Journal of Verbal Learning and Verbal Behavior*, **19**, 722–35.

Colle, H. A. and Welsh, A. (1976). Acoustic masking in primary memory. *Journal of Verbal Learning and Verbal Behavior*, **15**, 17–32.

Cowan, N. (1989). A reply to Miles, Madden and Jones: mistakes and other flaws in the challenge to the cross-modal Stroop effect. *Perception and Psychophysics*, **45**, 82–4.

Cowan, N. and Barron, A. (1987). Cross-modal, auditory–visual Stroop interference and possible implications for speech memory. *Perception and Psychophysics*, **41**, 393–401.

Frankish, C. R., Jones, D. M., and Hapeshi, K. (1992). Decline in accuracy of automatic speech recognition as a function of time on task: fatigue or voice drift? *International Journal of Man–Machine Studies*, **36**, 797–816.

Handel, S. (1989). *Listening*. MIT Press, Cambridge, Mass.

Jones, D. M. (1983). Loud noise and levels of control: a study of serial reaction. In *Proceedings of the Fourth International Congress on Noise as a Public Health Problem*, (ed. G. Rossi), pp. 719–38. Edizione Tecniche a Cura del Centro Ricerche e Studio Amplifon, Milan.

Jones, D. M. (1990). Recent advances in the study of performance in noise. *Environment International*, **16**, 447–58.

Jones, D. M. and Hapeshi, K. (1991). Final report of the contract: Information-processing under high workload. Army Personnel Research Establishment, Farnborough, Hants.

Jones, D. M. and Macken, W. J. (1993). Irrelevant tones produce an 'irrelevant speech effect': implications for phonological coding in working memory. *Journal of Experimental Psychology: Learning, Memory, and Cognition*, Vol. 19, No. 2, 1–13.

Jones, D. M. and Macken, W. J. (submitted). Pre-attentive streaming governs the disruption of serial recall by irrelevant speech: implications for attention and memory.

Jones, D. M. and Morris, N. (1992). Irrelevant speech and serial recall: implications for theories of attention and working memory. *Scandinavian Journal of Psychology*, **33**, 212–29.

Jones, D. M., Miles, C., and Page, J. (1990). Disruption of proof-reading by irrelevant speech: effects of attention, arousal or memory? *Applied Cognitive Psychology*, **4**, 89–108.

Jones, D. M., Madden, C., and Miles, C. (1992). Privileged access by irrelevant speech to short-term memory: the role of changing state. *Quarterly Journal of Experimental Psychology*, **44A**, 645–59.

Jones, D. M., Macken, W. J., and Murray, A. C. Disruption of short-term memory by changing-state auditory stimuli: the role of segmentation. *Memory and Cognition*. (In press.)

Kahneman, D. and Triesman, A. (1984). Changing views of attention and automaticity. In *Varieties of attention* (ed. R. Parasuraman and D. R. Davies), pp. 29–61. Academic Press, London.

Liberman, A. M. and Mattingly, I. G. (1985). The motor theory of speech perception revised. *Cognition*, **21**, 1–36.

Lieberman, P. (1984). *The biology and evolution of language*. Harvard University Press, Cambridge, Mass.

Marr, D. (1976). Early processing of visual information. *Philosophical Transactions of the Royal Society, London*, B, **275**, 483–524.

Martin, R. C., Wogalter, M. S., and Forlano, J. G. (1988). Reading comprehension in the presence of unattended speech and music. *Journal of Memory and Language*, **27**, 382–98.

Miles, C. and Jones, D. M. (1989). The fallacy of the cross-modal Stroop effect: a rejoinder to Cowan. *Perception and Psychophysics*, **45**, 82–4.

Miles, C., Madden, C., and Jones, D. M. (1989). Cross-modal, auditory visual Stroop interference: a reply to Cowan and Barron. *Perception and Psychophysics*, **45**, 77–81.

Miles, C., Jones, D. M., and Madden, C. (1991). The locus of the irrelevant speech effect in short-term memory. *Journal of Experimental Psychology: Learning, Memory, and Cognition*, **17**, 578–84.

Morris, N. and Jones, D. M. (1990a). Memory updating and working memory: the role of the central executive. *British Journal of Psychology*, **81**, 111–21.

Morris, N. and Jones, D. M. (1990b). Habituation to irrelevant speech: effects on a visual short-term memory task. *Perception and Psychophysics*, **47**, 291–7.

Morris, N. and Jones, D. M. (submitted). Multiple resources in verbal short-term memory.

Morris, N., Quayle, A., and Jones, D. M. (1987). Memory disruption by background speech and singing. In *Contemporary ergonomics* (ed. E. Megaw), pp. 494–9. Taylor and Francis, London.

Morton, J. (1979). Facilitation in word recognition: experiments causing change in the logogen model. In *Processing of visible language* (ed. P. A. Kohlers, M. Wrolstad, and H. Bouma), pp. 273–96. Plenum, New York.

Quayle, A. J., Morris, N., and Jones, D. M. (1988). Irrelevant speech effects on a range of short-term memory tasks. Paper presented at the BPS Cognitive Section Conference, Cambridge.

Rummelhart, D. (1991). Connectionist concepts of learning, memory and generalization. Paper presented at the International Conference on Memory, Lancaster University, UK.

Salamé, P. and Baddeley, A. D. (1982). Disruption of short-term memory by unattended speech: implications for the structure of working memory. *Journal of Verbal Learning and Verbal Behavior*, **21**, 150–64.

Salamé, P. and Baddeley, A. D. (1986). Phonological factors in STM: similarity and the unattended speech effects. *Bulletin of the Psychonomic Society*, **24**, 263–5.

Salamé P. and Baddeley, A. D. (1989). Effects of background music on phonological short-term memory. *Quarterly Journal of Experimental Psychology*, **41A**, 107–22.

Salamé, P. and Baddeley, A. D. (1990). The effects of irrelevant speech on immediate free recall. *Bulletin of the Psychonomic Society*, **28**, 540–2.

Thackray, R. A. and Jones, K. N. (1971). Level of arousal during Stroop performance: effects of speech stress and 'distraction'. *Psychonomic Science*, **23**, 133–5.

Thackray, R. A., Jones, K. N., and Touchstone, R. M. (1972). The colour-word interference test and its relation to performance impairment under auditory distraction. *Psychonomic Science*, **28**, 225–7.

Walsh, M. A. and Diehl, R. L. (1991). Formant transition duration and amplitude rise time as cues to the stop/glide distinction. *Quarterly Journal of Experimental Psychology*, **43A**, 603–20.

II. Attentional control of complex tasks

Introduction

Neville Moray

A s Henry Shaffer states in his paper on the study of musical performance, we have all learnt from Donald Broadbent that '. . . good research begins and ends in the real world'. Perhaps the only sense in which one might disagree with that assertion is by refusing to accept the distinction between the world of the laboratory and the so-called 'real' world, for I think that those of us who have inherited Donald's concern with the applicability of psychology have felt that his own approach did not see the two worlds as distinct. Certainly he has, throughout his career, moved readily between them as if there were no barrier. Good research may be carried out in either, and good method must apply equally to both.

It is interesting to look back on *Perception and communication* (Broadbent 1958) and find that, even though it provides an exhaustive review of its topics as of that time, the overall flavour of it is clearly the flavour of the laboratory, even if quite a number of the studies quoted in it were performed in applied contexts. By and large even the latter were performed using what one might call the 'atomic' model of experiments: isolate both the behaviour and the variables from the influence of outside disturbance, and try to find the atomic facts of behaviour, with the aim of subsequently assembling them into a general theory of what was then called information-processing and would probably now be called cognition. The model of attention and information-processing was an abstract flow-chart, and was not quantified. None the less it guided and supported a wide variety of research, even by those who sought to disprove it. Even in its original incarnation it included work on vigilance, and hence on complex systems such as radar and sonar watchkeeping; and some of the chapters ventured a long way from standard experiments to a consideration of individual differences and personality factors such as extraversion and introversion. Donald indicated clearly the route by which one could extrapolate from the limited experimental setting in which atomic variables were manipulated to the richer settings of the 'real' world.

The routes of such pilgrimages can be seen in all the papers in this section of the book. Shaffer and his colleagues have, over the years, traded the earnest keyboard of the typist for the more aesthetic keyboard of the concert pianist—a move perhaps to the sublime from the meticulous, and have in doing so bridged such a gap as may exist between the Two Cultures. Shallice and his group have followed the tradition in Donald's work of concern with personality and the changes in behaviour associated with clinical and neurological disorders, and in doing so can be seen as part of an even longer tradition which Donald himself inherited, namely the work of Bartlett and Head on schemata and neurological damage. Alan Baddeley is perhaps the most direct inheritor of the model proposed in *Perception and communication*. His work on short-term memory has ensured for the APU the role of guardian and cultivator of one of the most important elements of the model, even if the offspring has undergone considerable changes as it matured.

It is also in Baddeley's work that we can see how many of us have inherited not merely the respect for experimental methodology which has always marked Donald's work, but also an eagerness to use it in unusual settings, settings in which people live and make their livings. Although he does not mention it in his paper, Baddeley has of course worked in areas such as commercial diving, and has been able to apply the experimental methods and information-processing concepts even in that harsh and demanding environment. Similarly Moray has used ideas springing from *Perception and communication* in studying radar operators, and in investigating the cognitive abilities of people working in process-control and manufacturing industries. It is noteworthy that even when research is conducted in such rich environments, where there is far less control over what people do than is possible in classical laboratory research, both the methods and concepts which were proposed by Donald's early work stand up remarkably well, and can provide a framework for research which was impossible with the equipment and methods of the 1950s. And mental models, which might have been regarded as ghosts in the machines of the 1950s theories, have emerged as the souls of the new machines of the 1980s and 1990s.

In some respects Rabbitt's pilgrimage can stand for that undertaken by all of us. It is a far cry from his purist studies of choice-reaction time in the 1960s to his concern for the all-enveloping constructs of general intelligence as it waxes, flourishes, and wanes with age—if indeed it does, since some of his work makes one encouraged to believe that indeed the guile of the old may compensate for the vigour of the young. As we move from the limited certainties of experimental research to the application of behavioural science to the betterment of the human condition, it is apparent that Donald Broadbent's influence and ideas can support both, and have done so. As Shaffer says, there are tremendous insights to be gained if 'We can crystallize questions about the human mind by posing them as engineering questions about a potential robot.' This attitude, where we marry the techniques of basic science to the practicalities of engineering, both in research and application, is one which is closely related to Donald's concerns throughout his life, that the accumulation of knowledge be matched by its application to the general weal.

Perhaps the best way to end this introduction to the papers on behaviour in complex systems is to put the quotation from Shaffer's paper in consort with one from the end of *Perception and communication*, for the two together seem to me to sum up much of what I have felt to be Donald's philosophy and influence on my own research over the years, as I have tried to move from the simplicity of the laboratory towards the complexity of society, and to try to ensure that in applying behavioural science to the understanding of human nature I and my students retain a concern for the place of values in research: 'The scientific quest must be renewed: not to denigrate man but to raise him up. And to the writer the belief in experimental method seems merely a translation into the idiom of our time of the injunction to be, not only as innocent as doves, but also as wise as serpents. It would be well to combine it with other precepts from the same source.' —— *Perception and communication*, closing paragraph

REFERENCE

Broadbent, D. E. (1958). *Perception and communication*. Pergamon Press, Oxford.

SIX

Designing for attention

Neville Moray

As is well known, Broadbent's original model of attention was a single-channel limited-capacity model, in which observers directed their attention at successive instants to different parts of the environment. It is commonly thought that later research has rendered such a model obsolete, and more subtle and multifarious mechanisms have been proposed by many researchers in the last thirty years. While such subtlety may be required to account theoretically for the vast amount of data on attention which has been collected in research performed under the restricting constraints of laboratory tasks, a simpler attitude is sufficient when we consider how to apply a model of attention to the design of human–machine systems. In this latter case we are well advised to return to Broadbent's original Filter Theory, which is probably both necessary and sufficient to guide the efforts of the designer.

INTRODUCTION

I have two most pleasant memories of the days when I was carrying out doctoral research on attention in the late 1950s in Oxford. One is of what I suppose is best described as friendly competition with Anne Treisman in the development of research paradigms for selective attention. (She won the competition of course!) The second is of the great kindness and encouragement which I received as a young researcher from Donald Broadbent—even if, as I still maintain, he did not answer what I perceived as trenchant criticisms of his model in a paper I gave at the British Psychological Society meeting in 1958.

They were heady times for those of us who by chance had stumbled into the field of attention. For the first time almost since the days of Titchener there were real opportunities to make major breakthroughs, due to the new technologies which then became available. It is amazing to look back and reflect on the difference between 1958 and now. I took delivery of a two-channel tape recorder which had to be specially ordered and built from basic components because no stereo machines were available on the commercial market. I attended the second course ever given at Oxford on programming a computer, and learned to write Ferranti Mercury Autocode on five-hole punched paper tape in South Parks Road, where its first computer had just been installed by the University. And Donald Broadbent's book *Perception and communication* appeared, the first major work for decades to speak openly about attention, and destined to cause a major paradigm-shift in American psychology. (The impact in Britain was perhaps not as great, because British psychology had always retained an interest in perception, attention, and such areas of psychology, which subsequently came to be called 'information-processing', and led later to cognitive psychology as we now know it. We had never succumbed to the *grotesqueries* of the American passion for learning-theory.)

Perception and communication proposed a simple, elegant, and intuitively appealing model for attention, Filter Theory, which matched the common-sense view of how attention works. As no one needs reminding, it was an all-or-none switch which could be directed to one of many incoming messages, funnelling the information either into a limited-capacity system where, in a way never specified in the model, perception occurred, or alternatively into short-term memory buffers if there were more than one simultaneous input. At least some of the experimental work which I and others carried out in the following years could be explained by the model, and I have always felt, even in the face of much sophisticated work by others in the following years, that rather more data could be explained by the model than it was ever given credit for.

The following three decades saw an explosion of research of ever-increasing sophistication into the nature of attention. Anne Treisman completed the very elegant series of experiments on selective listening we began together, and has continued to study the underlying mechanisms of visual attention with elegance and determination. People with names spanning the alphabet at least from Allport (1980) to Wickens (1984) have produced evidence for multichannel or multiple-processor theories of attention. And with the increasing sophistication of experimental design, the happy days of a loaf of bread, a jug of wine, and a tape of dichotic prose have gone for ever. We certainly now know far more about the subtle mechanisms by which the brain controls the intake of information, its selective processing, and the means by which responses are organized and directed appropriately to their purpose. Our theoretical knowledge of attention, based on laboratory research, has developed out of all recognition.

One of Donald Broadbent's outstanding characteristics as a researcher has always been his interest in applying the results of laboratory research to the solution of what are sometimes called, curiously, 'real-world' problems. At the risk of inventing an ugly neologism I shall refer to them as 'extralaboratory' problems, since I find it offensive to think of laboratory research as occurring in some realm only of the imagination, and as conducted by colleagues who have the existential status of mere phantasmata. In this paper I wish to argue that for the practical purpose of the designer of human–machine systems in which operators must perform tasks in the data-rich world of extralaboratory tasks, Donald Broadbent's original model is not merely sufficient, but may even also be necessary. Whatever the deep structure of attention may be, its surface performance is, in the vast majority of cases, well described by a single, limited-capacity channel, which is switched discretely among the various inputs. The more elaborate explanatory models become too unwieldy to be used directly for design specifications.

Apart from being adequate, Filter Theory yields conservative design, which is desirable for both safety and efficiency. If we make the assumption that attention is a single-channel limited-capacity system, and it turns out that we are wrong, then people will do better than our design predicts. If our assumptions are correct, then at least they will do no worse than the model predicts. The single-channel limited-capacity (SCLC) model is therefore a sound basis for human–machine design. This is true because the vast majority of extralaboratory tasks involve vision as the primary mode of information-acquisition, and the structure of the visual system constrains strategies of attention in a way to which SCLC is a good approximation. In what follows it will be useful to remember that I am not seeking to understand the deep mechanisms underlying behaviour. I am concerned not to explain, but to predict behaviour. For the most part I shall not need to consider information-processing at the level of detail at which, for example, Anne Treisman does her research. I am not concerned to understand how attention is supported by mechanism, neural or conceptual, but to predict how attention as a skill for strategic behaviour will operate, and how to make use of such knowledge about strategic attention to couple operators to tasks effectively by means of systems design.

THE DESCRIPTIVE STATISTICS OF VISUAL ATTENTION

The reason that we can adopt a SCLC model as a working approximation for design is the nature of the visual system, and in particular the structure of the retina. As is well known, the acquisition of high-resolution visual information requires that an observer fixate the source of information with the fovea, because visual acuity falls off so rapidly as a function of visual angle away from the fovea, and because colour vision is at its most effective on the fovea. Hence it is characteristic of visual attention in extralaboratory situations that the observer scans the environment 'systematically' by pointing the fovea at relevant sources of information, using both eye-movements and head-movements to do so. The word 'systematically' is placed in quotes to anticipate some of the results I shall discuss below. It might indeed be better to use the word 'strategically', since 'systematic' can include 'random' as well as orderly patterns of fixation.

For the purpose of developing a model I shall take a deliberately extreme position. Although there is no doubt that information is acquired from the periphery of the retina (there would presumably be no peripheral retina did it not subserve some purpose), we can ignore that ability for most purposes. One obvious property of the peripheral retina is to respond to sudden changes in the pattern of light by causing the observer to fixate, at least momentarily, the region of the visual field where the sudden change occurred. Such sudden changes act as exogenous 'interrupts' to the pattern of attention. Our main concern, however, will be to examine the endogenously-driven pattern of visual attention to dynamic environments which are statistically in a steady state for periods which are long compared with the time constants of saccades.

The world of the extralaboratory observer is characterized by a pattern of information which is dynamic both in space and time. From moment to moment the direction from which important visual information arrives changes, and in general where there is a source of relevant information in a fixed location in the environment the probability of a signal's being emitted from that source varies as some function of time. Most commonly the dynamics of visual information require stochastic functions of time and space to describe their dynamics. Even when the distribution of information in the environment is relatively static and deterministic the behaviour of the observer is likely to make it dynamic. Observers in general do not stay in a fixed position in their environments, and do not maintain a fixed direction of gaze. Their movements about the environment therefore change the direction from which information may arrive, and the fact that their movements cause the pattern of information on their retinae to change means that they also cause a change in the probability of observing signals from the several sources which surround them.

The comparison of visual attention to a kind of searchlight or directional antenna sweeping over the environment has been made too often to make it worth while ascribing it to a particular author. And it is the particular appropriateness of that analogy which makes the SCLC model apposite. Visual attention in extralaboratory environments is realized by the observer's successively pointing his or her fovea at different parts of the environment. Since the visual angle subtended by the fovea is between 1° and 2°, a designer of human–machine systems should assume as a conservative approximation that visual attention consists of a pattern of discrete fixations each covering a region of about that size.

Visual attention is therefore limited by the rate at which fixations can be made. And if a designer wants to know whether an observer will, under the best possible conditions, be able to pay attention to all the necessary sources of information, what is required is a model of the dynamics of the visual SCLC. Fortunately there is abundant evidence about those dynamics. Typical distributions of eye-movement rates and fixation times are shown in Fig. 6.1.

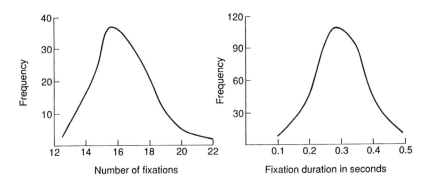

FIG. 6.1. Distribution of fixation rates (number of fixations per 5 seconds of free search) and distribution of fixation durations. (After Boff and Lincoln 1988, Reference 7.504.)

Note that these data are supported by a number of studies of extra-laboratory tasks, and not only by measurements of the fixation latency in a laboratory task where the observer is looking at a single source or a fixed pattern of sources and knows exactly when a signal will be presented, and where all that is required is to fixate the source where a signal appears. There is a remarkable consensus in the literature about fixation rates (Fitts *et al.* 1950; Moray and Rotenberg 1989; Moray *et al.* 1983; Moray *et al.* 1980; Boff and Lincoln 1988, reference 7.504; Miller *et al.* 1977; Senders *et al.* 1964; to name but a few). It may well be that much higher fixation rates can be obtained in laboratory settings; but they are not normally seen in extralaboratory tasks such as flying or driving, or when people are manning control panels in industrial settings. When greater rates do appear they last for only a very short time. The first well-established property of the visual SCLC is therefore that one cannot assume that it can sample different sources of information at rates greater than 2 times a second.

A second point to note in defining the basic characteristics of the visual SCLC is that the rates may be very much less than 2 per second, since to achieve that rate the observer must minimize the duration for which the gaze remains directed to a source of information. If for some reason a long fixation is required, then obviously the rate of switching will decrease. There are good theoretical reasons for expecting fixation durations to increase if the signal-to-noise ratio is low or the information content of the visual signal at a fixed signal-to-noise ratio is high (Senders *et al.* 1964; Sheridan and Ferrell 1974). Models of speed–accuracy trade-off and sequential decision-making suggest that fixation duration may vary considerably as a function of the pay-off structure of the task. But we may be able to make an estimate of the practical limit here also. If observers are to make 2 fixations per second, let us consider what is implied about the duration of fixations.

There are good data for the time it takes the eye to move as a function of visual angle. Let us consider two cases, one where the observer successively fixates two sources of information 5° apart, and another where the sources are 90° apart. Becker and Fuchs (1969) suggest that in the former case the movement time will be about 40 msec., and in the latter about 300 msec. If we assume that no head-movements are involved (though at 90° they will almost certainly occur, (Sanders 1963)) and that there is no latency involved in triggering them, this puts an upper limit of about 450 msec. for the duration of a fixation when a series of small visual angles are involved, and an upper limit of about 200 msec. when large angles are involved. Since the duration of saccades is approximately linear in visual angle, we can therefore assume that the visual SCLC is limited to about 2 samples a second, with the duration of each sample being in the range 200 to 450 msec. under the best conditions. If head-movements are involved and the fixation rate is to be maintained, then fixation durations must decrease. These results match the data shown in Fig. 6.1 quite well.

Another aspect of the data on which there is substantial agreement concerns changes in fixation time in dynamic situations. Consider a driver who manœuvres through traffic of varying density (Senders *et al.* 1966), an air-traffic controller who monitors airspace in which the separation of the aircraft changes from time to time (Moray *et al.* 1980, 1983), a helmsman who steers a boat among islands and other craft (Miller *et al.* 1977), and an operator who monitors a display to detect abnormal states of a process-control plant (Moray and Rotenberg 1989). Almost without exception there are only insignificant changes in fixation duration in the different phases of these tasks. What changes is the frequency of fixation, the sampling frequency. The duration of fixation seems to be related more to the quality of the display (which can be interpreted as the signal-to-noise ratio or to the number of possibilities between which the operator has to distinguish once a fixation is made), or to the time it takes for the display to respond to an action of the operator. The constancy of fixation duration is remarkable.

Let me again emphasize that I am not claiming that these values will always be obtained in experiments (although that is the case for saccade durations), but that they are sufficiently characteristic that a designer of human–machine systems would do well to assume that they limit the dynamics of visual attention in extralaboratory tasks. They provide a practical model for the bandwidth of visual attention. (I am using the term 'bandwidth' in a slightly loose sense here, to mean the maximum frequency at which attention can be switched between tasks. The appropriate measure is perhaps 'switches of attention per second' rather than Hz, but it is convenient to have a single word. Another interpretation would be that if attention is tracking a source of information, the bandwidth of attention means the maximum frequency of variation of the source which can be followed continuously. In this sense it could be measured appropriately in Hz, as is usually the case when a system's bandwidth is specified.)

THE DETERMINANTS OF VISUAL ATTENTION

The bandwidth of the world is not constrained to match the bandwidth of visual attention. It is interesting to speculate about the degree to which the two would match in a natural environment such as that in which humans first evolved. One must assume that if the bandwidth of visual attention did not match the bandwidth of significant events in the environment, humans would have been eliminated. Visual attention acts as a bandpass filter. One must assume that the distribution of occurrences and movements of predators and prey, the rate of signal generation caused by the voluntary movement of a human through the natural environment, and other significant natural events was such that the bandwidth of the SCLC was adequate, assisted by the interrupt system supplied by the orientating reflex. But the world which we design for people to occupy is by no means matched to the SCLC bandwidth. There are too many sources of information in control panels;

vehicles move too rapidly; processes unfold too quickly; and the complex interaction between people performing skilled tasks in teams put too great demands on the SCLC for everything to be attended. The fundamental reason to change the direction of one's attention is, as Senders has observed, to reduce one's uncertainty about the state of the environment (Senders *et al.* 1964). How then do people manage to perform so well amid the dynamics of the world as we create it?

The problem is to match the sampling limitations of the SCLC to the dynamics of information in the world. The rest of this paper will examine a small selection of data with the aim of identifying properties both of the environment and of the observer which allow this to be done. Essentially it is a question of developing *strategies* of attention, of scheduling sampling appropriately to match the expected distribution in time and space of the occurrence of significant events, subject to the constraints on the bandwidth of the SCLC which we have already discussed. If a designer is aware of the factors which determine strategies, then he or she should be able the better to design interfaces which couple the properties of the visual SCLC to the constraints of the task facing the observer. Scheduling is central, and it is curious that Scheduling Theory has never been used as a normative model for visual attention, since it would seem obvious that scheduling is the central problem for attention. If the SCLC can only sample one source of information at a time, when should it be directed to which source and for how long? We shall return to this approach later.

If we are to develop a model to use in systems design we need to make certain assumptions about the characteristics of the observers. In particular we must assume that they have had sufficient experience of the environment to have acquired a mental model of the temporal and spatial statistics of that environment. This will usually require at least several hours of interaction with the environment, and much longer for environments with many displays, rare events, or low-bandwidth signals.

It is convenient to distinguish between exogenous and endogenous determinants of attention. We shall now consider a small subset of experiments which will suffice to show some of the main determinants of attention, and one or two experiments which introduce some new approaches to designing for attention. A detailed review of them can be found in Moray 1986. We begun with exogenous sources of uncertainty.

Among the earliest and simplest models are those of Senders and his co-workers (Senders *et al.* 1964; Senders 1983). They proposed several normative analytical models for optimal attention to continuous signals, based on Information Theory. In a series of laboratory experiments

Senders showed that visual sampling was determined by the bandwidth
of the process observed, in approximate agreement with the Nyquist
Sampling Theorem. The tasks were to detect values in zero-mean
bandwidth-limited Gaussian processes which exceeded a well-defined
threshold. He verified empirically that for this task, where there were
no differences in cost and pay-off for observing different sources and no
interaction with the signal source other than reporting its value, the
model predicted the distribution of attention quite well, although
signals with bandwidths above about 1 rad. sec. $^{-1}$ were undersampled,
and bandwidths below that value oversampled. The slope of the function relating sampling to bandwidths was linear and monotonic. He
was later able to show that the undersampling could be well accounted
for on the assumption that higher bandwidths allowed observers to
detect rates of change as well as instantaneous values of the processes
(Senders 1983). The oversampling we shall consider later. His co-
workers (Senders *et al.* 1964) extended the model to take account
specifically of how close each process was to the threshold when it was
observed. The model predicted that if an observation showed that the
process was close to the value at which the observer had to report it as
being above the threshold limit, the next observation would be taken
sooner than if it was near the mean. Senders *et al.* (1966) later applied
the Sampling Theorem model fairly successfully to predicting visual
attention while driving. Senders also, in his original 1964 paper,
showed that Information Theory would predict that the fixation duration should remain constant for a display with a constant signal-to-
noise ratio, independent of the frequency with which it is sampled—a
result that explains the empirical finding, mentioned earlier, that
fixation frequencies, not fixation durations, are used by operators to
cope with changing demands of signal rate.

Related models were developed to include cases where the operator
tried to maximize the value of each observation (Sheridan 1970); and
cases where both the pay-off structure varied and the operator might
intervene to correct a divergent non-zero-mean process (Carbonell
1966). Carbonell reported very limited data which supported his model
(although we failed to replicate his results a few years ago), and Sheridan
and Rouse (1971) found that observers did not match the predictions of
Sheridan's model. However, they used very unpractised observers,
and it is clear that merely instructing people what are the pay-offs and
statistics of processes is insufficient to ensure optimal attention. Strategies for the latter must be learned by performance: instruction is
insufficient. Indeed there is good evidence to suggest that in general
one sees optimal performance in many tasks, not just attentional tasks,
only when conscious decision-making is replaced by internalized models

of which the operator is unaware. On balance, however, we can conclude that signal bandwidth is a major exogenous determinant of attention. Notice that while bandwidth can strictly speaking be ascribed only to continuous signals, it has an analogue in the probability of the occurrence of a signal as a function of time in the domain of discrete signals. This should be borne in mind in the following discussion, and the two equated.

The suggestion that costs and pay-offs are also determinants was confirmed by Kvalseth et al. (1977), who found that when observations were costly, the rate of observing decreased, while if the penalty (cost) of missing an important observation was high, the observing rate increased.

The above experiments, all (with the exception of Senders's work on driving) involving laboratory experiments of rather unreal data sequences, lead to two conclusions: signal bandwidth and the cost–pay-off structure of the task are major determinants of attention whose effect can be quantified in simple experimental settings. The work of Fitts and his co-workers (Fitts et al. 1950) on eye-movements in aircraft cockpits are compatible with the laboratory data.

I have referred to factors such as signal bandwidth, costs, and pay-offs, and signal information-content as exogenous factors, because they are properties of the environment. But it should be noted that observers only show optimal behaviour once the statistical structure of the environment has been internalized (a 'mental model' of the environment's statistical structure has been acquired in the head). In one sense, then, optimal attention only arises when the attentional demands of the environment become endogenous causal factors, and attention is then strategically driven from the mental model. The only exception would be for cases of attentional interrupt, such as the orientation reflex. As far as I have been able to discover there is no systematic body of research on what physical or psychological characteristics of a signal make it a good interrupt. Intuition and the common observation that the brain is sensitive to change would suggest that interrupt signals should have high rates of change, and that the magnitude of the change should be great to ensure that it functions as an interrupt. (Some hints are to be found in Boff and Lincoln 1988, reference 11.421). It is worth noting that an appeal to the 'salience' of a signal has no explanatory value. No doubt salient signals do function as effective interrupts: after all, that is part of the definition of salience. What we need in this regard is an operational definition of what physical and psychological properties characterize salience. We shall see later that while it is not at present possible to custom-design interrupts, it is possible to show one way in which this might be done (Moray and Pawlak, in preparation).

An attentional determinant which seems to be certainly an endogenous property of the observer is memory. We noted earlier that
Senders *et al.* (1964) found that signals with very low bandwidth are
sampled more frequently than would be predicted by the Sampling
Theorem. An obvious explanation would be that if the observer forgets
the value of the last observation, he or she will need to take another
observation not at the Nyquist instant, but when forgetting has increased uncertainty to an intolerable level. Several of my own investigations support the notion that forgetting is a determinant of the
frequency of visual sampling. Moray *et al.* (1973) found that, in a task
where observers themselves determined the rate of generation of uncertainty, sampling was at a fixed interval of about 7 seconds, regardless of the bandwidth of the process. Moray *et al.* (1980, 1983) recorded
the eye-movements of radar operators and noted that although the time
for the antenna to rotate was about ten seconds (and hence at any given
point on the display there was no new information at a frequency
greater than 0.1 Hz), operators refixated echoes at intervals of about
1.5 seconds when there were only two aircraft to be monitored. They
estimated the forgetting of radar-like displays to become significant at
around 5–10 seconds after an observation was made, and interpreted
their findings as being due to operators' having a very low tolerance for
memory-uncertainty. They developed a quantitative model of attention
to radar displays which included forgetting as a major factor in determining when visual attention would be next directed to a particular
source of information. If we want an estimate of the effect of forgetting
on attention which is accurate to an 'engineering approximation' suitable for design, the data suggest that if a source of information has a
bandwidth so low that it is not a first-order exogenous determinant of
attention, then it will be sampled about every 5–10 seconds—more
frequently if the cost of a missed signal is high, and less frequently if the
cost is low. A value of 7 seconds will do as an approximation for a first-
cut design parameter.

While the Information Theory approach of Senders *et al.* (1964) of
course amounts to the claim that exogenous uncertainty drives attention, and that claim is supported by experiments of Kvalseth (1977)
and Crossman *et al.* (1974), the results on memory just quoted suggest
that in situations where the exogenous generation of uncertainty is low,
forgetting is a potent endogenous source of uncertainty, and may
become the dominant determinant of attention.

Let us turn now to more complex determinants of attention. Suppose
that we had an accurate description of the bandwidth of the signal
sources in the environment, their associated costs and pay-offs, and the
forgetting functions. What biases might observers apply to their atten-

tional strategies due to what we might call their understanding of the semantic characteristics of the task? These are biases which stem from the overall goals of which the operator is conscious, although he or she will not in general be conscious of the details of his or her attentional strategy which will result. (People are not usually aware of the pattern of their visual attention in extralaboratory tasks.) We can think of these biases again as being strategic plans which provide overall programming of attention at a high level, with the tactical details being determined by the kind of factors we have already considered above.

The mathematical model of radar-operator attention developed by Moray *et al.* (1980, 1983) included a factor of this kind. The authors assumed that the operator was aware that there are very stringent limits on aircraft dynamics, and hence as the distance separating aircraft decreased it would be necessary to pay more attention to close pairs of aircraft and sacrifice attention to those with plenty of airspace. As has already been mentioned, the model was quite successful in modelling radar-operator eye-movements. Moray and Rotenberg (1989) recorded the eye-movements of operators controlling a simulated thermal hydraulic plant during fault-detection and fault-management. They observed the well-known phenomenon of 'cognitive lockup' or 'cognitive tunnel vision' following the detection of a fault. The operators switched the pattern of their visual attention so that the proportion of time spent attending to the faulty subsystem more than doubled, from about 17 per cent to about 37 per cent. Moreover, this prevented attention to a second subsystem, which subsequently became faulty. Attention to that subsystem declined from about 22 per cent to about 10 per cent while the first fault was managed, and did not return even to its former value for several minutes, during which the second subsystem diverged badly from its set points. One interesting observation was that during that time operators did occasionally look at the second faulty subsystem. In fact the first observation after it became faulty was not on the average delayed. What happened was that very few fixations were directed to it, and no steps were taken to handle the fault until the management of the first was more or less complete.

Another example of the relevance of strategic patterns of attention, or rather their absence, can be found in the paper by Miller *et al.* (1977). They noted changes in the pattern of eye-movements of helmsmen as a function of fatigue and as a function of the density of other boats and the difference between open water and water with islands when controlling a motorboat. The boating environment is interesting in that for long periods there may be little in the way of signals from the environment requiring monitoring. On the other hand there are certain situations in which one would expect very definite patterns of attention to emerge, patterns which would be similar to 'cognitive tunnel vision'.

Miller *et al.* comment on a case where one of their helmsmen failed to notice a boat which was approaching, because it was hidden by a structural member supporting the windscreen. Now several points can be made about appropriate strategies of attention in such a situation. The people they used as subjects were 'experienced' motorboat helmsmen, in that they had boating experience and were able to control and navigate the boat without difficulty. But clearly they did not have the appropriate mental model for pilotage. As should be well-known to anyone who helms a boat, it is critical to note whether other craft maintain a constant bearing with respect to one's own craft. A constant bearing means that sooner or later a collision will occur. A fundamental goal in pilotage is to ensure that the bearing of other craft with respect to one's own is constantly changing. This implies that a vessel could remain hidden by a pillar supporting the cabin roof precisely if it were on a collision course. Hence a major bias in determining attention should be a strategic bias in favour of repeatedly moving one's eyes and head so as to discover any craft thus hidden.

One would also expect, although Miller *et al.* do not report any such data, that if a craft appears to be on a bearing which is not changing the proportion of fixations directed to it should increase (because of the cost associated with failing to notice the constant bearing). One might also predict that the duration of fixations in this case would increase, since the object of the helmsman will be to determine whether there is a just noticeable difference in the bearing of the other craft. In crowded waters we would then have a nice instance of the conflict between the need to direct attention to the variety of hazards in the vicinity, and the need to repeatedly fixate the craft on a collision course at more and more frequent intervals as the distance closes, and one might be able quantitatively to predict the duration of fixation required to detect a change in relative bearing. The fact that none of these events were recorded in the study suggests that the pattern of attention revealed that the helmsman was lacking the 'pilotage semantics' in his mental model that should have programmed attention appropriately.

Another example of higher-level strategic controls of attention is found in the recent work of Muir (1989). She conducted experiments as part of a series which we are undertaking to understand the way in which an operator develops trust in a plant which is operated automatically under supervisory control. The relevant finding was that the more that an operator trusted a subsystem of the plant to perform well, the less often its state was sampled. Fondness makes the heart grow absent.

Finally, Liao (1990) and Moray and Liao (1988) modelled and measured the way in which attention was divided among four tasks with considerably different cognitive characteristics which had to be performed 'simultaneously'. The situation was designed to be a laboratory approximation to extralaboratory tasks such as cockpit management or control-room monitoring where there are both many sources of information and many actions to be taken, while the operator has an SCLC visual system and only one pair of hands. As the workload increased tasks were shed. The operators decided for themselves which task to abandon progressively when it was necessary to handle others. Moray and Liao were able to model the overall workload on the assumption of a visual SCLC and a single-channel response system.

All these experiments and field studies suggest that high-level semantics can bias the observer's visual attention in strategic ways. In some cases they seem to suggest suboptimal behaviour. The operators are meant to monitor all four subsystems, but lock on to one of them when a fault occurs; they are meant to perform all four tasks, but abandon one when overloaded, and so on. But as I have pointed out elsewhere (Moray 1981), 'lockup' can often be a rational strategy when dealing with complex environments. (If an abnormal reading is observed in a subsystem, the cause of the fault is in general more likely to be associated with other variables in that subsystem than in the set of variables in other parts of the plant which are less tightly coupled to the abnormal variable.) Hence much of what has often been thought of as pathological or suboptimal attention is actually the outcome of rational strategy. To predict such biases requires an extensive task-analysis of the operators' task from which a model of strategically optimal patterns of attention can be deduced.

We saw earlier that Scheduling Theory should provide a normative model for a SCLC. We are at present beginning a series of experiments using Scheduling Theory to predict the allocation of attention in manufacturing, process-control, and flight-management tasks. The analogy is with Scheduling Theory in manufacturing. In that domain Scheduling Theory is used to solve a problem such as the following. We have several jobs to do, which start at different times, must be finished by different due dates, and take different times to process. We have one (or more generally n) machines. In what order should we assign jobs to machines, when should the jobs be started, and when interrupted to insert another job? The problem can be solved for various criteria, such as minimizing the overall production time, minimizing the number of jobs which are completed late, providing the maximum amount of slack time, etc. In applying this as a model of attention to an SCLC, we identify 'attention' with the single machine, fixation duration with processing time, the times at which decisions have to be completed or observations completed with due dates, and the decision criteria with various psychological factors. For example, maximizing the amount of slack time would give the observer spare time free from the necessity of making observations; minimizing late jobs would ensure that all sources of information were as far as possible observed at or before the time when a critical event might occur, and so on. Our initial results appear promising (Moray *et al.* 1991). We envisage incorporating the parameters of attention as discussed in this paper into the definition of the 'plant' (the observer) whose 'work' is to be scheduled.

TOWARDS A DESIGN METHODOLOGY

The problem for a designer can be stated thus. An operator will be confronted with many sources of information in a visual environment. How can the designer be sure that there will be time to observe enough of the sources of information to maintain an accurate picture of system state from moment to moment so as to provide a basis for adaptive behaviour?

As an exercise, let us consider a variant of the system which was modelled by Moray *et al.* (1980, 1983). Let us assume that operators face a radar screen on which they are performing air-traffic control, but in addition there are a number of other instruments which must be observed. The radar might be an airborne collision-avoidance radar, and the other instruments flight-deck instruments giving the status of engine parameters. Let there be two classes of gauges other than the radar. One is a set of gauges on which no special regions are marked, but which the operator should monitor 'continuously' to keep track of their value—for example a compass heading. Let us call that class of instruments 'Full Range' instruments. The second group are instruments such as r.p.m., oil pressure, etc., where the important point is to observe how close to a 'danger zone' the value of the instrument is at all times. Let us call these instruments 'Limit' instruments. We wish to predict whether the operator will have time to view all the instruments and all the radar echoes.

The aim of the designer is to predict, from moment to moment, at which instrument the operator will look, and from those data to derive other statistics such as the transition probabilities between instruments, how often (at what interval) the operator will return to look at an instrument, etc. This in turn will allow the design to be evaluated using statistics derived from Markov analysis, which, as we shall see, provide a particularly useful guide to design evaluation.

The first step is to decide on a conservative level of detail for predicting behaviour. At what interval should the design model mimic behaviour? As we have seen, the empirical data suggest that the maximum rate of eye-movements is about 2 per second. This suggests that we should calculate where the operators will be looking at intervals of twice a second. If we are fortunate, and operators are able to exceed this rate, we will have an even more effective system. But choosing an interval of twice a second is certain to be fine enough to capture the vast majority of changes of state of the visual Filter. We first consider the Full Range instruments. From the engineering design characteristics of the aircraft, we can estimate the bandwidth of each of these instruments, and from the bandwidths in turn we can define the Nyquist sampling interval. The list of the Nyquist intervals for the Full Range instruments is a list of the sampling intervals which are necessary and sufficient for an ideal observer who wishes to track the values of the instruments. In particular at each instant it contains the list of those instruments (if any) which should be fixated at the next moment. We next consider the Limit instruments. We again estimate the bandwidth of these instruments, and also if possible obtain statistical data to describe the time function which will force the instrument under various operational conditions.

For both Full Range and Limit instruments we can approximate their behaviour by nominal mean Gaussian bandlimited noise functions if we do not have exact data. (By nominal mean, as distinct from zero mean, I imply that we know the mean value which is expected to appear on the instrument during normal operation, such as the normal oil pressure or the normal engine temperature, about which Gaussian fluctuations occur.) We can now apply a model such as that in Senders *et al.* (1964), which predicts the interval to the next sampling moment as a function of the distance of the observed value from the Limit for that instrument on the last observation, and the autocorrelation function of the forcing function. We can run a simulation of that process assuming various means and standard deviations for the Gaussian distribution, and derive a distribution of expected intervals to the next look for a range of conditions which cover the critical ranges of operation of the aircraft, based on engineering design specifications and the kind of missions which will be flown. The output of the simulation will be a further list of sampling intervals, and at each instant a flag indicating whether a particular instrument should be fixated at the next instant.

We can now model the sampling intervals for looking at echoes on the radar using the model of Moray *et al.* We assume that associated with each echo is a threshold for the tolerable uncertainty about its position, and that if the uncertainty is greater than that threshold, then the observer will look at that echo again to reduce the uncertainty to its minimum possible value, which is the uncertainty when fixating it, limited by observation noise. The threshold is determined by the relative importance of the various echoes, and by the separation of the aircraft: the closer two aircraft are together the greater the importance of sampling their positions.

The uncertainty of the memory for position is generated by a two-dimensional random walk which begins from the estimated location of the echo when it was last observed. Forgetting is modelled as

$$\% \text{ information retained} = a + b.\exp(-k.t)$$

and hence the uncertainty of the xth echo by

$$U_x = a_x + b.\exp(k_x.t).$$

where U_x is the standard deviation of the estimated position in memory, a_x is the standard deviation of the estimate of the position when it is fixated, t is the time in seconds since the last observation, and b, k_x are constants.

The relative importance of echoes is determined by the context of the situation (which represent large, fast aircraft, which represent small aircraft not approaching the airport, etc.). The increasing urgency as aircraft approach one another is calculated as the probability that there is a significant statistical overlap of the distributions of the estimated positions of the two aircraft. (As U_x, U_y increase for two aircraft the probability of their distributions overlapping to a significant extent will also increase.) If the urgency is greater than a threshold defined by the dynamics of the aircraft (rate of turn, climb, and dive for avoidance manœuvres) then it should be examined at the next instant.

Repeating these calculations will add the list of radar signals with unacceptable uncertainty to the list of signals to be sampled. We now associate with each item on the list a fixation duration appropriate to it. This is a weakness at present in the model, since there does not seem to be a way to determine *a priori* what these fixation times are. In the present state of our knowledge they will have to be estimated from empirical data, or examined over a range of plausible values using Monte Carlo methods. Having done this we now consider the resulting list and decide which signal to sample in the next instant. This can be done using Scheduling Theory (Moray *et al.* 1991). We consider each fixation duration to be the 'processing time' for the 'job' of examining the signal. The sampling instant, predicted either from the Sampling Theory, the Limit model, or the forgetting rate as appropriate is the 'due date' by which the previous 'job' should be finished. Let us assume that the ideal behaviour is that our observer will complete all jobs by their due dates. (That is, he or she will be able to sample each signal for long enough to determine its value at or before the next instant when the appropriate model says a new job should be sampled.) This amounts to defining our decision criterion as minimizing the number of jobs which are unfinished by their due dates, where both due dates and processing times are different for different jobs. It can be shown that the appropriate scheduling algorithm for that decision rule is the Moore–Hodgson algorithm (Moray *et al.* 1991). At each instant we apply the rule to the list of signals to be sampled, and fixate the item indicated by the algorithm.

The above process will guarantee that if the estimates of the time at which signals should be sampled and the estimates of fixation durations are correct, then the observer will, by using the Moore–Hodgson algorithm, perform visual sampling in the best possible order. Of course, as with many normative models, we do not assume that the operator consciously performs all these calculations, but that by prolonged performance of the task the brain has learned how to perform computations of which the observer is probably unaware, but which can be represented by the mathematics as described in our model.

We now wish to determine whether the performance limits of the visual SCLC Filter have been exceeded by the demands of the design. We collect the sequence of fixations predicted by the model over a long run, and from the sequence generate a transition matrix which describes the probability relations among the fixations. This matrix can be used to generate Markov Process statistics (Kemeny and Snell 1960). In particular we can generate the Mean First Passage Time (MFPT) matrix. The entries in that matrix are the means of the time which will elapse from the time that one of the row entries is fixated until the time when each of the column entries is next fixated. We can also generate a matrix which contains the standard deviations associated with each entry in the MFPT matrix. Now we saw earlier that there is good reason to think that in many visual sampling tasks significant forgetting sets in after about 7 seconds. Hence if we examine the MFPT matrix and the associated standard deviations, and find that any (mean + standard deviation) substantially exceeds 7 seconds, then we know that on the average that signal will not be sampled often enough to prevent the observer losing track of its value through forgetting on at least 15 per cent of occasions. (There will be approximately 15 per cent of the distribution which exceeds the mean + 1 standard deviation.) In that case we decide that the system design exceeds the ability of human observers to pay attention in a way adequate to perform the task.

Another evaluation criterion would be to look for cases where the MFPT is substantially greater than the sampling interval appropriate to the bandwidth of each variable. Other evaluation statistics which can be derived from the transition matrix include an estimate of fixation time (for empirical data) and the proportion of time spent on each signal source. Moray *et al.* (1980, 1983) used their model to predict at what point radar operators would be overwhelmed by increasing workload as more aircraft were added to the controller's scenario. They used the MFPT estimates to identify a scenario where there would not be time to pay attention to all the echoes before forgetting set in, and were able to identify the scenario where, in a subsequent empirical study, controllers did indeed lose control of the airspace. Their predictions matched the empirically recorded eye-movement MFPTs and other statistics reasonably well.

We see then that by assuming that in practical applications dynamic visual attention can be represented as a classical Broadbent Filter, with the properties of an SCLC, we are able to provide in principle a model both to design and to evaluate systems which are dependent on the dynamics of visual attention. No full-scale application of this methodology exists at present, although some aspects of it have been applied from time to time. (See, for example, Clement *et al.* 1968.) One interesting problem which the model raises is how any operators manage to track the state of any large system. If the eye-movement rate is limited to two fixations per second, and if forgetting sets in between 5 and 10 seconds after a signal is fixated, how can anyone monitor large industrial systems with hundreds of displays, such as power-station control room displays, or even the array of sources of information in a cockpit?

Although there are rather few data on this point, a likely solution is that the mental models which operators form of the systems with which they interact include models of the couplings between variables. Since the variables in a subsystem are tightly coupled, observing the value of one variable in a subsystem will give sufficient information about the probable values of other variables in that subsystem that a rather economical strategy could develop, with one sample per subsystem being used to establish the likelihood that the whole subsystem is in the normal operating range, instead of the observer's fixating all the variables. The theoretical implications of this strategy for the monitoring of both normal and faulty systems has been discussed by Moray (1981), and there is a small but suggestive set of empirical data in Iosif (1968, 1969*a*, 1969*b*). Much more work is needed on this topic, the higher-order strategies of visual attention. We are currently beginning such work in the context of Scheduling Theory and strategic behaviour in modelling pilot workload.

I have tried to outline here the general features of an approach to design for visual attention, in order to show the strength of Filter

Theory in applied problems, where what is required is not 'the truth' of an explanation of attentional mechanisms, but 'an engineering approximation' which can be used for the solution of practical problems. One problem of course is that the model assumes a statistically steady-state environment (although it can handle slowly evolving situations by treating them as piecewise stationary).

There remains the problem of how to capture the observer's attention when a process departs from its steady state, and an urgent situation arises. Can we specify the appearance of a display which will guarantee that an unusual signal will 'always' be noticed? Can we custom-design 'interrupts'?

TOWARDS A PSYCHOPHYSICS OF ALARMS AND INTERRUPTS

Let us consider the problem of designing alarms and interrupts. It seems to be a topic which has attracted remarkably little systematic, quantitative research. We want to ensure that as far as possible an observer who is locked into a well-scheduled pattern of visual attention none the less notices an abnormal signal and directs attention to it, at least until a decision can be made as to whether the overall strategy of attention should be disrupted. We have recently begun to look into the question of how to use classical psychophysical data, which define the value of a JND giving a 50 per cent probability of detection to define signals which will 'always' be detected. Our motivation is a response to the diatribes of Meister (for example 1989, and others too numerous to mention) claiming that human-factors 'research' (he means largely laboratory research) is useless for systems design.

The problem is to extrapolate from the psychophysical JND in such a way as to determine the magnitude of a signal which will 'always' be noticed. We have begun to develop a method for doing this, using a combination of Signal Detection Theory and classical psychophysics (Moray and Pawlak, in preparation). The results so far are interesting. We can predict, for example, by how much the mercury in a thermometer must rise (increase in length) in order for an observer to notice that its value has changed given that we know what miss and false-alarm rate the 'client' will tolerate. In order to do this we apply signal-detection theory to determine a range of probable values for the false-alarm rates which were present in the original psychophysical experiment. We then make assumptions as to what false-alarm rate will be tolerated in the situation for which we are designing the alarm, and assume that the operator will be trained to adopt an appropriate criterion.

When we do this we find actual performance to be less than that predicted by the model. The cause of this turns out to be the need to anchor the observation, and is related again to the fallibility of memory. If there is no uncertainty as to when the signal may change, then we obtain performance very close to what the model predicts. But that of course is useless, since abnormal readings occur in general at unpredictable times. It turns out that we can improve performance close to that predicted by the model by putting a marker on the scale at the normal set-point. When we do that we can predict the probability of hits and misses from classical psychophysical data which provide only the JND for the kind of judgement involved, with no estimate of false-alarm rates. That is, we can design the alarm based on a $p = 0.5$ of detecting the signal, and ensure a probability of detection at any value defined by the client, regardless of whether we know when the display will be sampled (Moray and Pawlak, in preparation). This is a first step towards a design methodology for displays which can be guaranteed to catch attention.

FILTER THEORY REDIVIVUS

Where does this leave us? There are of course, many kinds of filters, and few of them function like that proposed in *Perception and communication*. But there has been a steady increase in both theory and data about that single-channel limited-capacity filter with a rather low switching rate which is our peripheral visual system. Some particularly interesting work on the lack of processing during saccades is reported by Sanders in Chapter 2 of the present volume. We now understand rather well how the visual filter should work in order to handle the demands of a dynamic environment, filled with meaningful sources of information associated with costs and pay-offs, and requiring an observer to take appropriate action in response to the content of the information displayed. There's life in the old dog yet. Indeed that comment is perhaps unfair. No one has really found out just what tricks the dog has in its repertoire, since the history of attention research became so dominated by laboratory studies and the auditory domain in the years following the publication of Donald Broadbent's Filter Theory that visual attention to extralaboratory tasks was neglected. I propose that we put the animal through several new hoops, and I expect it to perform admirably.

There is a much deeper level of explanation needed if we are to understand many of the parameters which I have lightly glossed over. Why does memory fade in the way it does? What is that nature of decision-making such that the information captured in a fixation is processed at the rate which occurs? How does a strategic plan act to change decision criteria? If we are to have a complete cognitive psychology of attention all these questions will have to be answered. But in the mean time those of us who are interested in extralaboratory problems, in the applied psychology of the design of human–machine systems, have, I believe, an adequate basis on which to model and use a rejuvenated version of Donald's Filter Theory. What we now have are quantitative values to put into the model, and a much more detailed knowledge of its characteristics. The model is in one sense very different from the qualitative version which appeared in *Perception and communication*. But the visual version of Filter Theory is much closer to the original than the auditory version ever was. We are ready to produce a quantitative practical model for the design of human–machine systems requiring dynamic visual attention. In this paper I have not been able to develop a complete and detailed quantitative version of the model, but I hope I have given some indication of how we should approach the task.

CONCLUSION

I was fortunate enough to be a graduate student when Donald Broadbent's work launched the new wave of research on attention. It is a mark of the quality of that work that more than thirty years later I can still go back to it to provide a central organizing principle for my own work. And I would add just this. It is not just the quality of the research which has made it so rewarding to work in this domain, but also the kindness and friendship which over the years I have received from Donald. I hope that in some measure I can pass on to my students those influences, as I try to pass on the firm conviction that one can combine fundamental research with the application of their results to the betterment of the human condition, an aim which has been a hallmark of Donald Broadbent's own work.

REFERENCES

Allport, D. A. (1980). Attention and performance. In *New directions in cognitive psychology* (ed. G. L. Claxton), pp. 112–53. Routledge and Kegan Paul, London.
Becker, I. and Fuchs, A. F. (1969). Further properties of the human saccadic system: eye movements and correction saccades with and without visual fixation points. *Vision Research*, **9**, 1247–58.

Boff, K. and Lincoln, J. (1988). *Engineering data compendium*. Wiley, New York.

Broadbent, D. E. (1958). *Perception and communication*. Pergamon Press, London.

Carbonell, J. R. (1966). A queueing model for many-instrument visual sampling. *IEEE Transactions on Human Factors In Electronics*, **HFE-7**, 157–64.

Clement, W., Jex, H., and Graham, D. (1968). A manual control-display theory applied to instrument landings of a jet transport. *IEEE Transactions on Man–Machine Systems*, **MMS-9**, 93–110.

Crossman, E. R. F. W., Cooke, J. E., and Beishon, R. J. (1974). Visual attention and sampling of displayed information. In *The human operator in process control* (ed. E. Edwards and F. Lees), pp. 25–50. Taylor and Francis, London.

Fitts, P. M., Jones, R. E., and Milton, J. L. (1950). Eye movements of aircraft pilots during instrument landing approaches. *Aeronautical Engineering Review*, **9**, 1–5.

Iosif, G. (1968). La stratégie dans la surveillance des tableaux de commande. I Quelques facteurs déterminants de charactère objectif. *Revue roumanien de Science sociale-psychologique*, **12**, 147–61.

Iosif, G. (1969a). Influence de la correlation fonctionelle sur parametres technologiques. *Revue roumanien de Science sociale-psychologique*, **13**, 105–10.

Iosif, G. (1969b). La stratégie dans la surveillance des tableaux de commande. II Quelques facteurs déterminants de charactère sujectif. *Revue roumanien de Science sociale-psychologique*, **13**, 29–41.

Kemeny, J. G. and Snell, J. (1960). *Finite Markov chains*. Van Nostrand, New York.

Kvalseth, T. (1977). Human information processing in visual sampling. *Ergonomics*, **21**, 439–54.

Kvalseth, T., Crossman, E. R. F. W., and Kum, K. Y. (1977). The effect of cost on the sampling behavior of human instrument monitors. In *Monitoring behavior and supervisory control* (ed. T. B. Sheridan and G. Johannsen), pp. 393–404. Plenum Press, New York.

Liao, J. (1990). A simulation study of human performance deterioration and mental workload. Unpublished Ph.D. thesis, University of Toronto Department of Industrial Engineering.

Meister, D. (1989). *Conceptual aspects of human factors*. Johns Hopkins Press, Baltimore..

Miller, J. M., Gatchell, S. M., and Dykstra, D. R. (1977). *The visual behavior of recreational boat operators*, Technical Report, CG-31-77. Department of Transportation, United States Coast Guard, Washington, DC.

Moray, N. (1981). The role of attention in the detection of errors and the diagnosis of failures in man–machine systems. In *Human detection and diagnosis of system failures* (ed. J. Rasmussen and W. B. Rouse), pp. 185–98. Plenum Press, New York.

Moray, N. (1986). Monitoring behavior and supervisory control. In *Handbook of perception and human performance* (ed. K. Boff, L. Kaufmann, and J. Beatty), Vol. II, Chapter 45. Wiley, New York.

Moray, N. and Liao, J. (1988). *A quantitative model of excess workload, subjective workload estimation, and performance degradation*, Technical Report, EPL-88-03. Department of Mechanical and Industrial Engineering, University of Illinois at Urbana-Champaign.

Moray, N. and Pawlak, W. *Towards a psychophysics of display design*. (In preparation.)

Moray, N. and Rotenberg, J. (1989). Fault management in process control: eye movements and action. *Ergonomics*, **32**, 1319–42.

Moray, N., Synnock, G., and Richards, S. (1973). Tracking a static display. *IEEE Transactions on Systems, Man and Cybernetics*, **SMC-3**, 518–21.

Moray, N., Richards, M., and Low, J. (1980). *The behaviour of fighter controllers*, Technical Report. Ministry of Defence, London.

Moray, N., Neil, G., and Brophy, C. (1983). *The behaviour and selection of fighter controllers*, Technical Report. Ministry of Defence, London.

Moray, N., Dessouky, M. I., Kijowski, B. A., and Adapathya, R. (1991). Strategic behavior, workload and performance in task scheduling. *Human Factors*, **33**(6), 607–29.

Muir, B. M. (1989). Operators' trust in and use of automatic controllers in a supervisory process control task. Unpublished Ph.D. thesis, University of Toronto, Department of Psychology.

Sanders, A. (1963). *The selective process in the functional visual field*. Institute for Perception, TVO-TNO, Soesterberg, Netherlands.

Senders, J. W. (1983). *Visual scanning processes*. University of Tilburg Press, Tilburg, Netherlands.

Senders, J. W., Elkind, J., Grignetti, M. C., and Smallwood, R. P. (1964). *An investigation of the visual sampling behavior of human observers*, NASA-CR-434. Bolt, Beranek and Newman, Inc., Cambridge, Mass.

Senders, J. W., Kristofferson, A. B., Levison, W., Dietrich, C. W., and Ward, J. L. (1966). *An investigation of automobile driver information processing*, Technical Report. Bolt, Beranek and Newman, Inc., Cambridge, Mass.

Sheridan, T. B. (1970). On how often the supervisor should sample. *IEEE Transactions on Systems Science and Cybernetics*, **SSC-6**, 140–5.

Sheridan, T. B. and Ferrell, W. R. (1974). *Man–machine systems*. MIT Press, Cambridge, Mass.

Sheridan, T. B. and Rouse, W. B. (1971). *Supervisory sampling and control: sources of suboptimality in a prediction task*. 7th NASA Annual Conference on Manual Control, University of Southern California.

Wickens, C. D. (1984). *Engineering psychology and human performance*. Charles E. Merrill, Columbus.

SEVEN

Motor programs and musical performance

L. Henry Shaffer

For many years the study of motor skill has fallen between two theoretical stools, fitting neither the cognitive conception of mind nor the biological conception of behaviour. The cognitive study has been dominated by the Cartesian view of mind as essentially a contemplative system, interpreting its world through sense data and by abstract reasoning. In the extreme version of this view action is seen as a rather trivial extension of a decision process: the brain decides what to do and the body simply does it. In contrast, the biological view is of an organism involved in intimate interaction with its environment. Emphasis is given to the physical exchanges between the organism and the objects it manipulates. In this view, particularly as it has been presented by direct-action theorists (Kugler and Turvey 1987), cognition is seen as an unwanted ghost in the machine, a concept without explanatory value. This is unfortunate, because for many skills there is no better way to discuss them theoretically than in terms of a cognitive system organizing actions executed by a motor system. In particular the skills of music and language fall in this class.

The separate contributions of the cognitive and motor systems in organizing motor skill have become much clearer in recent years, following major developments in motor control theory. Central to this theory is an idea formulated in the 1930s by Bernstein (1967), that a motor system can autonomously compute a fluent movement to a given goal. The computational exercise of trying to get robots to perform human-like movements (Jordan 1989; Morasso and Tagliasco 1986) has demonstrated the feasibility of this idea, and has extended it to the co-ordination of a fluent motor sequence towards a series of motor goals. Thus the modern theory of motor skill is conceptually simple, describing an internal organization of action at two distinct levels: it assumes a cognitive system organizing a structured goal sequence for an action, and a motor system organizing the movements that can fluently achieve these goals. This separation of planning and execution allows the overall system to function flexibly (Sacerdoti 1974). It allows the cognitive system to improvise plans for action without the need to consider details of execution; and it allows the motor system to achieve an abstractly specified goal in a way that adaptively takes account of current contingencies of movement.

One of the consequences of integrating motor skill more fully within cognition is that it leads to a shift of perspective in an epistemology of mind: it leads us to think of mental activity more as a basis for action than as merely formulating knowledge about the environment. In effect the biological view is assimilated into cognitive theory. Knowledge is seen as a means of achieving goals in the real world. In a similar spirit, Winograd and Flores (1986) advocate a conceptual shift from the rationalist view of language as communication to a view of language as social interaction and as a means of persuasion. Musical performance too involves manipulation, both in the sense that it involves acting upon an instrument to produce sound, and that it involves expression that is used to persuade the listener to hear the music in a certain way.

Central to the modern conception of motor skill is the recursive concept of a system in the brain modelling the functional subsystems it controls. Thus it is supposed that the motor system contains models of the capabilities of the muscle plant; and the cognitive system contains models of the motor system and of the environment in which it acts. Planning an action entails constructing mental representation of its goals relative to a cognitive model, and these representations in turn serve as a basis for producing the action itself. I shall refer to the constructive process as motor programming, and to the representation as motor programs.

MOTOR PROGRAMMING

The terms 'motor programming' and 'motor program' have in fact been used inconsistently for many years. Control theorists working in a tradition of motor physiology have tended to identify programming as a process within the motor system organizing movement (Stelmach and Requin 1980), while linguists interested in speech have identified it with cognitive planning processes (Fromkin 1971; Kozhevnikov and Chistovich 1965). Interestingly, the latter concept arose from the work of Lashley (1951) and Bernstein (1967), both of whom were physiologists with intuitions about motor skill ahead of their time. In a more recent trend, the former concept of program is effectively replaced by the concept of a forward model, generated within a motor system that can autonomously compute the details of movement online (Jordan 1989).

Again, a motor program has been variously conceived as a declarative or a procedural entity. This has arisen from a confusion of two distinct metaphors: one is a theatre programme, which is a description of intent;

the other is a computer program, which contains procedures for realizing an intent. If it can be agreed that motor programming occurs within the cognitive system and that the computation of movement occurs within the motor system, then it becomes useful to focus on the declarative aspect of programming and define a motor program as the set of representations formed in planning an action, generating a goal structure for that action. As a consequence of such definitions the concept of motor program becomes a framework for an epistemology of motor skill. It offers a way of studying the information that has to be generated in the brain to support skilled performance.

A distinction previously made between a plan and a program (Shaffer 1981) loses much of its relevance in an epistemology of skill. It hinges on being able to partition the information for an action into what is latently relevant and what is actively being used in controlling the ongoing movement. Attempting to estimate the scope of the active component has been useful for understanding fluency in a transcription task (Shaffer 1976); but when we turn to expressive aspects of performance the validity of these estimates is thrown increasingly into doubt. For example, a musician may give a fluent performance of a piece of music by sight-reading the score only a bar ahead of playing, yet may choose to express it rather differently having had an opportunity to study the score. It thus appears that an interpretation of the score can shape expression over the whole performance.

Depending on the nature of the task, a motor program may have to be improvised during the performance, derived from a displayed text, or obtained from memory. A theory of motor programming must be able to describe the different modes of derivation, but it is important to suppose that the epistemology is unchanged between these: the same information must be generated in each case, and so the program for a given output should be invariant. Some theorists have adopted an arbitrarily narrow concept of a program as a memorized entity leading to a fixed motor sequence. There is little virtue in this narrowness, and it tends to arise in studying motor control, i.e. the control of movement, rather than motor skill.

A motor program may contain a hierarchy of representations. How many levels are needed will depend on the task, on the coding resources of the cognitive system, and on the input resources of the motor system. A program is hierarchic in the sense that one level is derived from another, making information explicit that was only implicit in the parent representation. For example, a speech act arises as a mental model of a state of a real or imaginary world. It achieves linguistic status as a semantic entity, representing something like root morphemes within a network of syntactic and semantic relations. There has to be at least one more level of representation making a lexical sequence explicit, but it is likely that a further level is used to make a phoneme sequence explicit. This last level is desirable on theoretical grounds: a motor system having to map each lexical form into a sound sequence would need a motor memory for every word, providing access to its phonetic pattern, whereas having to map phonemes into sound patterns requires memory for only a compact alphabet. This theoretical analysis of representational levels obtains full support from evidence on speech errors (Fromkin 1971).

There are reasons to suppose that the symbols in motor programs are not wholly abstract, but that in at least some levels they make explicit certain properties of the movements, or the acoustic consequences of these. In this sense they are analogue codes of motor output, and we thus see a theoretical symmetry between perceptual images (Kosslyn 1980) and motor programs. Analogue codes lack the universality of abstract codes, such as binary digits; but in mapping operations they allow faster computation, by facilitating content-addressable memory. The possibility of such codes provides a way of explaining such phenomena as signal–response compatibility and close shadowing (Marslen-Wilson 1973).

In short, we can think of a motor program as a choreography for action in a notation that can be readily interpreted by the motor system. It is derived in one or more levels from an abstract intention, making new information explicit at each level, but at its lowest level it is still sufficiently abstract to allow the motor system freedom to compute a movement adaptive to the current context. An epistemology of motor skill traces a choreography from its abstract formulation to its execution, revealing the kinds of knowledge that have to be recruited at each step.

MUSICAL PERFORMANCE

There have been studies of musical performance going back to the 1890s, when Binet and Courtier made smoked-drum recordings of keyboard performances. The early work was mainly descriptive, demonstrating such things as the use of rubato and chord spread as expressive devices (Seashore 1938). In my own early ventures into studying piano performance, made possible by connecting a piano to a computer and getting this to record the performances, I became interested in the motor problems of hand independence and timing (Shaffer 1981).

It seemed to me that piano playing contradicted the current theories of attention, which asserted either that the brain could control perform-

ance in only one task at a time, or that it could control multiple performances only if these made use of different input and output modalities.
In piano playing the hands may have to perform truly independent
tasks in pursuit of playing the single piece of music. Data from skilled
pianists demonstrated that the two hands can sustain quite different
patterns of movement, involving different motor logistic problems,
following different rhythms linked only by an abstract metre, and
involving different patterns of force and compliance. In polyphonic
music these differences can even extend to the fingers within a hand
playing different voices. Good pianists can expressively control one
hand's moving off the temporal beat, leading or lagging it. To obtain
this degree of independence motor programming must generate parallel
and independent streams of information which are similar in kind, and
when playing directly from a score these streams of information must
be derived from similar symbols on adjacent staves.

The issue of timing became interesting, particularly as it was observed that pianists could reproduce patterns of timing over a piece of
music with great precision in successive performances. Analyses of
timing variability across performances, in different levels of timed
musical unit, showed that this was often less at one of the metrical
levels of unit than would be expected from the variability in timing
individual notes. This leads us to suppose a hierarchy of timekeepers
(Vorberg and Hambuch 1978), consistent with the idea that an abstract
pulse is generated at the level of the metrical unit, while the motor
system arranges the kinematics and timing of playing notes in relation
to this. When the two hands play quite different rhythms the motor
system must be able to fractionate the pulse interval differently for each
hand.

We should be clear about the complexity of computation the motor
system faces in note timing, since what must be timed in relation to the
pulse is not the onset of each finger trajectory, but the moment of its
completion when it initiates a sound. This extends the problem of
inverse-kinematics in motor control (Morasso and Tagliasco 1986),
which requires the computation of a patterning of torques over a chain
of joints that will result in the end effector achieving a certain motor
target. That target has to include end-point timing as a component.

As every study of musical performance has shown, the formally
regular event of the metrical beat or bar is never played with an iso-
chronous pulse. Rather the tempo fluctuates expressively over the
music. This implies that the internal timekeeper is a kind of program-
mable clock that can modulate its pulse rate under instruction from the
motor program. Its demonstrable ability to return very accurately to a
particular tempo shows that this clock has stable referents. If we think

of the clock as a neural oscillator then the referents can be seen as attractor points of the oscillatory system, and the rubato excursions, of speeding up and slowing down, as perturbations away from an attractor (Kugler and Turvey 1987).

Timing and hand independence are matters of technical competence, and they are achieved mainly within the motor system. The results of the performance studies reveal a system considerably more complex than anything typically envisaged by motor-control theorists, and it becomes a benchmark of a control theory whether it can encompass these empirical findings. What has become a focus of interest in these studies, however, is the observed precision in the use of expression. This has prompted new questions about how expression is represented in the motor program, and what musical knowledge is needed to generate it. A musical score sometimes contains markings for tempo, dynamic (i.e. intensity), and articulation, but these are usually vague, and they usually prescribe only some key aspects of expression.

A player may use expression as a benign but uninformative gesture, but more often it is used didactically to emphasize for the listener some aspect of musical meaning. In order to be effective in this it must satisfy conventions shared with the listener. One of the more robust of these is phrasing. Music can be heard as moving continually between tension and relaxation, and a musical phrase typically rises to a peak of tension and ends in relative relaxation. This tension–relaxation trajectory tends to be conveyed in performance by a rise and fall in tempo and dynamic, and this has analogies with uses of expression in speech.

Since musical phrases can be embedded within a larger phrase, it is possible to apply the phrasing gesture recursively. A good example of this was observed in performances of the Chopin F sharp minor Prelude (Shaffer and Todd 1987). The piece lends itself naturally to this because it is based on a rhythmic grouping that repeats four times in each bar throughout the piece. Thus the phrasing gesture was observed over the four beats in a bar, over phrases of two or four bars, and over sections made up of groups of phrases. Yet performances obtained of Bach's C major Prelude, from the first book of *The 48 Preludes and Fugues*, did not show a recursive use of gesture, though this piece has a similar structure, also making use of a repeating rhythmic grouping. In effect a single phrasing gesture was observed spanning the whole piece. Thus it appears that structural grouping had a different significance in the two pieces, and it becomes interesting to ask what it was in the music that led to the different interpretations.

These contrasting results indicate that attempts to state context-free, or even limited-context, rules for expression (Sundberg *et al.* 1983) are of limited value. There is unlikely to be a simple mapping between local musical patterns in a score and expressive devices in a performance. Rather we have to think of a performer's overall interpretation of the piece of music mediating between a text and its performance. Thus we are faced with the complex problem of trying to explicate a hidden variable, the interpretation underlying a performance: it is complex because we cannot assume a simple mapping from the text to this variable, on the one hand, or from this variable to expression, on the other.

There are a few tactics which may simplify the problem. One is to ask the player to state his or her interpretation; but a difficulty with this is that the information in a motor program may not be fully accessible to verbal description. A variant of this tactic is to ask the player to annotate the score, which can reveal something of the player's understanding of the music, even if it incompletely reflects the interpretation.

A different tactic is to obtain a theoretical analysis of the music and use this as a model interpretation against which to examine a performer's use of expression. This is not an easy matter, since there is seldom a unique analysis for a piece. Analysts may bring different preconceptions to an analysis, but in any case composers often exploit structural ambiguity to achieve musical interest. It is part of the musical aesthetic. We have to assume, therefore, that when it arises the ambiguity can be constrained to a few alternatives, and so limit the range of valid interpretations. While there is no guarantee that the player's interpretation will be among these, we can compare actual expression with the interpretative options made available by the theory.

I have assumed that the theoretical analyst and the performer share a common goal of finding an interpretation for a piece of music. It may be, however, that the different aims of pedagogy and entertainment lead to different kinds of interpretation. They may share a common basis, but diverge in some significant aspects. A possible source of divergence is that theorists confine themselves almost wholly to the analysis of musical structure, for which there is a variety of abstract theories. They tend to identify musical meaning with structure. In contrast, the performer takes account of the expressive markings in the score and uses these to discern a patterning of mood in the music. Musical meaning for the performer embraces both its structures and its moods. It is, for instance, evident that the character of a piece of music can be considerably altered by playing it at a different tempo, though clearly its structure is left invariant. There is at present no good theory relating mood and structure, though there have been attempts at this by Meyer (1956) and others.

It may seem at this point that I have taken the concept of motor program out on a limb where it serves little useful purpose. On the contrary, my claim is that the concept provides an excellent framework within which to tackle the following question: What kinds of knowledge would we have to give a humanoid robot to enable it to perform music-ally (a requirement which goes beyond getting it to play music)? The ability to give a meaning to the music must be part of this. Thus we can crystallize questions about the human mind by posing them as engin-eering questions about a potential robot. I suggest that questions of musical aesthetics and musicianship can be made more precise, and therefore given a better chance of being answered, if they are taken from the realm of speculative philosophy and presented as questions about motor programs, since we know from the research data that these are precise entities used to control expressive performance.

Returning to the performances of the Bach and Chopin preludes, I shall examine possible bases for their differences in expression more fully than in the earlier study. Two such possibilities spring immedi-ately to mind, but it is a third that is potentially interesting here.

Different performers played each piece, and they may have had dif-ferent performing styles. As a check on this we have looked at the performances of both players playing the same Chopin mazurka, and in this they were found to be equally expressive (Shaffer and Todd 1987).

Again, the two pieces, separated by nearly a hundred years of musical development, belong to different musical idioms, Baroque and Romantic, and even though Chopin took the inspiration for his cycle of *Preludes* from the earlier Bach cycle of *Preludes and Fugues* his idiom was very different. The styles of playing music of different historical periods have varied with fashion, and there have been fashions of playing Bach with metrical rigidity and Chopin with huge expressive license; but modern scholarship has provided little support for such extremes, and modern professional performers are generally aware of this.

It is likely that a more substantial reason for the expressive differ-ences is to be found in the structural differences between the two preludes. They share the common structural feature of using mono-tonously repeating rhythmic patterns; but in terms of musical narrative, harmonic structure, melodic structure, and texture they are quite dif-ferent, and looking at some of these features we can see how the performances were differently shaped by them.

Bach's Prelude in C major

The piece is 35 bars long, of which the first 32 bars contain the same rhythmic figure, occurring twice in each bar. The figure contains an

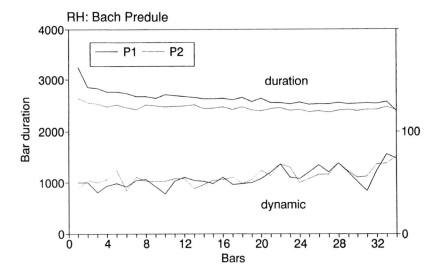

FIG. 7.1. Graphs of timing and dynamic for two performances, P1 and P2, of the Bach C major *Prelude* by the pianist RH. The abscissa is in the metrical unit of a bar and the left ordinate gives the played bar duration in msec., while the right ordinate gives the played bar dynamic in arbitrary units, but with a true zero.

arpeggiated chord, and only the chord changes from bar to bar. The piece is essentially a virtuoso demonstration of chord progression.

The pianist RH gave two performances, and these are summarized in Fig. 7.1 in terms of the played duration of each bar and of the peak dynamic, or intensity, in the bar.

The graphs of timing are very similar to each other, apart from a minor difference in tempo. They show a brief acceleration at the very beginning and from then on a slight, almost imperceptible, quickening of tempo up to about bar 24, levelling out until a final acceleration occurs in the penultimate bar. The last bar consists of a single chord and, as is common practice, this was sustained, allowing the piano sound to fade to silence. Thus this bar is omitted from the graph. The graphs of dynamic show more variation, though the total compass was not large, and there were minor differences between the performances. The scale of dynamic is in arbitrary units, but with a true zero. Broadly, dynamic remained fairly steady up to about bar 20, and then it built up in a series of climaxes to the end of the piece.

Note that in completely inexpressive performances all such graphs would be horizontal straight lines. In fact the score contains no express-ive markings, nor does it indicate a tempo, and this is fairly typical of music written in that period. It is interesting that RH was more expressive in dynamic than in timing, since the harpsichord, for which the music was written, allowed little variation in dynamic. Thus the performances have been adapted to the capabilities of the modern piano, and this supports my earlier suggestion that the performer was not bound by purist considerations of Baroque practice. To understand his uses of expression let us consider more fully the musical structure of the prelude.

Though the piece uses every semitone in the chromatic scale it never leaves the key of C major, developing in succession four tonal regions of tonic, subdominant, dominant, and tonic harmonies in this scale. Thus it forms a very basic tonal trajectory beginning and ending in the tonic, in which the subdominant acts as a preparation for the dominant, strengthening its tendency to return the music to the tonic. The music moves metrically in 4-bar phrases, except that bar 8 appears to act as both the last bar of the second phrase and the first bar of the third, and this overlap accounts for the odd number of bars in the piece.

The first section, bars 1–19, which takes up over half the piece, is a subtle but undramatic exploration of harmony around the tonic, C major, chord. It achieves minor tensions through an upward movement in melodic register in bar 5, in the rhythmic irregularity produced by elision at bar 8, and in the use of dissonant versions of the dominant chord in bars 12 and 14. The second section, bars 20–23, is a single phrase in subdominant harmony, i.e. built around the chord of F major. For all its brevity it achieves a major increase in tension through its use of dissonant and ambiguous harmony, which nevertheless prepares the following dominant harmony by the curious device of constructing a semitonal ascent of the bass, F, F sharp, A flat (= G sharp), omitting G, the dominant note. The third section, bars 24–31, is in dominant harmony, and it builds to the climax of the piece by a melodic ascent from note D, the dominant of the dominant, up to G, the dominant, over a continuous pedal note G in the bass. This climax is reached in bar 29, and the melody then descends again to F, preparing a return to the tonic. The final section, bars 32–35, is in the tonic, completing the harmonic trajectory of the piece. It restores not only harmonic stability but also melodic register: from bars 1 to 33 there has been more than an octave descent in melodic register, and this is abruptly restored in bar 34, which may be seen as giving the music a lyrical uplift.

The calm opening may be seen as setting the character of the piece, suggesting an unhurried tempo. The tempo chosen by RH, equivalent to about 5 notes per second, is consistent with this, as was his refusal to vary tempo over the performance. The early dynamic peak in performance at bar 5 coincides with the upward movement in melodic register in that bar. The three crescendos in performance occur in each of the sections moving the harmonic trajectory away from and back to the tonic. The first is in bar 22, the first of two dissonant bars preparing the dominant. The second is in bar 28, which takes the upward melodic movement from F to F sharp and so delays the entry of G. It is an interesting expressive gesture, since it allows the music to relax slightly at the actual melodic and harmonic peak in bar 29. The last crescendo occurs in the final section, and it took different forms in each performance. In the first performance it peaked in bar 33, in which the repetitive rhythm first gives way to a freer melodic line; while in the second it ascended up to the final chord, presumably responding to the melodic uplift in the final two bars.

It is instructive to compare these performances with those analysed by Cook (1987) from gramophone recordings of the piece by Helmut Walcha, playing a harpsichord, and Glenn Gould, playing a piano. They both played the opening section, bars 1–19, at a steadily decreasing tempo, the inverse of RH's gesture. At the same time Gould produced a steady lowering of dynamic. They also differed from RH by slowing progressively in the final section. None of the pianists produced a consistent end-of-section slowing: RH produced none at all, Walcha slowed at bar 23, the end of the subdominant phrase, and Gould ended the continuing trend of decreasing tempo at bar 20, the beginning of that phrase. He then accelerated progressively through that and the next section, thus underlining the raised tension in those sections. At the same time he steadily increased dynamic from bar 20 up to and including bar 29, and then let it decrease to a peaceful ending.

There seem to be some musically eccentric features of Walcha's use of timing making it unclear how he interpreted the piece; RH and Gould were in agreement with each other and with the usually accepted analysis of the piece, though it is perhaps Gould who conveyed the structure more clearly in his use of expression. Where the players differed in gesture in the outer sections, this reflects differences in the perceived character rather than in the structure of the piece. It is a matter of character whether the opening section should accelerate or decelerate in pursuing its uneventful course; or whether the final section should reach a peroration or fade peacefully, given the late ascent in register. The important point here is the demonstration that structure alone does not fully determine expression.

Finally, building a bridge to the next performance study, it is worth considering further why the performances examined here made little use of slowing at phrase boundaries. Though there are well-formed cadences in each phrase the melody line is more or less seamless throughout, so that there is little or no sense of rest within the piece, only a continuous unfolding of a harmonic progression towards the final cadence. This is in marked contrast with the next piece.

Chopin's Prelude in F sharp minor

This *Prelude* is just 34 bars long, but is more eventful than the Bach. It too can be assigned a hierarchic structure: it divides into an 18-bar exposition and a 16-bar recapitulation; these divide mainly into 4-bar phrases, but the third phrase of the exposition extends to 6 bars; some of the phrases have an antecedent–consequent structure of near-symmetric halves; finally, each bar has a metre of 4 beats, each beat containing the same rhythmic figure, except in the final two bars, which simplify to a series of chords.

The Chopin score, unlike the Bach, contains markings of expression and of slurs to indicate phrase articulation: it is marked *Molto agitato* ('very restless') at the beginning, it indicates dynamic levels and crescendos in several places, and it indicates a slowing at the end of the exposition and a quickening of tempo at the beginning of the recapitulation. These are vague markings, leaving much to the discretion of the performer.

The pianist this time was PB, who gave two performances. These are summarized in Fig. 7.2 in terms of beat duration and beat dynamic, the latter defined, as before, by the salient event within the beat. These graphs show pronounced variation both in tempo and in dynamic, and they show a considerable precision in reproducing this variation across performances, although the second performance made slightly less extreme use of slowing. Again, the last two bars, in which there was a major slowing on the final chords, are omitted from the graphs.

The graphs of timing clearly reflect the hierarchy of musical units. There is a large slowing at the end of bar 18, which ends the exposition; there is secondary slowing in bars 4, 8, 14, 22, 26, and 30, ending the respective phrases, and also at bars 16 and 28, marking the boundaries of the antecedent–consequent subphrases; finally one sees third-order slowing at the ends of bars within a phrase, which however becomes more pronounced towards the end of the piece. The variation in dynamic is more conservative, reflecting mainly section and phrase structure. For a more detailed account of the expressive patterning we need to turn to a fuller analysis of the musical structure.

The tempo marking *Molto agitato* defines the character of the piece, but this could anyway be seen from the obsessively repeating rhythm combined with the harmonic structure. The two phrases that make up the first 8 bars have an antecedent–consequent relationship. They each state the same theme in tonic harmony, F sharp minor, in their first

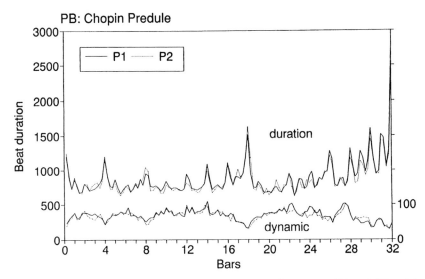

FIG. 7.2. Graphs of timing and dynamic for two performances, P1 and P2, of the Chopin F sharp minor *Prelude* by the pianist PB. The abscissa is marked in bars and the music has four beats in a bar. The left ordinate gives the played beat duration in msec., while the right ordinate gives the played beat dynamic in arbitrary units, but with a true zero.

half, and then dissipate tonality in a tonally ambiguous and dissonant sequence in the second half. They differ in that the first sequence returns to the tonic, whereas the second sequence has moved upward in register by a third, as though moving the music towards the relative major, but it leaves the harmony unresolved. The third phrase remains tonally ambiguous throughout, suggesting different keys at different moments. Thus a tension building in successive waves of more or less unresolved ambiguity is sustained up to bar 14, and is augmented by the rhythmic shift extending the third phrase from 4 to 6 bars. This phrase is marked in the score with a sustained crescendo leading to *ff*, 'very loud', at the beginning of the next and last phrase of the exposition. This last phrase has an antecedent–consequent structure in a remote key, and the subphrases differ only in that the second returns the music abruptly in its last beat to the home key of F sharp minor, so bringing it to a temporary rest. While the first subphrase is marked *ff* in the score the second is marked *p*, 'quiet', making a contrast between the earlier tension and the impending resolution.

   The opening of the recapitulation telescopes the opening phrases of the piece into a single phrase, and also takes the music upward in register by more than an octave, the overall effect being an explosive growth of tension in the space of 4 bars. This phrase is marked with a crescendo leading to an *ff* climax, but by the end of the phrase the harmony has returned to F sharp minor. From then on, for the remaining three phrases, the music stays in the home key, using F sharp major to provide a tonal colouring in bars 29–31, so giving the music a lyrical uplift by means of a major–minor contrast. The earlier register is restored by a gradual descent over bars 23–24, and from then on the melody too becomes almost static, spelling out very slowly over the remaining bars an approximate echo of the initial theme heard in bar 1. The score marks a progressive lowering of dynamic, going down to *pp*, 'very quiet', in bar 29.

I have tried to indicate that for the most part the expressive markings in the score are redundant, since there is enough internal evidence in the musical structure to reconstruct them. The exception is the transition from *ff* to *p* within the last bar of the exposition, in which Chopin has chosen a dynamic contrast of antecedent–consequent subphrases where other dynamic solutions would be feasible.

Returning to the performances, we have seen that PB has clearly understood the phrase structure of the music, and we can also see the large variations in tempo as responses to the fluctuations in tension in the music. It would have been inappropriate to play this piece in the manner of the Bach prelude. Also, whereas there was a lowering of dynamic in bars 4, 8, and 18 reflecting moments of relative relaxation at a phrase boundary, there was in fact an increase of dynamic in bar 14, in which the unresolved phrase takes the exposition to its climax. Thus in general these performances conform quite well with the theoretical analysis of the piece. We can conclude that the motor program underlying performance contains a description of the music similar to the one given here, and that this internal description has served as a basis for expression. Such correspondences between theory and performance provide strong evidence for the abstract representations of large-scale structures in motor programs.

There are, however, aspects of expression in these performances that are not supported by a theoretical description of structure, and we have to consider these.

At the end of the exposition, bars 15–18, a climax of tension is dissipated within a phrase that contains a subphrase in an alien key and a repetition of this which manages on the last beat to return the music to the home key. The ease with which it achieves the return makes the listener reconsider the apparent harmonic distance between the alien key and the home key. Like the alternate perspective of the Necker cube it should come as a sudden insight; but PB has played a gradual diminuendo over this phrase, though there is no harmonic progression within the phrase to support this.

The recapitulation builds rapidly to a climax in bar 22 and then dissipates tension progressively over the remainder of the piece. Structurally there are only a few moments of brief lyrical climax, achieved by melodic leaps to the tonic note, F, and by switches between major and minor coloration. It thus seems musically appropriate to allow the music to flow to a peaceful ending. PB broadly achieves this by building a diminuendo from bar 23 onwards and at the same time slowing the tempo, but has disrupted the flow in two ways. In bar 28 she builds a sudden loud climax, mainly through an accenting of the repeating melody note D. Yet neither the bar nor the note has a structural significance to support this. D is an upper neighbour note of the dominant note, C-sharp, which has sounded continuously over the previous three bars, but the transition carries little dramatic weight. Again, in the later bars she produces a massive slowing at the end of each bar. Combined with a falling dynamic the effect of this fluctuation of tempo is to create a sense of directional uncertainty in the music. Yet nothing is more certain than the harmonic progression of these bars towards the final cadence. It is as though PB has interpreted the marking *Molto agitato* as applying throughout the piece, overriding structural evidence to the contrary.

It goes beyond the scope of motor-programming theory to discuss aesthetic issues of expressive license in musical performance, but it is reasonable to point out that in each case of a mismatch between theoretical structure and expression examined here there seems to have been a loss of musical subtlety. One could go on to argue that the structure of a piece of music strongly constrains, though it does not fully determine, its character. The different kinds of tension created structurally can be expressed in different ways, but expressive gestures not supported by structural features may be regarded as representing a kind of expressive rhetoric. Sometimes the composer uses expressive markings to define a structural feature or to clarify a structural ambiguity. An example of the former has already been described, occurring at the end of the exposition; the latter tends to occur in modern atonal music, where it is not always easy to discern the musical structure.

CODA

The use of analysis to infer a player's interpretation has been taken a step further in a more recent study (Shaffer and Clarke, in preparation), comparing a published analysis of a late Beethoven piece with its performance by the author of the analysis. This has allowed us to explore further the relationship between the two kinds of interpretation. It becomes evident that the performer has to make expressive decisions, on matters of tempo, dynamic level, extent of modulation, and so on, having to do with the character rather than the structure of the music, and so not usually considered in formal analysis; while analysis uncovers musical structures that cannot always be readily expressed in performance.

I have taken the concept of motor program to the limit of its useful domain, and believe this to be both interesting and fruitful. I have used the examples of musical performance to illustrate the richness of information in a motor program and of the implicit knowledge drawn upon in constructing it. Finally, in this research I have tried to observe the principle that Donald Broadbent taught me thirty years ago, that good research begins and ends in the real world.

REFERENCES

Bernstein, N. (1967). *The coordination and regulation of movements.* Pergamon, London.

Cook, N. (1987). Structure and performance in Bach's C major Prelude (WTC 1): an empirical study. *Music Analysis*, **6**, 257–72.

Fromkin, V. (1971). The non-anomalous nature of anomalous utterances. *Language*, **47**, 27–52.

Jordan, M. (1989). Indeterminate motor skill learning problems. In *Attention and performance XIII* (ed. M. Jeannerod), pp. 796–836. MIT Press, Cambridge, Mass.

Kosslyn, S. (1980). *Image and mind.* Harvard University Press, Cambridge, Mass.

Kozhevnikov, V. and Chistovich, L. (1965). *Speech: articulation and perception*, Joint Public Research Service No. 30543. US Department of Commerce, Washington, DC.

Kugler, P. and Turvey, M. (1987). *Information, natural law, and the self-assembly of rhythmic movement.* Erlbaum, Hillsdale, NJ.

Lashley, K. (1951). The problem of serial order in behavior. In *Cerebral mechanisms in behavior* (ed. L. Jeffress), pp. 112–36. Wiley, New York.

Marslen-Wilson, W. (1973). Linguistic structure and speech shadowing at very short latencies. *Nature*, **244**, 522–3.

Meyer, L. (1956). *Emotion and meaning in music.* University of Chicago Press.

Morasso, P. and Tagliasco, V. (eds) (1986). *Human movement understanding.* North-Holland, Amsterdam.

Sacerdoti, E. (1974). Planning in a hierarchy of abstraction spaces. *Artificial Intelligence*, **5**, 115–35.

Seashore, C. (1938). *Psychology of music.* McGraw-Hill, New York.

Shaffer, L. H. (1976). Intention and performance. *Psychological Review*, **83**, 375–93.

Shaffer, L. H. (1981). Performances of Chopin, Bach and Bartok: studies in motor programming. *Cognitive Psychology*, **13**, 327–76.

Shaffer, L. H. and Clarke, E. (in preparation). Analysis and performance of Wo O 60.

Shaffer, L. H. and Todd, N. (1987). The interpretive component in musical performance. In *Action and perception in rhythm and music*, The Royal Swedish Academy of Music publication No. 55 (ed. A. Gabrielsson), pp. 139–52. The Academy, Stockholm.

Stelmach, G. and Requin J. (eds) (1980). *Tutorials in motor behavior.* North-Holland, Amsterdam.

Sundberg, J., Askenfelt, A., and Fryden, L. (1983). Musical performance: a synthesis-by-rule approach. *Computer Music Journal*, 7, 37–43.

Vorberg, D. and Hambuch, R. (1978). On the temporal control of rhythmic performance. In *Attention and performance VII* (ed. J. Requin), pp. 535–56. Erlbaum, Hillsdale, NJ.

Winograd, T. and Flores, F. (1986). *Understanding computers and cognition.* Ablex, Norwood, NJ.

EIGHT

Working memory or working attention?

Alan Baddeley

Unlike some of my younger colleagues, I can not claim to have become a psychologist as a result of reading *Decision and stress*, or indeed *Perception and communication*, which was in fact published the year I joined the Applied Psychology Unit. I can however claim that it played a major role in turning me into a cognitive psychologist. I arrived at the Unit having previously studied secondary reinforcement in rats, and enthusiastic to continue work on animal learning. My reason for straying from this particular path was certainly not due to Donald's active discouragement; as his subsequent book *Behaviour* (Broadbent 1961) indicates, he had a lively interest in theories of learning based on animal studies. He even considered from time to time the possibility of setting up an animal colony at the Unit, and looked benignly on my attempt to set up a breeding colony of woodlice behind the mechanical workshop, which alas came to nought as a result of my lack of skills in woodlouse husbandry. I went on to read *Perception and communication*, and rapidly forgot the poor woodlice in my enthusiasm for the exciting new prospects of cognitive psychology.

My post was funded by the British Post Office, who were persuaded by Conrad of the wisdom of considering psychological factors in designing their new postal codes, a project that was not easy to relate directly to my interest in theories of vigilance that had been stimulated by *Perception and communication*. Instead, at Donald's suggestion I collaborated with Peter Colquhoun who was working on vigilance, discovering an enthusiasm for collaboration that has never left me. Meanwhile I tackled the issue of human learning from an information-processing viewpoint, in subsequent years moving on to the long-term/short-term memory controversy. From there I moved into working memory, developing a model with Graham Hitch, who had just finished a PhD with Donald. It was only in retrospect that I realized how similar our model was to his earlier proposals. We were both strongly influenced by Donald's particular research style, and his flair for deriving important theoretical insights from the tackling of real-world practical problems, encouraging us to develop a model that might allow us to follow in Donald's footsteps. We are still using the model, and as will become clear later, still being influenced by him.

STM AS A WORKING MEMORY

Perception and communication argued for separate long- and short-term memory systems obeying quite different principles. In the decade that followed the publication of *Perception and communication*, the evidence for a dichotomy appeared to grow ever stronger, and in 1968 Atkinson and Shiffrin produced an influential model that was explicitly derived from Broadbent's earlier concepts. Their view differed, however, in proposing a single limited-capacity short-term memory system that combines the role of Broadbent's STM component with his limited-capacity attentional system. This model was characteristic of many other more or less similar conceptualizations of STM, and became known as the *modal model*. However, although it gave a good account of most of the available evidence, by the early 1970s it was running into difficulties.

One problem stemmed from its basic learning assumption, that the amount of long-term learning was a direct function of the length of time material was held in STM. A number of studies such as that of Craik and Watkins (1973) showed that simply maintaining an item by subvocal rehearsal did not guarantee good learning. A second problem stemmed from the study of patients with STM deficits. Shallice and Warrington (1970) showed that such patients had grossly reduced digit span, implying a severely impaired STM, and yet were capable of apparently normal long-term learning, and furthermore were able to live normal lives with few general cognitive impairments. If they were defective in the functioning of the kind of unitary limited-capacity STM system proposed by Atkinson and Shiffrin, then their learning and everyday cognition should in fact have been grossly disrupted.

Graham Hitch and I decided to tackle this paradox, and since we did not have access to such patients we attempted to simulate the deficit in normal subjects by means of concurrent task procedures. We loaded our subjects with concurrent activities that were assumed to occupy the STM system, and studied the impact of this on the performance of such cognitive skills as learning, comprehension, and reasoning (Baddeley and Hitch 1974). Our results were broadly consistent with the neuro-psychological evidence in suggesting that although clear effects could be detected, they were far from catastrophic.

In order to account for our results, and others in the literature, we proposed the simple model outlined in Fig. 8.1, which involves fractionating working memory into at least three subcomponents. The first of these, the *visuo-spatial sketchpad* or *scratchpad*, is assumed to be a subsidiary or slave system capable of holding and manipulating visuo-spatial information, and is regarded as responsible for visual imagery.

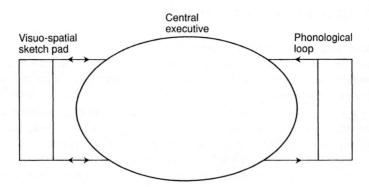

FIG. 8.1. A simplified representation of the working-memory model proposed by
Baddeley and Hitch.

The second slave system, the *phonological* or *articulatory loop*, is assumed
to perform a similar function for speech-based information. It is this
system that is assumed to be defective in patients with impaired STM.
Finally, we assume that these systems are co-ordinated, and linked to
LTM by an attentional control system which we termed the *central
executive*.

   In our development of the model, we have tended to concentrate
most strongly on the two slave systems, principally because we felt that
they offered more tractable problems than the central executive; if we
could not make progress with the slave systems, we felt we had little
chance of succeeding in understanding the executive. We have in fact
been reasonably successful in exploring these subsystems, with the
phonological loop proving particularly tractable since we already knew
a good deal about it as a result of the wealth of experiments done using
auditory digit span. We have in recent years been particularly concerned however, at the question of the functional role of the phonological loop; the possibility that evolution might have placed it there in
careful anticipation of the invention of the telephone seemed less than
totally convincing, leaving us with the fear that Jim Reason might have
been right in suggesting that it was little more than 'a pimple on the
face of cognition'.*

   A good deal of our effort over recent years has been concerned with
the issue of the functional relevance of the phonological loop, with the
picture eventually emerging of a system that plays some role in ongoing

---

* We are grateful to Jim Reason for pointing out at the *Festschrift* that this quote is inaccurate.
The location he proposed for the pimple was on a part of the anatomy that was somewhat less
elevated than the face.

speech comprehension (Vallar and Shallice 1990), but which plays an even greater role in language-acquisition. Our first hint of this came from a study of new phonological learning in a patient with a very specific deficit in short-term phonological memory (Baddeley *et al.* 1988). We found that despite a normal capacity to learn paired-associates in her native language, she showed an almost total inability to learn the vocabulary of an unfamiliar foreign language, Russian, when this was presented auditorily. Subsequent studies have indicated that short-term phonological memory capacity probably plays an important role in the acquisition of vocabulary by both normal children and children with a specific language disability (Gathercole and Baddeley 1989, 1990). Phonological loop capacity also appears to be crucial in the case of children learning a second language (Service 1989). It seems likely then that, far from being a mere pimple, the phonological loop plays a crucial role in the acquisition by children of their native language (see Baddeley 1992*a* for a more detailed overview).

By this time, some twenty-five years had passed since the publication of Broadbent's original ideas; we felt that we were making genuine if steady progress in understanding the two slave systems, but had always found reasons for postponing a direct attack on the central executive. The position finally came to a head in my attempt to bring together our research on working memory in a book written with the encouragement of Donald Broadbent, for the Oxford Psychology Series (Baddeley 1986). Having reached the last chapter and given nothing but the most shadowy account of the central executive, sheer embarrassment caused me to attempt to tackle the problem head-on.

The executive was assumed to operate as an attentional controller, and the obvious source of possible models would seem to be in the attentional literature. However, the literature on attention seemed to be bewilderingly diverse; where could one start? I was fortunate in that my dilemma occurred at a time when Donald had just published an invited review of the progress of research in attention (Broadbent 1982). This typically lucid account made it clear that my problems in applying existing attentional models to the analysis of working memory stemmed largely from the fact that most models were concerned with *perceptual selection* of one form or another, while the central executive was principally concerned with the *integration* of information and the *control* of action.

Fortunately there was one exception to this general trend, the model of attentional control proposed by Norman and Shallice (1980). The model is described in more detail in the contribution to this volume by Shallice, but can briefly be summarized as proposing two ways of controlling ongoing action. Routine activities are controlled by existing schemata, with the co-ordination between different routine actions achieved by a series of contention scheduling procedures which, for example, allow us to walk and talk at the same time. However, in cases of emergency, when an ongoing activity has to be overridden, or in performing novel tasks, a second procedure takes over, the Supervisory Attentional System, or SAS. The SAS is capable of modulating and modifying existing programmes, as well as creating new actions to cope with new problems.

As Shallice describes in Chapter 9, the model is capable of accounting for a rich array of data, including the attentional lapses and slips of action described by Reason (1979) and Norman (1981), as well as giving an account of the striking and diverse symptoms shown by patients with frontal-lobe damage. The model was particularly attractive in my own case, since it offered an account of some data collected in my Ph.D. thesis some twenty years before for which I had been unable to find an adequate interpretation.

RANDOM GENERATION AND THE CENTRAL EXECUTIVE

The data in question stemmed from the task of random generation, in which the subject tries to produce a random sequence from a given set of items, for example the letters of the alphabet. Subjects were instructed to imagine that all the letters were in a hat, that they were drawing out one letter at a time, speaking its name, returning it to the hat, and shaking before drawing again, hence producing a totally random sequence. When they were required to do this at a slow rate, for example at four seconds per item, subjects were capable of producing sequences that approximated closely to randomness. However, as rate of generation increased, so did redundancy, as measured by bias in the frequency of occurrence of individual letters or letter pairs, and also as indicated by the production of stereotypes, either from the alphabet (*AB, QR, XY*), or from frequent acronyms (*BBC, USA*).

The Norman and Shallice model can explain the limited capacity for randomization by assuming that the production of letter names is normally dominated by powerful pre-existing schemata such as those involved in reciting the alphabet, or in producing acronyms. Allowing such schemata to operate, however, is directly contrary to the instruction to maintain randomness, hence requiring the constant intervention of the SAS to break up the tendency to stereotypy, and to generate new retrieval plans. The more rapid the requirement to generate, the less opportunity the SAS has to intervene, and the greater the redundancy.

Randomness is also influenced by the informational demand of the generating task, with speed of generation being a function of number of alternatives, up to about seven or eight, after which the function levels off, just as occurs in the classic choice-reaction time function known as Hick's Law, provided that sufficient alternatives are demanded to allow the discontinuity to show up (see, for example, Seibel 1963). Finally, when random generation is used as a secondary task, the redundancy of the generated items can be used as a measure of the load imposed by the primary task. In one study (Baddeley 1966), subjects were required to sort cards into one, two, four, or eight alternatives at a rate of one response every two seconds. With each sorting response they were required to produce a letter of the alphabet. The redundancy of the letter-sequence produced increased linearly as a binary logarithmic function of the number of sorting alternatives, whether redundancy was measured in terms of individual items, pairs of letters, or alphabetic stereotypes.

As we shall see later, random generation proves to be a convenient secondary task that can plausibly be assumed to load on the central executive component of working memory. In a joint research programme with John Duncan and Hazel Emslie, we are currently attempting to refine and extend the measure, in particular exploring the possibility that randomly pressing keys may provide a suitable nonverbal analogue of alphabetic generation. A preliminary study has required subjects to generate 'chords' comprising the simultaneous pressing of one finger from each hand. Preliminary results suggest that redundancy increases with rate of generation, whether this is measured in terms of the frequency of occurrence of individual chords, of adjacent pairs of chords, or of stereotypes, which comprise chords comprising the same finger of each hand. The possibility of utilizing random generation in more than one modality should substantially increase the potential value of the technique. Random generation has in fact already proved useful in tackling a number of problems, including the analysis of the cognitive skills employed in playing chess.

WORKING MEMORY AND CHESS

The experiments that follow were carried out as a series of joint studies with Trevor Robbins and a series of undergraduates who chose to carry out their honours research project in this area (Robbins et al., in preparation). The research was stimulated by a line of argument developed by Holding (1985) in his book *The psychology of chess skill*.

Chess has most characteristically been interpreted as depending upon visuo-spatial processing and imagery; Holding, however, suggests that verbal coding may be equally important. Milojkovic (1982) proposes that stronger players depend to a greater extent on propositional rather than imagery encoding, while Holding has claimed that top players are often reported to exhibit superior verbal skills, often operating as professional writers. He attempted to test this proposal by requiring subjects to remember chess positions while counting backwards in threes. He observed a clear decrement, and concludes that this demonstrates the importance of the verbal component (Holding 1985, 1989). However, counting backwards is likely to place demands on the central executive as well as the phonological loop, making Holding's conclusion less than compelling. Our first experiment examined this issue in a study requiring subjects to memorize and recall chess positions while performing tasks that were known to disrupt either the phonological loop, the visuo-spatial sketchpad, or the central executive.

We tested a total of 20 subjects from Cambridge chess clubs, ranging in expertise from weak club players to the Grand Master level (Elo gradings ranged from 130 to 240). Positions were selected from the middle games of top-class tournaments. They were set up on one board that was placed behind a screen. This was removed to allow 10 seconds of study, after which the screen was replaced, and the subject was required to reproduce the position on the second board. Performance was tested using the method devised by de Groot (1965), in which a point is given for each piece placed in a correct location, and a point deducted for each erroneously placed piece. Four conditions were used, namely (1) *control*—no concurrent activity; (2) *articulatory suppression*—the subject was required to utter the word 'the' at a rate of one per second; (3) *visuo-spatial suppression*—the subject was required to tap the keypad of a computer at a one-second rate, following a predictable predetermined path; and (4) *random generation*—the subject was required to generate letters of the alphabet at a rate of one per second.

This paradigm has previously been used by de Groot (1965), who reports a high correlation between expertise and memory performance. We replicated this finding, showing a correlation of 0.624 between Elo rating and performance. While the games chosen were regarded as relatively obscure, we did have one striking instance of long-term memory from one of the subjects, a chess journalist who not only identified the source of one of the games, but also pointed out that we had slightly changed the position! The influence of the concurrent tasks is shown in Fig. 8.2, separately for the 12 relatively inexperienced and the 8 most expert players. While the overall level of performance in the

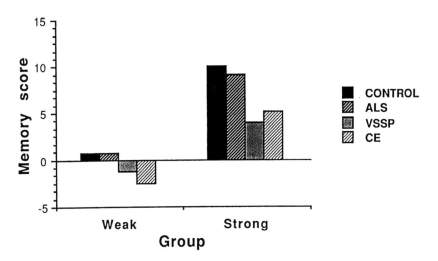

FIG. 8.2. The effect of concurrent task on memory for chess positions in weak and strong players. ALS = Articulatory suppression, VSSP = Suppression of the Visuo-spatial sketchpad, and CE involves disrupting the central executive by random generation.

two groups differed markedly, the pattern of interference was equivalent, with articulatory suppression having no effect, while both visuo-spatial suppression and random generation produced broadly equivalent amounts of disruption. Our results therefore suggest that Holding's conclusion regarding the importance of verbal encoding in memory for chess positions may have been premature.

Our next study attempted to go beyond memory and study the basis of strategic thinking in chess. We selected a number of chess positions from *Test your chess IQ (Book 1)* by A. Livshitz (1988), from which subjects were required to choose the optimal move and continuation. The various responses are analysed by Livshitz and given a grading, which we used as our score. The concurrent tasks were broadly the same as in the previous study, but with two exceptions. The undergraduate experimenters chose to replace the previous suppression word of 'the' with 'see-saw', on the grounds that it contained a richer array of phonemes, and the rate of random generation was reduced from one per second to one every two seconds, when it became clear that the one-second rate totally wiped out the capacity to perform the chess task. The subjects were 12 members of the Cambridge University Chess Club with Elo gradings from 120 to 206.

Performance again correlated with chess grading ($r = 0.493$), and also showed a comparable pattern of disruption for weak and strong players, with no effect of articulatory suppression, together with approximately equivalent disruption from the visuo-spatial suppression task and random letter generation. However, the fact that we had to slow down the rate of generation in order to allow subjects to perform the task at all suggests that this tactical task relies more heavily on executive processes than does the memory task.

Our third study involved two separate conditions. The first required subjects to count the number of squares to which a king could move

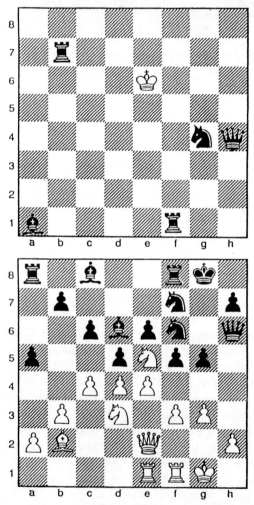

FIG. 8.3. Examples of the chess positions used in the third experiment. The upper position represents the King's flight-square problem, while the lower represents the strategic evaluation problem.

without going into check. The second involved making strategic judgements, assessing which side was winning in a series of complex middle
games taken from two Grand Masters, Petrosian and Botvinnick, both
of whom are renowned for the complexity of their strategic play (see
Fig. 8.3). The same secondary tasks were used as in the previous study,
with the exception that we excluded articulatory suppression, since our
own work, and comparable studies by Saariluoma (in press) indicated
that this had no effect on chess performance. Twelve undergraduate
chess players from the University of Cambridge served as subjects,
their ratings ranging from 120 to 205.

The tactical judgement task, in which the subject had to count escape
squares for the king, gave results that were broadly consistent with the
previous tactical and memory studies, with performance being impaired by both visuo-spatial suppression and random generation. On
this occasion, however, the correlation with chess grading did not reach
significance $(r = 0.245)$. The pattern of results for the strategic judgement task was however, quite different, with no effect of concurrent
task on performance. Performance was in fact rather poor, but was
above chance, showing a healthy correlation with chess grading
$(r = 0.528,\ p < 0.01)$, indicating that the failure to find an effect of
secondary task was not simply due to the presence of a floor effect.
While this unexpected result clearly requires further investigation, we
have tentatively interpreted it as indicating that the strategic evaluation
task is simply too complex to carry out analytically, thus forcing the
subject to rely on a relatively automatic assessment, presumably based
on some process analogous to pattern recognition.

Our analysis of chess has moved from studying the retention of chess
positions through to the investigation of tactical and strategic play. We
have used secondary tasks based on spatial tapping and on the generation of random letter-sequences, neither of which is obviously a memory
task. Are we therefore still justified in using the term working *memory* to
describe our studies, or could they better be characterized as studies of
working *attention*? Before going on to discuss this issue, it may be
helpful to consider a second series of experiments that aimed to investigate the operation of the central executive, on this occasion focusing
on patients suffering from Alzheimer's disease (AD).

WORKING MEMORY AND ALZHEIMER'S DISEASE

My research on Alzeimer's disease resulted from an invitation from
two Italian colleagues, Hans Spinnler and Sergio Della Sala, to collaborate in a multi-centre study of AD. They hoped that I and my

colleague Bob Logie would provide the cognitive-psychology input to a more detailed understanding of the functional deficits found in such patients. Our first study (Spinnler *et al.* 1988) examined the perform-ance of AD patients on a range of memory tasks, finding a memory deficit that resembled the classic amnesic syndrome in showing im-paired long-term memory, but differed in that our AD patients also showed poor performance on tests of both verbal and visuo-spatial memory span. While this might indicate specific deficits in both verbal and spatial STM, it seemed more economical to account for the disrup-tion in terms of a central executive deficit. Work carried out by Morris (1984, 1986) using the phonological loop as a framework for studying memory in AD, and other results reviewed by Morris and Baddeley (1988) are also consistent with the hypothesis of a central-executive deficit. How could one test a central-executive hypothesis, given that instructions for random generation would almost certainly be too difficult for AD patients to understand? We argued on *a priori* grounds that one of the central functions of working memory is to co-ordinate information from the two slave systems. By selecting tasks that weighed principally on the two slave systems, we felt that we could minimize interference from the overloading of either peripheral system, thus producing a task that is principally dependent upon central-executive function.

We chose as our primary task pursuit tracking; the subject was required to keep a lightpen in contact with a spot of light that moved about randomly on a computer display. When the pen deviated from the target, the target changed colour; the percentage of time on target was automatically recorded, and the speed of movement of the spot increased to a point at which each subject was on target for approxim-ately 60 per cent of the time. Tracking was combined with three other tasks. (1) Articulatory suppression: this was expected to make minimal demands on the central executive, other than those involved in ensur-ing that both tasks are performed at the same time. (2) Simple reaction time: the subject was presented with clearly-audible tones, and required to respond by pressing a foot pedal. (3) Digit span: after establishing the subjects' digit span, they were given digit sequences at span length while performing the concurrent tracking task. This last condition has the advantage that both tasks are titrated to a point at which level of performance is equivalent for the AD patients and the two control groups, normal elderly and normal young subjects (Baddeley *et al.* 1986).

The results of this study were broadly in line with the predictions based on a CE deficit hypothesis. Articulatory suppression showed a trend in the direction of disruption for AD patients, although this did not reach significance. The other two conditions showed a clear tendency for AD patients to be disproportionately disrupted by the requirement to carry out tracking simultaneously with the concurrent task, whether this was simple reaction time or digit span. This disruption occurred on both tracking and on performance on the two concurrent tasks.

The results were consistent with the proposal that AD patients are particularly sensitive to the requirement to co-ordinate the performance of two tasks, as the central-executive hypothesis would predict. However, this conclusion is open to two objections. Firstly, the reaction-time task may have been more difficult for the AD patients than the controls, hence disproportionately penalizing them when it was performed while tracking. This reduces our firm conclusions to those based on the digit-span task, for which performance was adjusted across groups. A second problem concerns the possible objection that we had simply shown that anything that makes a task more complicated will differentially penalize Alzheimer patients.

We tackled both of these in a subsequent study (Baddeley *et al.* 1991), in which the same AD patients were tested on three occasions, separated by intervals of six months, hence allowing the progress of the disease to be studied longitudinally. The first part of the study involved exactly the same procedure as was used in the previous investigation. We tested a control group of normal elderly on two occasions separated by six months; since we found no evidence of change we did not persevere to a third test six months later.

The overall pattern of results revealed in Experiment 1 was repeated when AD patients and elderly controls were compared. Of rather more significance however, were the longitudinal comparisons of performance on the AD group. These are shown in Fig. 8.4, which indicates that whereas the performance on the individual tasks shows little deterioration over the period of a year, dual-task performance shows a steady and significant decline, even in the case of the simplest task of concurrent tracking and articulatory suppression. Equivalent decrements were also shown on both tracking and secondary-task performance. Since we are using subjects as their own controls, and since individual task-performance does not decline, these results are not open to the objection that the observed decrement reflects differential difficulty of the individual tasks; hence they speak more clearly to the issue of central executive disruption in AD.

These results are, however, still open to the objection that performing tasks simultaneously simply makes them more difficult, with difficult tasks being more vulnerable to AD. While this is not a very attractive hypothesis, since it allows a *post hoc* explanation of virtually

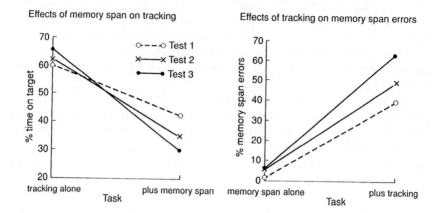

FIG. 8.4. The effects of memory span on tracking and tracking on memory span in patients suffering from Alzheimer's disease. The patients are tested on three occasions separated by six months, and the progress of the disease is reflected clearly in performance on combined tasks, but not on either task performed alone (data from Baddeley *et al.* 1991*a*).

any results obtained, it would clearly be desirable to refute it if we wished to make a strong case for a central-executive deficit in AD. We carried out a second experiment which bears on this point by varying difficulty within a single experiment, an experiment that does not involve dual-task performance.

The study is based on Yntema's (1963) experiment on keeping track of multiple targets, modified so as to make it simple enough to be performed by AD patients. The subjects were presented with a single item from a semantic category and required to decide whether it belonged to any of one, two, or four possible categories. In each case, the one, two, or four category names were presented underneath the item, so as to minimize memory load. In performing this task, normal subjects typically increase their decision latency with the number of available categories. The question at issue is whether AD patients will show a similar increase, and more importantly, whether the magnitude of this increase will become disproportionately greater as the disease progresses.

AD patients and normal elderly controls were tested on two occasions separated by approximately six months; patients were significantly slower than control subjects in categorization on both occasions. Both groups showed an increase in latency with number of alternatives, and neither showed a significant difference in performance across the two tests. The AD patients differed from control subjects, however, in showing a much higher error-rate. Frequency of erroneous responses increased with number of alternatives, and was significantly greater on the later test session, when the disease had progressed. There was however, no suggestion of an interaction between number of alternatives and test session, suggesting that increased difficulty does not necessarily make the task more sensitive.

Hence, although it would be unwise to place too much emphasis on the results of one or two experiments, our data do appear to be consistent with the proposal that AD patients show a particularly marked deficit in the operation of the central-executive component of working memory, and that this does not merely represent a tendency for increased difficulty to lead to increased sensitivity. Having said this however, it is of course important to bear in mind that AD patients are far from uniform, and that what we have observed is a general tendency that holds across patients, rather than a reliable characteristic of all AD patients (see Baddeley *et al.* 1991 for a discussion of this point).

Once again, we have performed a series of experiments on the central executive using tasks in which functions other than memory are manipulated. To what extent are we therefore justified in referring to the system as working *memory*?

WORKING MEMORY OR WORKING ATTENTION?

Before discussing the status of our own model, it may be instructive to examine briefly the role of memory in other contemporary working memory models. These fall into two broad categories, production-system models deriving from the work of Newell and Simon (1972), and individual difference-based models of working memory such as that employed by Daneman and Carpenter (1980).

The concept of a limited-capacity working memory plays a central role in production-system modelling. The working memory system is assumed to be capable of holding a limited number of chunks, each of which contains a series of 'pointers' to relevant information in long-term memory. Hence, while the number of chunks held by the system is strictly limited, if more can be packed into a chunk as a result of prior learning, then the effective capacity of the working memory system can be expanded. This lies at the heart of such models as Anderson's ACT* (Anderson 1983), Kintsch and Van Dijk's (1978) model of comprehension, and Ericsson's (1985) account of expertise.

Temporary storage of such pointers in working memory lies at the heart of the production-system implementation of such models, making working memory an essential component of the whole enterprise. This

166 WORKING MEMORY OR WORKING ATTENTION?

is both a strength and a weakness. It is a strength in that the concept of working memory provides a crucial component of a modelling technique that has clearly been extremely productive and adaptable. Its weakness is that it results in a working memory whose characteristics are postulated, rather than empirically investigated. Since I suspect that we rarely guess correctly first time in trying to understand how cognitive processes work, I myself regard this as a major weakness. Someone who believes more strongly in implementation as the *sine qua non* of successful modelling would no doubt take the opposite view. An interesting case of the two approaches meeting is offered by the elegant series of studies on the role of phonological coding in memory span for Chinese carried out by Zhang and Simon (1985).

Zhang and Simon were concerned to contrast the production-system approach to memory, which argues for a constant number of chunks, with that proposed by the phonological loop, where phonological similarity and word-length are assumed to have major influences on span over and above the influence of number of chunks. Chinese is a beautiful language for carrying out such experiments, since it allows visual and phonological similarity to be completely dissociated. In one of their experiments, for example, Zhang and Simon tested memory span for a series of visually presented words that were very dissimilar in both meaning and appearance, as represented in the pictographic script used, but which were all pronounced identically, as *gong* with a high tone. As the phonological-loop model would predict, performance was extremely poor.

A second series of experiments was concerned with separating the effects of spoken duration and chunk size, again producing results that were broadly compatible with the word-length effect (Baddeley *et al.* 1975). Zhang and Simon incorporate these findings into an equation which, they argue with some justification, suggests that similarity and word-length do not account for all the variance, and that a smaller component due to chunking is probably also necessary. At an empirical level, their equation appears to give a good account of their data, but I find it difficult to work out whether their underlying model has been changed at all significantly by data that manifestly fit the alternative phonological-loop model more closely than the chunking model. One has the slight suspicion that any result could be fitted into an expanded equation without presenting a serious challenge to the existing model. Once again, whether one regards that as a strength or a weakness depends on one's preference on an empiricist–rationalist dimension. As someone who spent nine years working in Donald Broadbent's Unit, there is little doubt as to which end of the dimension I myself find most comfortable.

The second approach to working memory that I want to consider is the one that has perhaps been most influential in North America in recent years, and which occurs in one form or another in the work on reading comprehension in adults by Daneman and Carpenter (1980, 1983). This approach essentially takes an operational definition of working memory, defining working-memory tasks as those which involve the simultaneous storage and manipulation of material. A typical study (for example, Daneman and Carpenter 1980) devises a task which involves combined storage and processing, and uses it to predict performance on other tasks, such as reading comprehension. This approach has been very productive in analysing comprehension, and has more recently been shown to give a good account of the performance on reasoning tests of the type that are typically used to measure intelligence (Kyllonen and Chrystal 1990).

I would regard the approach taken by Daneman and Carpenter and by Kyllonen and Chrystal as entirely compatible with the Baddeley and Hitch working-memory model, and as offering a valuable tool for analysing complex but important real-world tasks (see Oakhill *et al.* 1986 and Baddeley 1992*b*, for a more detailed discussion). The current weakness of this approach, however, in my own view stems from the fact that the measures so far used tend to be relatively global, containing unspecified contributions from slave systems such as the phonological loop, and possibly from aspects of long-term memory such as vocabulary knowledge. Failure to take this into account can lead to problems of interpretation. An example occurs in the proposal by Daneman and Tardif (1987) that their results indicate a separate working-memory system for language. This conclusion is potentially confounded by the differential contribution of the phonological loop, an interpretation that is consistent with the subsequent evidence against a specific working-memory system for language presented by Turner and Engle (1989).

Another problem with the operational definition of working memory in terms of concurrent memory and processing is that it would apparently require one to assume that working memory was operative only in studies that require obvious storage, hence ruling out most of the previously described experiments on chess and on the functional deficit in AD. To the extent that memory and non-memory studies form a coherent pattern of results, this relatively arbitrary separation would seem to be unfortunate.

I myself suggest that the central-executive component of working memory does not itself involve storage, which produces the apparently paradoxical conclusion that not all working-memory studies need involve memory. I suspect that all working-memory tasks draw at least minimally on the central executive, so should we therefore rename the system *working attention*?

I think we should not rename working memory, for three reasons. First, I dislike the term 'working attention', since it seems to imply that there can also be 'non-working attention', which seems an unhelpful concept. Secondly, I dislike the frequent changing of terminology, unless this implies an important underlying conceptual change. I have in fact been somewhat guilty already in more recently preferring 'sketchpad' to 'scratchpad', and 'phonological loop' to 'articulatory loop', on the grounds that they give a more accurate account of the underlying processes proposed. However, changing 'working memory' to 'working attention' would represent a much more radical modification. The third and most important reason for preferring to retain the term 'working memory' stems from my assumption that although the central executive may be primarily attentional in nature, temporary storage is an absolutely essential feature of the working-memory system as a whole. While space does not permit the justification of this view, it is argued in detail elsewhere (Baddeley, 1992c). Hence, I propose to continue to use the term working memory for the system as a whole, despite my assumption that its most crucial component, the central executive, is concerned with attention and co-ordination rather than storage.

In conclusion, it could be argued that the term 'working memory' is a misnomer, a historical accident that reflects the fact that the model evolved from the earlier and more limited concept of short-term memory. There is no doubt that memory storage is only one component of the system, which depends crucially on attentional control processes, revealed in a range of tasks from chess strategy to task co-ordination in AD. Nevertheless, I would argue that the temporary storage of information continues to be central to the system, which I suggest we continue to refer to as working memory.

REFERENCES

Anderson, J. R. (1983). *The architecture of cognition.* Harvard University Press, Harvard.

Atkinson, R. C. and Shiffrin, R. M. (1968). Human memory: a proposed system and its control processes. In *The psychology of learning and motivation: advances in research and theory,* Vol. 2 (ed. K. W. Spence), pp. 89–195. Academic Press, New York.

Baddeley, A. D. (1966). The capacity for generating information by randomization. *Quarterly Journal of Experimental Psychology,* **18**, 119–29.

Baddeley, A. D. (1986). *Working memory.* Oxford University Press.

Baddeley, A. D. (1992a). Is working memory working? The Fifteenth Bartlett Lecture. *Quarterly Journal of Experimental Psychology,* **44A**, 1–31.

Baddeley, A. D. (1992b). Working memory. *Science*, **255**, 556–9.

Baddeley, A. D. (1992c). Consciousness and working memory. *Consciousness and Cognition*.

Baddeley, A. D. (in press). Working memory and conscious awareness. In *Theories of memory* (ed. A. Collins, S. Gathercole, M. Conway, and P. Morris). Erlbaum, Hillsdale, NJ. (In press.)

Baddeley, A. D. and Hitch, G. (1974). Working memory. In *Recent advances in learning and motivation*, Vol. 8 (ed. G. A. Bower), pp. 47–90. Academic Press, New York.

Baddeley, A. D., Bressi, S., Della Sala, S., Logie, R., and Spinnler, H. (1991). The decline of working memory in Alzheimer's disease: a longitudinal study. *Brain*, **114**, 2521–42.

Baddeley, A. D., Della Sala, S., and Spinnler, H. (1991). The two-component hypothesis of memory deficit in Alzheimer's disease. *Journal of Clinical and Experimental Neuropsychology*, **13**, 372–80.

Baddeley, A. D., Logie, R., Bressi, S., Della Sala, S., and Spinnler, H. (1986). Dementia and working memory. *Quarterly Journal of Experimental Psychology*, **38A**, 603–18.

Baddeley, A. D., Papagno, C., and Vallar, G. (1988). When long-term learning depends on short-term storage. *Journal of Memory and Language*, **27**, 586–95.

Baddeley, A. D., Thomson, N., and Buchanan, M. (1975). Word length and the structure of short-term memory. *Journal of Verbal Learning and Verbal Behavior*, **14**, 575–89.

Broadbent, D. E. (1958). *Perception and communication*. Pergamon Press, London.

Broadbent, D. E. (1961). *Behaviour*. Eyre & Spottiswoode, London.

Broadbent, D. E. (1982). Task combination and selective intake of information. *Acta Psychologica*, **50**, 253–90.

Craik, F. I. M. and Watkins, M. J. (1973). The role of rehearsal in short-term memory. *Journal of Verbal Learning and Verbal Behavior*, **12**, 599–607.

Daneman, M. and Carpenter, P. A. (1980). Individual differences in working memory and reading. *Journal of Verbal Learning and Verbal Behavior*, **19**, 450–66.

Daneman, M. and Carpenter, P. A. (1983). Individual differences in integrating information between and within sentences. *Journal of Experimental Psychology: Learning, Memory and Cognition*, **9**, 561–84.

Daneman, M. and Tardif, T. (1987). Working memory and reading skill re-examined. In *Attention and performance XII* (ed. M. Coltheart), pp. 491–508. Erlbaum, Hove.

de Groot, A. D. (1965). *Thought and choice in chess*. Basic Books, New York.

Ericsson, A. (1985). Memory skill. *Canadian Journal of Psychology*, **39**, 188–231.

Gathercole, S. E. and Baddeley, A. D. (1989). Evaluation of the role of phonological STM in the development of vocabulary in children: a longitudinal study. *Journal of Memory and Language*, **28**, 200–13.

Gathercole, S. and Baddeley, A. D. (1990). Phonological memory deficits in language-disordered children: is there a causal connection? *Journal of Memory and Language*, **29**, 336–60.

Holding, D. H. (1985). *The psychology of chess skill*. Erlbaum, Hillsdale, NJ.

Holding, D. H. (1989). Counting backward during chess move choice. *Bulletin of the Psychonomic Society*, **27**, 421–4.

Kintsch, W. and van Dijk, T. A. (1978). Toward a model of text comprehension and production. *Psychological Review*, **85**, 363–94.

Kyllonen, P. C. and Chrystal, R. E. (1990). Reasoning ability is (little more than) working-memory capacity?! *Intelligence*, **14**, 389–433.

Livshitz, A. (1988). *Test your chess IQ (Book 1)*. Pergamon Press, Oxford.

Milojkovic, I. D. (1982). Chess imagery in novice and master. *Journal of Mental Imagery*, **6**, 125–44.

Morris, R. G. (1984). Dementia and the functioning of the articulatory loop system. *Cognitive Neuropsychology*, **1**, 143–57.

Morris, R. G. (1986). Short-term forgetting in senile dementia of the Alzheimer's type. *Cognitive Neuropsychology*, **3**, 77–97.

Morris, R. G. and Baddeley, A. D. (1988). Primary and working memory functioning in Alzheimer-type dementia. *Journal of Clinical and Experimental Neuropsychology*, **10**, 279–96.

Newell, A. and Simon, H. A. (1972). *Human problem solving*. Prentice Hall, Englewood Cliffs, NJ.

Norman, D. A. (1981). Categorization of action slips. *Psychological Review*, **88**, 1–15.

Norman, D. A. and Shallice, T. (1980). *Attention to action: willed and automatic control of behavior*, CHIP Report 99. University of California, San Diego.

Oakhill, J. V., Yuill, N., and Parkin, A. J. (1986). On the nature of the difference between skilled and less-skilled comprehenders. *Journal of Research in Reading*, **9**, 80–91.

Reason, J. T. (1979). Actions not as planned: the price of automatisation. In *Aspects of consciousness, Vol. 1: Psychological issues* (ed. G. Underwood and R. Stevens), pp. 67–89. Academic Press, London.

Robbins, T. W., Barker, D. R., Bradley, A. C., Burton, J. B., Fearneyhough, C., Gillespie, P. H., *et al*. Working memory in chess. (In preparation.)

Saariluoma, P. Visuo-spatial and articulatory interference in chess players' intake. *Applied Cognitive Psychology*. (In press.)

Seibel, R. (1963). Discrimination reaction time for a 1023-alternative task. *Journal of Experimental Psychology*, **66**, 215–26.

Service, E. (1989). *Phonological coding in working memory and foreign-language learning*, General Psychology Monographs, No. B9. University of Helsinki.

Shallice, T. and Warrington, E. K. (1970). Independent functioning of verbal memory stores: a neuropsychological study. *Quarterly Journal of Experimental Psychology*, **22**, 261–73.

Spinnler, H., Della Sala, S., Bandera, R., and Baddeley, A. (1988). Dementia, ageing, and the structure of human memory. *Cognitive Neuropsychology*, **5**, 193–211.

Turner, M. L. and Engle, R. W. (1989). Is working memory capacity task dependent? *Journal of Memory and Language*, **28**, 127–54.

Vallar, G. and Shallice, T. (eds) (1990). *Neuropsychological impairments of short-term memory*. Cambridge University Press.

Yntema, D. B. (1963). Keeping track of several things at once. *Human Factors*, **5**, 7–17.

Zhang, G. and Simon, H. A. (1985). STM capacity for Chinese words and idioms: chunking and acoustical loop hypothesis. *Memory and Cognition*, **13**, 193–201.

NINE

Supervisory control of action and thought selection

Tim Shallice and Paul Burgess

*P*erception and communication contained the first real scientific theory of the moment-to-moment control of the cognitive machinery in the carrying out of mental operations. It was also the first major example of the adoption of the human experimental psychology methodology that is now standard to test a complex information-processing model. Preceding applications such as those of Hick (1952) and Miller (1956) were restricted to individual processes only.

Over the last thirty years, continued application of the same methodology to the problem of how attentional control of the processing of perceptual input is carried out has led to a convergence of views on a position which is a clear descendant of that advocated in *Perception and communication* (see for example Posner 1978; Treisman, this volume, Chapter 1). There has been less concordance over the mechanisms of the attentional control of action and thought processes which are not directly tied to perceptual input. They are much more difficult to investigate by human experimental psychology procedures, and in particular by chronometric techniques. If one considers, as well as how routine thought-processes are selected, what mechanisms are involved in dealing with novel tasks, then the standard experimental psychology procedures are no longer adequate. Multiple-trial investigations of a cognitive system in essentially steady-state operation would not work, as by the end the formerly novel task will have ceased to be one.

A second complication that exists when one moves from the attentional control of perceptual processes to attentional control of cognitive ones is that there is an increasing need to take into account qualitative differences in types of processing mechanism. Over the last twenty years the assumption that cognition is carried out by a variety of separable processors has received support both from human experimental psychology paradigms (Allport *et al.* 1972; Baddeley and Hitch 1974; Posner 1978) and from cognitive neuropsychology (see Shallice 1988, for a review). This means that the hypothesis that there are attentional processes which enforce serial or near-serial processing (see Broadbent 1982) cannot be directly inferred from the existence of only a single on-line processing mechanism.

Over ten years ago Don Norman and one of us, Shallice (1980 [1986]), accepted the assumption that a variety of processors are used in action and thought-processes and suggested that the control of their on-line operation involved two qualitatively different types of mechanism (see Fig. 9.1). The lowest control level was held to utilize action or thought *schemas*—a concept derived from Piaget's (1936) *schemes*—program-like entities, one for each qualitatively distinct basic well-learned type of action or thought operation. The selection of which schema or schemas is or are to be operative at a time was carried out by *contention-scheduling*, a mechanism which resolved conflicts through lateral inhibition between independently activated schemas.

Contention scheduling, however, was held to involve *routine* selection between potentially demanding competing schemas, which are themselves well-learned. Coping with novelty was held to involve a separate mechanism—the Supervisory System—which modulates the operation of contention scheduling by providing additional activation or inhibition of schemas competing in the lower-level mechanism.

Of these concepts, both those of the existence of separable program-like entities controlling individual well-learned skill or thought operations and their characterization as 'schemas' are frequent assumptions in cognitive science theorizing on thought and action. The former is,

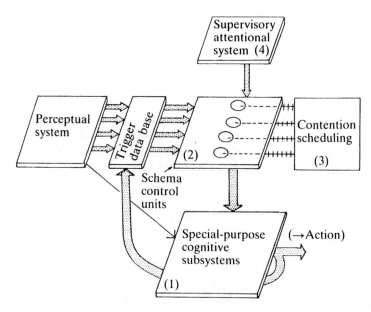

FIG. 9.1. The Norman–Shallice model, reproduced from Shallice *et al.* (1989) by permission of Oxford University Press.

for instance, present in production-system models (for example, Newell and Simon 1972) and the latter in such theorizing as that of Schmidt (1975) and Rumelhart and Ortony (1977). That such entities receive activation and are in mutually inhibitory competition for control of the machinery for thought and action is again part of the *Zeitgeist*. However, the assumption that there is a separable Supervisory System, while far from original—indeed it is a reformulation of a position held by Luria (1966), and has a family resemblance to Baddeley and Hitch's (1974) assumption of an executive store—is often criticized as merely postulating a controlling homunculus.

In fact, the idea that a central aspect of the organization of a cognitive system can be a mechanism with the primary function of co-ordinating how an appropriate course of action is produced in novel situations is now well established in artificial intelligence (see for example Fahlman 1974; Sussman 1975). The most dramatic example of this idea in operation in AI is SOAR (Laird *et al.* 1987), held by its inventors to be a general theory of cognition (see Newell 1990). One of its basic principles is that problem-solving is 'impasse'-driven, where an impasse is the state of affairs that occurs when the system is uncertain about what is its most appropriate course of action. Impasse-detection switches the goal of the system's problem-solving capacities to that of producing a procedure likely to resolve the impasse. It initiates special memory processes ('chunking') that will in due course lead to an alteration to its basic knowledge (its set of productions) to incorporate how the impasse has been resolved on this occasion. The 'impasse' is the fulcrum on which the problem-solver turns, and the purpose of the 'impasse' is to confront novelty.

The idea that a distinction between routine and non-routine processing may be represented by a qualitative division within the cognitive system is therefore placed on the intellectual agenda by developments in AI. However, this by itself does not show that the human cognitive system is so structured. Moreover the empirical evidence gathered by Newell (1990) from human experimental psychology to support the distinction—at least as it is represented in SOAR—is far from compelling. Indeed, for the reasons given earlier, human experimental-psychology methodology may not be the most suitable approach for tackling this issue. In this paper we intend to review evidence from another approach—cognitive neuropsychology—to see whether it supports the distinction as it is represented in the Norman–Shallice theory, and in particular whether patients exist whose difficulties are well characterized as arising from any impairment to the Supervisory System.

On the Norman–Shallice model the Supervisory System modulates the operation of contention-scheduling. Testing whether the behaviour of a particular type of patient would correspond to that of the model with a damaged Supervisory System could therefore be carried out in one of two ways, which we call 'negative' and 'positive'. The negative approach is to consider how contention-scheduling *operating alone* would be expected to behave in particular situations. The patient should show those types of behaviour. The positive approach is to consider the sorts of operation which the Supervisory System would be required to carry out. The patient should have difficulty with tasks involving those operations.

In the initial specification of the model (Norman and Shallice 1980 [1986]) the Supervisory System was held to be necessary for behaving appropriately in five types of situations:

1. Situations that involve planning or decision-making.
2. Situations that involve error-correction or 'trouble-shooting' (see Mandler 1975).
3. Situations where the responses are not well learned or contain novel sequences of actions.
4. Situations judged to be dangerous or technically difficult.
5. Situations that require the overcoming of a strong habitual response or the resisting of temptation.

There is one group of patients whose deficits seem to arise in these sorts of situation—patients with lesions of the prefrontal cortex, the region anterior of the premotor cortex. Indeed, the model can be seen as an information-processing analogue of the theory Luria (1966) put forward to account for the problems exhibited by such patients.

The results of more recent neuropsychological studies are also broadly in agreement with this type of characterization. Slower-responding than is shown by normal control subjects on moves *following* the initial one in the Tower-of-London test (Owen *et al.* 1991) is most easily explained in terms of the prefrontal patients' not creating or following a plan of action (see also Shallice and Burgess 1991*a*); this fits with characteristic 1. The 'stuck-in-set' perseverative errors they make on the Wisconsin Card-Sorting Test (Milner 1963; Drewe 1974; Nelson 1976) represent an inability to correct errors (type 2). The difficulty of learning random cross-modality associations (Petrides 1985) is an example of a type 3 situation. The Stroop test is clearly an example of overcoming a strong response-tendency (characteristic 5). It has been held to be impaired after frontal-lobe lesions (Perret 1974, but see also Stuss *et al.* 1981; Shallice 1982). The only one of these situations where an impairment in frontal-lobe patients has yet to be reported is the fourth; but to set up an appropriate experimental test for it is clearly much more difficult.

These five types of situation were, however, only intuitively generated by Norman and Shallice from two more general types. The first is where an incorrect response has been or is liable to be generated by contention-scheduling operating alone. In these respects 'positive' tests of the hypothesis reduce to 'negative' ones. The second is where no well-learned line of action is available to the system to produce an appropriate response—i.e. certain components of the situation are novel.

It has recently been argued that it is inappropriate to conceive of the deficit shown by frontal-lobe patients as a problem in tackling novel situations. Karnath et al. (1991) examined the performance of frontal-lobe patients and controls on the task of learning a series of fairly easy covered mazes. Prefrontal patients took longer to learn the mazes than did patients with more posterior lesions. However, the authors argued that, as there was no difference on error measures between the frontal patients and the controls on the first trial, it is not on the new and unfamiliar situation that the impairment manifests itself. Instead, as many more errors occurred on the second trial, they argued that 'patients with frontal lobe damage are not generally incapable of dealing with non-routine situations . . . they profit more slowly from experiences made in new and unfamiliar situations'. However, the construction of the mazes was such that the optimal strategy for making least errors on the first trial was to obey the simple rule that, on arrival at a dead-end, one should return to the last choice point and select a new path. Clearly for later passages through the maze it would be important to attempt to memorize on the first trial what one did at choice-points. On the first trial frontal patients spent only about 0.7 sec. in deciding which way to go at choice-points. Normal controls, by contrast, took about 1.7 sec.—significantly more. It seems plausible, then, that the prefrontal patients' greater error scores on the second trials derived from their less appropriate behaviour on the first. More critically, though, coping with novel situations does not just refer to the behaviour on the very first attempt to solve a problem. It only ends when a set of well-learned schemas and their triggers appropriate to the situation have been created.

This example, though, illustrates the way that a concept like coping with novelty is not easily operationalized. Indeed, this applies rather generally to the different types of situation for which the Supervisory System is held to be required. What exactly is planning, for instance? The issue is one much disputed in the AI literature; contrast, for instance, Sacerdoti (1975) with Suchman (1987). What exactly is 'trouble-shooting' or 'temptation'? This suggests that a more direct test of the theory could come from the 'negative' predictions, assessing whether the behaviour of prefrontal patients is well represented as unmodulated contention-scheduling.

UNMODULATED CONTENTION-SCHEDULING

What characteristics will the behaviour of an unmodulated contention-scheduling system have? The basic control elements in contention-scheduling—the schemas—have activation levels determined by 'triggers' in a trigger data-base, analogous to a production system working memory. In Shallice (1982) it was argued that the behaviour of unmodulated contention-scheduling would depend on the overall task situation. In particular, it is critical whether it contains salient aspects which lead to the strong activation of a trigger or triggers, which in turn strongly activate one or more schemas. If such trigger–schema links are activated, then behaviour would necessarily be controlled by the strongly activated schemas. On the other hand if no task-relevant schemas are strongly activated by triggers, capture of behaviour by virtually any schema could occur if its triggering stimulus is currently present. Thus it was argued that 'stuck-in-set' perseveration should occur in one of these situations, and distractability should occur in the other.

As has been discussed earlier, stuck-in-set perseveration is a standard way of characterizing the performance of frontal patients on the Wisconsin Card-Sorting Test. However, the test involves many factors (see Downes et al. 1989 for discussion); in particular it involves memory of what the patient did on the previous trial and what happened then, which might on the argument of Karnath et al., discussed earlier, be held to be a critical factor. If patients fail to remember what they did, then it would not be possible for them to alter their performance rationally.

Failures by frontal-lobe patients on tasks demanding continued attention have been described by a number of authors (for example Knight et al. 1981; Salmaso and Denes 1982; Wilkins et al. 1987; but see also Stuss et al. 1981). With the exception of the ERP study of Knight et al. these studies depend on the assumption that errors occurring in easy but continuous and slowly-paced tasks are due to failures of concentration; the inference is indirect.

The idea that unwitting triggering of inappropriate schemas may be the cause of these lapses of concentration is supported by individual case-accounts of (so-called) utilization behaviour. Utilization behaviour was originally described by Lhermitte (1983). The clinician seated opposite the patient places an object on the desk between them and pushes it towards the patient, saying nothing. Frontal-lobe patients have a tendency to pick up and use the object, for instance picking up a glass with water in it and drinking. Interpretation of the behaviour is made problematic by the demand characteristics inherent in the doctor–patient interaction. However we have recently observed a second form, which we call incidental utilization behaviour, in which the patient will pick up and use a variety of objects even when they are supposed to be doing something else, such as carrying out a psychometric test (Shallice *et al.* 1989; see also De Renzi and Barbieri 1992 for a review of related disorders). For instance, the patient L.E. picked up and dealt a pack of cards lying on the testing desk (appropriately for the number of people in the room).

Utilization behaviour provides more direct corroboration of how unmodulated contention-scheduling might be expected to operate in the absence of strong task-relevant triggers than does the occurrence of what appear to be excessive lapses of concentration. Uncontrolled selection of irrelevant schemas requires, however, that one assume that data-driven activation alone is sufficient for schema selection; this fits with observations of action lapses on normal subjects (Reason 1979; Norman 1981), but is an additional assumption. However, the most direct prediction would be that if trigger–schema links are weak no schema is activated.

TWO NEW 'NEGATIVE' TESTS OF THE HYPOTHESIS

We have recently developed two new tests (Burgess and Shallice, in preparation *a,b*), which can be viewed as providing more straight-forward situations where the two negative predictions can be contrasted—one requires inhibition of a strongly activated response and the second produces a state of affairs where no schema is strongly activated by a stimulus.

In the first task (Hayling Sentence-Completion test), the subject is presented with a sentence which has the last word omitted. What this last word should be is strongly cued by the rest of the sentence. The first part of the test requires the subject to give a word which appropriately completes the sentence. In the second part a word that makes no sense in the sentence context must be produced by the subject. An actual completion-response receives an error score of 3, a word semantically related to a word in the sentence receives an error score of 1, and an unrelated word one of 0. Thus for the sentence *Most sharks attack very close to the* . . . *coast* would receive an error score of 3, *whales*, one of 1, and *banana*, one of 0. Patients who satisfied a number of criteria, including have a lesion involving no more than two lobes, were tested. Patients whose lesions involved the frontal lobes (anterior group) and those with purely posterior lesions were closely matched on age (45.1, 43.0), NART IQ (109.3, 111.5) and FSIQ (102.6, 106.1). Twenty controls matched on age (49.7) and NART IQ (112.0) were also tested. On the critical part of the test, patients with anterior lesions had a much higher average error score than either the posterior group or the controls (see Table 9.1). There was no interaction with hemisphere. The anterior group found it much more difficult not to produce the triggered response than did the other groups.

In a second test, by contrast, no response was prepotently triggered by the stimulus situation. This was the Brixton Spatial Anticipation test, where subjects were presented with a 2×5 array of circles numbered 1 to 10. On each trial a single circle was filled, the rest being in outline only. The task of the subject was to predict which circle would be the filled one on the next trial. The position that was correct could be determined from that correct on the current trial by a simple rule, which changed after between 3 and 8 trials. The experiment involved eight rule changes and six different rules; typical ones were to move to the next-lowest number and to alternate between circles 4 and 10.

TABLE 9.1. Error scores on the Hayling Sentence Completion Test of two patient groups, each with unilateral lesions involving no more than 2 lobes, and normal control subjects.

	n	Error score (per question)
Anterior group	40	0.76*
Posterior group	24	0.32
Normal controls	20	0.20

* Significantly different from the other two groups at the 0.005 level.

Virtually the same set of patients carried out this test as the previous one. Responses made on trials in which the rule-changes are scored as if the previous rule still operated, as the patient has no way of knowing that a rule-change will occur. Since the subject has no way of rationally inferring the rule in this test until at least two trials have occurred, it is not realistically possible to obtain a perfect score. The results are shown in Table 9.2. The anterior group made significantly more errors than both the posterior group and the normal control group.

TABLE 9.2. Percentage of errors on the Brixton Spatial Anticipation test in two patient groups, each with unilateral lesions involving no more than two lobes, and normal control subjects.

	n	Percentage errors
Anterior group	40	45.3*
Posterior group	24	33.9
Normal controls	24	33.6

* Significantly different from the other two groups at the 0.01 level.

To obtain more information about the nature of the anterior group deficit on this task, errors made by patients were classified into three types. *Type 1* represented stimulus or response perseverations. It also included all responses that were preservations of the last previously corrected rule. *Type 2* represented the inappropriate application of a strategy. It included all error responses which represented either the application of a strategy formerly correct to the latest stimulus or response or in which the currently correct strategy was misapplied. Any other response made by any member of the normal control group was included with this error type, since it was conservatively assumed to arise from a different (incorrect) strategy that the normal subject had applied. Any other possible response, i.e. essentially one that could not arise from the application of a reasonable strategy to the last stimulus or response, was placed in group 3. The percentage of error responses of the three different types is shown in Table 9.3. The percentages of error types 1 and 2 did not differ between the anterior and posterior groups, but the anterior group made well over twice as high a percentage of apparently random responses as did the posterior group.

This test operates on a related principle to that of Wisconsin Card-Sorting (Milner 1963), in that the subject must learn arbitrary rules

TABLE 9.3. Percentage of the different types of error responses produced by the two patient groups in the Brixton Spatial Anticipation test.

	Anterior group	Posterior group
Error type 1 (Perseverations)	21.4	21.7
Error type 2 (Inappropriate Strategy)	63.9	72.9
Error type 3 (Guessing)	14.7*	5.4*

* $p < 0.02$.

which change fairly frequently. There are, however, two important differences between the two tests. First, the three relevant rules on the Wisconsin Card-Sorting (sort-by-colour, sort-by-shape, and sort-by-number) can be directly abstracted from the perceptual display. The four alternative targets in that test differ very clearly on colour, shape, and number, and, with the possible exception of number, these are very salient aspects of the stimuli. The present situation is different. Any particular stimulus gives no guide to the rule that may currently be in operation, as the rules relate to the relation between a stimulus and the preceding one—for example *decrease by one*. There is nothing about the stimulus situation *per se* from which such rule can be abstracted. We will assume that to follow a possible rule requires the activating of a particular schema. In the Wisconsin Card-Sorting test the colour, say, in the display can help to activate the schema *sort by colour*. No particular aspect of the stimulus in the present situation will help to activate, say, the schema *move to next lowest position*.

Secondly, in the Wisconsin Card-Sorting task a rule does not change until a sequence of a fixed number (6 or 10 in different versions) of correct responses occurs. This rule only changes when the preceding rules are overlearned. According to the present theory the relevant schema becomes strongly triggered by the context. Turning to the present situation and assuming that a guess or an incorrect strategy will give the correct response on 10 per cent of occasions, the average frontal patient will give the correct response by using the correct rule on approximately 3 trials per rule; and for the weaker subjects—who contribute most of the errors—the value will be even less. Thus overlearning does not occur, and the relevant schemas for rule-following will not be strongly triggered by the context.

For two different reasons, then, one would expect in the present task that strong triggering of relevant schemas would not develop, for weaker subjects at least. Thus in the absence of a Supervisory System no relevant schema would be strongly triggered. One would predict some form of random behaviour—or 'guessing'—to occur; and the nature of the errors bears out this prediction.

FRACTIONATION WITHIN THE SUPERVISORY SYSTEM

The rationale for the negative predictions is that the elimination of the Supervisory System will produce different types of behavour depending on the strength of trigger–schema connections relevant in the task situation. Thus the *same* lesion (to the Supervisory System) would give rise to two different types of behaviour depending on the state of another part of the cognitive system (contention-scheduling). This means that the correlation between performance on the two types of test would be expected to be high. In fact the correlation between the Brixton scores and the Hayling Sentence-Completion error scores is only 0.48, somewhat less than the correlation of Brixton with age (0.56), and not much greater than that between the Hayling score and age (0.37).

Since both age and the patients' level of current general intellectual functioning were influential in determining test performance, the effects of these factors were removed by partial correlation techniques. Under these circumstances the correlation between the Brixton and Hayling Test performances fell to 0.32, which suggest a rather low overall relationship between performance on the two tests. Moreover, certain individual cases showed difference scores on the two tests which, once estimates of test split-half reliability were taken into account (0.78 and 0.82 for the Hayling and Brixton respectively) were significant at the <0.01 level. Each of these individual cases had a frontal lesion—no posterior-lesion patient showed a discrepancy in performance on the two tests of such magnitude.

These results suggest that, while there are common components involved in performance of the tasks, the Supervisory System does not just act as a single resource as far as the effects of damage on task performance is concerned. While this complicates the 'negative' testing of the model, it makes excellent neuropsychological sense. Anatomically it appears that the prefrontal regions fall into two systems, with interconnections of areas on the whole *but not exclusively* confined within one so-called 'architetonic line' (Barbas and Pandya 1991); these are the orbital (basoventral) and mediodorsal prefrontal regions. The orbital–mediodorsal division also seems to be reflected in functional differences in animals. Thus the orbital cortex, which has major anatomical connections to the limbic system, has been classically associated in animals with deficits in inhibiting responses to negative stimuli and in emotional processing in general (see Butler and Snyder 1972; Fuster 1989). The dorsolateral part of the prefrontal lobe receives strong input through multi-synaptic pathways from the different cortical perceptual processing systems and from the hippocampus. It has been associated classically in animals with spatial delayed-response deficits (see for example Goldman-Rakic 1987), although much further fractionation of its functions is probable (see Petrides 1987).

Turning to human neuropsychology the possible fractionation of Supervisory System functions suggests the possibility of observing selective Supervisory deficits within individual patients. In a study of three frontal head-injury patients we obtained a possible candidate for such a selective disorder (Shallice and Burgess 1991*b*). All three patients had WAIS FSIQ scores of between 120 and 130. Moreover, on 13 tests held to have a frontal component, such as Wisconsin Card-Sorting, Word Fluency, Stroop, and Trail-Making, two of the patients (AP, DN) performed within the normal range on all tests; indeed AP scored above the median on all but one task. AP also performed well on a range of memory tests, although DN had problems on visual memory tests.

The three patients undertook few self-planned activities in daily life, and two at least had lost jobs through their disorganization. In daily life, they seemed to have particular difficulties when a number of different tasks had to be interleaved. For instance, on a shopping trip when a variety of different types of things will need to be obtained from different shops, they might well return with only half the necessary items. Their ability to schedule and carry out a number of fairly simple activities was tested in two different test situations—one test was carried out in a hospital room, but the other was a test where the patients were required to shop for items in a pedestrian precinct. Thus in this second test 'multiple errands' the subject had to carry out eight tasks, most being very simple, such as buying a lettuce. One task, though, required the subject to be in a particular place at a particular time, and the eighth required that four sets of information should be obtained and written on a postcard, which then had to be posted. Subjects had to obey a number of simple rules while carrying out the test. Shops could only be entered to buy something; anything bought had to be reported to a monitor; and anything used in performing the test had itself to be bought on the street. The three patients were all at least 3 SDs worse than a group of matched control subjects on the task. They each made over three times as many inefficient actions, and broke three times as many rules as did normal controls. Their behaviour was also qualitatively unusual. Two had difficulties with shopkeepers. In one case the patient decided that yesterday's newspaper would provide useful information for the postcard test. He entered a newsagent's shop, where surprisingly they were able to provide the newspaper he requested. As, so he later claimed, the previous day's newspaper was of no value he left the shop without paying for it—breaking the rule that only bought items might be used, but more critically being pursued by an angry shopkeeper. The patients performed at a similarly poor level in a more standard laboratory task situation that involved self-generated switching between tasks.

Behaviour frequently needs to be guided by explicit intentions generated previously or needs to conform with broad rules or decisions made at an earlier time which are not yet well learned. It is often the case in such situations that there is no explicit cue to remind one of the intention or rule. Thus there is nothing about the stimulus situation when entering a shop which will help to remind the subject in our multiple-errands test that the shop must not be entered unless something is to be bought. We developed a hypothesis relating to such intention- or rule-retrieving situations that would explain the inappropriate behaviour of the patients both within the experimental tasks and in everyday-life ones. We proposed that markers are activated when intentions are created or rules temporarily set up, which will be triggered if a relevant situation occurs; and that these patients have lost the facility to activate or trigger such markers. More standard frontal-lobe tasks operate as typical psychometric tasks in that they have an experimenter who is closely involved and task material which also directs the attention of the subject. We therefore presumed that such a marker to activate and trigger processes would be required less in such more standard tasks, so explaining the preserved performance of two of our patients on them.

A very interesting parallel suggestion has been made by Damasio *et al.* (1991) concerning work on a patient, EVR. An earlier study of EVR (Eslinger and Damasio 1985) had in fact been a major stimulus for our study, as EVR had many characteristics in common with our subject: he had a very high measured IQ and good performance on a variety of frontal-lobe tasks, while being incapable of holding down a job or planning his activities either on a daily basis or into the future. Damasio *et al.* contrasted GSR responses to *target pictures* 'depicting social disaster, mutilation and nudity' with *non-target pictures* depicting neutral scenes. In a PASSIVE condition no instructions were given. In an ACTIVE condition the subjects had to comment on the slide and the emotional impact it had on themselves. In the PASSIVE condition EVR showed no GSR response to *target(T)* or *non-target(NT)* stimuli (T 0.003 vs. NT 0.006; brain-damaged controls T 0.949 vs NT 0.289). In the ACTIVE condition he performed very like those controls (T 0.598 vs NT 0.012; controls T 0.594 vs. NT 0.137). Damasio *et al.* suggest that EVR has a defect in the activation of 'somatic markers', which they view as providing a 'conscious "gut feeling" on the merits of a given response' and likely to 'force attention on the positive or negative nature of given response options based on their foreseeable consequences' (pp. 320–1).

EVR had received a bilateral ablation of the ventromedial frontal cortices to remove a meningioma. Damasio *et al.* therefore ascribe their 'somatic marker' system to the anatomically specified orbital (or baso-ventral) region, and its hypothetical function certainly has a family resemblance to the functions classically associated with that region, as contrasted, say, to those attributed to the dorsolateral region.

The functions Damasio *et al.* ascribe to their 'somatic marker' system and those we ascribe to our activation and triggering of markers are not identical, but they have a distinct family resemblance, as they are both involved in the directing of ongoing behaviour by signals not explicitly presented perceptually. Moreover, the intact functions in EVR and in our patients AP and DN are similar. It seems possible that EVR and our patients have damage to the same subcomponent of the Supervisory System, and it may be possible too to link this subdivision to a neurological basis.

The two new 'negative' tests of the model were therefore individually successful. However, within individual frontal patients, performance on the Hayling Sentence-Completion Test and the Brixton Spatial Anticipation Test dissociated. As these patients were in the anterior group it seems implausible that the dissociations arise from damage to an on-line processing system. In this case it would seem to be inappropriate to consider the Supervisory System as a single resource, so the purer logic of the original testing of the theory is undermined. However, the strategy of making the more complex assumption that a Supervisory System exists but that it can fractionate is already bearing fruit.

REFERENCES

Allport, D. A., Antonis, B., and Reynolds, P. (1972). On the division of attention: a disproof of the single channel hypothesis. *Quarterly Journal of Experimental Psychology*, **24**, 225–35.

Baddeley, A. D. and Hitch, G. J. (1974). Working memory. In *The psychology of learning and motivation*, Vol. 8 (ed. G. H. Bower), pp. 47–89. Academic Press, New York.

Barbas, H. and Pandya, D. N. (1991). Patterns of connection of the prefrontal cortex in the rhesus monkey associated with cortical architecture. In *Frontal lobe function and dysfunction* (ed. H. S. Levin, H. M. Eisenberg, and A. L. Benton), pp. 35–58. Oxford University Press, New York.

Broadbent, D. E. (1982). Task combination and selective intake of information. *Acta Psychologica*, **50**, 253–90.

Butter, C. M. and Snyder, D. R. (1972). Alterations in aversive and aggressive behaviors following orbital frontal lesions in rhesus monkeys. *Acta Neurobiologica Experimentalia*, **32**, 525–65.

Damasio, A. R., Tranel, D., and Damasio, H. C. (1991). Somatic markers and the guidance of behavior: theory and preliminary testing. In *Frontal lobe function and dysfunction* (ed. H. S. Levin, H. M. Eisenberg, and A. L. Benton), pp. 217–29. Oxford University Press, New York.

De Renzi, E. and Barbieri, C. (1992). The incidence of the grasp reflex following hemispheric lesion and its relation to frontal damage. *Brain*, **115**, 293–313.

Downes, J. J., Roberts, A. C., Sahakian, B. J., Evendon, J. L., and Robbins, T. W. (1989). Impaired extra-dimensional shift performance in medicated and unmedicated Parkinson's disease: evidence for a specific attentional dysfunction. *Neuropsychologia*, **27**, 1329.

Drewe, E. A. (1974). The effect of type and area of brain lesion on Wisconsin Card Sorting Test performance. *Cortex*, **10**, 159–70.

Eslinger, P. J. and Damasio, A. R. (1985). Severe disturbance of higher cognition after frontal lobe ablation: patient EVR. *Neurology*, **35**, 1731–41.

Fahlman, S. E. (1974). A planning system for construction tasks. *Artificial Intelligence*, **5**, 1–49.

Fuster, J. M. (1989). *The prefrontal cortex* (2nd edn). Raven, New York.

Goldman-Rakic, P. S. (1987). Circuitry of primate prefrontal cortex and regulation of behaviour by representational memory. In *Handbook of physiology: The nervous system*, Vol. 5 (ed. F. Plum), pp. 373–417. American Physiological Society, Bethesda, MD.

Hick, W. G. (1952). On the rate of gain of information. *Quarterly Journal of Experimental Psychology*, **4**, 11–26.

Karnath, H. O., Wallesch, C. W., and Zimmerman, P. (1991). Mental planning and anticipatory processes with acute and chronic frontal lobe lesions: a comparison of maze performance in routine and non-routine situations. *Neuropsychologia*, **29**, 271–90.

Knight, R. T., Hillyard, S. A., Woods, D. L., and Neville, H. J. (1981). The effects of frontal cortical lesions on event-related potentials during auditory selective attention. *Electroencephalography and Clinical Neurophysiology*, **52**, 571–82.

Laird, J. E., Newell, A., and Rosenbloom, P. S. (1987). SOAR: an architecture for generated intelligence. *Artificial Intelligence*, **33**, 1–64.

Lhermitte, F. (1983). 'Utilization behavior' and its relation to lesions of the frontal lobes. *Brain*, **106**, 237–55.

Luria, A. R. (1966). *Higher cortical functions in man*. Tavistock, London.

Mandler, G. (1975). Consciousness: respectable, useful, and probably necessary. In *Information-processing and cognition: the Loyola Symposium* (ed. R. Solso), pp. 229–54. Erlbaum, Hillsdale, NJ.

Miller, G. A. (1956). The magical number seven, plus or minus two: some limits in our capacity for processing information. *Psychological Review*, **63**, 81–97.

Milner, B. (1963). Effects of different brain lesions on card-sorting. *Archives of Neurology*, **9**, 90–100.

Nelson, H. E. (1976). A modified card sorting test sensitive to frontal lobe defects. *Cortex*, **12**, 313–24.

Newell, A. (1990). *Unified theories of cognition*. Harvard University Press, Cambridge, Mass.

Newell, A. and Simon, H. (1972). *Human problem solving*. Prentice-Hall, Englewood Cliffs, NJ.

Norman, D. A. (1981). Categorisation of action slips. *Psychological Review*, **88**, 1–15.

Norman, D. A. and Shallice, T. (1980). *Attention to action: willed and automatic control of behavior*, Center for Human Information Processing, Technical Report No. 99. (Reprinted in revised form in *Consciousness and self-regulation*, Vol. 4 (ed. R. J. Davidson, G. E. Schwartz, and D. Shapiro), pp. 1–18. Plenum Press, New York, 1986.)

Owen, A., Downes, J. J., Sahakian, B. J., Polkey, C. E., and Robbins, T. W. (1990). Planning and spatial working memory following frontal lobe lesions in man. *Neuropsychologia*, **28**, 1021–34.

Perret, E. (1974). The left frontal lobe of man and the suppression of habitual responses in verbal categorical behaviour. *Neuropsychologia*, **12**, 323–30.

Petrides, M. (1985). Deficits in conditional associative-learning tasks after frontal— and temporal—lobe lesions in man. *Neuropsychologia*, **23**, 601–14.

Petrides, M. (1987). Conditional learning and the primate frontal cortex. In *The frontal lobes revisited* (ed. E. Perecman). IRBN, New York.

Piaget, J. (1936). *La naissance de l'intelligence chez l'enfant*. Delachaux et Niestlé, Neuchâtel.

Posner, M. I. (1978). *Chronometric explorations of mind*. Erlbaum, Hillsdale, NJ.

Reason, J. T. (1979). Actions not as planned. In *Aspects of consciousness*, Vol. 1 (ed. G. Underwood and R. Stevens). Academic Press, London.

Rumelhart, D. E. and Ortony, A. (1977). The representation of knowledge in memory. In *Schooling and the acquisition of knowledge* (ed. R. C. Anderson, R. J. Spiro, and W. E. Montague). Erlbaum, Hillsdale, NJ.

Sacerdoti, E. D. (1975). *A structure for plans and behavior*. Stanford University Press.

Salmaso, D. and Denes, G. (1982). Role of frontal lobe on an attention task: a signal detection analysis. *Perceptual and Motor Skills*, **54**, 1147–50.

Schmidt, R. A. (1975). A schema theory of discrete motor skill learning. *Psychological Review*, **82**, 225–60.

Shallice, T. (1982). Specific impairments of planning. *Philosophical Transactions of the Royal Society London*, **B**, **298**, 199–209.

Shallice, T. (1988). *From neuropsychology to mental structure*. Cambridge University Press.

Shallice, T. and Burgess, P. (1991a). Higher-order cognitive impairments and frontal lobe lesions in man. In *Frontal lobe function and injury* (ed. H. S. Levin, H. M. Eisenberg, and A. L. Benton), pp. 125–38. Oxford University Press.

Shallice, T. and Burgess, P. W. (1991b). Deficits in strategy application following frontal lobe damage in man. *Brain*, **114**, 727–41.

Shallice, T., Burgess, P., Schon, F., and Baxter, D. (1989). The origins of utilization behaviour. *Brain*, **112**, 1587–98.

Stuss, D. T., Kaplan, E. F., Benson, D. F., Weir, W. S., Naeser, M. A., and Levine, H. L. (1981). Long-term effects of prefrontal leucotomy. An overview of neuro-psychologic residuals. *Journal of Clinical Neuropsychology*, **3**, 13–32.

Suchman, L. A. (1987). *Plans and situated actions*. Cambridge University Press.

Sussman, G. J. (1975). *A computational model of skill acquisition*. Elsevier, New York.

Wilkins, A. J., Shallice, T., and McCarthy, R. (1987). Frontal lesions and sustained attention. *Neuropsychologia*, **25**, 359–65.

TEN

Crystal quest: a search for the basis of maintenance of practised skills into old age

Patrick M. A. Rabbitt

In order to discover how normal ageing of our brains affects our intellectual abilities we have to screen as many people of different ages as possible on as many different cognitive tests as they will agree to take. When we do this the most striking general conclusions are that variability in performance both between and within individuals sharply increases in successive age-decades. The increase in between-individual variance implies that as a cohort ages the differences in ability between its most and least able members steadily widens. Many different factors must simultaneously contribute to this increased variability. There is good presumptive evidence that longevity, and consequently prolongation of intellectual competence, are genetically inheritable; certainly women live longer, and probably retain intellectual competence proportionately later than do men (Plomin and McClearn 1990). As people grow older they are increasingly likely to suffer from one or more chronic pathologies (Siegler and Costa 1985). There is also mounting evidence that illnesses such as diabetes or respiratory and cardiac insufficiency, which become increasingly common in old age, can accelerate cognitive decline. Widening gaps in intellectual ability between the most and least competent members of ageing populations may partly reflect different genetically programmed trajectories of ageing, but also, and to an even greater extent, increasingly wide variations in health between individuals (Holland and Rabbitt 1991).

A quite different possibility is that ageing also increases variability in performance *within* individuals: that is, that differences between people's levels of competence at their best- and least-preserved skills tend to increase as they age. This can be illustrated by data collected by Rabbitt and Bent from 1400 residents of Manchester. All were aged between 50 and 86 years. Fig. 10.1a shows the levels of Pearson rank-order correlation coefficients between scores in, on the one hand, the Cattell Culture-Fair IQ test, a letter/letter coding task, a visual search task, and Baddeley's Syntactic Reasoning Task and, on the other hand, the WAIS Vocabulary Test for each of three Third Age groups from 50 to 59, 60 to 69, and 70 to 86 years. We see that the strengths of predictions for scores on a Vocabulary test (WAIS) from a performance IQ test (Cattell) or from tasks which are good measures of information-processing speed (Visual Search and Syntactic Reasoning) decline with sample age. The pattern of relationships shown in Fig. 10.1a is consistent with that seen in all previous similar comparisons reported in the literature. Figure 10.1b shows data collected by Rabbit and Abson from a similar sample of 1980 individuals resident in Newcastle-upon-Tyne. Unadjusted scores on the Mill Hill Vocabulary Test, on the AH 4 (Part 1) IQ test, on a test of cumulative learning of lists of words, on a test of free recall of a list of 30 words, and d' scores for recognition memory for 40 line drawings were all transformed to standard scores. This allowed us to compute the average differences between Mill Hill scores on the one hand, and scores on each of the other tasks on the other for each age-decade between 50 and 90 years. These are shown in Fig. 10.1b. We see that, on all measures, the average difference between attainment on the vocabulary test and on each of the other tasks increases with decade of age.

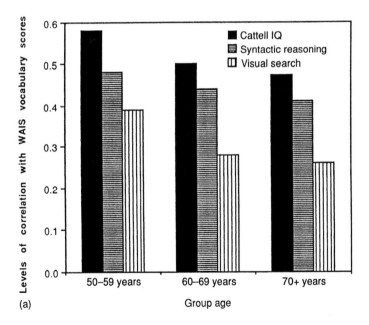

(a)

FIG. 10.1a. Correlations between WAIS vocabulary test scores and scores on Cattell IQ Baddeley Syntactic Reasoning and Visual Search tasks for groups of volunteers aged 50–59, 60–69, and 70–79 years.

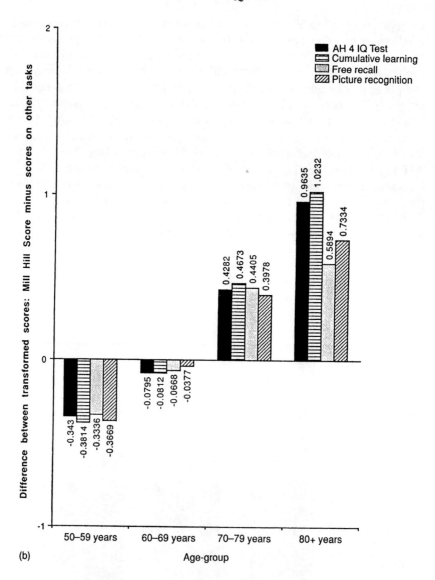

FIG. 10.1b. Differences between standardized scores on the Mill Hill Vocabulary scale and on the AH4 IQ test, a Cumulative Recall Task, a Free Recall task and a picture recognition task for groups of volunteers aged 50–59, 60–69, and 70–79.

There have been several distinct lines of speculation as to why, as people grow older, they lose ability at some cognitive tasks, such as performance IQ, while retaining their ability, or even perhaps improving it, at others, such as vocabulary tests. These ideas have usually been presented as analogies or metaphors rather than as functional models from which testable predictions can be derived. The purpose of this paper is to analyse these metaphors and models, to discuss some of the methodological and functional assumptions they conceal, and to try to evaluate the alternative frameworks now available to us for discussing functional distinctions between age-vulnerable and age-robust cognitive skills.

SUGGESTIONS FOR SOURCES OF FUNCTIONAL DIFFERENCES BETWEEN SKILLS WHICH CHANGE WITH AGE AND THOSE THAT DO NOT

1. Different parts of the brain age at different rates

A central premiss of contemporary neuropsychological models is that the human brain supports a cognitive system which has a 'modular' architecture in which physically different components independently subserve different functions. A natural speculation is that with advancing age these modules may degrade at different rates so that the various cognitive skills that they support begin to decline at different points in the lifespan and to different extents.

2. Possible qualitative differences between very 'old' and more recently acquired memories

A recent suggestion has been that, irrespective of the relative rates of ageing of the neurological locations in which they happen to be stored, the functional properties of 'very old' memories, including memories of useful information and problem-solving procedures, which have been retained for periods of many years, gradually become distinct from those of 'younger' memories which have been retained only for a period of days or months (for example Bahrick 1979, 1983, 1984; Bahrick et al. 1975; Bahrick and Phelps 1987). These studies overcame the obvious logistic problems of investigating memory over decades in the laboratory by studying very-long-term retention of coherent bodies of formally acquired information, such as Spanish learned at High School or University, or the topography of once-familiar towns. Bahrick's most general conclusion was that a rapid loss of remembered information over the first few years eventually asymptotes at a point where substantial data are still retained but no further decline occurs. Bahrick termed this basal level of recall the 'permastore'. This choice of terminology is not merely ornamental, because it carries the innuendo that after some time the neurological substrate of memory may some-how become 'frozen' in a way that halts further change. If we accept this concealed implication that 'old' and 'new' memories have quite distinct neurobiological bases we may also implicitly contrast age-robust skills acquired over a lifetime, which are no longer affected by the passage of time, and age-labile recently acquired skills, which may be lost over a few months or years. Note that this hypothesis does not entail the idea that some skills may be degraded and others spared by particular changes associated with the ageing process, *per se*. We need only suppose that 'permastore' memories persist into old age because they have long since gained the status of invulnerability to the passage of time. The nature and time-course of ageing of the brain can be left aside as a quite separate question, to be discussed as a pathological rather than as a normal process.

Neisser (1984) suggested an alternative, less physiologically loaded, hypothesis that 'permastored' memories may be relatively robust not because the functional mode of their representation has changed but because they represent a residue of 'schemata', or dynamic systems of rules and associations, which allow people to reconstruct events, rela-tionships between items of information, and plausible past scenarios. If this is the case, although the functional neurophysiological basis of storage may be the same for memories of all ages, bodies of information which are indefinitely retained as 'permastored' memories should be qualitatively different in terms of their structure and content from bodies of information which are more rapidly forgotten. Long-surviving memories should be records of linked concepts, rather than of particu-lar, isolated details. In Neisser's model, as in the others we shall discuss, the process by which a body of information is honed by time to a core residue of concepts does not necessarily tell us anything about the neurophysiological bases of cognitive ageing. Permastored memories may be age-resistant simply because their informational structure has been stripped down to a basic framework of linked rules and proposi-tions, rather than because the mode of their functional representation has changed.

Conway *et al.* (1991) report qualitative differences between 'perman-ent' and 'impermanent' memories which are consistent with Neisser's hypothesis. They had access to a unique resource; a large and enthusi-astic body of ex-students of the UK Open University who had studied, and been examined in, Cognitive Psychology at some time during a period of 12 years. This allowed them separately to test recall of names of theories, psychologists, and technical terms, and of concepts and their mutual relations. The wide age-distribution of OU students also allowed them to ask whether the characteristics of long-term memory remain unaltered throughout the life-span or whether, as age advances, the 'permastore' becomes less permanent, either because of changes in the way information can be laid down in the brain or because efficient distinction between procedures and concepts and names begins to be lost. Access to students' original terminal examination results allowed them to test whether the rate at which material is forgotten is proportional to the level of knowledge initially attained.

Conway et al.'s findings broadly replicate and extend Bahrick's in so far as they also found apparent asymptotes to forgetting. However, as Neisser suggested, there were differences in the rates at which qualitatively different kinds of material were forgotten. Names were lost earlier than concepts, with a lower asymptote, at 29 as against 39 months after examination. A contrast that will astound any teacher of psychology who has laboured against students' initial intellectual difficulties with, and vividly-expressed repugnance for, courses on research methodology is that recall of this material showed no decline at all, remainng at 30 per cent above chance throughout a 12-year recall interval. Slightly adapting Neisser's hypothesis Conway et al. take this as evidence for schema theory: 'schemata . . . do not represent detailed knowledge, but rather . . . knowledge abstracted from sets of experiences . . . e.g. encounters with various sets of concepts in different contexts such as laboratory reports, different parts of the course material and so on. This makes them different from material such as proper names which, as Cohen (1990) has argued, may lack semantic associates and so are not part of the semantic knowledge network'.

Conway et al. found some slight, but significant evidence of greater decline in recall in students over 60. This may be the first solid evidence for that most debatable of all cognitive changes in later life: 'age-specific memory impairment'. To the extent that they are correct this is evidence against, rather than for, the invulnerability of 'permastored' memories to the ageing process.

3. Psychometric models. The functional aetiology of 'fluid' and 'crystallized' abilities

Horn and Cattell (1966) were the first to point out that when data from psychometric test batteries applied to older and younger people are factor-analysed age-vulnerable and age-robust cognitive skills consistently fall into different clusters. They introduced the attractive terms of 'fluid intelligence' to designate general abilities that do not seem to be acquired or modified by practice and which seem to decline sharply with age, and 'crystallized intelligence' for bodies of acquired information and learned procedures, techniques, and skills that must be built up by practice over long periods of time and that seem to decline very little as people grow old. Horn (1982, 1986) showed that psychometric tests that load on a single common factor of 'fluid' general intelligence, ('g', Spearman 1927) cluster with performance indices from laboratory tests of efficiency of attention, of information-processing speed, and of learning-rate. In contrast, these laboratory-performance indices are very weakly represented in factors incorporating 'crystallized' intelligence, such as vocabulary or acquired knowledge of the world.

It is easy to illustrate that there are indeed marked differences in the extent to which Horn's categories of 'fluid' and 'crystallized' skills are retained into old age. Rabbitt and Abson collected data from 2100 residents of Newcastle-upon-Tyne aged between 50 and 86 years. Figure 10.2a gives distributions of scores from a subset of 983 individuals of this group (within which are separately represented people aged 50 to 59, 60 to 69, and over 70 years) on part 1 of the AH 4 intelligence test. This is an instrument known to be highly loaded for the single factor 'g', which is associated with 'fluid' intellectual abilities such as the ability to solve novel problems, and also with laboratory measures of information-processing speed (Nettelbeck and Rabbitt, in press; Rabbitt and Goward, in press a) and of learning-rate (Rabbitt et al. 1989) derived from simple laboratory tasks. Figure 10.2b shows distributions of scores obtained from the same volunteers on a test of 'crystallized intelligence', the Mill Hill vocabulary scale.

Figure 10.2a shows that older individuals more frequently obtain low AH 4 test scores, so that distributions of scores become increasingly skewed as group age increases. In contrast Fig. 10.2b shows that distributions of Mill Hill scores remain identical for all age-decades between 50 and 80 years.

It may be objected that this demonstration is much less dramatic than it first seems because, like other tests of recognition vocabulary, the Mill Hill vocabulary test is a relatively undemanding task in which volunteers have to identify the closest synonym out of a set of 6 alternatives given for each of a set of target words. More difficult tests of precision of vocabulary, such as recalling, rather than recognizing, exact definitions for target words might possibly pick up differences by age that are missed by the Mill Hill. Figure 10.3 uses imaginary data to illustrate how the presence or absence of age effects may depend on the level of task-difficulty at which groups are compared. When tasks are very easy, differences between age-groups may appear only late in life, or not at all, because they are all performing near their ceiling. As task-difficulty increases age-differences will be detected progressively earlier during the life-span, and we may also begin to see interactions between task-difficulty and age-differences in performance, such that differ-

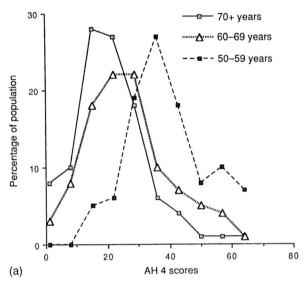

FIG. 10.2a. Distributions of scores on the AH4 (1) IQ test for groups of volunteers
aged 50–59, 60–69, and 70 + years.

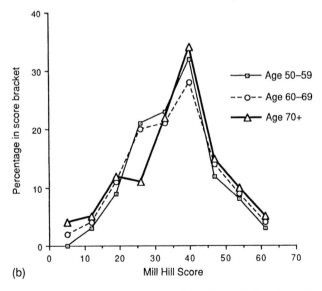

FIG. 10.2b. Distributions of scores on the Mill Hill Vocabulary Test for the same
groups of volunteers where AH4 (1) scores are shown in Fig. 10.2a.

ences between younger and older groups become more marked as task-difficulty rises. In contrast, when tasks become very difficult indeed increasing numbers of individuals in older groups may be able to attain only minimal scores, so that 'floor' effects appear and, while overall age-differences remain, interactions between task-difficulty and age may disappear or even reverse in sign.

It may also be argued that the retention into old age of overlearned data about words is too trivial an effect to justify use of the rather portentous term 'crystallized intelligence'. Both in everyday discourse and in psychometric theory the use of the term 'intelligence' typically carries the meaning of the ability to understand relationships or to use remembered information to solve problems, as distinct from rote recall of fragments of data. The term 'crystallized intelligence' would seem more apt if we could show that extensive and continued practice can also ensure the survival of particular sets of rules or procedures for solving complex problems.

In response to the first objection it seems unlikely that Rabbitt and Abson's observation of invariance of Mill Hill distributions across decades can be explained by ceiling effects. In these data the standard deviations of AH 4 test scores and Mill Hill scores were closely com-

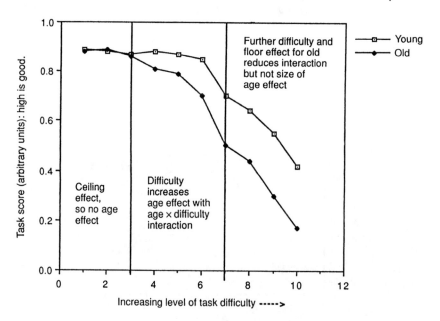

FIG. 10.3. Imaginary data illustrating how appearance of age differences may be present or absent depending on the level of task difficulty at which they are assessed.

parable. An amusing commentary on the second point can be made from data collected by Winder and Rabbitt (unpublished) from a group of 57 individuals who were expert solvers of cryptic crossword puzzles, and their novice controls, with whom each of them was exactly matched in terms of age, gender, and current level of fluid IQ (unadjusted AH 4 test score). Both experts and novices had been scored on the same open-ended (i.e. 'ceilingless') test of cryptic crossword-solving ability which required them to solve crossword-puzzle clues without time-pressure.

It is uninteresting that the experts were better than the novices at solving crossword clues since the two groups were selected precisely to ensure this. The interesting points are, rather, that among novices crossword-solving ability was strongly and positively predicted by their IQ test score $(r = 0.719)$ and negatively predicted by their ages $(r = -0.248)$, while among older experts crossword-puzzle solving ability was, if anything, positively correlated with age $(r = 0.241)$ and was not predicted by AH 4 test scores: $(r = 0.124)$. Thus experts' current crossword-solving abilities appear to have become independent of either their current ages or their current levels of 'fluid intelligence' (g). It seems that besides ensuring the simple retention of information about the meanings of words practice at solving cryptic crossword-puzzles can build up, and possibly also preserve, competence with the complex and arcane (albeit, in absolute terms, probably quite restricted) set of logical tricks, deductive procedures, coding conventions for clues, and accurate information about the structure sound patterns and relationships between words that are necessary to solve difficult cryptic crosswords.

To reverse the actual chronology of the development of ideas we may recast Horn and Cattell's (1966) distinction between age-vulnerable 'fluid' abilities and age-resistant 'crystallized abilities' as a modified version of the 'permastore' hypothesis. Within this framework the key emphases would be that most, perhaps all, cognitive skills are not 'hard-wired', but acquired during the life-span, and that different cognitive skills may have very different functional histories. Skills that are learned early in life and are continually practised into old age may be preserved by this prolonged development and sustained use while unpractised skills may be relatively rapidly lost.

This intuitively plausible general idea may be given two quite different implications. One is that continued use of a particular skill must benefit the neurophysiological substrate that supports it, so that the relative rates of *physiological* ageing of different parts of the brain are determined by the relative extents to which they continue to be actively used. A quite different implication is that although continued employment may not necessarily preserve the physiological health of local areas of the brain, the alterations in these structures which form the basis of learned skills are robust to adverse changes in direct proportion to the length of time over which they have been built up. So, for example, we may suppose that the acquired structures that support language skills which begin to be built up very early in life, and which continue to be used into old age, will be less affected by global age-related changes in the brain than will other, less diligently practised, and so less strongly 'stamped in', structures supporting other learned cognitive abilities.

The argument in this paper will move towards a third, hitherto undiscussed, possibility: that some of the differences between age-vulnerable and age-robust performance characteristics can be explained by the assumption that when modelling neural networks we must assume that units and connections between them have many different performance characteristics which are relatively independent of each other. These different performance characteristics may not all be equally vulnerable to age-related changes. Evidence for this speculation is still only illustrative rather than definitive, but at least suggests ways in which current models for differences in the relative resistance to age of different indices of cognitive performance can be reassessed and extended.

4. Attempts at a functional description for differences between fluid and crystallized intellectual skills

Although the concepts of 'fluid' and 'crystallized' intelligence have been widely documented and insightfully discussed by psychometricians it is curious that we still have no useful 'functional' or 'process' models to explain the ways in which these two categories of human information-processing differ, or why they are not equally affected by age-changes in the brain. Instead of testable functional models we have only pictur-esque analogies which at first sight seem to be harmlessly entertaining heuristic devices, but, when closely examined, turn out to imply strong covert assumptions about the architecture and dynamics of the ageing brain. One particularly genial analogy has been Salthouse's (1988) comparison of ageing memory to a reference library run by an increasingly frail librarian. The books and their contents may be unaffected by the passage of time, but the librarian becomes increasingly slow and inaccurate at accessing the information that they still preserve. The covert functional implication of this metaphor is that 'data-storage' and 'data-retrieval' are managed by discrete systems, and that the latter is affected by age while the former is not. The practical implication is that while sustained practice may perhaps preserve indefinitely the availability of data, or of learned information-processing procedures, the efficiency with which these data or procedures can be accessed, the speed with which they can be used, and the efficiency of support systems such as 'working memory' which are necessary to implement stored information-processing routines may all deteriorate with age. In short, as people grow old even highly-practised skills may become potentially available but inaccessible.

A parallel analogy might be with a computer program, which can be indefinitely preserved on a storage disc, but which eventually can no longer be read and run by a decaying machine which is gradually losing memory and processing-power. A slightly different version of this latter analogy seems to underlie Anderson's (1992) recent attempt to offer a 'functional' or 'process' model for the development of 'crystallized' and 'fluid' intelligence in young children. For Anderson (1992) the acquisition of 'crystallized' intelligence involves the rapid development of 'modules' of acquired skills and bodies of knowledge and procedures that may reside in specific brain areas and be subject to different, genetically imposed, limitations on their relative maximum levels of development. Thus particular individuals may be very high or relatively low achievers in particular 'modular' skills, depending on their idiosyncratic genetic legacies and opportunities for specific training. In contrast, 'fluid' abilities are performance parameters, such as information-processing rate and working-memory capacity. These are independent of specific modules, and represent performance characteristics of the entire central nervous system that (on Anderson's somewhat questionable assumptions) remain invariant throughout development. Anderson (1992), following previous studies such as those by Eysenck (1986), Jensen (1982, 1985), and Nettelbeck and Lally (1981), suggests that levels of these latter fluid skills can be picked up sensitively by psychometric tests loaded for Spearman's 'g', or by laboratory tasks such as 'inspection time' (i.e. tachistoscopic recognition thresholds) or Choice-Reaction Time (CRT) that provide simple, and so especially direct and reliable, indices of information-processing speed. Current levels of fluid skills determine both the rates at which 'modular' skills can be acquired and the efficiency with which they can be used once they are available.

No studies have yet rejected an obvious, plausible counter-proposal. This would be that skills may come as functional 'packages', in which elementary information-processing operations and higher-level planning, control, and data-storage and retrieval are all inseparably related aspects of a special-purpose programme developed to carry out a particular task. On these assumptions indices of the efficiency of higher-

and lower-level processes will be strongly correlated within, but not necessarily beyond, specific task domains. A limiting case of this model would be that we cannot measure people's 'information-processing capacity' or 'working-memory capacity' in the abstract, but only in the context of some particular concrete task; that is, with a particular type of material with which they may have had more or less practice in the context of their lifetime's experience. For example, it is plausible that the speed with which a person can make decisions about words or can formulate grammatically acceptable sentences may be a very poor guide to the speed with which he or she can make decisions about other types of input, such as relationships between numbers, complex patterns, or colour patches. Similarly, rate of attainment of language may be relatively unrelated to efficiency at mastering motor skills.

Some rationale for this point of view derives from demonstrations by Ericssen and associates (Chase and Ericssen 1982; Ericssen 1988; Ericssen et al. 1980; Ericssen and Polson 1988). With very prolonged practice people can develop extraordinary competence at particular skills, such as memory for restaurant orders or for strings of random digits or letters. However, these skills are intensely 'domain-specific' to particular types of material. For example, given sufficient practice, most young adults can achieve surprisingly long immediate-memory spans by inventing and using particular encoding strategies for lists of digits or letters. However, these encoding strategies are typically useful only for the particular material for which they have been developed, and attainment of remarkable spans for digits may yield no improvement in spans for letters, and vice versa. Within this conceptual framework the question arises as to what, precisely, is the level at which practice operates to produce these enormous improvements in performance? For example, very extended practice at a complex information-processing skill such as reading will certainly develop associated higher-order cognitive skills such as vocabulary and comprehension for text. However, does practice at reading also develop and preserve even relatively low-level component skills, such as speed of letter- and word-recognition? If it does we can further ask whether improvement at these particular elementary information-processing skills remains specific only to letters and words, or whether this training may also generalize to other simple information-processing tasks with non-verbal material. This question has some practical urgency in the field of cognitive ageing, where it is important to know whether continued practice at a general activity such as reading, or crossword-puzzle solving, preserves only the specific components of the skill that are practised, or whether it can generalize to benefit a wide range of other everyday competences.

A quite different line of explanation becomes possible if we shift our attention from the integrity or decay of entire modular structures, and focus instead on the elementary performance characteristics of the hypothetical information-processing networks of which all brain 'modules' must be constructed. Note that this change of emphasis does not contradict the ideas that the brain may have a 'modular' organization, or that different 'modules' (defined in a different way, as by Anderson, in press) may be developed to varying levels of efficiency by differential practice, or that ageing may affect some parts of the brain earlier and more drastically than others. Leaving all these questions open we can ask whether factors that operate in a global way to degrade overall neuronal efficiency in the entire brain will affect all the performance characteristics of elementary neural networks to the same extent, or will affect some performance characteristics earlier and more severely than others. To clarify this idea it is necessary to distinguish between the *performance characteristics of a system*, which are the indices we can objectively derive from laboratory tasks designed to give quantitative measures of its efficiency, and *the functional properties of the system*, which are logically quite distinct from these performance characteristics, and which we infer and model from relationships between these performance characteristics. So, for example, in simulations of networks, performance characteristics such as information-transmission rate, learning-rate, and forgetting-rate usually turn out to be only very modestly correlated with each other. Within this framework of explanation this is understandable, because our functional models for information-processing rate, learning-rate, and forgetting-rate derive their predictions of these performance characteristics from quite different hypothetical properties of the architecture of the Central Nervous System and of the units of which it is composed. In all our functional models some hypothetical system properties will affect only one, and others two or several different performance characteristics. Further, these relationships will vary with the particular choice of tasks from which performance indices are derived. For example, in some connectionist simulations of networks that process and learn information, maximum information-processing rate may depend *both* on the average time taken by one unit to activate another (for example, in very simplistic neurophysiological models, on synaptic delay) *and* on the extent to which the abundance and interconnectivity of units within the network allow distributed parallel processing. In the same simulations learning-rate may also depend on abundance and interconnectivity of units, but may be even more strongly determined by the rate of change of unit activation thresholds with repeated stimulation. Thus information-transmission rate and learning-rate are jointly affected by one functional property of the network, and quite separately affected by two others. To press this analogy further, different kinds of simulated degradation or, picturesquely, 'ageing' of a neural network, such as reductions in the numbers of its component units, losses of inter-connectivity between its units, or increases in 'random noise' may affect some of its performance characteristics much more than others. These distinctions, and the kinds of evidence we need to test them, may be clarified by reviewing some recent studies.

Some recent experiments by Bryan (1986) can be used to annotate Salthouse's (1988) metaphorical contrast between the ageing librarian and the intact reference library or the intact program disc and the failing computer. Within this framework of description we would expect that even if age leaves a body of acquired information intact it may nevertheless affect the efficiency with which it can be accessed. Bryan (1986) selected groups of individuals in their 50s, 60s, and 70s who had relatively high and relatively low scores on a test of fluid intelligence (the AH 4 parts 1 and 2). She compared them on two tests of vocabulary in which their responses were timed. In one of these tasks they were shown the pictures in the Warrington and McKenna vocabulary test one at a time, and their naming latencies and errors were recorded. In another task she recorded the speed and accuracy with which they matched spoken target words to the appropriate one of four pictures on each successive card of the British Picture Vocabulary Scale. The first comparison of interest was between subgroups of individuals in their 60s and 70s who achieved the same overall scores on both tests: that is to say these groups had identical scores for items correctly named or matched, and so equally good vocabularies as assessed by these tests. Naming latencies for the Warrington and McKenna task are plotted in Fig. 10.4a, and for the BPVS task in Fig. 10.4b.

Figures 10.4a and 10.4b show that, as might be expected from a voluminous literature, latencies for picture-naming and matching increase with the item difficulty (in this case with item rarity). Bryan's new finding was that the slope of the function relating latency to item difficulty becomes steadily greater as group mean AH 4 test scores decline (Fig. 10.4a,b). Bryan's data fit (albeit only modestly well) the pattern of the extremely general 'age–complexity interaction' first elegantly demonstrated by Cerella (1985). Across all levels of difficulty within and between all the laboratory CRT tasks for which he plotted data, Cerella found that, across all levels of task difficulty, response latencies of older people were simple multiples of those of young adults. That is, Choice Reaction Times (CRTs) for elderly subjects could accurately be estimated by multiplying CRTs for young adults by a

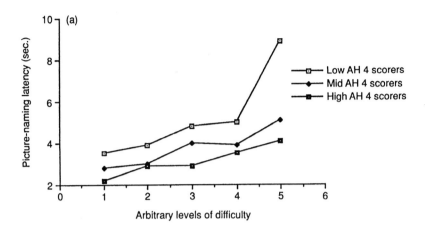

FIG. 10.4a. Data by Bryan (1986) for naming latencies on the Warrington and McKenna picture identification task for individuals with equal accuracy scores aged 60–69 and 70–79 years.

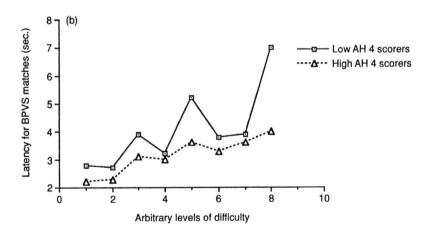

FIG. 10.4b. Data by Bryan (1986) for naming latencies for items on the British Picture Vocabulary scale for individuals with equal accuracy aged been 60–69 and 70–79 years.

simple constant (a number in the range between 1.3 to 1.7). Most of the tasks that Cerella (1985) analysed made no demands on memory. In Fig. 10.5 Cerella's graphical technique is used to re-plot Bryan's data on memory-retrieval latencies (retrieval of names for pictures and of words to match BPVS items) already given in Fig. 10.4a. Just as for straightforward CRT tasks, in which no retrieval of information from memory is involved, retrieval times for the elderly are quite well expressed as simple multiples of those for the young at all levels of item difficulty.

It seems that even if the size and precision of people's vocabularies do not diminish as they grow older, people nevertheless begin to take much longer to access them. Retrieval times for both rare and common words are increased by the same proportion, but this has the effect that the absolute increases in retrieval times are greater for slowly accessed rare than for rapidly accessed common words. It also seems that the speed and accuracy with which people can solve simple IQ test problems is a good index of the speed with which they can retrieve words from their internal dictionaries.

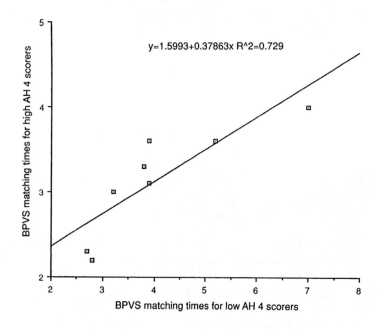

FIG. 10.5. Brindley/Cerella plot for Warrington and McKenna latencies given in Fig. 10.4a.

Rabbitt (in press) repeated Bryan's experiments in a context that directly exploits the constancy of Mill Hill scores across all age groups shown in Fig. 10.2b above. In a computerized version of the Mill Hill test target words appeared one at a time, each accompanied by its menu of 6 alternative possible synonyms. Volunteers made their choices from this menu by pressing one of the digit keys 1 to 6 on the computer keyboard. The next test item then immediately appeared. The computer program timed each choice to within 0.01 sec. and verified it for accuracy. This allowed gradients of decision latencies against item difficulty to be plotted for 58 individuals aged from 20 to 32 years and for 60 individuals aged 64 to 76 years. As we would expect from data from the pencil-and-paper version of the Mill Hill scale plotted in Fig. 10.2b, if we score the task by assigning a point for each word for which they chose the correct synonym, older and younger groups achieved almost identical Mill Hill scores ($F < 0.2$). However the older group made these decisions much more slowly and, as in Bryan's (1986) experiments, absolute differences in average latencies between the two groups increased with item difficulty. Fig. 10.6 plots mean latencies for the older group against those of the younger group across 8 (arbitrarily selected) levels of item difficulty. Once again, at all levels of item difficulty, decision times for the older subjects are simple multiples of those for the younger.

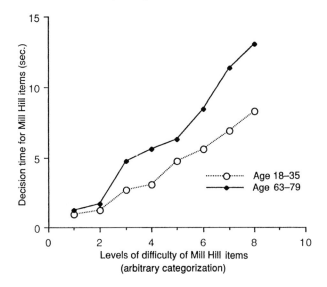

FIG. 10.6. Plot of latencies to answer Mill Hill items. Mean RTs for a group of 58 individuals aged from 20–32 years and 60 individuals aged from 64–76 years are compared.

A series of studies by Perfect (1989) again repeatedly showed differences in the times taken by older and younger people to retrieve complex bodies of acquired information from memory. He gave a computerized 'Trivial Pursuit' general knowledge task to older and younger adults who were either novices or experts in the various fields of knowledge probed. Once again, for both experts and novices, and across all levels of item difficulty, decision latencies of older individuals or low IQ test scorers could be derived by multiplying decision latencies of younger individuals or high test scorers by a simple scaling constant.

All these results can be interpreted as evidence of the aptness of Salthouse's analogy of the intact library and the decaying librarian: that is, although learned information, rules, or procedures may remain potentially accessible in memory until late in life, the efficiency with which they can be used will depend on the degree of integrity of the quite different functional systems by means of which they are accessed. We may further argue with Anderson (1992) that these 'other' systems do not seem to be tied to any domain-specific activity, such as retrieval of some, but not of other, particular kinds of information from memory, since their 'global' level of functional integrity can be well predicted by the speed and accuracy of solution of simple IQ test problems. The picture that emerges from these experiments is, therefore, very congenial to the metaphor of an intact data-storage system and a failing computer processor which gradually ceases to be able to read the information or to run the programs that it stores. It is also congenial to Anderson's (1992) idea that 'modules' of 'crystallized' skills are accessed by a single common information-processing system, or control system, or 'central processor' which services all of them in common. However, these experiments do not comment on the further possibility that very extended domain-specific practice may not merely build up and maintain a passive 'database' or 'reference library' of specific information about the world and a tool-kit of 'higher level procedures' to solve particular problems, but may also develop and preserve lower-level information-processing and retrieval procedures which are specific to some acquired skills and do not generalize to others.

This contrast can be illustrated by analysing data collected by Ian Stuart-Hamilton and Helen Papadeleloui at the University of Manchester Age and Cognitive Performance Research Centre to study how reading efficiency is maintained in old age. Seventy-two people aged from 50 to 80 years were each given a series of tasks related to various aspects of reading ability. These ranged from tests of higher-order abilities such as vocabulary, comprehension and memory for text, and reading speed (for example the NART, Mill Hill, and WAIS vocabulary, tests of memory and comprehension of printed texts, and measurements of reading-rate and eye–voice span) through tests of relatively lower-level skills such as speed and accuracy of word- and letter-recognition (for example, RTs to detect reversed letters in text; lexical decision tasks; RTs for physical identity and name identity of letters; random letter-strings in words printed in identical and in different cases; and latencies for recognition of homonyms and homophones). All volunteers were also scored on the AH 4 IQ test. A subset of 40 of these individuals were also given an easy 4-alternative serial choice-response task by Mrs Yang Qian. In addition Ian Stuart-Hamilton tried to obtain reliable estimates of individuals' amounts of lifetime practice at reading by recording their experience of education, their amount of use of reading during their professional lives, and their self-reports of the number of hours per day or week they currently spent reading books, newspapers, or magazines. However although all these measures correlated positively and significantly both with each other and with objective measures of language ability such as NART and vocabulary test scores, and scores on a spelling test, the most sensitive overall indices of individuals' reading involvement turned out to be their scores on an *ad hoc* 'literary quiz' in which they were asked to name authors of listed books, titles of works by listed authors, and characters and events in well-known works of fiction.

These data allow us to examine three questions. The most general is how well levels of current and lifetime practice preserve performance at reading into old age. The next is whether practice has its effects on all aspects of the task, that is at all levels of information-processing, or only on some aspects of the task and not others. For example, does practice maintain, and so predict, reading performance only in the sense that it affects higher-level reading skills such as overall reading rate and accuracy, eye–voice span, and memory and comprehension of text? Or does practice also alter and maintain levels of performance at lower-level component skills, such as speed of letter- or word-recognition and comparison? The final question is whether maintenance of performance at these lower-level skills also entails maintenance of performance at other, logically identical, skills using different material: i.e. if specific practice at reading maintains speed and accuracy at lexical decision, letter-identification, and symbol- and word-matching, does it also generalize to maintain performance at other easy choice-reaction-time tasks in which people identify or compare quite different kinds of stimuli? In other words, to what degree does practice generalize across skill domains?

As has been remarked, scores on the *ad hoc* 'Literary quiz', quite unexpectedly, turned out to be the best index of lifetime and current reading experience. Stepwise regression analyses compared literary quiz scores, chronological age, and AH 4 and vocabulary-test scores as predictors of scores on all the other tasks described above. It was clear that, as judged from scores on this quiz, lifetime and current practice at reading predicted higher-order reading skills. Once variance associated with literary-quiz scores had been partialled out chronological age had no significant effect on higher-level skills, such as eye–voice span, reading speed, and memory comprehension of text. In contrast, even after the effects of individual differences associated with AH 4 test scores *and* of chronological age had been taken into consideration, literary-quiz scores and subjective accounts of reading habits still significantly predicted variance in eye–voice span, in memory and text comprehension, and in reading speed. It seems that for these higher-level skills the amount and quality of lifetime and current practice is more important than age, and is at least as important as current level of IQ-test performance.

The same relationships could not be detected for 'lower-level' skills, such as recognition of letters, lexical decision tasks, and same–different letter- and word-matching tasks. Whether or not the effects of age and AH 4 test-score differences had been taken into consideration, neither volunteers' subjective estimates of the amount of time they spent reading nor their objective literary-quiz scores predicted their current performance on any of these more elementary information-processing skills. In contrast, levels of performance on all of these skills were well predicted by AH 4 IQ-test scores, and modestly predicted by chronological age. However, when variance associated with individual differences in AH 4 test scores had been taken into consideration, chronological age made no independent prediction.

Our third question was, whether any relationship observed between continued practice at reading and preservation of performance at particular lower-level skills concerned with letter- and word-identification and comparison might also generalize to improved performance at other simple information-processing tasks using different stimuli and response sets. This question lapsed because we found no evidence that practice at reading benefited or maintained lower-level skills at comparing and identifying words and letters. However, 40 participants in the reading study had also been screened by Qian Yang on a 4-alternative serial choice-response task using signal lights and keys. Their choice-response times significantly slowed with age and reduced with higher AH 4 test-scores, but when variance in AH 4 test-scores had been partialled out, age was no longer significant. These individuals' choice-reaction times significantly predicted their latencies on lexical decision tasks, symbol-identification tasks, and same–different comparison tasks ($r > 0.46$ in all cases). When effects of individual differences in AH 4 test-scores had been taken into consideration predictions of latencies on symbolic tasks from latencies on the non-symbolic CRT task were reduced, but still remained significant. There does seem to be a speed factor which is common to all elementary information-processing tasks, which is picked up by pencil-and-paper IQ tests, which is markedly affected by age, and which, as far as we can tell from this particular set of data, is not greatly affected by practice with particular stimulus materials and choices between responses.

At first sight these results seem to sharpen the distinction that Horn and others have made between 'crystallized' and 'fluid' cognitive skills. Practice can build up bodies of information and repertoires of higher-order procedures to a point at which their integrity and efficiency is not longer predicted by current levels of performance on simple problem-solving tasks (i.e. tests of 'fluid intelligence').

This distinction between the effects of practice on 'higher'- and 'lower'-order information-processing operations becomes less satisfactory when we consider how perverse it would be to deny that practice can also markedly improve the efficiency of lower-order elementary information-processing operations. For example, among many other studies, experiments described by Rabbitt and Banerji (1989) show that, even after many thousands of responses, practice continues to improve speed and accuracy at very easy choice-reaction time tasks. However, when closely examined, the relationships between practice, chronological age, and intelligence-test scores reveal some interesting paradoxes. For example Rabbitt and Goward (in press a) practised 90 individuals aged from 53 to 76 years who were divided into 9 equal groups balanced in terms of age-decade (50 to 59; 60 to 69; and 70 to 76) and in terms of IQ-test score (Low, 14 to 17; Medium, 27 to 28; and High, 41 to 43 points on the AH 4 test). All groups were given 10 blocks of trials each on an easy, four-choice CRT task. Figure 10.7 plots practice curves for the three IQ-test score groups.

Throughout the experiment the high IQ-test score groups responded fastest, the medium group more slowly, and the low IQ-test score group most slowly. The paradox is that the fast, high-IQ group shows little, the medium test-score group shows some, and the low test-score group shows considerable improvement with practice. From these results we must conclude that IQ-test scores *negatively* predict learning-rate. A similar paradox appears when the data are replotted to show the effects of age on practice. The youngest group are fastest, but show least improvement, and the oldest are slowest, but show most improvement. Can it really be that the older or less gifted people are, the more and faster they learn?

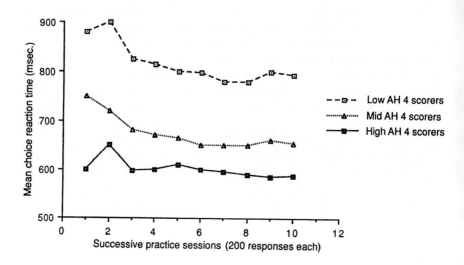

FIG. 10.7. Effects of practice on CRTs of groups of individuals with High, Medium, and Low scores on the AH4 (1) IQ test.

The key to this paradox seems to be task complexity. Rabbitt *et al.* (1989) found that young adults' AH 4 test scores predicted the rate at which they learned a very complex video game ($r = 0.68$) much better than they predicted their initial performance on this task ($r = 0.3$). This seems to be true of other complex tasks. Figure 10.8 plots unpublished data collected by Stollery, Rabbitt, and Moore from 94 individuals aged from 50 to 80 years. Within this population decade samples were matched for AH 4 test-scores. Figure 10.8a plots data from an easy four-choice serial CRT task in which they responded with a different finger to each of four spatially distinct targets for 4 runs of 200 signals and responses on each of 5 days. Figure 10.8b plots parallel data from a different version of this task, in which they made the same responses to the same signals but, on each trial, answered the signal that had appeared on the immediately previous trial rather than the one which was currently present. Figure 10.8c plots their data from a letter-categorization task with constant targets, background, and response to target mapping for 2 runs of 100 displays, and responses on each of 36 successive days of practice.

Results on the easy 4-choice CRT task illustrated in Fig. 10.8a replicate those obtained by Goward and Rabbitt in two respects: individuals with higher AH 4 test-scores respond faster than individuals with lower IQ-test scores, but High AH 4 test-scorers show slightly, but significantly (F = 5.6) less improvement with practice than low test-scorers. The correlation between AH 4 test-scores and rate and amount of improvement with practice is *negative*. An especially interesting point is that in this simple task the absolute difference in mean RTs associated with individual differences is greater than the maximum difference in mean RTs associated with practice. Results on the more difficult 'one-back' 4-choice CRT task illustrated in Fig. 10.8b present quite a different picture. High AH 4 test-scorers are, again, faster than low AH 4 test-scorers and improve less with practice. However, in this case, for both IQ-test score groups, the absolute differences between CRTs associated with differences in practice are very much larger than the maximum differences between mean CRTs associated with individual differences in AH 4 test performance. The data plotted in Fig. 10.8c showing the effects of very prolonged practice on a constant mapping visual-search task help us to interpret these differences and to develop this contrast further. The absolute size of the difference between IQ-test score groups did not vary significantly over 36 practice sessions. If we sample data from the third practice session we note that on this simple task, as on the easy four-choice CRT task, differences in mean RTs associated with individual differences in IQ-test score (118 msec.) are significantly greater than changes due to practice (at maximum 88 msec.). After 36 practice sessions differences associated with IQ-test scores still remain roughly constant (94 msec.), but the reduction in RT due to practice has increased to 332 msec. (Fig. 10.8d).

It seems that when tasks are very simple young adults and individuals with relatively high IQ-test scores may perform quite close to their eventual performance asymptote even when they first encounter the task. Older individuals and low test-scorers take longer to reach their best performance. As tasks become increasingly difficult no group can reach asymptote very early in practice, and the advantages of youth and better IQ-test performance also appear in faster learning-rates and in much greater overall improvement. In very easy tasks variance associated with individual differences exceeds variance associated with levels of practice; as tasks become more difficult the reverse is increasingly the case (Rabbitt *et al.* 1989). Data from very extended practice on constant mapping visual search adds a further caveat. In this task, if comparisons are made early in practice, individual difference effects (IQ test-score effects) appear to be much greater than practice effects. If data are sampled after very substantial practice the reverse is the case.

We have discussed the story, received from Horn and Cattell (1966) and Horn (1982, 1986), that prolonged practice results in marked domain-specific gains and in robust age-stabilization of 'higher-order'

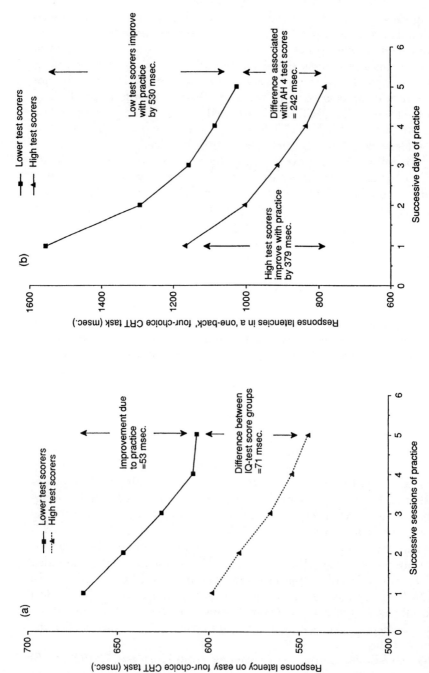

FIG. 10.8b. Effects of practice on CRTs in the 4 choice 'I-back' tasks. Groups with High and Low IQ test scores compared.

FIG. 10.8a. Effects of practice on 4 choice CRTs of groups of individuals with High and Low IQ test scores.

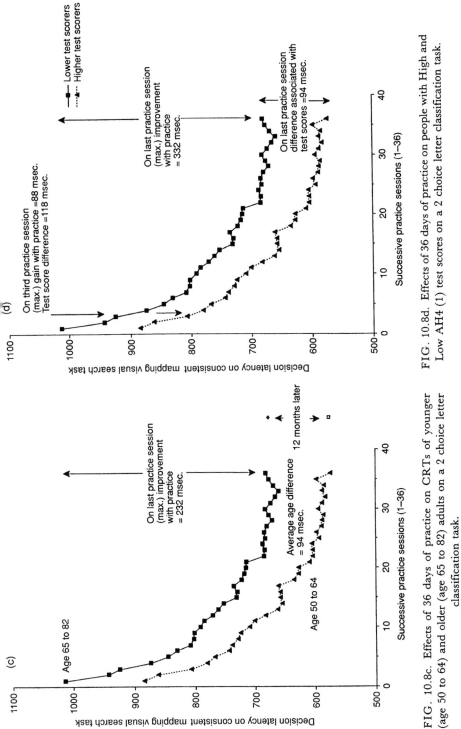

(c)

Age 65 to 82

On last practice session
(max.) improvement
with practice
= 232 msec.

Average age difference
= 94 msec.

Age 50 to 64

12 months later
♦
◀
▷
□

Decision latency on consistent mapping visual search task

Successive practice sessions (1–36)

FIG. 10.8c. Effects of 36 days of practice on CRTs of younger (age 50 to 64) and older (age 65 to 82) adults on a 2 choice letter classification task.

(d)

— Lower test scorers
·····■··· Higher test scorers

On third practice session
(max.) gain with practice =88 msec.
Test score difference =118 msec.

On last practice session
(max.) improvement
with practice
= 332 msec.

On last practice session
difference associated with
test scores =94 msec.

Decision latency on consistent mapping visual search task

Successive practice sessions (1–36)

FIG. 10.8d. Effects of 36 days of practice on people with High and Low AH4 (1) test scores on a 2 choice letter classification task.

complex information-processing tasks. In this framework of explanation, as particular cognitive skills are practised so they will be increasingly freed from association with current levels of IQ-test score, and so also, it has been inferred, they will increasingly be less strongly correlated with the individual differences in general intellectual ability (Spearman's 'g'), which are picked up by scores on pencil-and-paper IQ tests. Some authors (for example Anderson 1992; Eysenck 1986; Jensen 1982, 1985; Vernon 1985; Vernon and Jensen 1984) suggest that because performance indices derived from very simple information-processing tasks correlate modestly with psychometric measures of 'g', both these indices and the general factor 'g' must directly reflect some especially fundamental biological characteristic that sets limits to all other performance characteristics of the human information-processing system.

Most of the results obtained in our laboratory have been consistent with this tacit assumption. We found, as we would expect, that a lifetime's practice naturally results in markedly improved performance on complex tasks such as reading; but it also seemed that these advantages can be highly domain-specific. Prolonged training can apparently render particular higher-order aspects of complex tasks relatively independent of current level of IQ-test score or of current age. In contrast, we have not been able to show that practice on a complex task produces domain-specific benefits on some of its simple information-processing component operations, nor that practice weakens the relationship of performance on simple laboratory information-processing tasks with psychometric measures of 'g' and so, also, with current age. Up to this point our conclusions congenially fit the received description. However the data shown in Figs. 10.7 and 10.8 suggest that this apparent agreement may be very misleading.

Figures 10.7 and 10.8 force us to recognize that the relative effects of practice and of individual differences depend on the levels of difficulty of the tasks we compare and, more than this, on the precise point of practice at which we compare our subjects. In Rabbitt and Goward's (in press, *a*) very easy 4-choice CRT task individual differences in age or IQ-test score had much larger effects than did 10 blocks of practice. Moreover, older individuals and those with lower IQ-test scores improved significantly *more* than the young or those with higher IQ-test scores. The combination of these two trends makes it inevitable that, when we analyse data from such easy tasks, individual differences associated with practice will be overshadowed by the much larger effects of individual differences in age and IQ-test scores. The individual difference effects and associated differences in CRTs, moreover, run precisely counter to the effects of practice. In any principal-component analysis across tasks, age-groups, and psychometric measures, such as those reported by Horn (1982, 1986) it must inevitably be the case that scores on simple tasks which show small practice effects and large individual difference effects fall into common factors with individual difference measures such as chronological age or scores on tests of 'fluid intelligence'. They will thus be identified as age-sensitive indices of current levels of 'fluid intelligence'.

These relationships are entirely reversed in the study of Rabbitt *et al.* (1989) of prolonged practice on a difficult video game and in that of Stollery *et al.* of practice on a 'one-back' 4-choice CRT task (Fig. 10.8b). Here we see that the absolute magnitudes of practice effects can be very much greater than those of individual differences in age or in IQ-test scores. Performance on tasks like these, which is certainly much more strongly affected by a lifetime's practice than by individual differences in age or intelligence, will fall into correspondingly distinct factors in a Horn-type analysis, and so will be identified as indices of 'crystallized intelligence' which are relatively indifferent to current levels of age and of fluid IQ-test attainment.

The data of Stollery *et al.* on extended practice at visual search make the further point that either practice effects or individual difference effects may appear dominant, depending on some combination of the intrinsic difficulty of the task which we examine and the precise level of practice at which we compare our age or IQ-test score groups. This means that a performance index which appears to be a sensitive index of current 'fluid intelligence' if it is measured early in practice may appear to be an equally sensitive index of 'crystallized intelligence' if it is measured late in practice.

In this context it is misleading to suppose that practice makes the 'higher-level' processes in complex tasks less vulnerable to the effects of ageing and less sensitive to the effects of individual differences in IQ, but that it does not have either of these effects on the simple component information-processing operations that complex tasks entail. It is rather the case that for very simple tasks, similar to those considered in Stuart-Hamilton, Rabbitt, and Papadeleloui's analysis as 'lower-level' components of reading skills, the effects of individual differences in age and in IQ-test scores seem to be, in absolute terms, much greater than the effects of practice. Further, in these simple 'component' tasks, the correlation between improvement in performance with practice and individual differences in age and IQ-test performance *are often negative*. Practice reduces the already small differences between younger and older or higher and lower test-score groups by improving the performance of the less able while leaving the performance of the more able relatively unchanged. In contrast, as putatively 'elementary component skills' have to be jointly deployed in increasingly complex patterns in order to meet increasingly complex task demands, such as in the complicated video-game of Rabbitt *et al.* (1989), so current levels of performance depend much more strongly on levels of practice than on individual differences in age or in IQ.

The next step in this argument is to consider whether prolonged disuse, resulting in forgetting, may have relatively different effects on simple 'component' tasks and on more complex skills. Let us suppose that in both cases disuse causes performance to regress by a constant amount, or by a constant proportion (for example 50 per cent). For simple 'component' tasks, because practice has hardly produced any improvement in performance, it must be the case that, even after prolonged disuse, individual differences associated with age or IQ must still remain larger than individual differences associated with previous experience. For very complex tasks the enormous differences due to previously attained levels of practice will, after the same period of disuse, still remain much larger than 'baseline' individual differences associated with age or IQ-test performance. Within such a pattern of results it is no longer necessary to invoke the idea that prolonged practice 'protects' complex tasks, but not simple tasks, against the ravages of age or of forgetting. It also becomes irrational to argue that because indices of information-processing rate derived from simple tasks show very modest positive correlations with current IQ-test attainment and even more modest negative correlations with chronological age they must be uniquely direct reflections of some 'master' performance parameter which sets limits to the efficiency of the entire human cognitive system. Nor can we suppose that simple information-processing tasks, such as 'inspection time' or 'choice-reaction time' tasks are uniquely sensitive indices of the ravages of brain-ageing or of genetically determined 'biological bases' of individual differences in intelligence (Eysenck 1986). This last point is easily dismissed by a simple comparison. Individual differences in performance on apparently 'simple' and 'basic' laboratory performance indices such as choice-reaction time (Jensen 1982; Eysenck 1986; Vernon 1985; Vernon and Jensen 1984) or inspection time (Nettelbeck and Lally 1981) can hardly be regarded as exceptionally sensitive indices of individual differences in intelligence. On the contrary, they correlate negatively with IQ-test scores at very modest levels indeed; i.e. 0.2 to 0.5, as compared with correlations between quite different IQ tests (typically 0.7 and above) or between attainment on a particular pencil-and-paper intelligence test (the AH 4) and practised performance on a complex video game (0.68; Rabbitt *et al.* 1989).

It may be objected that this misses the crucial point that individual differences in age or in IQ-test performance must exaggerate individual differences in performance of complex tasks, because they strongly determine both the rate at which skill is acquired and, probably also, the maximum performance asymptote which can be attained. For example, in the study of Rabbitt *et al.* (1989), IQ-test scores correlated only modestly with initial video-game performance (at about $r = 0.3$), and accounted for only about 9 per cent of the variance between individuals. However, because on this task rate of improvement with practice correlated markedly and positively with IQ-test score, individuals with higher scores progressively moved ahead of the rest, so that, late in practice, the correlation between test-score and game performance had improved to 0.68, and eventually accounted for over 42 per cent of the variance between individuals. We might infer that because age and IQ-test score strongly determine learning-rate they should always predict performance late in practice more strongly than performance early in practice. As we have seen, this is only the case with *complex* tasks. In very simple tasks individual variance in performance associated with age or IQ-test ability may always remain as large as, or larger than, individual differences due to practice. Further, in these cases the relationship between IQ-test attainment and improvement may be negative—high scorers begin nearer asymptote, and therefore improve less, than low scorers.

These considerations apart, the key point that we must recognize is that we are not discussing absolute relationships but rather the balance between two separate effects which sometimes potentiate each other and sometimes cancel each other out. This is illustrated graphically in Fig. 10.9, which contrasts two cases in which different groups of individuals with high and low IQ-test scores show different learning curves, and in which the rates at which they learn a task increase with their IQ test scores. In Fig. 10.9a high test-scorers learn faster and have a higher performance asymptote than low test-scorers; but, at any level of practice, the absolute improvement from unpractised baseline achieved by the low test-scorers is always greater than the difference between their current level of attainment and that achieved by the high test-scorers. When data from both groups are pooled for analysis duration of practice will always be a better predictor of individual performance than IQ-test score. Figure 10.9b illustrates a case in which the absolute difference in level of performance between a high test-score group and a low test-score group very rapidly exceeds the asymptote that the low test-scorers can achieve. As soon as we pass this cross-over point at which the differences in attainment between the groups exceed the maximum benefits which practice brings to the low test-score group, performance will increasingly be determined by individual differences in test-scores rather than by individual differences in practice. Indeed, in the example shown in Fig. 10.10, as we sample pooled data

CRYSTAL QUEST

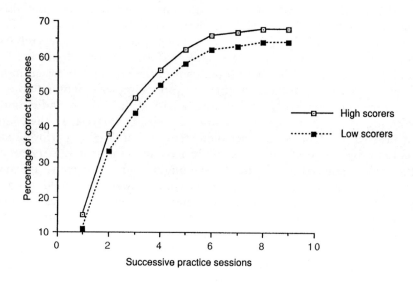

FIG. 10.9a. Hypothetical data showing a case where ceiling effects operate, and High test scorers both learn faster and have a higher performance asymptote than Low test scorers.

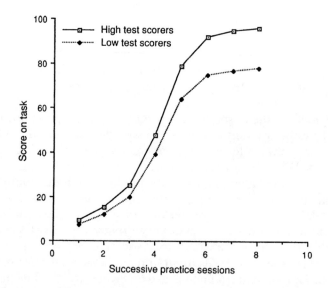

FIG. 10.9b. Hypothetical data showing a case where ceiling effects do not operate so that High Test Scorers increasingly surpass Low Test scorers as practice continues.

from both groups at increasing durations of practice *after* the cross-over point has been passed, predictions of individual performance from individual durations of practice computed from pooled data for the two groups will steadily fall, and, eventually, will become progressively *negative*. The high test-score group will perform increasingly better than the low test-scores, although all of them have had relatively less practice.

These patterns of change in relationships become intuitively obvious when we consider how practice and ability may account for differences in performance at very complicated intellectual skills such as chess, music, or mathematics. In these difficult skills people of high innate ability may continue to improve with practice, while people with lower ability reach, and may permanently stall at, much earlier and lower asymptotes. Given an appropriate scoring system for excellence at performance at these complex skills it is easy to see that highly-practised low-ability performers will perform better than high-ability novices until, after a given level of practice, the latter rapidly begin to surpass them. Until this point, when data from both groups are combined for analysis, current level of practice will be a better predictor of momentary current performance than will innate ability. However, beyond the critical point these predictions will reverse, and IQ test scores will first become as good as, and then increasingly a much more powerful predictor of current task performance than will current level of practice. Beyond this critical point, if we again examine correlations in the *combined* data from a very highly practised low-ability group and a less practised, but now superior, high-ability group, we will obtain the surprising result that level of attainment is *negatively* correlated with amount of practice. This case is illustrated in Fig. 10.10 below.

Of course, these logical quirks do not mean that there may not be qualitative differences between the skills that are preserved and those that are lost with age, nor even that we cannot detect or study any differences that may exist. However they do mean that we must be cautious in trying to investigate these differences by the correlational and factor-analytic techniques which have traditionally been used by psychometricians to distinguish between 'fluid' and 'crystallized' intelligence, and to identify the 'components' of these abilities. Such analyses have always entailed comparisons of levels of correlations between task-performance indices and, on the one hand, individual differences variables, such as age and test-score, and on the other (in effect, even if it is not directly so labelled), amount of practice experienced over a lifetime.

However, these logical quirks do mean that the presence or absence of such correlations is not good evidence that practice brings about

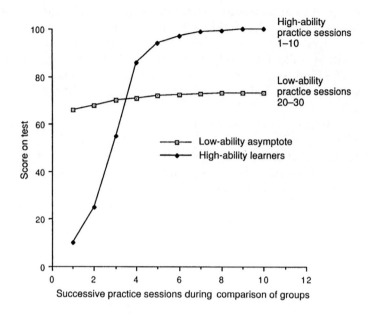

FIG. 10.10. Hypothetical data illustrating how individual differences in ability may lead to a situation where task attainment is negatively correlated with individual differences in practice.

changes in the internal representations of complex skills that make them more robust, or 'resistant', to the effects of ageing. More importantly, we see that, contrary to the practice of investigators such as Eysenck (1986), Jensen (1982, 1985), Nettelbeck and Lally (1981), and Salthouse (1982, 1985, 1991), we cannot use such correlations as evidence that very simple information-processing tasks somehow provide much more direct and revealing indices of 'fundamental' performance parameters of the human cognitive system than do much more difficult and 'cognitive' higher-order skills. Reaction times and inspection times (tachistosopic recognition thresholds) are no more 'fundamental' measures of performance than are gross scores on complex video games or on pencil-and-paper IQ tests. Performance indices from very simple tasks are interesting only in the sense that they are altered relatively slightly by practice, so that individual differences in amount of experience may do correspondingly little to mask the effects of individual differences in ability. For more complex tasks the effects of individual differences in age, or in IQ-test performance, can much more easily be masked by individual differences in lifetime practice on the task. Finally, the data from the study of Stollery *et al.* of a constant mapping visual search task (Fig. 10.8c above) show that the benefits of very extended practice may eventually exceed the initial advantages of higher IQ-test attainment. Even on very easy tasks a very highly practised person with a low IQ-test score may eventually perform better than a much less practised person with a high IQ-test score. In this sense, and in this sense only, we have evidence that even very simple 'components' of higher-order complex skills may become 'crystallized' by practice so as to appear relatively independent of current attainment on tests of 'fluid intelligence'.

IS THERE A FRAMEWORK OF DESCRIPTION WITHIN WHICH WE CAN SENSIBLY TRY TO ANSWER THE QUESTION WHETHER OR NOT SOME PARAMETERS OF PERFORMANCE ARE MORE AFFECTED BY AGE THAN OTHERS?

Rabbitt (in press) suggested a quite different framework to explain how, and how strongly, the *performance indices* derived from different laboratory tasks might be correlated with each other, and how individual differences in the levels of each of these indices, and in the patterns of correlations between them, and changes in these patterns of correlations with age might be related to the *functional properties* of units in a hypothetical information-processing network.

One obvious performance characteristic of such a hypothetical network will be the rate with which it can process information. We may suppose that the information-processing rate is ultimately limited by at least two distinct functional properties of the network. It will obviously depend on the speed with which any unit can fire, and with which it can activate any other unit. It will less obviously depend on the number of viable units in the network and on the richness of the connections between them. These latter factors will determine the extent to which the net can operate as a parallel distributed processing system, in which responses are captured by the first of several simultaneous and independent processes which terminates in response to a particular input.

A second performance characteristic, the efficiency with which the network can learn and store new discriminations between inputs, might also be expected to improve with the overall number of units and their mutual connections. This is because the more complex the system the larger the number of different encoding patterns that it can simultaneously test in parallel during learning until the optimal input–output configurations emerge. Further, the more complex the network the greater will be the number of different possible input and output conditions which it can potentially learn to classify. However, the rate at which the network can learn will be even more tightly restricted by another, quite distinct, functional property: the rate at which the activation thresholds of its units alter in response to repeated stimulation from each other.

A third performance characteristic might be the rate at which the network loses information that it has 'stored' as patterns of activation pathways between its units. This will also probably vary with the number and connectivity of its component units, because, as McClelland *et al.* (1986) and other connectionist modellers have pointed out, if we suppose that information is represented in terms of many different schemes of connections, loss of some connections will lead only to partial, but not total, loss of information: i.e. the network will have the property of 'graceful degradation'. Forgetting will also not depend entirely on survival of units and connections, because it will also be influenced by the rate at which the mutual activation thresholds between units change over time or with interference when they are not refreshed by continued use.

From this it follows that one hypothetical form of 'age degradation' of the system, programmed as deletion of units and of connections between them, may very well slow information-processing rate, reduce learning-rate, reduce the complexity of the categorizations that the network can learn, and also lead to loss of learned information (forgetting). Thus, if we can measure each of these performance characteristics independently we shall find that information-processing rate, learning-rate, complexity of categorizations, and forgetting rate all correlate positively with each other. However we may also find that these correlations are relatively weak, because, while all three performance parameters depend, to some degree, on the number and connectivity of units in the network, two performance parameters, learning-rate and forgetting-rate, will be strongly influenced by quite other properties of units than their number or connectivity: i.e. by stability or change in the mutual activation thresholds between units. This simplistic description of a hypothetical system allows us to see that the 'functional properties' of a network (such as numbers of units, richness of connectivity, unit activation thresholds, and rates of spontaneous change of unit activation thresholds over time), may be affected in quite different ways by different types of 'degradations' imposed on the network, such as deletion of units or of connections, or increases in levels of random noise. Let us, fancifully, consider that 'ageing' of the system is analogous to the operation of one or more of these different kinds of 'degradation' of its properties, and that the basic level of 'intelligence' of the system is determined by the initial levels at which we set its functional properties. These might include unit activation speed, number and connectivity of units, rates of change of unit thresholds with repeated stimulation, and rates of relapse of unit thresholds with the passage of time. The properties of the system which we can measure as its 'performance parameters' are, in general, likely to correlate modestly with each other, and to be affected jointly, *but to different degrees*, by most hypothetical kinds of global 'degradation' (or ageing) and by settings of initial levels (intelligence). However, the effects of degradation and of initial properties will be complex, and none of them is likely to be directly and faithfully mirrored by any *single* performance parameter which we can measure by getting the network to perform simple tasks. Even in this simplistic simulation the data of interest will not be the level of any single 'master' performance index which we can empirically isolate and quantify, but rather the nature, and the rate of change, in patterns of correlations between different performance indices as we compare different levels of degradation or different patterns of adjustments of initial settings of the levels of functional properties of the system.

It is important to emphasize how very different this framework of description is from the ones recently proposed by Anderson (1992), Eysenck (1986), Jensen (1982, 1985), and Nettelbeck and Lally (1981) as a context for discussions of the effects on performance of individual differences in general ability (i.e. Spearman's 'g'), and by Salthouse (1982, 1985, 1991) for discussions of changes in performance in old age. All these authors imply that individual differences or age-related changes in cognitive ability can most parsimoniously be described as secondary consequences of variation in a *single* 'master' performance parameter, information-processing rate. It is, of course, obvious that variations in information-processing rate will have entrained effects on variations in other measurable performance parameters, such as rate of learning and memory efficiency. For example, in terms of Craik and Lockhart's (1972) demonstrations that the efficiency with which items are learned depends on how deeply they have been processed on first inspection it is obvious that the faster individuals can generate associations and mnemonics to any new material that they encounter the deeper and more elaborately they will be able to process it within any fixed period of time, and the better their subsequent recall will be. Similarly, in Baddeley's (1986) model of the 'working memory system' the capacity of the 'articulatory loop' relates letter and digit spans directly to articulation-rates and to reading-rates. The momentary capacity of the loop is determined by the maximum rate at which items can be cycled around it. The capacity of the loop in turn determines the number of different items of information or alternative plans and procedures which can simultaneously be considered and compared, and so, also, the efficiency with which problems can be solved. It is therefore plausible that differences in information-processing rate can have 'knock-on' effects on all, or most, other cognitive abilities, among them the ability to solve intelligence-test problems rapidly and correctly.

The network model can accommodate the idea that changes in levels of a single simple performance parameter may have entailments for a variety of complex cognitive functions. However, it shifts our goal in the study of individual differences in age and in ability from discovery, or arbitrary selection, of a single 'master' performance parameter which entrains changes in all other cognitive skills. We move instead to *the study of changes in the mutual relationships between as many different performance indices as we can simultaneously measure.* Note that in doing this it shifts emphasis from a single index of the 'biological basis of intelligence' (Eysenck 1986) to a set of distinct performance parameters which may each vary independently between individuals, which may each degrade independently with age, and, most importantly, which may each be determined by the joint settings of a number of quite different functional properties of the system that supports them.

The key to studying these relationships is to devise experimental paradigms which allow us simultaneously to measure how two, or preferably several, performance indices co-vary in the context of the same task. Some recent studies show that this is possible, and suggest that individual differences in age and intelligence can be accompanied by marked changes in some indices but no detectable change in others.

One such paradigm was used by Rabbitt and Goward (in press *b*) and Maylor and Rabbitt (1987) to examine effects of age, intelligence, and ingestion of alcohol on information-processing speed, memory, and forgetting. The task was a computerized version of one developed by Shepherd and Teightsoonian (1961) in which 200 words appeared one after the other and subjects had to respond to each, indicating whether it was an 'old' word which had appeared before in the series or a 'new' word which had not already been seen. The sequence of words was controlled so that the probability of a word's being 'old' or 'new' was equal on every trial, and the number of items intervening between the first appearance of a 'new' word and its reappearance as an 'old' word was, equally often, and at random, 1, 4, 9, 19, and 49. This task allows four performance parameters to be simultaneously measured; information-processing rate, as the speed with which subjects make decisions; overall efficiency of recognition-memory accuracy, computed as d' or an equivalent non-parametric index; level of confidence, measured as the signal detection parameter Beta, and rate of forgetting, measured as the slope of the function for the decline in recognition accuracy with increasing interval between the first and subsequent appearance of target words.

Rabbitt and Goward tested 90 subjects, 30 in each of the three age-decades 50 to 59, 60 to 69, and 70 to 79 years. Decade samples were matched for unadjusted scores on the AH 4 IQ test. In each decade-sample ten fell into each of 2 test-score bands, 'low', from 10 to 26 points, or 'high', from 40 to 58 points.

As expected 'old/new' decision latency was directly related to chrono-logical age and inversely related to IQ-test score. Recognition-memory accuracy, as indexed by d', also fell with age and improved with test-score. Confidence levels did not differ with age or test-score. However for all age and test-score groups the probability that an old item would be correctly identified declined as a function of the number of items intervening between its first and second appearance at exactly the same rate. This illustrates that individual differences can have independent effects on different performance parameters, since age and test-ability predict decision speed and recognition-memory accuracy, but not forgetting-rate. However the demonstration is unconvincing, because when age and test-score have any effects at all these are similar in kind, and merely opposite in direction, as models for their operation offered by Eysenck (1986), Jensen (1982, 1985), and Salthouse (1982, 1985, 1991) might predict. Forgetting-rate may be a robust parameter that is not affected by any individual differences, or this paradigm may not be sufficiently sensitive to detect any individual variations in forgetting-rate that may in fact exist.

This uncertainty was resolved by a parallel study in which Maylor and Rabbitt (1987) used precisely the same task to examine differences between performance of young adults when they had, and when they had not, ingested alcohol. Alcohol slowed decision speed and reduced overall d', but also accelerated forgetting. It seems that these perform-ance parameters can indeed be functionally separate, since some treat-ments affect all of them, while others affect only two. In this sense it is reasonable to speculate that some performance parameters, such as rate of forgetting, may in Horn's (1982, 1986) terminology be robust or 'crystallized', while others may be labile or 'fluid' with respect to dif-ferent treatments or conditions. It becomes a dangerous assumption that any performance parameters may be 'crystallized' in the sense of becoming robustly indifferent to all task manipulations, individual differences, or drugs. The concept of 'crystallization', as it were, shatters, and we see that different performance parameters, and so inferentially the patterns of functional properties of the system that support them, may have characteristic signatures in terms of the patterns of vulnerability they expose to different task demands, individual differences, and neurophysiological insults.

These conclusions are reinforced by a study described by Goward (1986) which tested the stringent implications of Baddeley's (1986) model for the articulatory loop system in working memory. A very large number of studies have shown that in children and young adults immediate memory span for letters, digits, or words is linearly related to the speed with which individuals can process information (i.e. reading-rate or maximum articulation-rate). In Baddeley's model this constancy depends on two parameters: the first is the rate at which representations of input can be circulated around an 'articulatory loop'. This is because unless they are continually circulated and 're-freshed' representations will decay and become unavailable. Thus the faster items can be circulated, the more items can be held within a loop, and the greater will be immediate memory span. This model implies that, apart from information-processing speed, a second performance parameter of the loop must also limit immediate memory span. This is the rate at which items decay unless they are refreshed by being circulated. Goward showed that individual differences in span associated with differences in age or in IQ-test score were, indeed, directly related to individual differences in information-processing rate, but, in contrast, found no evidence for individual differences in decay rates. Once again one performance parameter altered with age and with IQ-test performance while another did not. The implications of changes in one parameter cannot be properly interpreted unless the presence or absence of correlated changes in others is simultaneously investigated.

CONCLUSIONS

This paper has discussed some alternative frameworks in which we may interpret the general finding that, as people grow old, they may retain high levels of performance in some highly-practised cognitive skills, such as the use of vocabulary, while simultaneously showing marked decrements in others, such as the rapid and accurate solution of novel IQ-test problems on which (if we take the meaning of 'novel' as rigorously as is necessary in the design and validation of IQ tests) they have had little or no practice.

A dichotomy between 'crystallized' bodies of acquired information and procedures and the more 'fluid' performance characteristics which are necessary to access or to use them seems to be unhelpful. The distinction between two hypothetical mechanisms or modules, one age-robust and the other age-vulnerable, seems needless because the availability and accessibility of stored information can more parsimoniously be modelled as two quite different, though possibly weakly correlated, performance characteristics of the same hypothetical network.

Also unhelpful is the assumption that once information in memory has remained available for a long period of time it enters some qualitatively different mode of functional representation ('permastorage'). The relative robustness of information in memory seems as much related to the availability of appropriate schemata as to the period for which it has been held in store.

Equally unnecessary seems a different distinction that is drawn between 'lower-level skills' which are more affected by age and the supposedly less affected 'higher-level skills' of which they may be 'components'. This rests on particular assumptions about the patterning of an unexplored set of relationships: between the relative magnitudes of differences in ability which directly reflect individual differences in levels of practice and those which relate to other sources of variation between individuals, such as age or performance on IQ-tests; and also between the relative extents to which these two different sources of variance in task-performance between individuals survive the passage of time and disuse.

A more fruitful framework seems to be one which (at last!) admits that an information-processing network must have several distinct and different parameters of performance, such as information-processing rate, learning-rate, and rate of forgetting, and that each of these performance parameters may depend on different subsets of elementary functional properties of the units of the network and of their patterns of connections with each other. At any moment in the network's history these performance parameters will correlate with each other to the extent to which they depend on the same subsets of functional properties, and will be independent of each other to the extent to which they depend on distinct properties. Factors such as age or alcohol, which, as we must suppose from the evidence available to us, tend to degrade network operation, may thus affect some of its properties, and so some of its measurable performance parameters, more than others. As an example, while marked individual differences in information-processing rate and in learning-rate are correlated with individual differences in age or in IQ-test score, individual differences in rates of forgetting seem, in our data, to be at least relatively unaffected by these two particular variables, although they are affected by the ingestion of alcohol. Any additional demonstrations that forgetting-rates are relatively independent of age and IQ-test score, and so of information-processing rates, would add to accumulating evidence for a new interpretation of differences between acquired and novel skills. To the extent that age does not affect the rate at which we forget the data and procedures that we have acquired, while it does markedly effect the rates at which we process and learn new information, we have a useful basis to begin to discuss individual differences in the extent to which acquired and novel skills can resist the changes which accompany old age.

REFERENCES

Anderson, M. (1992). Intelligence and development: a cognitive theory. Blackwell, Oxford.

Baddeley, A. D. (1986). Working memory. Oxford University Press.

Bahrick, H. P. (1979). Maintenance of knowledge: questions about memory we forgot to ask. *Journal of Experimental Psychology: General*, **108**, 296–308.

Bahrick, H. P. (1983). The cognitive map of a city: fifty years of learning and memory. *Psychology of Learning and Motivation*, **17**, 125–63.

Bahrick, H. P. (1984). Semantic memory content in permastore: fifty years of memory for Spanish learned at school. *Journal of Experimental Psychology: General*, **113**, 1–29.

Bahrick, H. P. and Phelps, E. (1987). Retention of Spanish vocabulary over 8 years. *Journal of Experimental Psychology: Learning, Memory, and Cognition*, **10**, 82–93.

Bahrick, H. P., Bahrick, P. O., and Wittlinger, R. P. (1975). Fifty years of memory for names and faces: a cross-sectional approach. *Journal of Experimental Psychology: General*, **104**, 54–75.

Bryan, J. (née Core) (1986). Old age and memory for complex material. Unpublished D.Phil. thesis, University of Durham.

Cerella, J. (1985). Information processing rates in the elderly. *Psychological Bulletin*, **98**, 67–83.

Chase, W. G. and Ericssen, K. A. (1982). Skill and working memory. *The Psychology of Learning and Motivation*, **16**, 1–58.

Cohen, G. (1990). Why is it difficult to put names to faces? *British Journal of Psychology*, **81**, 287–98.

Conway, M., Cohen, G., and Stanhope, N. (1991). On the very long term retention of knowledge acquired through formal education: twelve years of Cognitive Psychology. *Journal of Experimental Psychology. (General)*, **120**, 395–409.

Craik, F. I. M. and Lockhart, R. S. (1972). Levels of processing: a framework for memory research. *Journal of Verbal Learning and Verbal Behaviour*, **11**, 671–84.

Ericssen, K. A. (1988). Memory skill. *Canadian Journal of Psychology*, **38**, 188–231.

Ericssen, K. A. and Polson, P. G. (1988). An experimental analysis of the mechanisms of a memory skill. *Journal of Experimental Psychology, Learning, Memory, and Cognition*, **14**, 305–16.

Ericssen, K. A., Chase, W. G., and Faloon, S. (1980). Acquisition of a memory skill. *Science*, **208**, 1181–2.

Eysenck, H. J. (1986). The theory of intelligence and the psychophysiology of cognition. In *Advances in the psychology of human intelligence*, Vol. 3, (ed. R. J. Sternberg), pp. 1–34. Erlbaum, Hillsdale, NJ.

Goward, L. M. (1989). An investigation of the factors contributing to scores on intelligence tests. Unpublished Ph.D. thesis, University of Manchester.

Holland, C. A. and Rabbitt, P. M. A. (1991). The course and causes of cognitive change with advancing age. *Reviews in Clinical Gerontology*, **1**, 81–96.

Horn, J. L. (1982). The theory of fluid and crystalised intelligence in relation to concepts of cognitive psychology and aging in adulthood. In *Aging and cognitive processes* (ed. F. I. M. Craik and S. Trehub), pp. 237–78. Plenum, New York.

Horn, J. L. (1986). Intellectual ability concepts. In *Advances in the Psychology of Human Intelligence* (ed. R. J. Sternberg), pp. 35–75. Erlbaum, Hillsdale, NJ.

Horn, J. L. and Cattell, R. B. (1966). Age differences in primary mental ability factors. *Journal of Gerontology*, **21**, 210–20.

Jensen, A. R. (1982). Reaction time and psychometric 'g'. In *A model for intelligence* (ed. H. J. Eysenck), pp. 93–102. Springer-Verlag, Heidelberg.

Jensen, A. R. (1985). The nature of the black–white difference on various psychometric tests: Spearman's hypothesis. *The Behavioral and Brain Sciences*, **8**, 193–219.

McClelland, J. C., Rumelhart, D. E., and the PDP Research Group (1986). *Parallel distributed processing: explorations in the microstructure of cognition*. MIT Press, Cambridge.

Maylor, E. A. and Rabbitt, P. M. A. (1987). Effect of alcohol on rate of forgetting. *Psychopharmacology*, **91**, 230–5.

Neisser, U. (1984). Interpreting Harry Bahrick's discovery: what confers immunity against forgetting? *Journal of Experimental Psychology, (General)*, **113**, 32–5.

Nettelbeck, T. and Lally, M. (1981). IQ put to test. *Nature*, **290**, 440.

Nettelbeck, T. and Rabbitt, P. M. A. (1992). Ageing, cognitive performance, and mental speed. *Intelligence*, **27**, 211–34.

Perfect, T. J. (1989). *Age, expertise, and long-term memory retrieval*. Unpublished Ph.D. thesis, University of Manchester.

Plomin, R. and McClearn, G. E. (1990). Human behavioral genetics of aging. In *Handbook of the psychology of aging* (3rd edn), (ed. J. E. Birren and K. W. Schaie), pp. 231–59. Academic Press, San Diego.

Rabbitt, P. M. A. Does it all go together when it goes? The 19th Sir Frederick Bartlett lecture to the Experimental Psychology Society. To appear in the *Quarterly Journal of Experimental Psychology*, 1992. (In press.)

Rabbitt, P. M. and Banerji, N. (1989). How does prolonged practice affect decision speed? *Journal of Experimental Psychology, (General)*, **67**, 234–42.

Rabbitt, P. M. A. and Goward, L. M. Age, IQ, retrieval speed memory and rate of forgetting. To appear in the *Quarterly Journal of Experimental Psychology*. (In press *a*.)

Rabbitt, P. M. A. and Goward, L. M. Age, IQ test score, practice, and individual differences in reaction times. To appear in the *Quarterly Journal of Experimental Psychology*. (In press *b*.)

Rabbitt, P. M., Banerji, N., and Szemanski, A. (1989). *Space Fortress* as an IQ test? Predictors of learned and practised performance in a complex, interactive videogame. *Acta Psychologica*, **71**, 243–57.

Salthouse, T. A. (1982). *Adult cognition: an experimental theory of cognitive aging*. Springer-Verlag, New York.

Salthouse, T. A. (1985). *A theory of cognitive aging*. Amsterdam, N. Holland.

Salthouse, T. A. (1988). Effects of age on verbal abilities: an examination of the psychometric literature. In *Language and memory in old age* (ed. L. L. Light and D. M. Burke), pp. 17–35. Cambridge University Press, New York.

Salthouse, T. A. (1991). *Theoretical perspectives on cognitive aging*. Erlbaum, Hillsdale, NJ.

Shepherd, R. N. and Teghtsoonian, M. (1961). Retention of information under conditions approximating to a steady state. *Journal of Experimental Psychology*, **62**, 302-9.

Siegler, I. C. and Costa, P. T., jun. (1985). Health behaviour relationships. In *Handbook of the psychology of aging* (ed. J. E. Birren and K. W. Schaie), pp. 599-612. American Psychological Assoc., Washingdon DC.

Spearman, C. (1927). *The abilities of Man*. Macmillan, London.

Vernon, P. A. (1985). Individual differences in general cognitive ability. In *The neuropsychology of individual differences: a developmental perspective* (ed. L. C. Hartledge and C. F. Telzrow), pp. 125-50. Plenum, New York.

Vernon, P. A. and Jensen, A. R. (1984). Individual and group differences in intelligence and speed of information processing. *Personality and Individual Differences*, **5**, 411-23.

III. Conscious awareness

Introduction

Lawrence Weiskrantz

There has been a remarkable coalescence between ideas emerging from human experimental psychology and from neuropsychology, well represented in these chapters, and which also reflects Donald Broadbent's breadth of concerns. There was a time, at the early stages of his career, when the two fields were quite disparate, and indeed experimenters of normal function were almost patronizingly dismissive of studies of brain-damaged patients. Such findings, the normative theorists maintained, could only tell one of the peculiarities that might emerge from the perturbation of any complex system, like the squeaks from a damaged radio receiver.

It is ironical, in a way, that the coalescence has focused so sharply on the question of conscious awareness, especially when Donald himself has urged caution in tackling such difficult and ambiguous topics. But characteristically, he has fostered studies that admit of experimental analysis, and also invented a computer-based task as an appropriate ball-park for one set of such studies. Diane Berry's contribution is a convenient and valuable summary of her collaborative work with Donald and other colleagues in this domain. It contains a summary of the conditions under which they find a dissociation between subjects' ability to control the simulated task and the sometimes surprisingly small extent of their own knowledge of this ability. She also relates their findings to the larger literature and controversies in 'implicit learning', especially in the field of learning of artificial grammars, and helpfully provides a working specification of the features that characterize implicit learning.

Jacoby provides a paper that clearly bridges normal experimental psychology and neuropsychology, and offers an original general strategy that has application to both fields. Given that individual tasks are never process-pure, and given the uncertainty of interpretation and logical inconclusiveness of dissociations between tasks, he advocates a 'process-dissociation procedure', in which conscious and intentional modes are placed in opposition to automatic modes of control, allowing for a quantitative estimate of both modes. This general approach is applied to a broad range of examples in the fields of memory and attention, and also reflects original situations in which such an opposition can be contrived. It is a powerful and broad approach that offers an original strategy that contrasts with many of the contemporary approaches, and one that boldly addresses issues of conscious vs. automatic control in a manner that admits of quantification but also is congenial to folk-psychology intuitions.

Tulving grasps the nettle of the need to study questions of consciousness with his customary vigour and originality. His domain is the field of memory, but his discussion and suggestions range widely and provocatively. He outlines a classification of five different memory systems, and relates them to implicit vs. explicit retrieval, drawing on material from both neuropsychology and the study of the normal human memory (including subjects under anaesthesia) with adults as well as children. He advances a hierarchical schema, integrated in terms of 'the coordination hypothesis'—that information cannot be retrieved from a system into which it was not originally encoded, and that information encoded at a given level can be later retrieved or used at the same level and at lower levels, but not at higher levels. It is a bold and integrative thesis. It is a pity that Tulving, alone amongst the contributors, was forced to be absent from the actual *Festschrift* meeting (although a draft of his paper was available on the day), because his presence would have evoked much lively discussion. But the responses to his published contributions will certainly make up for that.

Finally, Weiskrantz reviews some recent evidence that is wholly in the neuropsychological domain, 'blindsight'. Among all the so-called examples of 'implicit processing' and of 'covert knowledge' it is probably the most counter-intuitive, and hence the most likely to elicit controversy (although implicit processing in amnesia was also not without its sceptical commentators in the early days of that story). He reviews some conflicts in the literature, and their resolution through empirical study of some of the critical psychophysical parameters. This is an the area of 'unconscious processing' that has aroused the greatest interest among philosophers, and hence provides a bridge between the experimental studies and some of the traditional problems in the philosophy of mind.

Experimental psychology as a discipline proceeds in a cumulative and progressive manner, absorbing new evidence and gradually embracing new theoretical frameworks. But it is doubtful if this set of papers could even have been anticipated at the beginning of Donald Broadbent's career. The gradual accretion has opened up new, challenging, and deep areas of research, emerging from the broad and tolerant background combined with experimental rigour that so characterizes Broadbent's own approach.

ELEVEN

Search for the unseen

Lawrence Weiskrantz

One of the very many areas in which Donald Broadbent has researched is implicit processing of learning in cognitive tasks. This has been done, as with all his research, on normal human subjects. My own research has approached the subject from the direction of neuropsychology and neurobiology, both human and animal. It might seem, therefore, that we are really in different camps, and in some places this would be a reasonable assumption. But Donald has a breadth of view that is remarkable and his attitude is one that encourages convergence from different approaches. As long ago as 1972 he co-edited *Biology of memory* with Karl Pribram, and in 1982 Donald and I co-organized and published a Royal Society symposium on *The neuropsychology of cognitive function*.

There are some areas of implicit processing in which relatively neutral terms can be substituted or used—'procedural', 'automatic', 'covert'. But there is one field of neuropsychological research, 'blindsight', in which it is very difficult to avoid using terms such as 'nonconscious', 'unconscious', or 'lack of awareness'. Blindsight refers to the ability of subjects with 'blind' field defects, caused by visual cortex damage, to discriminate visual stimuli in their impaired fields with forced-choice guessing or by implicit method, even though they do not 'see' the stimuli. Whatever 'neutral' terms one would prefer, it was undoubtedly the fact that patients claimed to be *unaware* of the stimuli they could nevertheless be shown to discriminate in their 'blind' fields that caught the attention and surprise of investigators as well as philosophers and, indeed, even the general public. Calling it either 'implicit' or 'covert' processing does not remove either the excitement or the mystery of the discovery, even if there are those who would wish to inhibit the use of folk-psychological terms. This aspect of the problem has also tended to raise metaphysical hackles, or alternatively, either delight or scepticism in some quarters, even in extreme instances to the extent of declaring it not to be a proper subject for scientific study.

By now there is sufficient evidence from a number of investigators using a variety of methods to remove any doubt that 'blindsight' is a robust phenomenon in some subjects; but it is not clear whether it is universal in *all* subjects with visual cortex destruction. With modern advances in imaging, indeed, it will no doubt become clear whether certain anatomical structures or parts of the visual system are critical. The situation is bound to be confounded by the age at which the lesion was sustained, its aetiology, and above all by the type of visual function being assessed. *Prima facie*, those tasks that tap non-cortical function, acting for example via the midbrain targets of the retina, would seem to be more likely candidates for universal residual function following visual cortex damage than cortical targets for specialized functions such as colour. Be that as it may, all these sources of variance are amenable to empirical enquiry, and indeed such enquiry will also lead directly to theoretical understanding. In that sense, one embraces any existing variance that can be potentially comprehended.

There are other sources of variance, however, that are *prima facie* incomprehensible (quite aside from those that arise from perverse misinterpretation of control procedures—an attribution which the aficionados of blindsight will understand!). One such arises when directly contradictory results are obtained on the *same* subject. This happened in the case of subject G.Y., on whom positive evidence for residual function had been found by a number of workers, including myself (Barbur *et al.* 1980, 1988; Blyth *et al.* 1986; Marcel, personal communication; cf. Weiskrantz 1990). There was a large body of formal psychophysical evidence on G.Y.'s ability to detect, locate, and discriminate the direction of moving and flickering stimuli, among other discriminations. Indeed, Barbur and I had made an informal video film showing G.Y. tracing the paths of moving targets in his 'blind' field by following them with arm movements, and this film had been viewed at a number of conferences and lectures.

But it happened that G.Y. was included in a study in 1989 by two Cambridge physiologists that surprisingly yielded strongly negative conclusions, cast in uncompromising terms: 'Using experimental conditions which would be expected to reveal even the most restricted and rudimentary spatiotemporal visual capacity, we can report no evidence for residual visual function in any region of the perimetrically-blind hemifield of any of our hemianopic patients.' Moreover, they wrote that they 'deliberately set out to optimize stimulus parameters for testing in the blind fields of our subjects. Despite careful attention to spatial frequency [*sic*], temporal frequency, contrast and visual field test locus using well localized stimuli we could find no evidence of any residual function in the perimetrically-blind hemifield of any of our 3 subjects' (Hess and Pointer 1989). The paradox was so puzzling that John Barbur and I decided to retest G.Y. over an intensive two-year period. In the course of those studies we have, in fact, become quite grateful to that uncompromisingly negative outcome of the Cambridge study, because it led us into a domain of stimulus control that not only

enabled us, we think, to resolve the paradox, but also to make some
new discoveries. And so this essay is an expression of a useful advance
from a situation that seemed to be both incomprehensible and even
damaging.

The Cambridge study introduced the use of stimuli that were
bounded by Gaussian temporal and spatial functions, in which both
the onset/offset functions and the spatial borders were gradual in a
precisely specified way. In fact, they used both temporal and spatial
envelopes for studying the intact hemifields of their subjects, but their
negative results with temporal Gaussian envelopes apparently led them
to abandon any effort to study spatially *structured* stimuli in the blind
hemifields, i.e., spatial frequency was not one of their variables. Their
results in the intact fields were nicely systematic and sensitive, and the
identical Gaussian parameters that were so well adjusted to the intact
field were also used without amendment in the blind hemifields. They
used a stimulus that was bounded by a spatial Gaussian with a standard
deviation of 2°. The entire extent of the spatial unstructured 'blob' was
theoretically about 8°, but of course only a smaller fraction of the
stimulus was actually visible. The temporal Gaussian envelope had a
standard deviation of 250 msec., which again theoretically yielded a
stimulus of 1 sec. in duration, but in practical terms somewhat less.

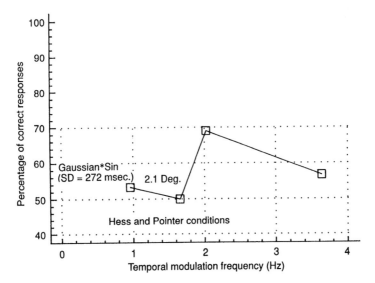

FIG. 11.1. Replication of results with subject G.Y. using size and temporal Gaussian
parameters similar to those of Hess and Pointer (1989). Chance with the two-alternative
forced procedure is 50 per cent. The subject performed at or close to chance levels, as in
the original study.

The stimuli were also sinusoidally modulated temporally at various rates. The appearance of such a stimulus in normal vision is of a relatively small unstructured 'blob', fading gradually to nothingness at its borders, with each presentation starting and ending gradually.

When we tested G.Y. with the same parameters as in the Cambridge study, requiring him to guess in a two-alternative forced-choice paradigm which of two intervals contained the 'blob', we too obtained negative results (Fig. 11.1). But we set out to *vary* the standard deviation of the Gaussian temporal onset and offset functions across a broad range (see Figs 11.2 and 11.3), and, as that also changes the total

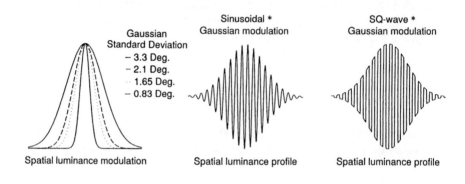

FIG. 11.2. Schematic profiles of stimulus spatial distributions. All spatial displays were Gaussian-weighted, but the standard deviation, and thus the size, could be varied, as shown in the left-hand figure. The stimuli could be either unstructured 'blobs' or square-wave or sine-wave gratings (from Weiskrantz *et al.* 1991).

duration of the stimulus presentation, we arranged conditions such that we could also vary the duration of the stimulus at its maximum contrast level. The results were very clear: merely by making the onset/offset envelope a bit more rapid, by a difference in the standard deviation of as small as 50 msec., G.Y.'s performance was excellent, virtually perfect. Conversely, a temporal SD as great as 250 or more yielded chance discrimination. Total stimulus duration itself was irrelevant (Figs. 11.4 and 11.5).

As it is also clear from the 'blindsight' literature that stimulus size is an important variable, we also examined this and confirmed that G.Y. was also sensitive to this factor: with a size that would be well within the limits of normal vision, he was at chance, but rose to very high success rates as size was increased (Fig. 11.6). These findings have recently been published (Weiskrantz *et al.* 1991).

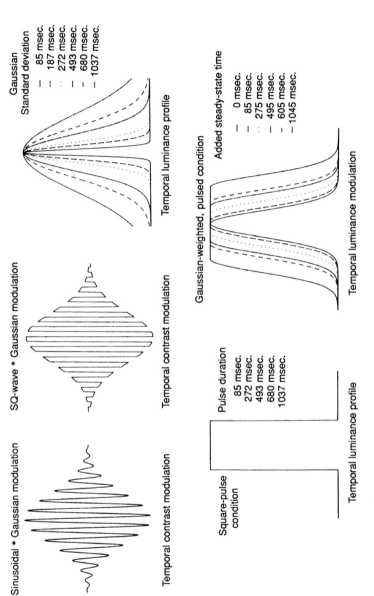

FIG. 11.3. Schematic profiles of the temporal distributions of stimuli. They could be Gaussian-weighted (top row), or pulsed for variable durations (bottom left). The duration of a temporally Gaussian-weighted stimulus could be 'stretched' (bottom right) (from Weiskrantz et al. 1991).

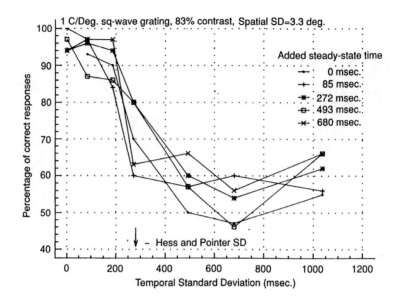

FIG. 11.4. The effect of magnitude of the standard deviation of the temporal Gaussian on performance with a square-wave grating. The duration of the stimulus presentation could be 'stretched' by varying amounts (from Weiskrantz *et al.* 1991). G.Y.'s performance was excellent with temporal standard deviations of 200 msec. or less.

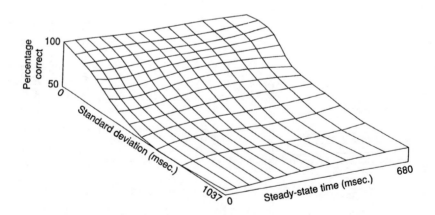

FIG. 11.5. Three-dimensional plot of performance as a function of temporal standard deviation and total added duration with a square-wave grating. It can be seen here and in Fig. 12.4 that temporal duration was of critical importance, and that total added duration was of minimal importance (from Weiskrantz *et al.* 1991).

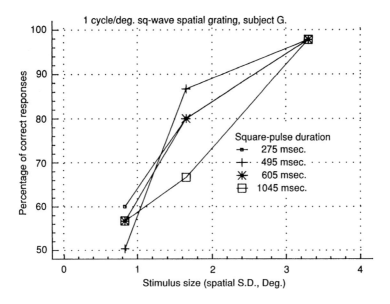

FIG. 11.6. The effect of stimulus size of a square-wave grating presented temporally as a square-wave pulse of varying durations (from Weiskrantz *et al*. 1991).

Having identified the temporal Gaussian and stimulus size appropriate to this particular subject, G.Y., Barbur and I were then in a position to exploit them to examine other properties of his residual capacity. In particular we were interested in knowing whether he had any capacity for spatial *structure, per se*. Previous studies had not discovered any such capacity in this subject (although positive results have been reported in others: cf. Weiskrantz 1990 for a review). In order to study this it was important to eliminate temporal transient phenomena as a critical parameter for the onset and offset of the stimuli. We chose a temporal Gaussian with a SD of 500 msec., which is well outside the limit at which it could allow detection by G.Y. based on temporal onset by itself. Spatial frequency of a sine wave grating was then varied, as well as temporal modulation rate. This revealed a sharply tuned, bandpass response, spatial channel, with a peak at just over 1 cycle/degree, provided the stimulus was temporally modulated at more than approximately 5 Hz, with a peak modulation rate of 10 Hz (Barbur *et al.*, in preparation). It is important to stress that this stimulus did not entail any change in the average level of light flux: the bright bars and the dark bars of the grating had a mean luminance equal to the background.

This was not the only capacity to be uncovered: G.Y. also responded to luminance *per se*, in the absence of spatial structure, with a similar dependence on temporal modulation rate. This, in itself, was less surprising, but it was not to be expected from any of the earlier results that G.Y. had *two* independent visual channels—or, possibly, one channel with two different capacities. It is interesting that both channels required temporal modulation to be revealed. Having eliminated the transient control at offset/onset by using a shallow Gaussian envelope, the temporal modulation reintroduced transients into the system. Direct comparison of the Gaussian SD and the sine wave slopes during temporal modulation is not really possible or strictly legitimate, but it is interesting nevertheless that a minimum temporal modulation rate of about 4 Hz is required for good performance, especially for the spatial-structure channel. This is approximately equivalent to an onset time of 125 msec., which is of the same order of magnitude for good performance using a Gaussian onset/offset envelope. (The details of the experiments on these two visual channels will appear in a paper by Barbur *et al.*, in preparation.)

The specification in precise quantitative terms not only has the advantage of allowing theoretical spatio-temporal response models to be developed, but the two putative channels for this particular subject also account for much of the assorted sets of results earlier reported for him, especially his ability to detect suddenly presented or moving stimuli, within certain limits.

They also led to a further extension: the pupillary response has been explored by Barbur and colleagues as an implicit method of studying residual function (cf. the review by Weiskrantz 1990). In normal vision it is clear that a small pupillary constriction can be observed in response to a wide range of stimuli, including gratings and coloured stimuli. Indeed, it is possible to obtain a curve that parallels the contrast-sensitivity function, and to obtain measures of visual acuity. Heretofore a pupillary response to a grating has not been found in the 'blind' hemifields of subjects with cortical damage, including G.Y. (although of course a response to luminance increase is found, although somewhat diminished, as is well known). Given that we found parameters that would yield a psychophysical capacity to detect a low spatial frequency grating, with narrow tuning, such a stimulus was therefore presented to G.Y. afresh, and his pupil responses measured. Gratifyingly, in preliminary experiments a small pupillary constriction was found to a 1.2 cycle/degree grating.

It should not be assumed that these two putative channels provide an exhaustive account of G.Y.'s residual capacities. It is already known that he can respond to the spatial locus of an effective stimulus, and more recently Stoerig and I have examined his wavelength discrimination (paper in preparation). Nor, of course, can it be assumed that the profile for G.Y. will be the same for all other 'blindsight' subjects. On the contrary, given the vagaries of lesion disposition in human clinical cases, the profiles are almost certain to be different; but the dissociations are potentially likely to provide very useful information about visual modularity in the human brain.

The general message is the gratifying nature of the outcome of our efforts to resolve a superficially incomprehensible conflict of evidence. If the Cambridge study had been expressed in less uncompromising or dogmatic terms, or appeared in a less prestigious journal, perhaps the resolution and the novel extensions would never have emerged. Paradoxically, while 'blindsight' is perhaps the most strongly counter-intuitive of all the implicit processing phenomena that have been reported, it is also perhaps the one that permits the most precise specification to be made of the stimuli that are effective.

It is also the area of implicit processing that currently probably holds the greatest promise of identifying a neurobiological basis. The anatomical and physiological properties of the visual pathways have been studied in some detail, from the types of retinal ganglion cells to the various targets in the brain, including subdivisions within particular routes, such as the lateral geniculate pathways. The physiological properties of extra-striate visual cortical areas suggest specializations for colour, orientation, movement, spatial locus, and form that could potentially be linked with particular aspects of residual functions. With advances in improving resolution of non-invasive imaging techniques, there is a promise of making such a link in individual cases, with the further promise that PET scanning and related methods could provide an identification of particular dimensions of ongoing visual activity. Some of the aspects of the current state of knowledge of the neurobiology of blindsight view have been reviewed in a recent article by Cowey and Stoerig (1990).

There have been other conflicts in the blindsight domain that have never reached the light of day (i.e., have never been published). A highly original phenomenon had been reported from a Western European laboratory regarding the effect of a stimulus in the one hemifield (whether normal or 'blind') on an adapted detection threshold in a mirror-symmetric portion of the other hemifield (Singer et al. 1977). We tried hard to replicate that finding in normal subjects, given its potential usefulness for clinical screening. We could not do so. Happily, the matter was resolved by the senior author's accepting an invitation to demonstrate the procedure of their experiment using apparatus made available to us at Moorfields Hospital in London. We together were able to follow the procedure using the precise parameters of the original study, especially the range and schedule of inter-stimulus intervals—such parameters can never be exhaustively specified in every detail in a published paper. In our original efforts to replicate we had assumed a precisely fixed inter-stimulus interval, whereas the success of the method depended upon a random schedule of intervals, and this turned out to be critical. The outcome led to a double positive outcome: we could then repeat the findings, but the size of the effect was smaller than originally published, although still robust. This, in turn, led to the realization that there was a simple error in the scaling of the calibrations of the curves in the published paper, which needed adjusting.

In passing, I cannot claim to have always had a constructive response to conflict of evidence in other areas in which I have worked, especially with evidence that is counter-intuitive, and thus inherently controversial—for example, as in the amnesia field, where the evidence for intact priming was certainly resisted when it was first reported by Warrington and me in 1968 (although it now seems to be an industry). Indeed, there has not always been an opportunity to respond in such a positive way, nor can one always rise to a tolerant response to persistently and transparently destructive misinterpretations, or worse. But it is comforting to be able to report these examples, and again express gratitude for having been tempted into finding an answer to a conflict of evidence that also allowed new ground to be ploughed. The examples I have cited also reflect an attitude that epitomizes Donald's own strong insistence on empirical resolutions rather than arguments from supposed first principles or a popular appeal to a show of hands.

Blindsight, as an example of 'implicit' processing, under a subheading of 'covert processing', arises from neuropsychological evidence in clinical cases, with a background of experimental research with animals. Donald's research has been entirely with normal human subjects. One of the truly gratifying developments over the past decade has been the interplay between the neuropsychological and the normal human experimental interests, both at the empirical and the theoretical levels. Along these lines, various links can be seen between 'covert' discriminations in neuropsychological cases and subliminal or automatic processing in normal subjects. I have argued that these two domains, blindsight and subliminal or near-supraliminal detection in normal vision, are not the same, although they might well be in other comparisons of explicit and implicit processing. Warrington and I have found double dissociations between the capacities of the intact hemifield and the 'blind' hemifield in an intensively studied subject, D.B. (cf. Weiskrantz 1986), which leads to a strong inference (but, of course, no proof) that blindsight and normal vision are qualitatively as well as quantitatively different. There will no doubt be examples of implicit processing where the two domains map more directly on to each other, as has been argued, for example, in the area of implicit processing in prosopagnosia and normal face-perception (Young 1992); but regardless of whether blindsight turns out to be one of them, as I doubt, nevertheless the methodologies used by the two fields are closely similar, and both present similar theoretical challenges, and thus each enriches the other. Whether or not the wavelengths are different, it is good to be part of the same spectrum being illuminated by Donald.

REFERENCES

Barbur, J. L., Ruddock, K. H.,, and Waterfield, V. A. (1980). Human visual responses in the absence of the geniculocalcarine projection. *Brain*, **103**, 905–28.

Barbur, J. L., Forsyth, P. M., and Findlay, J. M. (1988). Human saccadic eye movements in the absence of the geniculocalcarine projection. *Brain*, **111**, 63–82.

Blyth, I. M., Bromley, J. M., Kennard, C., and Ruddock, K. H. (1986). Visual discrimination of target displacement remains after damage to the striate cortex in humans. *Nature*, London, **320**, 619–21.

Broadbent, D. E. and Weiskrantz, L. (eds) (1982) *The neuropsychology of cogntive function*. The Royal Society, London.

Cowey, and Stoerig, (1990). The neurobiology of blindsight. *Trends in Neuroscience*, **29**, 65–80.

Hess, R. F. and Pointer, J. S. (1989). Spatial and temporal contrast sensitivity in hemianopia. A comparative study of the sighted and blind hemifields. *Brain*, **112**, 871–94.

Pribram, K. H. and Broadbent, D. E. (eds) (1970). *Biology of memory*. Academic Press, New York.

Singer, W., Zihl, J., and Poppel, E. (1977). Subcortical control of visual thresholds in humans: evidence for modality specific and retinotopically organized mechanisms of selective attention. *Experimental Brain Research*, **29**, 173–90.

Warrington, E. K. and Weiskrantz, L. (1968). New method of testing long-term retention with special reference to amnesic patients. *Nature*, London, **217**, 972–4.

Weiskrantz, L. (1986). *Blindsight. A case study and implications*. Oxford University Press.

Weiskrantz, L. (1990). Outlooks for blindsight: explicit methodologies for implicit processes (The Ferrier Lecture). *Proceedings of the Royal Society of London*, **239B**, 247–78.

Weiskrantz, L., Harlow, A., and Barbur, J. L. (1991). Factors affecting visual sensitivity in a hemianopic subject. *Brain*, **114**, 2269–82.

Young, A. W. (1992). Face recognition impairments. In *Processing the facial image* (ed. V. Bruce, A. Cowey, and D. I. Perrett), pp. 47–54. Oxford University Press.

TWELVE

Implicit learning: reflections and prospects

Dianne Berry

In recent years a considerable debate has arisen over the extent to which cognitive tasks can be learned non-consciously or implicitly. On the one side of the debate, a large number of studies have demonstrated a discrepancy between measured performance and explicit verbalizable knowledge (for example Reber 1989; Berry and Broadbent 1984, 1988). On the other side of the debate, however, a number of researchers have claimed that these discrepancies can be accounted for without resorting to the notion of implicit learning (for example Dulany *et al.* 1984; Perruchet and Pacteau 1990). Instead, they argue that the lack of explicit knowledge may be attributed to factors such as inadequate testing methods. This chapter reviews many of the studies which have contributed to the debate. In particular, it focuses on the two research paradigms that have generated the most research—artificial-grammar learning, pioneered by Arthur Reber, and the control of complex systems, pioneered by Donald Broadbent.

EARLY STUDIES

Reber's (1967) study is seen as the starting-point for current work on artificial-grammar learning. In the first part of this experiment subjects were shown a series of letter strings, which were generated by a finite-state grammar. They were not told about the existence of the grammar, and were simply told to memorize the letter strings. A control group of subjects were given random strings to learn. In the second phase of the experiment subjects were told about the existence of the grammar, and were given an unexpected classification task. They were given a new set of strings (half of which were grammatical and half ungrammatical) and had to classify them as being grammatical or not. Reber found that subjects given grammatical strings to memorize in phase one showed superior memory performance to those given random strings. More importantly, subjects given grammatical strings performed significantly above chance on the unexpected classification task, even though they were not able to explain how they made their decisions, or what the rules of the grammar might be.

As far as the control of complex systems is concerned, the earliest studies looking at the implicit–explicit distinction were carried out by Broadbent (1977) and Broadbent and Aston (1978). In the initial study people took on the role of controller of a city transport system. Their task was to control the number of passengers using the buses and the number of empty car-parking spaces, by varying the time-interval between buses and the car-parking fee. The experiment was set up so that subjects were given starting values for all four variables, and were asked to reach specified target values of bus load and number of parking spaces. Broadbent found that although people improved in their ability to make the right decisions, they did not improve in their ability to answer questions about the relationships within the system on a post-task questionnaire. There was also no correlation between ability to control the system and scores on the post-task questionnaire. He concluded that ability to control the system bore little connection to the ability to answer verbal questions about it. A similar dissociation was noted by Broadbent and Aston (1978). They found that teams of managers taking decisions on a model of the British economy improved in decision-making performance with practice. Yet individuals making up the team did not improve on multiple-choice questions about the principles governing the economic model.

IDENTIFYING A DISSOCIATION

In both areas the early studies were very important in that they aroused considerable interest and stimulated a large number of studies. The early findings were extended and refined in these follow-on studies (for example Reber 1976; Reber and Lewis 1977; Reber and Allen 1978; Berry and Broadbent 1984; Broadbent et al. 1986), and considerable evidence seemed to be emerging for a dissociation between task performance and verbalizable knowledge. In the case of artificial-grammar learning, Reber (1976), for example, compared the original neutral memorization procedure (where subjects simply memorized the letter strings and were then given the unexpected classification task), with one where subjects were told during the memory phase that the strings conformed to certain grammatical rules. They were told that it might help them to memorize the strings better if they tried to work out what the rules might be. Reber found that this explicit search instruction, as he called it, had a negative effect on performance on both the memorization phase and the subsequent classification task.

In the case of the control tasks, Berry and Broadbent (1984), for example, required subjects to control either a sugar-production factory or a computer-simulated person. (The tasks were in fact mathematically identical.) It was found that in both cases practice significantly improved ability to control the tasks, but had no significant effect on ability to answer post-task written questions. In contrast, verbal instructions about the best way to control the tasks had no significant effect on control performance, although they did make people significantly better at answering the questions. Moreover, across the set of experiments there was a significant negative correlation between task performance and question-answering. People who were better at controlling the tasks were significantly worse at answering the questions. Berry and Broadbent concluded that these tasks might, under certain conditions, be performed in some implicit manner. Broadbent *et al.* (1986) came to a similar conclusion using the city transport system. They found that subjects improved in ability to control the tasks with practice, but there was not a corresponding increase in the number of correct answers to verbal questions about the system. They also found that verbal explanation had no effect on task performance (although in this case the verbal explanation simply consisted of presenting the written questionnaire with the correct answers filled in).

CONDITIONS AND MODES OF LEARNING

It became apparent, following these studies, that, rather than simply demonstrating or denying dissociations, a more interesting approach is to look at the conditions that give rise to dissociations or the lack of them. Some progress has been made in this direction. As far as artificial-grammar learning is concerned, Reber *et al.* (1980) followed up Reber's (1976) study, which showed the negative effect of the explicit search instruction. Reber *et al.* found that the explicit search instruction interacted with what they termed 'structural salience', that is, the degree to which the critical patterns of letter-ordering were obvious to subjects. They found that when the stimuli were presented in a structured display so that the rules for letter-ordering were more obvious or salient, then the search instruction had a positive effect on grammar-learning.

A similar finding in relation to the control tasks was observed by Berry and Broadbent in 1988. In this study subjects interacted with one of two computer-simulated people. In one case the underlying relationship was relatively obvious or salient—the computer person responded a certain amount lower on a friendliness scale than the subject. (The friendliness scale consisted of 12 adjectives, ranging from Very Rude to Loving.) In the other case the relationship was less obvious (non-salient)—a slight response lag was introduced. In the case of the salient-person-task, performance improved with practice, subjects scored highly on the post-task written questionnaire, and performance was positively associated with question-answering. In the case of the non-salient task, although performance improved with practice, subjects were not able to answer the questionnaire, and performance was uncorrelated with question-answering. Like Reber, Berry and Broadbent also found that salience interacted with the provision of an explicit search instruction. Telling people to search for the underlying rule had a detrimental effect on controlling the non-salient person, but a beneficial effect on controlling the salient person.

Further evidence for a distinction between implicit and explicit learning modes was provided by Hayes and Broadbent (1988) and Berry (1991). In the latter case it was found that experience of watching another person interacting with the salient-person control task had a beneficial effect on subsequent control performance with the same task, whereas experience of watching another person interacting with the non-salient-person control task had no beneficial effect on subsequent control performance.

On the basis of the 1988 results, Berry and Broadbent postulated two different possible modes of learning in complex situations where people have to acquire knowledge about the relationships between a number of variables without necessarily knowing in advance what the key variables are. We suggested that one mode is an implicit or unselective one, in which a person observes the variables unselectively and attempts to store all the contingencies between them. The contingencies could be represented as a set of procedures or as some form of look-up table. In either case, a particular set of circumstances would give rise to a particular response. An alternative mode of learning is an explicit or selective one, in which a few key variables are selected, and only the contingencies between these key variables are stored. Provided that the correct variables are selected, this can be a fast and effective method of learning. It-is also likely to result in knowledge that can be made explicit because of the relatively small number of relationships involved. However, if the task contains many variables and the wrong variables are selected, learning with this mode will do badly compared with the implicit one.

I think that it is fair to say that we now see this characterization as being a little extreme, and believe that it is more useful to think in terms of there being a continuum of modes. It also seems unlikely that each mode operates in isolation. Rather, performance in complex learning situations is likely to involve a subtle combination of implicit and explicit processes. Similarly, knowledge gained is likely to involve both implicit and explicit aspects, rather than relying solely on one or the other. (See Jacoby *et al.*, this volume, Chapter 13 for a different approach to assessing the strength of dissociations between implicit and explicit components in tasks.)

CHALLENGES AND QUALIFICATIONS

The early studies aroused considerable interest, but also a certain amount of scepticism. The debate over whether learning should or should not be characterized as being implicit has been stronger in the area of artificial-grammar learning, but there have also been some new findings in relation to the control tasks that require certain qualifications to be made. First, some people have been concerned that the apparent lack of verbalizable knowledge might be due to the particular questions asked. Although it is difficult to argue against this, a range of question types have been used, and generally similar results have been obtained (see for example Berry 1984). Also, Stanley *et al.* (1989) asked subjects to practice at either the sugar-production or personal-interaction task and then to describe to somebody else how to control it. Although in this case people were free to choose their own words, performance was still found to improve before they could tell somebody else how to succeed. However, although there was a marked dissociation at moderate levels of practice, Stanley *et al.* did find that highly experienced subjects (570 trials) were able to give verbal statements that helped novices to perform more successfully. McGeorge and Burton (1989) also used this method of getting subjects to provide instructions for subsequent subjects. However, they used the protocols to develop computer simulations of subjects' performance. They found that after 90 trials of practice about one-third of subjects were able to report heuristics that resulted in simulated performance equivalent to observed performance.

Finally, Sanderson (1989) also reported positive associations between performance and verbalizable knowledge with high levels of practice, using Broadbent's city transport task. She also stressed the weakness of assessing verbalizable knowledge solely by means of post-task questionnaires. Instead, she advocated use of a mental-models analysis technique, in which subjects' question answers are compared with those that would be produced by a number of different mental models. She suggested that such a mental-models analysis made it clear that verbal knowledge can show a distinct change before it is reflected in raw questionnaire score. Taken together, the Stanley *et al.*, McGeorge and Burton, and Sanderson studies suggest that dissociations might not be as complete as was at first thought. It seems that people clearly develop some explicit knowledge as a result of experience.

Turning now to artificial-grammar learning, the strongest criticisms have come from Dulany and colleagues and from Perruchet and Pacteau. They both argue that there is no evidence that knowledge acquired during artificial-grammar learning is implicit in nature. Dulany *et al.* (1984) used a forced-choice technique whereby during the classification task subjects were asked to underline that part of a string that 'made it right' if it was classified as grammatical or that part that violated the rules if it was classified as ungrammatical. Dulany *et al.* argued that the features marked by the subjects were sufficient to account for the full set of decisions made; that is, knowledge of the grammar was held consciously. This has led to somewhat of a debate between Reber and colleagues and Dulany and colleagues, which will be discussed later in this chapter.

The second major line of attack has come from Perruchet and Pacteau (1990). They have argued that exposure to grammatical strings results in little more than knowledge of particular pairs of letters or bigrams that occur in the grammar. Their claim is based on two main findings. First, subjects exposed to pairs of letters rather than whole strings in phase one of the experiment performed just as well on the subsequent classification task. Secondly, in a separate experiment subjects were exposed to complete exemplars and were asked to rate isolated bigrams for their legitimacy. It was found that their ratings could predict observed classification performance without error. However, while subjects undoubtedly did acquire appreciable bigram knowledge, there are other studies which show that subjects do learn more than just bigrams (see, for example, Mathews 1990; Reber 1990).

RECENT CLARIFICATIONS

To recap, there is evidence for a dissociation between performance and verbalizable knowledge at moderate levels of practice with the control tasks, but positive associations emerging with more extensive practice. In the case of artificial-grammar learning, there is a fairly strong debate between those in favour of the existence of implicit learning and those against it. The aims of this section are, firstly, to describe some recent experiments that have carried out a more fine-grained analysis of performance on these tasks. And secondly, to suggest that much of the debate arises because of the failure of authors to define their terms and to say what they really mean by terms like 'implicit' and 'unconscious'.

As far as the control tasks are concerned, Marescaux *et al.* (1989), and Marescaux *et al.* (1990) have recently carried out a more fine-grained analysis of subjects' knowledge following experience with the sugar-production task. After practising at the task, subjects were asked a number of questions in the form of a series of problems on the computer. The questions varied along two basic dimensions. The target sugar output was either the same or different to that experienced while controlling the task, and the mini-history given to subjects at the start of each question was either taken from their own immediately preceding interaction, or was taken from a hypothetical interaction. The results showed superior questionnaire performance when subjects had to reach the same target as they had experienced while interacting with the task, and when the mini-histories were taken from their own past experience. The key factor seemed to be whether subjects were tested on specific situations which they themselves had experienced while interacting with the task. They did not seem to have learned anything that could be used in other novel situations. These findings have been replicated and extended by Dienes *et al.* (in press), and Dienes has recently shown that they can be successfully modelled using a connectionist look-up table.

Dienes (Dienes *et al.* 1991) has also carried out a fine-grained analysis of performance on artificial-grammar learning tasks. In one experiment, following the memorization and classification phases, subjects were asked to describe as fully as possible the rules or strategies that they used to classify the strings. The rules elicited were used to simulate classification performance. It was found that the simulated performance was considerably lower than the classification performance. Subjects were also given a new knowledge test in which they were asked which letters could occur after different stems varying in length from zero letters upwards. Performance on this task was significantly above chance and not significantly different from subjects' classification performance. This latter result is in line with Perruchet and Pacteau's study. It also extends their study by showing that subjects' knowledge of positional dependence of bigrams could be elicited out of context of particular exemplars.

Putting the various findings together, it seems clear that grammar-learning knowledge cannot be fully elicited by free recall, but can be elicited using various forced-choice measures. The same has been shown to some extent for the control tasks (Berry and Broadbent 1987). But the question is, should these forced-choice tests be considered as being tests of explicit or of implicit knowledge? It is interesting to note that in the neuropsychological literature (for example Schacter *et al.* 1988; Weiskrantz, this volume, Chapter 11) forced-choice tests have been used to demonstrate implicit knowledge. Patients firmly deny any explicit knowledge, even when they are given no feedback on a forced-choice outcome. They believe that they are guessing, but their performance is still above chance.

The question of the interpretation of forced-choice tests brings me to the second point mentioned above; that is, the failure of authors (including ourselves) to define what they mean by terms like 'implicit' or 'unconscious'. In terms of the artificial-grammar learning debate, both Reber and Dulany use the term conscious in different ways. Broadbent himself has made this point in a recent theoretical paper (Broadbent, in press). Reber believes that Dulany's underlining task and Perruchet's bigrams task are tests of implicit or unconscious knowledge. He suggests that subjects' underlinings could be the result of vague guesses which could be made on the basis of implicit knowledge. In contrast, Dulany and Perruchet seem to believe that data can only be called 'unconscious' if it can never reveal itself by any event that the person can report. According to them, if people can correctly underline key letters, an act of which they are conscious, then that knowledge cannot be unconscious. The trouble is that neither side gives a good account of what they mean by 'unconscious' or 'implicit', and neither present adequate criteria for deciding if a test is a test of implicit or of explicit knowledge. Dulany and Perruchet use their results as evidence that there should be no distinction between implicit and explicit. Yet this does not seem to be a particularly profitable way forward.

Berry and Dienes (1993) have recently come up with the following working characterization of implicit learning, in that we believe it to be associated with the following features:

1. Transfer specificity:
   (a) relative inaccessibility of knowledge with free recall (for example Reber 1967; Berry and Broadbent 1984; McGeorge and Burton 1990; Dienes *et al.* 1991);
   (b) limited accessibility of knowledge with forced-choice tests (for example Dulany *et al.* 1984; Berry and Broadbent 1987; Perruchet and Pacteau 1990; Dienes *et al.* 1991); and
   (c) limited transfer to related tasks (for example Berry and Broadbent 1988; Squire and Frambach 1990; Berry 1991).
2. Tends to be associated with incidental learning conditions, rather than with deliberate hypothesis-testing (for example Reber 1976; Berry and Broadbent 1988).
3. Gives rise to a phenomenal sense of intuition (for example Reber 1967; Berry and Broadbent 1984).

4. Relatively robust in the face of:
   (a) time (for example Allen and Reber 1980);
   (b) psychological disorders (for example Abrams and Reber 1989).

The point is that arguing that there are no grounds for an implicit–explicit distinction because subjects can underline key features in strings or can rate bigrams evades the question of why certain types of learning are associated with these characteristics. Why does learning in some situations give rise to procedural knowledge which is highly context-bound, whereas in other situations it tends to give rise to knowledge which can be characterized as being context-free, symbolic, and manipulable? As Berry and Broadbent suggested in 1988, and Reber in 1989, we still need to identify the key factors that give rise to the different types of learning and the different types of knowledge.

PROSPECTS

So what are the prospects for implicit learning? Should it continue to be a flourishing research area, or should it be dismissed as being of little interest? Recent progress in three fields biases me towards the former alternative. These fields are computational modelling, neuropsychology, and experimental studies.

Computational modelling

Some interesting advances have been made in this area. As far as artificial-grammar learning is concerned, Dienes (1990, 1992) attempted to model grammar-learning using a range of connectionist and exemplar models. The data used to evaluate the models was taken from Dienes et al. (1991) and Dulany et al. (1984). Dienes found that the only model to pass all the set criteria was a connectionist simultaneous delta-rule model. He argued that this class of model can be regarded as abstracting a set of representative but incomplete rules of the grammar. Cleermans and McClelland (1991) have also recently applied a connectionist model to the learning of finite-state grammars, but their model incorporates hidden units. They used the recursive network model of Elman (1990) to model sequential learning of a noisy finite-state grammar in a reaction-time paradigm. They found that with an augmented version of the model the match to subject data was good.

Other approaches to modelling artificial grammar learning include the THIYOS classifier system of Druhan and Mathews (1989) and the Competitive Chunking model of Servan-Schreiber and Anderson

(1990). On the basis of the current evidence it is not possible to choose any one of the different approaches to modelling as being clearly superior to the others. In each case there is some content available to consciousness, whether in the form of rules, chunks, or activation patterns. The implicit knowledge seems to be in the pattern of strengths determining what content is made available to consciousness.

Dienes (1990) has also applied the delta-rule auto-associator model to learning of the control tasks. He found that when the model coded context not by distinct units, but by persisting activation in the units, it could learn the Clegg person task used by Berry and Broadbent (1984) and the salient and non-salient person tasks used by Berry and Broadbent (1988). However, it could acquire appreciable predictive knowledge only for the salient-person task. A second version of the auto-associator model, which coded behaviours on both the current and previous trials with distinct units, matched less well with the empirical data. Dienes has also shown that recent results with the control tasks (Dienes *et al.*, in preparation) can be successfully modelled using a connectionist look-up table.

Neuropsychological studies

The second reason for feeling optimistic about the future of implicit learning comes from neuropsychological studies.

In recent years there have been a large number of studies of neuro-psychological patients which support the notion of a distinction between implicit and explicit processing. Studies have demonstrated that patients with various lesions and deficits frequently show implicit knowledge of stimuli that they cannot explicitly perceive, identify, or process semantically. This pattern of normal or near-normal perform-ance on implicit tests, compared with severely impaired performance on explicit tests, has been observed in patients suffering from blindsight (see also Weiskrantz, this volume, Chapter 11), alexia, prosopagnosia, neglect, amnesia, aphasia, and agnosia. In the case of amnesia, Squire and Frambach (1990) actually tested patients on the Berry and Broad-bent (1984) sugar-production task. They found that the amnesics per-formed just as well as the controls in the initial training session. However, in the second session they performed significantly worse than the controls. Squire and Frambach suggested that this is because by this stage of practice the normal control subjects were starting to build up explicit knowledge that could be used to improve performance still further. The amnesics, in contrast, were not able to do this.

Considering all the syndromes together, it seems uncertain at the present time whether the implicit–explicit dissociations in each of the syndromes can be accounted for by a single common mechanism (see, for example, Schacter *et al.* 1988). Our level of understanding is not sufficiently advanced to make such a claim. However, in the current context, evidence from neuropsychological studies does add considerable weight to the importance of implicit processing.

Experimental studies

As far as experimental research is concerned, there is evidence for implicit learning using new paradigms, as well as new findings with existing paradigms.

Implicit learning in new paradigms In terms of new paradigms, McGeorge and Burton (1990) carried out an experiment in which subjects were initially exposed to 30 four-digit numbers while performing an incidental cover task (for example mental arithmetic). Each set of digits contained a number 3, although subjects were not explicitly informed of this. In the second phase subjects were given pairs of four-digit numbers, and for each pair they were asked to choose the one seen before. In fact, neither had been seen before; but one contained a number 3. McGeorge and Burton found that subjects were more likely to recognize numbers as 'old' if they contained a 3. However, in post-task interviews subjects were not aware of the importance of number 3. We have recently replicated this effect in our laboratory, but using a far more extensive test of explicit knowledge. We still found no evidence that subjects were aware of the importance of the number 3, or of the type of rule that was being used.

New findings with existing paradigms In terms of new findings with existing paradigms, the final line of work I want to mention is some research by Cheng Chan, a graduate student of Donald Broadbent and mine. Chan (1992) has adapted the artificial-grammar learning paradigm in two interesting ways. In his first set of studies he used non-verbal symbols, rather than letters, as the elements in the grammar. Using these symbols he replicated Reber's basic finding. Chan went on to perform a number of experimental manipulations and carried out some very fine-grained analyses of the data. Contrary to the findings of Perruchet and Pacteau, he provided converging evidence for a dissociation between classification and bigrams knowledge. Firstly, he showed that on the bigrams test subjects only have good knowledge for letters that come at the beginning and end of strings. They do not know about bigrams that occur in the middle of strings. In contrast, in the classification test subjects are sensitive to violations that occur in the middle of strings. Secondly, he showed that performance on the bigrams test is affected by changes in surface information, whereas this is not the case for classification performance. Finally, by carrying out an analysis of confidence ratings, he showed that subjects are sensitive to the accuracy of their responses on the bigrams test, but that again this is not so for the classification test. Chan has put forward a Confidence Accuracy Slope (CAS) model which he says can be used as a criterion for deciding whether performance is implicit or explicit. The CAS model is a computational model which computes the slope of the regression line (the CAS value) for performance accuracy and a self-reported metamemory measure. The underlying assumption of the model is that implicit processes are dissociated from metacognition (confidence, feeling of knowing), which is known to be associated with explicit processes. According to Chan, the assumption of a dissociation between implicit processes and metamemory is borne out by a number of his experiments using various implicit and explicit tasks. Implicit processes usually produce a CAS value of zero, while explicit processes usually produce a CAS value of greater than zero.

Following on from another of Perruchet and Pacteau's results, Chan compared a bigrams-trained group with an exemplar-trained group. He found that although the bigrams-trained subjects performed significantly above chance on the subsequent classification task, they performed significantly less well than the exemplar-trained subjects. He also found that Confidence Accuracy Slope values were different for the two groups, that is, performance levels could be predicted on the basis of confidence ratings for the bigrams group, but not for the exemplar-trained group.

In a second adaptation of the Reber paradigm, Chan (1992) has looked at the effect of using semantically meaningful stimuli as the elements in the grammar, rather than meaningless shapes or letters. To do this he has simulated a simplified database system. Subjects therefore had to deal with meaningful computer-file operations, such as 'create', 'open', 'append', and 'edit'. Again the results are promising. Chan has been able to replicate many of the basic effects found with letter strings using these meaningful operations as the grammatical elements. He found that after exposure to a number of permissible operational sequences, people were able to discriminate permissible sequences from non-permissible ones. In addition, they were also able to generate novel sequences. In fact, he found that subjects had a fair degree of knowledge about bigrams, trigrams, and higher-order chunks of associative knowledge. Interestingly, however, this sequence-generation test was associated with a CAS value of zero. Following on from these experiments, Chan has also suggested a way in which research on artificial-grammar learning could be applied to computer-system design.

So, putting all this together, I think that the prospects for research on implicit learning are good. Not only are new experimental paradigms being developed and existing ones being extended and refined, but converging work is taking place within the areas of computational modelling and neuropsychology.

CONCLUSION

The aim of this chapter has not been to provide an exhaustive review of research on implicit learning. Rather, the intention has been to use selected studies to illustrate the development of work in this area and to highlight the contribution of Donald Broadbent. On the basis of the studies reviewed here, I think that implicit learning will continue to be a flourishing research area for some time to come. I think that the contribution that Donald Broadbent has made is quite obvious, through his own work and now through the work of others he has supervised, such as Dienes and Chan.

ACKNOWLEDGEMENTS

I am grateful to Zoltan Dienes, Cheng Chan, and Tony Gillie for their helpful comments on an earlier draft of this chapter. I am especially grateful to Donald Broadbent for his long-standing contribution to my thinking in this area.

REFERENCES

Abrams, M. and Reber, A. S. (1989). Implicit learning in special populations. *Journal of Psycholinguistic Research*, **17**, 425–39.

Allen, R. and Reber, A. S. (1980). Very long term memory for tacit knowledge. *Cognition*, **8**, 175–85.

Berry, D. C. (1984). Implicit and explicit knowledge in the control of complex systems. Unpublished D.Phil. thesis, University of Oxford.

Berry, D. C. (1991). The role of action in implicit learning. *Quarterly Journal of Experimental Psychology*, **43**, 881–906.

Berry, D. C. and Broadbent, D. E. (1984). On the relationship between task performance and associated verbalisable knowledge. *Quarterly Journal of Experimental Psychology*, **36**, 209–31.

Berry, D. C. and Broadbent, D. E. (1987). The combination of explicit and implicit learning processes. *Psychological Research*, **49**, 7–15.

Berry, D. C. and Broadbent, D. E. (1988). Interactive tasks and the implicit–explicit distinction. *British Journal of Psychology*, **79**, 251–72.

Berry, D. C. and Dienes, Z. (1991). The relationship between implicit memory and implicit learning. *British Journal of Psychology*, **82**, 359–73.

Berry, D. C. and Dienes, Z. (1993). *Implicit learning: theoretical and empirical issues.* Erlbaum, London.

Broadbent, D. E. (1977). Levels, hierarchies and the locus of control. *Quarterly Journal of Experimental Psychology*, **29**, 181–201.

Broadbent, D. E. (1991). Recall, recognition and implicit knowledge. In *Essays in honor of George Mandler* (ed. W. Kessen, A. Ortony, and F. I. M. Craik), pp. 125–34. Erlbaum, Hillsdale, NJ.

Broadbent, D. E. and Aston, B. (1978). Human control of a simulated economic system. *Ergonomics*, **21**, 1035–43.

Broadbent, D. E., Fitzgerald, P., and Broadbent, M. H. P. (1986). Implicit and explicit knowledge in the control of complex systems. *British Journal of Psychology*, **77**, 33–50.

Chan, C. (1992). Implicit cognitive processes: theoretical issues and applications in computer system design. Unpublished D.Phil. thesis, University of Oxford.

Cleermans, A. and McClelland, J. (1991). Learning the structure of event sequences. *Journal of Experimental Psychology: General*, **120**, 235–53.

Dienes, Z. (1990). Implicit concept formation. Unpublished D.Phil. thesis, University of Oxford.

Dienes, Z. (1992). Connectionist and memory array models of artificial grammar learning. *Cognitive Science*, **16**, 41–79.

Dienes, Z., Broadbent, D. E., and Berry, D. C. (1991). Implicit and explicit knowledge bases in artificial grammar learning. *Journal of Experimental Psychology: Learning, Memory and Cognition*, **17**, 875–87.

Dienes, Z., Fahey, R., and Berry, D. C. (in press). The role of specific instances in controlling a dynamic system. *Journal of Experimental Psychology: Learning, Memory and Cognition*.

Druhan, B. and Mathews, R. (1989). THIYOS: a classifier system model of implicit knowledge of artificial grammars. *Proceedings of the 11th Annual Conference of the Cognitive Science Society*, pp. 66–73. Erlbaum, Hillsdale, NJ.

Dulany, D. E., Carlson, R., and Dewey, G. (1984). A case of syntactical learning and judgement: how concrete and how abstract? *Journal of Experimental Psychology: General*, **113**, 541–55.

Elman, J. (1990). Finding structure in time. *Cognitive Science*, **14**, 179–211.

Hayes, N. and Broadbent, D. E. (1988). Two modes of learning for interactive tasks. *Cognition*, **28**, 249–76.

McGeorge, P. and Burton, M. (1989). The effects of concurrent verbalisation on performance in a dynamic systems task. *British Journal of Psychology*, **80**, 455–65.

McGeorge, P. and Burton, M. (1990). Semantic processing in an incidental learning task. *Quarterly Journal of Experimental Psychology*, **42**, 597–610.

Marescaux, P., Luc, F., and Karnas, G. (1989). Modes d'apprentissage sélectif et nonsélectif et connaissances acquises au control d'un processus. *Cahiers de Psychologie Cognitive*, **9**, 239–64.

Marescaux, P., DeJean, K., and Karnas, G. (1990). *Acquisition of specific or general knowledge at the control of a dynamic simulated system.* Esprit BRA Action 3219, Report PR2GK.

Mathews, R. (1990). Abstractiveness of implicit grammar knowledge: comments on Perruchet and Pacteau's analysis of synthetic grammar learning. *Journal of Experimental Psychology: General*, **119**, 412–16.

Perruchet, P. and Pacteau, C. (1990). Synthetic grammar learning: implicit rule abstraction or explicit fragmentary knowledge? *Journal of Experimental Psychology: General*, **119**, 264–75.

Reber, A. S. (1967). Implicit learning of artificial grammars. *Journal of Verbal Learning and Verbal Behaviour*, **5**, 855–63.

Reber, A. S. (1976). Implicit learning of synthetic languages: the role of instructional set. *Journal of Experimental Psychology: Human Learning and Memory*, **2**, 88–94.

Reber, A. S. (1989). Implicit learning and tacit knowledge. *Journal of Experimental Psychology: General*, **118**, 219–35.

Reber, A. S. (1990). On the primacy of the implicit: a comment on Perruchet and Pacteau. *Journal of Experimental Psychology: General*, **119**, 340–2.

Reber, A. S. and Allen, R. (1978). Analogy and abstraction strategies in synthetic grammar learning: a functionalist interpretation. *Cognition*, **6**, 189–221.

Reber, A. S. and Lewis, S. (1977). Toward a theory of implicit learning: the analysis of the form and structure of a body of tacit knowledge. *Cognition*, **5**, 331–61.

Reber, A. S., Kassin, S., Lewis, S., and Cantor, G. (1980). On the relationship between implicit and explicit modes in the learning of a complex rule structure. *Journal of Experimental Psychology: Human Learning and Memory*, **6**, 492–502.

Sanderson, P. (1989). Verbalisable knowledge and skilled task performance: associations, dissociations and mental models. *Journal of Experimental Psychology: Learning, Memory and Cognition*, **15**, 729–47.

Schacter, D. L., McAndrews, P., and Moscovitch, M. (1988). Access to consciousness: dissociations between implicit and explicit knowledge in neuropsychological syndromes. In *Thought and language* (ed. L. Weiskrantz), pp. 242–78. Oxford University Press.

Servan-Schreiber, E. and Anderson, J. R. (1990). Learning artificial grammars with competitive chunking. *Journal of Experimental Psychology: Learning, Memory and Cognition*, **16**, 592–608.

Squire, L. and Frambach, M. (1990). Cognitive skill learning in amnesia. *Psychobiology*, **18**, 109–17.

Stanley, W. B., Mathews, R., Buss, R., and Kotler-Cope, S. (1989). Insight without awareness: on the interaction of verbalisation, instruction and practice on a simulated process control task. *Quarterly Journal of Experimental Psychology*, **41**, 553–77.

THIRTEEN

Redefining automaticity: unconscious influences, awareness, and control

Larry L. Jacoby, Diane Ste-Marie, and Jeffrey P. Toth

One of the most exciting developments in the last decade has been the discovery of effects on memory and perception that are not accompanied by awareness of the source of those effects. Dissociations between performance on direct and indirect tests supply striking examples of perceptual analysis in the absence of seeing, and effects of the past in the absence of remembering. In blindsight, patients make visual discriminative responses without the subjective experience of seeing (Weiskrantz 1986). In Korsakoff amnesia, patients give correct memory responses without the subjective experience of remembering (for example, Warrington and Weiskrantz 1974). Normal subjects also show dissociations between their performance on direct versus indirect tests of memory and perception (for reviews, see Richardson-Klavehn and Bjork 1988; Hintzman 1990; Bornstein and Pittman, in press). Similarly, in 'implicit learning', people exposed to complex stimulus environments can make decisions and categorizations that are well above a chance level of accuracy, even though they are unable to verbalize the basis of their performance (Broadbent 1977; Broadbent *et al.* 1986; Lewicki 1986; Reber 1989).

In this chapter, we identify unconscious influences of the sort revealed by indirect tests with automaticity. We realize that the term 'automaticity' raises a lot of issues for those studying attention. Indeed, Broadbent (1982) has questioned the utility of the concept, while others have shown that the criteria used to define automaticity are seldom simultaneously met (Bargh 1989; Neumann 1984). However, we believe that effects taken as evidence for automaticity and effects revealed by indirect tests of memory and perception are so closely related as to be best treated together (Jacoby 1991). Following Neumann (1984), we argue that, contrary to accepted definitions, automaticity is not a characteristic of processing controlled by stimuli, but rather is an emergent property of the exercise of specific skills in an environment. That is, automaticity is not driven by stimuli separately from skills that are brought into play by intentions. By treating unconscious influences within the context of intention, our research has led us to emphasize the role of selection and control processes—the same processes that

Donald Broadbent has spent much of his career investigating. A major goal of this chapter is to redefine automaticity (unconscious influences) in terms of a measure of intentional, consciously-controlled responding.

We begin by arguing that awareness is a prerequisite for conscious control, and then describe the methodological advantages of arranging a situation such that consciously-controlled processing acts in opposition to unconscious processes. We then describe a 'process-dissociation procedure' and show how it can be used to derive separate quantitative estimates of the effects of consciously-controlled and unconscious processes. It is this procedure, and the theoretical framework that underlies it, that provides a redefinition of automaticity. Next, we describe a series of experiments that used a flanker paradigm to investigate spatial selection and automatic influences of memory. Those experiments produced some surprising results. To anticipate, they support a very relativistic view of automaticity, showing that automaticity depends on a combination of task orientation and prior experience. We conclude by discussing the advantages of redefining automaticity in terms of conscious control.

THE ADVANTAGES OF OPPOSING CONSCIOUS AND UNCONSCIOUS INFLUENCES

There are two major difficulties for a research programme that assumes a distinction between conscious and unconscious processes. First is the obvious problem of establishing the existence of the two types of processes. Given that this goal can be achieved, a second and ultimately more important problem is that of identifying factors which selectively influence the two forms of processing.

Dissociations between performance on direct and indirect tests of memory have been useful for establishing the existence of unconscious influences. For example, it has been shown that earlier reading of a word can enhance later perceptual identification (Jacoby and Dallas 1981), as well as later completion of a fragment of the earlier read word (Tulving *et al.* 1982). These effects on indirect tests of memory occur even though a person shows no evidence of memory for earlier reading the word when given a direct test, such as a test of recognition memory. The direct test serves as a self-report measure of awareness, and is used to show that people were unaware of the prior presentation of studied items. Given such lack of awareness, effects on indirect tests are said to originate from unconscious influences of memory or from implicit memory.

However, performance on indirect tests can be difficult to interpret. Most indirect tests of memory and perception (for example, fragment-completion, priming in lexical decision) constitute 'facilitation paradigms' in that unconscious influences would serve to facilitate performance of those tasks, just as would aware, intentional uses of memory or perception. For fragment-completion performance, as an example, memory for earlier reading of a word might facilitate performance by means of unconscious influences, but intentional use of memory would produce the same result. Consequently, supposed demonstrations of unconscious influences may often be due to the conscious use of information that goes undetected by the experimenter (Holender 1986; Richardson-Klavehn and Bjork 1988). Indirect tests cannot legitimately be treated as selectively measuring only unconscious processes; that is, as being process- or factor-pure (Jacoby 1991; Jacoby and Kelley 1991; Reingold and Merikle 1990). Also, there is good reason to believe that self-report measures do not always provide an accurate index of conscious processing or of awareness (Kelley and Jacoby 1990; Reingold and Merikle 1990; White 1982).

Rather than relying on self-report measures and indirect tests, we have used effects on the control of behaviour to infer differences in awareness. Although we see the nature of awareness as an important issue in its own right (see, for example, Kelley and Jacoby 1990), our main interest in awareness is in the extent to which it can be translated into control over thought and behaviour (Jacoby *et al.*, in press). It is common to argue that awareness serves as a prerequisite for consciously-controlled processing of the sort that is necessary for intentional action (for example, Kuhl 1986; Shallice 1988). However, awareness also serves the equally important function of allowing one to inhibit action by opposing influences that would otherwise prevail (for example, Bowers 1975, 1984). Freudian slips serve as a colourful example. In that case, awareness of a distorted word or phrase prior to its verbalization would allow one to oppose the slip. We have used the opposition of consciously-controlled and unconscious processes as a methodological tool to identify factors which selectively influence the two forms of processing. Placing aware and unaware processes in opposition holds important methodological advantages over the use of facilitation paradigms.

Consider the effects of dividing attention. It has been argued that attention to an event is required for later intentional use of memory, but not for automatic or unconscious influences of memory (for example, Eich 1984; Grand and Segal 1966; Koriat and Feuerstein 1976; see Dixon 1981 for a review). One way to investigate that possibility would be to use a facilitation paradigm, such as fragment-completion, to assess the effects of dividing attention during study (for example, Parkin *et al.* 1990). However, if any effects of divided attention were found, we would be unable to interpret those effects; we couldn't tell if the influence of dividing attention was on automatic or intentional uses of memory, because a reduction in either of the two uses of memory would produce an effect in the same direction. In contrast, by constructing a situation such that automatic and intentional uses of memory have opposite effects, we would be in a better position to detect any differential effects of divided attention.

In a series of 'false-fame' experiments (Jacoby *et al.* 1989), conscious and unconscious influences were set in opposition so as to examine the effects of dividing attention. In the first phase of one of those experiments, people read a list of non-famous names under conditions of either full or divided attention. Attention was divided by requiring subjects to listen for runs of 3 odd numbers while reading names. In the second phase, those old names were mixed with famous and new non-famous names, and presented for fame judgements. We correctly informed subjects that all of the names they had read in the first list were non-famous, so if they recognized a name on the fame test as one from the first list, they could be certain that the name was non-famous. Thus conscious recollection of a name from the first list opposed any increase in familiarity the name would gain from being read in that list. Given this arrangement, any increase in the probability of mistakenly calling an old non-famous name famous must result from an unconscious influence of memory for its prior presentation, because conscious recollection would produce an opposite effect. Formally, old non-famous names would mistakenly be called famous only if the name was familiar (F) but subjects did not recollect (R) the name as being earlier presented: $F(1-R)$. Dividing attention was expected to reduce the probability of recollection, and thereby make it more likely that the effects of earlier reading a name on its familiarity would be revealed.

Results showed that when full attention was given to the reading of names, old non-famous names were *less* likely to mistakenly be called famous than were new non-famous names. In that case, people could recollect that old non-famous names were earlier read, and, consequently, were able to be certain that those names were non-famous. The opposite occurred when attention was divided during the reading of non-famous names. Dividing attention resulted in old non-famous names' being *more* likely to be mistakenly called famous than were new non-famous names; that is, a 'false-fame' effect. Following divided attention, people were less able to use conscious recollection to oppose the familiarity produced by the earlier reading of non-famous names.

The fame experiments demonstrate how placing conscious and unconscious processes in opposition allows effects of the two types of processes to be clearly separated. We have also used this opposition procedure to separate the contributions of recollection and familiarity to recognition-memory performance (see below). Our interest in the processes underlying recognition memory is related to our more general interest in the nature of unconscious processes. We view familiarity as an unconscious or automatic influence of memory, whereas recollection is seen as an intentional use of memory. Some might be uncomfortable hearing familiarity being called an unconscious or automatic influence of memory. However, the results of other experiments justify doing so.

Effects on familiarity are observed in memory-impaired populations. The aged as well as amnesics show the false-fame effect (Dywan and Jacoby 1990; Squire and McKee 1992). Even more impressive, the false-fame effect is shown when names are presented to patients under general anaesthesia (Jelicic *et al.*, submitted). To ensure that patients were unaware of the auditory presentation of names, the input list was not initiated until the first surgical incision had been made, and was ended before suturing that incision. The false-fame effect found for anaesthetized patients is nearly as large as the ones we have found after divided attention. Effects on familiarity remain in the absence of recollection, thus supporting the notion of familiarity as an unconscious or automatic influence of memory.

THE PROCESS DISSOCIATION PROCEDURE

By placing familiarity and recollection in opposition, the false-fame experiments showed that dividing attention reduces recollection, leaving effects of familiarity largely unopposed. However, from those results we cannot be certain that dividing attention did not also influence familiarity. The probability of calling an old non-famous name famous reflects a combination of automatic and intentional influences $(F(1-R))$. What is needed is a means of separately estimating effects on automatic and consciously-controlled processing. If we could separately estimate effects, we might be able to show that dividing attention influences recollection but has no influence on familiarity. Also, it might be possible to show that memory impairments such as those produced by ageing are restricted to effects on recollection, and leave automatic influences of memory unchanged.

In the false-fame experiments subjects were told at test that all earlier-read names were non-famous, so as to place familiarity and recollection in opposition. We refer to this test as the 'exclusion' condition, because recollection served to exclude names that were earlier read. In contrast, suppose that we misinformed subjects that all the earlier-read names were actually obscure famous names. In this case (the 'inclusion' test condition) both recollection and familiarity would produce judgements of 'famous'. That is, in contrast to the exclusion condition, recollection would serve to include earlier-read names as famous. An old name could be judged famous either because it was recollected as being on the earlier-read list, or because, although recollection failed, the name was sufficiently familiar to be accepted as famous: $R + F(1 - R)$. Thus the effect of calling an earlier-read name 'famous' would reflect automatic and intentional uses of memory acting in concert.

By combining results from an inclusion and an exclusion condition, one can separately estimate the effects of intentional and automatic processes. The probability of calling a name famous on the exclusion test can be subtracted from that probability on the inclusion test to estimate the probability of recollection: $R = (R + F(1 - R)) - (F(1 - R))$. Given an estimate of recollection, one can easily compute an estimate of familiarity. In summary, what we have done is to combine results from a test for which automatic and intentional processes act in concert with results from a test for which automatic and intentional processes act in opposition to separately estimate the effects of the two types of processes.

The probability of recollection provides a measure of consciously-controlled processing defined in terms of selective responding. For the inclusion test, people are to *select for* old names, whereas, for the exclusion test, people are to *select against* old names. If the probability of recollection were 1.0, people would always call old names famous on the inclusion test, and never call those names famous on the exclusion test. In contrast, if the probability of recollection were 0, people would be as likely to call an old name famous on an exclusion test as on an inclusion test. To gain an intuitive grasp of the way that R measures conscious control, consider the problem of measuring the amount of control that one person has over another person, such as the control a parent has over a child. If a child is as likely to engage in an act when told not to as when told to, then the parent has no control (i.e., $R = 0$). Control cannot be measured by only telling a child to or not to engage in some act; rather, control is assessed by the difference in performance between the two conditions. Automatic processes are defined in relation to the measure of intentional, consciously-controlled processing. In contrast to consciously-controlled processing, automatic processes (familiarity) do not support selective responding, but, rather, produce the same effect regardless of whether that effect is in concert with or opposed to one's intentions.

We call this the process-dissociation procedure, because what we are looking for are factors that produce dissociations in their effects on the estimates of the different types of processes. It is important to us that we should be able to find such dissociations. One of the strongest assumptions underlying the procedure is that automatic and intentional uses of memory are independent. If this assumption is valid, then we should be able to identify factors which have large influences on one process but leave the other process unchanged. Returning to the effects of divided attention and of ageing, we expect those factors to influence recollection but to have no influence on familiarity.

Jennings and Jacoby (submitted) used the process-dissociation procedure to examine the effects of dividing attention and of ageing. In their experiment, young subjects read a list of names under either conditions of divided or full attention. An elderly group of subjects read the names under conditions of full attention. For an exclusion test, people were told that all the earlier-read names on that test were non-famous. For an inclusion test, people were told that all the earlier-read names on the test were famous.

Looking at the results from their experiment (Table 13.1), the exclusion test conditions largely replicate the results from our earlier experiments. Young subjects in the full-attention condition were less likely to mistakenly respond 'famous' to old as against new non-famous names. An opposite effect was found after divided attention and for elderly subjects. Because of a reduction in recollection, subjects in the divided-attention condition and elderly subjects were less able to exclude old names. This reduction in recollection also showed itself in performance on the inclusion test, a test for which recollection would result in old names' being included among those selected as famous. Both dividing attention and ageing reduced the probability of old names' being called famous on that test. The difference between the inclusion and exclusion tests in the probability of calling old names famous provides an estimate of the probability of recollection. That difference is larger for the young, full-attention condition than for the other two conditions.

Using the process-dissociation procedure to separately estimate effects, we see that dividing attention and ageing substantially reduced the probability of recollection (Table 13.1). For subjects in the full-attention condition, the probability of recollection was 0.60. For subjects in the divided-attention condition and for elderly subjects, the probabilities were 0.34 and 0.31. In contrast to effects on recollection, familiarity remained largely unchanged across the conditions. The results are not perfect. One would have liked to have found that estimates of familiarity were identical across the three conditions, so as to show that conscious control can be manipulated without changing unconscious influences. However, the differences are in the wrong direction to what would be expected if familiarity were truly being affected

TABLE 13.1. Observed probabilities of accepting test items ('famous') and estimated probabilities of recollection and familiarity

Group	Observed probabilities		Estimated probabilities	
	Old	New	Recollection	Familiarity
Young—Full attention				
Inclusion	0.73	0.19	0.60	0.33
Exclusion	0.13	0.19		
Young—Divided attention				
Inclusion	0.59	0.22	0.34	0.38
Exclusion	0.25	0.22		
Elderly				
Inclusion	0.58	0.29	0.31	0.39
Exclusion	0.27	0.23		

Estimated recollection = P('famous'/inclusion) − P('famous'/exclusion)

Estimated familiarity = $\frac{P('famous'/exclusion)}{(1-Recollection)}$

Example: For the elderly subjects, estimated recollection was $0.58 - 0.27 = 0.31$, and estimated familiarity was $0.27/(1.0 - 0.31) = 0.39$.

by the attentional manipulation. Also, the small differences in estimated familiarity that were observed might have been produced by differences in criterion among the conditions. As is shown by performance on the new non-famous names, young subjects in the full-attention condition were slightly less willing to call names famous than were subjects in the other two conditions. That difference in criterion might account for the estimated probability of familiarity's being slightly lower for the young, full-attention condition as against the other two conditions.

We have also used the process-dissociation procedure to separate different bases for recognition-memory judgements (see Jacoby 1991, in preparation; Jacoby and Kelley 1991). Many of those experiments have used forced-choice procedures so as to avoid the criterion differences noted above. Among the results obtained so far are that words presented in related pairs are better recollected than words presented in unrelated pairs; low-frequency words are better recollected than high-frequency words; and words presented as anagrams to be solved are better recollected than those that were simply read. In each case, dividing attention during the presentation of words radically reduced recollection. In terms of familiarity, words in related pairs, low-frequency words, and words presented as anagrams to be solved all produced higher levels of familiarity than words presented in corresponding conditions. Most important, dividing attention had little if any effect on the estimates of familiarity. Other experiments have shown that dividing attention at the time of test or inducing fast recognition responses through the use of deadlines produce effects that are similar to those of dividing attention during study. Thus, under a wide range of conditions, effects of ageing, manipulations of attention, and speeded responding have been shown to reduce recollection while leaving familiarity unchanged.

The use of the process-dissociation procedure to measure automaticity can be contrasted with procedures that have been used as attempts to produce a factor- or process-pure measure of automatic responding. For example, dividing attention has been used to define automatic responding, the notion being that automatic responding does not rely on the availability of attentional capacity. Problems for that approach are that one can never be sure that consciously-controlled processing has been fully eliminated or that the procedures used to eliminate consciously-controlled processing did not also influence automatic processing. In contrast, with the process-dissociation procedure, it is not necessary for us to eliminate consciously-controlled processing to measure the effect of automatic processes. The same is true for speed of responding. Others (for example, Dovidio and Fazio 1992) have used fast responding as a defining characteristic of automaticity, whereas we have used the process-dissociation procedure to reveal differential effects of requiring fast responding (Toth, in preparation). The procedure provides us with a means of empirically testing the extent to which dividing attention or requiring fast responses eliminates consciously-controlled processing and leaves automatic or unconscious processes unchanged. If consciously-controlled processing is fully eliminated (i.e., $R = 0$), responding in an in-concert (inclusion) test condition will be the same as that in an opposition (exclusion) test condition. More generally, other people's definitions of automaticity become our independent variables. For us, automaticity and conscious control are measured by relations between performance in a condition in which the two types of processes act in concert and a condition in which they act in opposition.

We have used process-dissociation procedures to estimate automatic and consciously-controlled processes in a variety of domains in addition to fame judgements and recognition memory. Debner and Jacoby (submitted) have used the procedure to separate conscious from unconscious perception in a way that parallels the procedure used to separate consciously-controlled from automatic uses of memory. Ian Begg, a colleague at McMaster, has extended the procedure to separate logic from intuition in syllogistic reasoning. Later, we describe other possible extensions of the process-dissociation procedure. Before doing so, we consider a further refinement of the notion of automaticity.

SPONTANEOUS RECOGNITION IN THE FLANKER PARADIGM: THE RELATIVITY OF AUTOMATICITY

How spontaneous is recognition memory of an item? Recognition memory is typically tested by directing people toward the fact that some of the tested items were previously presented, as was done in our experiments described above. Recognition directed in that fashion might differ in important ways from the spontaneous recognition that occurs in the absence of any explicit question about the 'pastness' of an event. As a commonplace example, the factors that are important for spontaneous recognition of an acquaintance encountered on the street might be different from those important for the recognition of the same acquaintance in response to a direct question. The distinction between spontaneous and directed remembering is an old one, dating back at least to Ebbinghaus (1913). Our interest in that distinction relates to our interest in automaticity. Spontaneous recognition is unintentional in the sense of not being directed by instructions, and may be more automatic than is directed recognition. For spontaneous recognition to occur, it may be necessary for the pastness of an event to 'capture' attention, whereas directed recognition involves the 'giving' of attention (cf. James 1890). At issue is the question of how divorced from intention is spontaneous recognition. As we describe later, that question is equivalent to the question of the relativity of automaticity (cf. Neumann 1984).

To measure spontaneous recognition, what is needed is some means of measuring recognition of an item that does not require asking people whether they recognize the item. To do this, Diane Ste-Marie, a graduate student at McMaster, used the flanker paradigm, introduced by Eriksen and Eriksen (1974; see also Shaffer and LaBerge 1979). Her experiments were designed to determine the conditions under which the 'oldness' of a word that is to be ignored influences recognition judgements about a target word (cf. Eriksen et al. 1986). In the first phase of her experiments, a long list of words was presented for study. For a recognition test, each old and each new target word was presented flanked above and below by either an old word or a new word. The flanker presented above a target was always the same word as that presented below a target. Subjects were to make their recognition decision about the target (middle) word while ignoring the flankers. The effect of the relation between the flanker and the target was used to measure spontaneous recognition in the form of automatic processing of the flanker. If the flanker was processed despite instructions that it should be ignored, recognition decisions should be fastest when the flankers and target were compatible (old flankers, old target; new flankers, new target) rather than incompatible (new flankers, old target; old flankers, new target).

A first experiment examined the effects of dividing attention at the time of test. In the experiments described earlier, consciously-controlled processing in the form of recollection served to localize events in time, and was reduced by requiring subjects to engage in a secondary task so as to divide attention at test. Similarly, requiring subjects to engage in a secondary task might limit people's ability to localize events in space. Focus of attention has been described as analogous to a spotlight (Broadbent 1982; LaBerge 1983) or a zoom lens (Eriksen and Rohrbaugh 1970; Eriksen and St. James 1986). A common feature of those analogies is that the 'breadth' of attention is treated as varying across situations. Items that are to be ignored (i.e., distractors) are said to influence responding to target items only if the distractors are within the visual field that is 'illuminated' by attention. Returning to the question of spontaneous recognition, the suggestion is that, for an item to be spontaneously recognized, that item must appear within the field of attention. Requiring subjects to engage in a secondary task might prevent their focusing attention to a degree of precision that is sufficient for flankers to be totally ignored. If dividing attention by means of a secondary task does reduce control over spatial localization, one would expect larger flanker effects under conditions of divided as against full attention.

Subjects in a divided-attention condition engaged in a listening task while simultaneously making recognition-memory judgements to visually presented target words surrounded by flankers. Subjects in a full-attention condition only made recognition-memory judgements. The results showed no flanker effect when full attention was given to the recognition test, but a good-sized flanker effect when attention was divided (Table 13.2). In the divided-attention condition, decisions were faster when the flanker and target were compatible rather than incompatible. Just as engaging in a secondary task reduces people's ability to accomplish the intentional processing that is necessary to localize an event in time, engaging in a secondary task reduces people's ability to localize events in space.

TABLE 13.2. Recognition times and accuracy
as a function of flankers

Target	Full attention Flanker:		Divided attention Flanker:	
	Old	New	Old	New
Old	869	860	1396	1565
New	1008	1025	1698	1510

Having found a flanker effect, we were in a position to ask about factors influencing automatic uses of memory. That is, what factors are important for the 'oldness' of a flanker to have an effect? One obvious factor is the number of prior presentations of the flanker. A very familiar acquaintance should certainly be more likely to be spontaneously recognized that would be a person we had previously met only once. Automaticity has traditionally been assumed to develop as a function of the number of presentations of an item (for example, Logan 1988). Thus a flanking word that had been previously presented several times would be expected to have a larger effect than would a flanker that had been presented only once. A second factor that would be expected to influence spontaneous recognition is the similarity in the appearance of an item between its prior study and its test presentations. A visually-presented flanking word would be expected to have a larger effect if the word had earlier been presented visually rather than aurally. In that vein, studies employing perceptual identification as an indirect test of memory have shown that earlier reading of a word enhances its later visual perceptual identification to a substantially larger extent than does earlier hearing of a word (see, for example, Jacoby and Dallas 1981; Morton 1979). Results of that sort have been used to argue for the existence of a perceptual representation system in which separate representations (logogens or word forms) correspond to the written and to the spoken version of a word (Morton 1979; Tulving and Schacter 1990). A prior encounter with a word is said to enhance its later identification by priming its modality-specific representation.

To examine the effects of repetition, the number of prior presentations of words that served as flankers was varied. Flankers were new, presented once or presented four times during study. All old targets on the recognition test had been presented only once during study. Recognition was tested under conditions of either full or divided attention.

However, only the results for the divided-attention condition will be described, because performance in the full-attention condition failed to show any flanker effects.

If automaticity is increased by the number of prior presentations, one should expect larger flanker effects when flankers had earlier been presented four times rather than only once. However, the results showed that once-presented flankers produced a larger effect than did four-times presented flankers (see Table 13.3). Old targets surrounded by once-presented flankers were responded to faster (1391 msec.) than were those surrounded by four-times presented or new flankers (1775 msec. and 1712 msec., respectively). Similarly, new targets flanked by once-presented items yielded slower responses (1803 msec.) than did those flanked by either four-times presented or new items (1624 msec. and 1460 msec., respectively). These results were sufficiently surprising for us to do another experiment to determine whether the results could be replicated. The results of the second experiment agreed with those described above in showing that words that should have been very familiar because of their repeated presentation were less effective as flankers than were words that had earlier been presented only once.

TABLE 13.3. Flanker effects of presentation frequency

Target	Divided attention Flanker:		
	4 ×	1 ×	New
Old (1 ×)	1775	1391	1712
New	1624	1803	1469

One explanation for the decline in the effectiveness of flanking words produced by their repetition focuses on the fact that all old words that were presented as targets for the test of recognition memory had been presented only once. That is, it may be the similarity in prior processing between the targets and flanking words, rather than the absolute familiarity of the flankers, that is important for the effectiveness of the flankers. This 'relativity of automaticity' would account for once-presented flankers' being more effective, as compared to four-times presented flankers, when the target words were also once presented. A prediction made by this account is that if all the target words had been presented four times, four-times presented flankers would be more effective than would be once-presented flankers. We tested that possibility, and failed to find any effect of flankers, even when recognition was tested under conditions of divided attention. It seems that if target words are made easy to recognize by their repetition, flanking words lose their effectiveness. That result left the relativity of automaticity untested. However, the possibility that effectiveness of a flanking word depends on the similarity in processing history between the flanking and target words arose again when we examined the effects of modality of prior presentation.

As was described earlier, the results from experiments that have used visual perceptual identification of words as an indirect test of memory suggest that the effects of a flanker will be specific to the modality in which the flanking word was previously presented (for example, Jacoby and Dallas 1981). Because of the modality-specificity of effects of prior exposure on visual word identification, words that were earlier read should be more effective as flankers than are words that were earlier heard. We tested that prediction by varying the modality of the prior presentation of words that served as flankers. Importantly, all the words that were presented as targets for the test of recognition memory were words that had been earlier heard. The results of that experiment (Table 13.4) showed that words that had been earlier *heard* were more effective as flankers than were words that had been earlier read. That is, the results were opposite to what would be expected if it were modality-specific priming or transfer from prior exposure of a word that was important for the word's effectiveness as a flanker.

The lack of effectiveness of flanking words that were earlier read is understandable if it is the relation between the modality of prior presentation of target and flanking words that is important for the effectiveness of flankers. Had the target words been words that were earlier

TABLE 13.4. Flanker effects as a function of modality

Target	Flanker:		
	Heard	Read	New
Old (heard)	1585	1867	2029
New	2265	2166	2212
Old (read)	1851	1486	1846
New	1788	1951	1643

read, flanking words that were also earlier read might be more effective than flanking words that were earlier heard. In fact, the results of a later experiment showed this to be the case (Table 13.4). In combination, results from these experiments show that it is the relation between the processing history of the target and flanking words, rather than the absolute history of the flanking word, that determines whether flanker effects will be observed.

Returning to the question of spontaneous recognition, the flanker experiments suggest that spontaneous recognition is not a function of the recognized stimulus alone, but depends to a large degree on a person's task orientation. Factors that would be expected to influence spontaneous recognition—repetition and physical similarity between study and test—were found to have little or no effect on their own. Rather, attention to the target word resulted in the adoption of an unconscious 'set' that determined the type of distractor items that were spontaneously recognized. We refer to this set as unconscious because none of the subjects, when asked, claimed to have noticed the homogeneity of old target words (for instance, that they were all words that had earlier been read), although that homogeneity created the set for the particular class of items. The result is similar to one observed in investigations of 'release from proactive interference' in short-term memory (see Wickens 1972, 1970; Turvey 1974): subjects' awareness of a change in a dimension of words that are to be remembered is not required for the change to produce release from proactive interference.

One important difference between spontaneous recognition of an acquaintance and spontaneous recognition as measured in the flanker paradigm is that the former (usually) eventuates in awareness of the evoking stimulus (the acquaintance). In contrast, subjects claimed to have successfully ignored the flanking words and to have not noticed that their performance was sometimes facilitated or interfered with by the presence of those words. This difference is most probably due to a difference in focus of attention. In the flanker task, subjects are instructed to ignore the flankers and selectively attend to the target; in contrast, the awareness that accompanies the spontaneous recognition of an acquaintance usually occurs when attention is more 'dispersed' (James 1890). Results from the flanker paradigm suggest that the effects of spontaneous recognition are not fully reliant on the awareness that usually accompanies its occurrence.

Our flanker-effect experiments provide evidence of the relativity of automatic, unconscious influences of memory. In theories of attention, Neumann (1984) and others have used findings of relativity to argue that automaticity cannot be described as stimulus-driven, but, rather, must be understood in terms of levels of control (see Broadbent 1977;

Shallice 1972, 1988). Much the same can be said for automatic or unconscious influences of memory. As has been shown using the process-dissociation procedures, it is possible to separate the effects of automatic and consciously-controlled processes. However, automatic influences of memory are not stimulus-driven in a context-free manner. Our flanker experiments showed that automatic influences of memory (spontaneous recognition) were dependent on the relation between the processing history of the flanker and that of the target. Rather than being totally stimulus-driven, automatic influences of memory are automatic only in the context set by intentional processes.

TOWARD REDEFINING AUTOMATICITY: CONCLUSIONS

Although not introduced as doing so, the 'flanker' experiments conform to the process-dissociation procedure for separating automatic from intentional influences of memory. The experiments described earlier measured intentional, consciously-controlled processing in terms of the relation between performance on inclusion vs. exclusion tests, with the test conditions being produced by a manipulation of instructions. Depending on test instructions, automatic and intentional influences of memory acted either in concert (inclusion test) or in opposition (exclusion test). In contrast, for the flanker experiments, the manipulation was one of the compatibility of the flanker and target words. Depending on the presence or absence of that compatibility, automatic and intentional influences acted in concert (for instance, old flankers, old target) or in opposition (for instance, old flankers, new target). For manipulations of compatibility, it is possible to use the process-dissociation procedure to gain separate quantitative estimates of the effects of automatic and intentional processes. A deadline procedure can be used so as to allow one to work with probabilities of a correct response rather than response times. Lindsay and Jacoby (in preparation) did this for the Stroop (1935) task, and were able to produce process-dissociations to show differential effects of factors on automatic and intentional processes in that task. The equations used by Lindsay and Jacoby to separate the effects of the two types of processes were different from those used in the inclusion/exclusion experiments. However, the general procedure was the same.

For both the manipulation of inclusion/exclusion instructions and for analysing Stroop-like situations, we define automatic processing in relation to intentional, consciously-controlled processing so as to gain separate quantitative estimates of the effects of the two types of processing. Having gained such estimates, we are then in a position to search for process-dissociations so as to validate our procedure, and to specify factors that differentially influence the two forms of processing. By use of the process-dissociation procedure, we centre on the issue of intentional, conscious control of responding. We hold that to measure the effects of automatic (unintentional) processing, the effects of intentional, consciously-controlled processing must also be measured. Automatic processes are defined as those that produce the same effects regardless of whether those effects are in concert with or in opposition to one's intentions.

In contrast, the traditional definition of automatic processing is a fast process that consumes no attentional capacity, is under the control of stimuli rather than intention, and occurs without awareness (see, for example, Posner and Snyder 1975; Shiffrin and Schneider 1977). Similar characteristics have been attributed to implicit memory, the form of memory that is measured by an indirect test. It is the characteristic of lack of awareness that most obviously relates the use of indirect tests to the traditional definition of automaticity. For an indirect test, people are not made aware of the relation between the test and the prior experience whose effects are tested. There is, of course, the worry that performance on an indirect test is sometimes contaminated by intentional uses of memory or perception. To guard against such contamination, subjects are typically instructed to respond as rapidly as possible when given an indirect test (see, for example, Graf and Schacter 1989). Presumably, the rationale for that instruction is that fast responding does not allow sufficient time for intentional use of memory. That is, reliance on implicit memory, like automaticity, is assumed to be more likely when rapid responding is required. Further, implicit memory has been assumed to be stimulus-driven, as is automaticity by its traditional definition. For example, findings that amnesics show priming on perceptual tasks, such as fragment-completion and word-identification, have been taken as evidence for the existence of a perceptual representation system that is preserved by amnesics (Tulving and Schacter 1990). The perceptual representation system is described as capable of supporting responding in a variety of tasks, and as stimulus-driven in that it reflects only the perceptual characteristics of an event, not its meaning.

Our redefinition of automaticity in terms of the process-dissociation procedure changes the status of characteristics that have traditionally constituted its definition. As stated earlier, others' defining characteristics of automaticity become our independent variables. Divided attention, fast responding, etc., probably limit the opportunity for intentional, consciously-controlled processing, but not so completely as to allow those conditions to serve as a satisfactory definition for auto-maticity. Just as the inclusion/exclusion experiments showed that dividing attention reduces the possibility of using consciously-controlled processing (recollection) to localize events in time, the flanker experi-ments showed that dividing attention at test limits the possibility of using consciously-controlled processing to localize events in space. However, in neither set of experiments did dividing attention fully eliminate the possibility of intentional, consciously-controlled process-ing. Research guided by the traditional definition of automaticity has suffered from the practice of fully identifying automaticity, a form of processing, with performance on a particular task chosen to instantiate one of the defining characteristics of automaticity; that is, tasks are treated as if they were factor- or process-pure. Rather than identifying automatic and consciously-controlled processes with different tasks, the process-dissociation procedure separately estimates the contributions of the two types of processes to performance of a particular task. By doing so, we avoid assuming that tasks are process-pure.

By separately estimating the contributions of the different types of processes, we are able to show that the contribution of one process can remain invariant over manipulations that have large effects on the contribution of the other process. For example, the 'false-fame' experi-ments done by Jennings and Jacoby (submitted) showed that ageing re-duced recollection, but had no effect on familiarity. Invariance of that sort cannot be revealed by identifying processes with tasks and then finding task dissociations. Task dissociations are useful for revealing differences in the processes involved in two tasks, but cannot reveal invariance across subject populations or across experimental manipula-tions for any particular form of processing. By use of the process-dissociation procedure we hope to specify better the nature of deficits produced by normal ageing and by various neurological insults. How-ever, our concerns with the relativity of automaticity make us hesitant to describe preserved functions of perception or memory as arising from the preservation of some particular form of perceptual or memory representation. Given the relativity of automaticity, it might be better to speak in terms of a *preserved skill* reflected by performance of a particular task, rather than in terms of a preserved system (perceptual or memory representation) whose *general* status is diagnosed by per-formance of a specific task (cf. Tulving and Schacter 1990).

The process-dissociation procedure redefines automaticity in terms of a measure of consciously-controlled processing. The automaticity measured by that means is not totally stimulus-driven. Our flanker experiments showed that the automatic use of memory which underlies spontaneous recognition reflects the similarity in processing history between the target and flanker words. That 'relativity' is of the same sort that has led others to describe automaticity in terms of levels of control (for example Neumann 1984; Norman and Shallice 1980). How does this relativity of automaticity weigh on our claim that the process-dissociation procedure measures the independent contributions of automatic and intentional, consciously-controlled processing? Although the two types of processing function independently, consciously-controlled processing sets the context for automatic processing. This means that automatic processing, along with its estimated contribution, is expected to change across tasks that involve different intentions or goals. In our fame experiments, for example, the automatic effect of prior exposure to non-famous names arose in the context of the fame-judgement task; prior exposure to those names might have had a different automatic effect—or no effect at all—in other contexts. In our flanker experiments, target words set the context for flanker effects; having earlier heard a flanking word had a large effect, or no effect, depending on the modality in which target words were earlier presented.

A great appeal of the notion of automaticity has been the wide range of domains in which it can be applied. By redefining automaticity in terms of a measure of intentional, consciously-controlled processing we mean to preserve the generality of the notion while correcting its faults. In discussions of automaticity and of unconscious influences, the important issue typically is one of conscious control over thought and behaviour. The process-dissociation procedure centres on that issue, and can be applied in a wide variety of domains. For example, in addition to applications described earlier, it should be possible to extend the procedure to measure individual differences in personality and cognitive factors that influence control (cf. Reason, this volume, Chapter 20; Revelle, this volume, Chapter 17) as well as the effects of emotion (cf. Teasdale, this volume, Chapter 18). Regardless, it should now be obvious that investigation of unconscious influences of memory leads to issues that have formerly been the preserve of attention theorists. That is to say that memory theorists are now in the same wilderness that has long been inhabited by attention theorists. Donald Broadbent's contribution to navigating that wilderness has been invaluable. We are sorry that he is retiring before fully leading us into the clear.

ACKNOWLEDGEMENTS

Preparation of this chapter was supported by a Natural Science and Engineering Research Council (NSERC) operating grant to Larry L. Jacoby and by a postdoctoral fellowship awarded to Jeffrey Toth by the North Atlantic Treaty Organization.

REFERENCES

Bargh, J. A. (1989). Conditional automaticity: varieties of automatic influences in social perception and cognition. In *Unintended thought* (ed. J. S. Uleman and J. A. Bargh), pp. 3–51. Guilford Press, New York.

Bornstein, R. F. and Pittman, T. *Perception without awareness.* Guilford Press, New York. (In press.)

Bowers, K. S. (1975). The psychology of subtle control: an attributional analysis of behavioural persistence. *Canadian Journal of Behavioural Science,* 7(1), 78–95.

Bowers, K. S. (1984). On being unconsciously influenced and informed. In *The unconscious reconsidered* (ed. K. S. Bowers and D. Meichenbaum), pp. 227–73. Wiley, New York.

Broadbent, D. E. (1977). Levels, hierarchies, and the locus of control. *Quarterly Journal of Experimental Psychology,* 29, 181–201.

Broadbent, D. E. (1982). Task combination and selective intake of information. *Acta Psychologica,* 50, 253–90.

Broadbent, D. E., FitzGerald, P., and Broadbent, M. H. P. (1986). Implicit and explicit knowledge in the control of complex systems. *British Journal of Psychology,* 77, 33–50.

Debner, J. A. and Jacoby, L. L. (submitted). Unconscious perception: attention, awareness, and control. Submitted for publication.

Dixon, N. F. (1981). *Preconscious processing.* Wiley, Chichester, England.

Dovidio, J. F. and Fazio, R. H. (1992). New technologies for the direct and indirect assessment of attitudes. In *Questions about questions: inquiries into the cognitive bases of surveys* (ed. J. Tanur), pp. 204–37. Sage, New York.

Dywan, J. and Jacoby, L. L. (1990). Effects of aging on source monitoring: differences in susceptibility to false fame. *Psychology and aging,* 5, 379–87.

Ebbinghaus, H. (1913). *Memory.* Teachers College, Columbia University, New York.

Eich, E. (1984). Memory for unattended events: remembering with and without awareness. *Memory and Cognition,* 12, 105–11.

Eriksen, B. A. and Eriksen, C. W. (1974). Effects of noise letters upon the identification of a target letter in a nonsearch task. *Perception and Psychophysics,* 16, 143–9.

Eriksen, C. W. and Rohrbaugh, J. W. (1970). Some factors determining efficiency of selective attention. *American Journal of Psychology,* 83, 330–42.

Eriksen, C. W. and St James, J. D. (1986). Visual attention within and around the field of focal attention: a zoom lens model. *Perception and Psychophysics,* 40, 225–40.

Eriksen, B. A., Eriksen, C. W., and Hoffman, J. E. (1986). Recognition memory and attentional selection: serial scanning is not enough. *Journal of Experimental Psychology: Human Perception and Performance,* 12, 476–83.

Graf, P. and Schacter, D. L. (1989). Unitization and grouping mediate dissociations in memory for new associations. *Journal of Experimental Psychology: Learning, Memory, and Cognition,* 15, 930–40.

Grand, S. and Segal, S. J. (1966). Recovery in the absence of recall: an investigation of color-word interference. *Journal of Experimental Psychology,* 72, 138–44.

Hintzman, D. L. (1990). Human learning and memory: connections and dissociations. *Annual Review of Psychology,* 41, 109–39.

Holender, D. (1986). Semantic activation without conscious identification in dichotic listening, parafoveal vision, and visual masking: a survey and appraisal. *Behavioral and Brain Sciences*, **9**, 1–23.

Jacoby, L. L. (1991). A process dissociation framework: separating automatic from intentional uses of memory. *Journal of Memory and Language*, **30**, 513–41.

Jacoby, L. L. and Dallas, M. (1981). On the relationship between autobiographical memory and perceptual learning. *Journal of Experimental Psychology: General*, **3**, 306–40.

Jacoby, L. L. and Kelley, C. M. (1991). Unconscious influences of memory: dissociations and automaticity. In *Neuropsychology of consciousness* (ed. D. Milner and M. Rugg), pp. 201–33. Academic Press, London.

Jacoby, L. L., Woloshyn, V., and Kelley, C. M. (1989). Becoming famous without being recognized: unconscious influences of memory produced by dividing attention. *Journal of Experimental Psychology: General*, **118**, 115–25.

Jacoby, L. L., Toth, J. P., Lindsay, D. S., and Debner, J. A. Lectures for a layperson: methods for revealing unconscious processes. In *Perception without awareness* (ed. R. Bornstein and T. Pittman). Guilford Press, New York. (In press.)

James, W. (1890). *Principles of psychology*. Henry Holt & Co, New York.

Jelicic, M., De Roode, A., Bovill, J. G., and Bonke, B. (submitted). Unconscious learning established during anesthesia. Submitted for publication.

Jennings, J.M. and Jacoby, L. L. (submitted). Automatic versus intentional uses of memory: aging, attention, and control. Submitted for publication.

Kelley, C. M. and Jacoby, L. L. (1990). The construction of subjective experience: memory attributions. *Mind and Language*, **5**(1), 49–68.

Koriat, A. and Feuerstein, N. (1976). The recovery of incidentally acquired information. *Acta Psychologica*, **40**, 463–74.

Kuhl, J. (1986). Motivation and information processing: a new look at decision making, dynamic change, and action control. In *Handbook of motivation and cognition: foundations of social behavior*, Vol. 1, (ed. R. M. Sorrentino and E. T. Higgins), pp. 404–34. Guilford Press, New York.

LaBerge, D. (1983). Spatial extent of attention to letters and words. *Journal of Experimental Psychology: Human Perception and Performance*, **9**, 371–9.

Lewicki, P. (1986). *Nonconscious social information processing*. Academic Press, New York.

Logan, G. D. (1988). Toward an instance theory of automatization. *Psychological Review*, **95**, 492–527.

Morton, J. (1979). Facilitation in word recognition: experiments causing change in the logogen model. In *Processing of visible language*, Vol. 1, (ed. P. A. Kolers, M. E. Wrolstal, and H. Bonma), pp. 259–68. Plenum, New York.

Neumann, O. (1984). Automatic processing: a review of recent findings and a plea for an old theory. In *Cognition and motor processes* (ed. W. Prinz and A. F. Sanders), pp. 255–93. Springer-Verlag, Berlin.

Norman, D. A. and Shallice, T. (1980). Attention to action: willed and automatic control of behaviour, Center for Human Information Processing Technical Report No. 99. Reprinted in revised form in *Consciousness and self regulation*, Vol. 4 (ed. R. J. Davidson, G. E. Schwartz, and D. Shapiro), pp. 1–18. Plenum, New York, 1986.

Parkin, A. J., Reid, T. K., and Russo, R. (1990). On the differential nature of implicit and explicit memory. *Memory and Cognition*, **18**, 507–14.

Posner, M. I. and Snyder, C. R. R. (1975). Attention and cognitive control. In *Information processing in cognition: The Loyola Symposium* (ed. R. L. Solso), pp. 55–85. Erlbaum, Hillsdale, NJ.

Reber, A. S. (1989). Implicit learning and tacit knowledge. *Journal of Experimental Psychology: General*, **118**, 219–35.

Reingold, E. M. and Merikle, P. M. (1990). On the inter-relatedness of theory and measurement in the study of unconscious processes. *Mind and Language*, **5**, 9–28.

Richardson-Klavehn, A. and Bjork, R. A. (1988). Measures of memory. *Annual Review of Psychology*, **39**, 475–543.

Shaffer, W. O. and LaBerge, D. (1979). Automatic semantic processing of unattended words. *Journal of Verbal Learning and Verbal Behavior*, **18**, 413–26.

Shallice, T. (1972). Dual functions of consciousness. *Psychological Review*, **79**, 383–93.

Shallice, T. (1988). Information-processing models of consciousness: possibilities and problems. In *Consciousness in contemporary science* (ed. A. J. Marcel and E. Bisiach), pp. 305–33. Clarendon Press, Oxford.

Shiffrin, R. M. and Schneider, W. (1977). Controlled and automatic human information processing: II. Perceptual learning, automatic attending, and a general theory. *Psychological Review*, **84**, 127–90.

Squire, L. R. and McKee, R. (1992). Influence of prior events on cognitive judgments in amnesia. *Journal of Experimental Psychology: Learning, Memory, and Cognition*, **18**, 106–15.

Stroop, J. R. (1935). Studies of interference in serial verbal reactions. *Journal of Experimental Psychology*, **18**, 643–62.

Tulving, E. and Schacter, D. L. (1990). Priming and human memory systems. *Science*, **247**, 301–5.

Tulving, E., Schacter, D. L., and Stark, H. A. (1982). Priming effects in word-fragment completion are independent of recognition memory. *Journal of Experimental Psychology: Learning, Memory, and Cognition*, **8**, 336–42.

Turvey, M. T. (1974). Constructive theory, perceptual systems, and tacit knowledge. In *Cognition and the symbolic processes* (ed. W. B. Weimer and D. S. Palermo), pp. 165–80. LEA, Hillsdale, NJ.

Warrington, E. K. and Weiskrantz, L. (1974). The effect of prior learning on subsequent retention in amnesic patients. *Neuropsychologia*, **12**, 419–28.

Weiskrantz, L. (1986). *Blindsight: a case study and implications.* Oxford University Press.

White, P. (1982). Beliefs about conscious experience. In *Aspects of consciousness*, Vol. 3, (ed. G. Underwood), pp. 1–25. Academic Press, London.

Wickens, D. D. (1970). Encoding categories of words: an empirical approach to meaning. *Psychological Review*, **77**, 1–15.

Wickens, D. D. (1972). Characteristics of word encoding. In *Coding processes in human memory* (ed. A. W. Melton and E. Martin), pp. 191–215. Wiley, New York.

FOURTEEN

Varieties of consciousness and levels of awareness in memory

Endel Tulving

Consciousness as an object of intellectual curiosity is the philosopher's joy and the scientist's nightmare. It is delightfully easy to generate all sorts of thoughts about consciousness, thoughts that can be related to other thoughts, supported by logical arguments, and illustrated with suitable anecdotes. It is distressingly difficult to come up with any hard data that clarify such thoughts by sorting out useful from less useful ones or, even more desirably, eliminating some thoughts as false altogether.

The problems plaguing the study of consciousness are well known. They include uncertainty as to what consciousness is, the uncertainty concerning its general status in the biological or psychological order of things, doubts about the reliability and validity of empirical observations claimed to be 'about' consciousness, the multitude of ways in which these observations can be interpreted, the difficulty of measuring consciousness, and many others. A pervasive symptom of the current state of affairs is the permeation of discussions of consciousness with intolerable vagueness.

One possible reason for the rather chaotic state of affairs in the scientific study of consciousness has to do with the widely accepted implicit assumption that consciousness is in some sense unitary, the assumption that consciousness is consciousness is consciousness. In this view, the major defining characteristic of consciousness is its distinction from unconsciousness. Although theorists sometimes go beyond a simple 'contrastive analysis' between conscious and unconscious processes (Baars 1988), and differentiate between 'levels' of consciousness—for instance, conscious, preconscious, subconscious, and unconscious processes (Kihlstrom 1987)—these levels typically represent quantitative degrees of the same qualitative entity. Thus the prevailing view is that of a homogeneous consciousness, that is, that there exists a 'single conscious mechanism' (for example Schacter *et al.* 1988, p. 270). This assumption is manifest in the tendency to describe and discuss consciousness as an undivided whole, to ask what *consciousness* is, how *it* is to be defined, what *it* does, what function *it* serves, where in the mental activity *it* appears or does not appear, and how and in what sense *it* differs from non-consciousness (for example Baars 1988; Mandler 1975; Marcel and Bisiach 1988; Velmans 1991). At the early stages of inquiry this was a perfectly reasonable orienting attitude. But today it is less appropriate.

Every now and then the assumption of unitary consciousness is questioned. For instance, Churchland recently observed that 'what we now lump together as "consciousness" may not be so much a unitary phenomenon admitting of a unitary explanation, but a rag-bag of sundry effects requiring a set of quite different explanations' (Churchland 1988, p. 281). Similar opinions have been expressed by a few others as well (for example Allport 1988; Farthing 1992; Gazzaniga 1985) but they have not yet become a basis of concerted action at the empirical level.

In this essay I will explore the possibilities of a more analytical approach to the study of consciousness. I do so by (a) dealing with consciousness only as it manifests itself in phenomena of memory, (b) distinguishing between consciousness and awareness as separable concepts, and (c) exploring the notion that different forms of memory and different aspects of the operations of memory are correlated with different kinds of awareness. The general issue that ties together the various strands of the argument concerns the meaning of the claims that some forms of memory are 'conscious' whereas others are 'non-conscious'. This kind of claim is frequently made, but it has not been sufficiently explicated. What does it mean?

The essay consists of five main sections, in addition to the present introduction and a final summary and conclusions: (1) Multiple memory systems; (2) Conscious awareness and memory; (3) The relation between consciousness and awareness; (4) Semantic 'learning' without noetic awareness? and (5) The co-ordination hypothesis.

MULTIPLE MEMORY SYSTEMS

Everybody knows about Donald Broadbent's *Perception and communication*, a book that changed the history of experimental psychology (Broadbent 1958). Everybody also knows about the distinction that he made in the book, between the S system and the P system. It represents an early important step on the road that psychology has taken toward the acknowledgement of the biological reality of the modularity of the brain.

The early dichotomies between short-term and long-term memory and other similar distinctions have now developed into more complex classificatory schemes. These schemes in their various versions (for example, Roediger 1990; Squire 1987, 1992; Squire and Zola-Morgan 1991; Tulving 1987, 1992; Tulving and Schacter 1990, 1992; Weiskrantz 1987, 1990) represent tentative resolutions of what now, thirty years after *Perception and communication*, has turned into one of the hot issues of the science of memory—how many different forms of learning and memory, or how many systems, are there?

Memory systems are defined in terms of property lists, statements of the kinds of behaviour or cognitive information they mediate, the characteristics of their operation, and their neural basis (for example, Sherry and Schacter 1987; Squire 1987; Tulving 1984; Tulving and Schacter 1990; Weiskrantz 1987, 1990). Different systems usually collaborate in the execution of tasks that confront the individual in its interaction with the environment. The untangling of the web of the complex system–task interactions is a major objective of the systems-oriented research. The relevant evidence is provided by empirical observations at different levels of analysis, in different divisions of neural, behavioural/cognitive, and computational sciences. Various aspects of this evidence have been reviewed by Mitchell (1989), Polster *et al.* (1991), Schacter (1987, 1990), Sherry and Schacter (1987), Shimamura (1986), Squire (1987, 1992), Tulving (1987, 1992), Tulving and Schacter (1990, 1992), Tulving *et al.* (1991), and Weiskrantz (1987, 1990), among others.

A classificatory scheme of five major memory and learning systems is shown in Table 14.1. The five are *procedural* memory, perceptual representation system (PRS), *short-term* memory, *semantic* memory, and

TABLE 14.1. Classification of human memory systems—1991

Major system	Other terms	Retrieval
1. Procedural memory	Skill learning Non-declarative	Implicit
2. Perceptual representation (PRS)	Perceptual priming Quasi-memory (QM)	Implicit
3. Short-term memory	Primary memory Working memory	Explicit
4. Semantic memory	Knowledge system Generic memory Categorical memory	Implicit
5. Episodic memory	Autobiographical Personal memory	Explicit

episodic memory. Table 14.1 also shows some other closely related terms. Each of the five systems is large and complex, comprising a number of subsystems for which evidence at the present stage of our knowledge is of variable quality, as it is for the main systems themselves.

It can be conjectured that the ordering of these systems in the overall classification scheme corresponds roughly to their developmental sequence, with the procedural system the earliest, and the episodic the latest. Another conjecture is that the ordering of the systems also reflects the relations among them: the operations of the higher systems depend on, and are supported by, the operations of the lower ones, whereas lower systems can operate essentially independently of the higher. The systems are also assumed to vary, roughly in the same order, with respect to the extent to which their operations involve consciousness, conceived in its unitary formulation, or with respect to the *kinds* of consciousness or awareness that accompany their functions.

The procedural system is an *action* system. Its operations are expressed in behaviour; they can occur independently of cognition, and do not require conscious awareness of a kind that characterizes other forms of memory (Cohen and Squire 1980; Squire 1987).

The other four are *cognitive* systems. Their operations are expressed in cognition that need not be converted into behaviour. (1) Perceptual repetition priming is a *non-conscious* form of learning that consists in the facilitation of the perceptual identification of words and objects. It is subserved by the perceptual representation system, PRS (Schacter 1990; Tulving and Schacter 1990). PRS is a pre-semantic system, that is, its operations can be carried out independently of the semantic and other higher memory systems. (2) Short-term memory, or primary memory, retains perceptual and conceptual information for a period of time measured in seconds after the input. It makes possible a lingering conscious awareness of recently presented stimuli, or of recently contemplated thoughts. It is dissociated from long-term (episodic and semantic) memory (Shallice 1988; Shallice and Warrington 1970). (3) The semantic memory system makes possible acquisition, retention, and use of organized information in the broadest sense; its principal function is cognitive modelling of the world (Lockhart *et al.* 1976; Tulving 1983). It is also assumed to mediate conceptual repetition priming, which is distinguished from perceptual priming (Keane *et al.* 1991; Tulving and Schacter 1990). (4) Episodic memory enables the individual to consciously remember personally experienced events embedded in a matrix of other personal happenings in subjective time. Episodic memory shares many properties with semantic memory. It depends on semantic memory for many of its operations, but it also uniquely transcends the range of the capabilities of semantic memory (Kinsbourne 1989; Kinsbourne and Wood 1975; Tulving 1983, 1987; Tulving *et al.* 1991).

As a historical footnote appropriate to the occasion that the present volume helps to celebrate, it is of interest to note that Donald Broadbent was an early proponent of the distinction between semantic and episodic memory, agreeing wholeheartedly with the same distinction made by Sir Frederic Bartlett, although not quite using the terms that we use today. The interested student of history can read all about it in Chapter 3 of *Perception and communication* (Broadbent 1958). Implicit in Broadbent's discussion of conscious recollection of personal events is a reference to one of the important albeit little discussed differences between retrieval from semantic and from episodic memory: with practice, the former can but the latter cannot become automatic or 'non-conscious'.

CONSCIOUS AWARENESS AND MEMORY

I have suggested elsewhere that it may be useful to imagine a rough parallel between various forms of consciousness and different kinds of memory. Specifically, the retrieval operations governed by different memory systems from procedural to episodic may be associated with an ordering of forms of consciousness, from anoetic (non-knowing) at the lower end, through noetic (knowing) at the level of the perceptual and semantic systems, to an autonoetic (self-knowing) consciousness that characterizes episodic memory (Tulving 1985). This speculative idea is not without its problems (Natsoulas 1986; Schacter 1989), but it can serve as a heuristic basis for formulating more specific hypotheses.

Evidence concerning the relation between consciousness and *procedural* memory is still scant, although a beginning has been made (for example, Nissen 1992). One possible method of empirical assessment of the role of consciousness in procedural memory tasks might take the form of systematic comparisons of first-person and third-person accounts (Marcel 1988; Olson and Astington 1987; Velmans 1991) of performance on tasks systematically varying in their reliance on procedural memory. Discrepancies between the two accounts reflect the involvement of subjective experience, and therefore could be used as empirical indices of the role that consciousness plays in procedural and other forms of memory.

Systematic evidence regarding the issue of consciousness and *short-term memory*, or primary memory, is also meagre, despite, or perhaps because of, William James' (1890) and others' (for example Atkinson and Shiffrin 1971; Craik and Lockhart 1972) identification of primary memory with consciousness.

The issue of conscious awareness becomes more central, and its study more systematic, in the distinction between explicit and implicit memory, or explicit and implicit retrieval (Graf and Schacter 1985; Schacter 1987). These labels refer to the presence or absence of the subject's awareness, at the time of retrieval, of the relation between present and past experience. The awareness of the referential relation between the present and the past is usually referred to as 'remembering', 'conscious recollection', or 'recollective experience'. In the GAPS theory (Tulving 1983), it is based on 'ecphoric information', a product of the interaction between stored memory traces and current retrieval information. In implicit retrieval a similar referential awareness is said to be absent: the person's present cognitive activity has been influenced by past experience, but the person is unaware of this fact.

It is important to note that despite the close relation between the two, explicit memory is not the same as episodic memory. Apart from definitional differences—one is a form of retrieval, the other a memory system—relevant evidence also points to separation. Research by John Gardiner, his associates, and others, for instance, based on the distinction between 'remembering' and 'knowing' in explicit memory tasks, suggests that people can arrive at knowledge about the 'contents' of past episodes, even in word-list experiments in the laboratory, not only on the basis of episodic memory, but also, less effectively, on the basis of semantic memory, or some other system whose identity is not yet clear (for example Gardiner 1988; Gardiner and Java 1990; Gardiner and Parkin 1990; Gregg and Gardiner 1991; Rajaram 1991; Tulving 1985). And there is some preliminary evidence, from a study of event-related potentials, that this distinction between remembering and knowing reflects a difference in brain activity at the time of encoding (Smith 1992).

Thus, the distinction between explicit and implicit retrieval cuts across the classification systems shown in Table 15.1: procedural memory, PRS, and semantic memory retrieval are assumed to be implicit, whereas primary and episodic memory retrieval are explicit.*

The literature on comparative studies of implicit and explicit memory is expanding rapidly. The core studies of implicit memory have been concerned with repetition priming (for example Richardson-Klavehn and Bjork 1988). Repetition priming (henceforth simply 'priming') is

---

* Not all writers accept this organization. Squire and Zola-Morgan (1991), for instance, still lump episodic and semantic memory together into declarative memory, which they identify with explicit memory. In their scheme, declarative memory deals with the acquisition of 'information about *facts* and *events*' (Squire and Zola-Morgan 1991, p. 1381, emphasis added).

said to have occurred when the identification of an object, such as a word, is facilitated by a prior encounter or encounters with the same object or similar objects. Two basic forms of repetition priming have been identified (Keane *et al.* 1991; Roediger 1990; Schacter 1990; Tulving and Schacter 1990). *Perceptual* priming, observed and measured in situations in which the test cue is perceptually or physically (in word priming, lexically) related to the target object, occurs independently of the cue's or the target object's meaning. *Conceptual* priming, observed and measured in situations in which the test cue is conceptually related to the target object, can occur independently of the cue's and the target's perceptual appearance.

Unlike the problematic and empirically uncertain statements concerning the presence or absence of consciousness in the operations of procedural memory, the non-conscious nature of priming, especially perceptual priming, is well established. A person who identifies many different patterns of retinal stimulation as one and the same familiar object, or recognizes a string of letters such as 'percptual' as a familiar word, despite a missing letter, is perfectly aware that she is perceiving the object or the (misspelled) word, and totally unaware that she is engaging in an act of memory, that is, that she is in any way using information stored in memory. Specifically, we could say that the person in our example is anoetically aware of priming and noetically aware of the perceived object, and that she has no autonoetic awareness of its earlier occurrences.

Such autonoetic awareness can be evoked in an explicit recognition test, in which the subject is asked whether he remembers having seen a particular word in the previously presented study list. In a certain proportion of cases, the autonoetic awareness leads the subject to identify a test item as 'old'. In the same situation we can also test the subject's ability to identify incompletely specified words, words not spelled out completely but instead represented by graphemic fragments such as -N-V-R-E and U-I-E-S-. It is well known that a single previous encounter with the corresponding words may enhance the probability that the subject can complete the fragment, that is, that he can identify the incompletely described word. This is perceptual priming. It is also well known that such perceptual priming is (stochastically) independent of episodic recognition of studied words: priming effects are as large for the study-list words that the subject consciously recollects (recognizes) as having been in the study list as they are for the study-list words that the subject does not remember having seen in the study list (for example Tulving *et al.* 1982). This type of contingent dissociation provides objective empirical support for the notion that priming is 'non-conscious'.

We must nevertheless hasten to qualify the statement that perceptual priming is non-conscious because, like many other similar statements one finds in the literature, it too is intolerably vague. Surely the subject-participant in the experiment is as fully conscious an individual —wide awake, alert, aware of herself, aware of her surroundings and the task on hand—when she is performing the fragment-completion test as she is when she is making decisions about earlier occurrences of test items. And surely she is as conscious an individual when she contemplates the products of her performance on the 'non-conscious' priming task as she is when she is looking at an 'old' test item in the 'conscious' explicit recognition task. What does it mean then to talk about 'non-conscious' priming?

THE RELATION BETWEEN CONSCIOUSNESS AND AWARENESS

It is useful to draw a distinction between two aspects of consciousness, or subjective experience, that are frequently confused, or discussed indiscriminately (cf. Bunge and Ardila 1987, Ch. 11). One is a *general capacity* that an individual possesses for particular kinds of subjective experience; I refer to it as *consciousness*. The other is a *particular manifestation* of this general capacity; I refer to it as *awareness*.*

It is also useful to postulate the existence of different kinds of consciousness, and, therefore, different kinds of awareness. Thus, it seems reasonable to assume that the consciousness of a young child differs from that of an adult, and that the consciousness of an intoxicated person differs from that of a sober person. Different states of consciousness also characterize sleeping people, anaesthetized persons, comatose people, those who have suffered certain kinds of brain damage, and so on.

Consciousness is determined by the properties of the individual's brain and its general state at any given time. A given kind of consciousness determines what kinds of awareness or subjective experience the person *can* have; it provides the individual with a potential for particular kinds of awareness. Consciousness is not directed at anything, whereas awareness is always of something (cf. Bunge and Ardila 1987, p. 236). To be aware of something means to have a particular subjective experience that is determined by both the current (general) state

---

* This choice of terms to designate the distinction between the general capacity and its particular expressions is arbitrary, and by no means optimal. But the use of existing terms is preferable to the adoption of new ones, because psychologists, by and large, tend to be suspicious of, and even averse to, new terms.

of consciousness *and* the current (particular) stimulation from external and internal sources. Thus, awareness presumes consciousness, but consciousness does not imply awareness: consciousness is a necessary but not a sufficient condition of awareness. A sleeping person's consciousness, but not that of a waking person, allows him to *dream*; but that does not mean that all sleep is dreams.

The relation between awareness and consciousness is analogous to seeing something, or visually perceiving a particular scene or object, on the one hand, and the sense of sight, on the other: consciousness *allows* certain kinds of subjective experiences, but does not dictate any particular ones, as the sense of sight *allows* certain kinds of sensory achievements, but in and of itself does not prescribe any.

Within a given state or kind of consciousness there are levels of awareness. We have already discussed three such levels—anoetic, noetic, and autonoetic—within normal, waking, alert consciousness. In our earlier example of recognition and primed fragment-completion, the subject's consciousness was constant throughout the experiment, yet her awareness of the relation between a present object—the recognized word or the word completed from its fragment—and the earlier study episode varied with the task: she was autonoetically aware of the relation in the explicit recognition test, noetically aware of the cues and completed targets, and anoetically aware of priming in the implicit memory test.

Within a given level of awareness many particular kinds of subjective experiences may occur. We can think of (selective) *attention* as the primary process that determines the aspects of the stimulus situation of which the individual is aware.

As a concrete illustration of the application of the notions discussed, consider two (related) questions that for a long time have been of interest to students of consciousness: (1) Does 'non-conscious perception' occur? and (2) Can people 'remember' semantic information non-consciously?

SEMANTIC LEARNING WITHOUT NOETIC AWARENESS

In several recent experiments it has been demonstrated that surgical patients are capable of encoding, storing, and subsequently retrieving information presented to them while they are in a 'non-conscious' state under general anaesthesia (for example, Jelicic *et al.* 1992; Roorda-Hrdlicková *et al.* 1990). In these experiments, subjects undergoing surgical operations were presented, via headphones, with a small set of categorized words. They were tested for the retention of these words a few hours after they came out of the surgery. As usual (for a review, see Kihlstrom and Schacter 1990), they had no conscious recollection of having heard anything during surgery. Yet their performance on a conceptual priming task—assumed to reflect the operations of semantic memory (Tulving and Schacter 1990)—showed significant retention: given the names of different conceptual categories and asked to produce instances, the subjects were more likely to produce the words that had been presented to them under anaesthesia than words that had not been presented.

Because of the absence of appropriate controls, it is not known how the magnitude of the priming effects observed in the anaesthetized subject compares with the same effects in subjects with normal consciousness.* But, if we assume that the anaesthetized subjects were not noetically aware of the auditory messages presented to them, then the fact that at least some conceptual priming occurs under these conditions is noteworthy. It suggests that 'conscious perception' is not necessary for the encoding of novel semantic information into memory: 'learning', or registration, of semantic information can occur in the absence of awareness.

The fact that semantic priming can occur in the (presumed) absence of autonoetic or noetic awareness, in the state of consciousness produced by anaesthesia, naturally leads to the question of the nature of the relation between two kinds of alternations in awareness—those correlated with different kinds of consciousness (such as 'normal' versus anaesthetic), and those achieved through the manipulations of stimulus presentation and attentional processes within 'normal' consciousness. How are these alterations in awareness similar; how are they different? The answer to the question has implications for the controversy as to whether normally conscious people who are not aware of the occurrence of a word can nevertheless 'perceive' something of its semantic meaning (for example, Cheesman and Merikle 1986; Holender 1986; Marcel 1983, 1988; Reingold and Merikle 1988).

THE CO-ORDINATION HYPOTHESIS

Perhaps the most interesting implication of the findings of conceptual priming in anaesthetized subjects has to do with the *relation* between awareness at encoding and awareness at retrieval. The findings suggest

---

* It is conceivable, although not very likely, that the *conceptual priming* effect is no smaller in anaesthetized than in normal subjects. But an appropriate comparison is possible only under conditions in which normal subjects could not rely on their episodic memory in the conceptual priming task.

what I will refer to as the co-ordination hypothesis. It holds that retrieval or use of information stored in memory is limited to a level of awareness no higher than the level of awareness at the time of original experience or encoding.

In the experiments with anaesthetized subjects (Jelicic *et al.* 1992; Roorda-Hrdlicková *et al.* 1990), the subjects did discriminate and encode the semantic information presented to them. We can say that the subjects were aware of the input at some low level: they were aware of it anoetically (non-knowingly). At the time of the test, the subjects could not retrieve anything at the level of autonoetic awareness— explicit recall and recognition was zero. Furthermore, the subjects' *noetic* awareness of their performance in the semantic memory task of producing primed category instances was presumably the same for primed and unprimed targets. The *difference* between primed and unprimed production—the difference classified by the experimenter as the conceptual priming effect—thus expressed itself at the level of anoetic awareness.

A similar kind of relation between awareness at encoding and awareness at retrieval is found in analyses of childhood amnesia. Perner (submitted) has reported evidence suggesting that in children younger than three or four years episodic memory and autonoetic awareness are greatly impoverished, and may be absent altogether. These children, of course, are highly capable learners and memorizers; they have acquired a great deal of knowledge about the world. They can act on that knowledge, and report it verbally, and they can retain it over shorter or longer periods of time. What they cannot do, according to Perner, is to *remember the experience* of their own personal involvement in the acquisition of this knowledge: they lack autonoetic consciousness. One consequence of young children's inability to encode happenings *as experienced*, autonoetically, is their inability to remember these happenings as adults—the phenomenon of childhood amnesia.

Yet another example of the co-ordination hypothesis is provided by patients with anterograde amnesia (Talland 1965). The inability of such patients to remember autonoetically any personal happenings from the postmorbid period could reflect the failure of the establishment of requisite memory traces because of damage to neural pathways of the episodic memory system. Such episodic-memory damage, however, does not necessarily prevent amnesic patients from acquiring new semantic knowledge, or encoding and retrieving it at the level of noetic awareness. (For further discussion, see Tulving *et al.* 1991.)

These kinds of phenomena—semantic learning in the absence of autonoetic remembering under anaesthesia, in early childhood, and in anterograde amnesia—suggest that high-level semantic information, which can be encoded and retained in different systems, can be retrieved at a level of awareness no higher than the level of awareness accompanying the original encoding of the information into 'remembery'.* It is this idea—that information encoded at a given level can be later retrieved or used at the same level and at lower levels of awareness, but not at higher levels—that I refer to as the *co-ordination hypothesis*. The co-ordination hypothesis parallels a comparable assumption about the relations among memory systems: information encoded only into a lower system cannot be retrieved from a higher system.

A similar idea was suggested by Eich (1984). He pointed out that unattended events usually cannot be recollected consciously, but this fact does not rule out the possibility that 'even though the effects of memory for unattended events may not—*and probably cannot*—be revealed in tests of retention that require remembering to be deliberate or intentional, such effects might become manifest in tests that do not demand awareness of remembering' (Eich 1984, p. 105, emphasis added).

The co-ordination hypothesis helps us to re-evaluate some of the issues concerning consciousness that have been of considerable interest to contemporary cognitive psychologists (for example Baars 1988; Cheesman and Merikle 1986; Holender 1986; Marcel 1983, 1988; Marcel and Bisiach 1988; Velmans 1991)—such as whether it is possible for human observers to extract semantic information from words of whose presence they are unaware. Many assert that people cannot perceive and 'consciously recollect' semantic information of which they were unaware at the time of presentation (for example Holender 1986). Others, relying on the kinds of phenomena summarized above, believe that people are capable of 'learning' high-level semantic information of which they are not consciously aware. The co-ordination hypothesis resolves the apparent conflict between these two propositions. The sceptics' denial may be true in situations in which the subjects are tested for awareness of the presented information at a higher level of awareness than that prevailing at encoding; the believers' assertion may be true if the encoded information is used or retrieved at a level of awareness stipulated by the co-ordination hypothesis.

SUMMARY AND CONCLUSIONS

In this essay I have reflected on the claim that some forms of memory are conscious while others are non-conscious. I suggested that such a

* 'Remembery' is a term recently suggested by William James Morrow, which I use here in the sense of 'neural record of the encoded information that enables synergistic ecphory' (Tulving 1992). William James is James McGaugh's grandson. He is 60 years younger than Donald Broadbent. I thank William James's grandfather for making me aware of the word.

claim is too vague to be of much scientific value. The major problems with such a formulation have their roots in the tendency to assume that consciousness is a unitary concept, as well as the failure to distinguish systematically between different kinds or states of consciousness, on the one hand, and different levels of awareness of particular aspects of experience within a given kind or state of consciousness, on the other hand.

I outlined a general classificatory scheme of five memory systems, and related these systems to the distinction between implicit and explicit retrieval. I then raised the question of what it means to say that implicit retrieval—which characterizes the use of information in procedural memory, in the perceptual representation system, and in semantic memory—is non-conscious. To answer the question I proposed a distinction between consciousness and awareness: consciousness is the general capacity for having subjective experiences, whereas awareness refers to the particular exercise of that capacity. Implicit retrieval, in this scheme, refers to the cognitive act, performed by a normally conscious individual, of using previously stored information in the absence of either autonoetic or even noetic awareness of the relation between the present and the past.

I then briefly described experiments reported by Bonke and his associates, as well as observations by Perner regarding the origin of later-life childhood amnesia in dysfunctional autonoetic remembering in early childhood, and I mentioned the phenomenon of anterograde amnesia. All of them illustrate what I referred to as the co-ordination hypothesis: retrieval or use of information stored in a memory system is restricted to a level of awareness not exceeding the level of awareness characterizing the system's operations at the time of the original experience or encoding.

ACKNOWLEDGEMENTS

The author's research is supported by the Natural Sciences and Engineering Research Council of Canada, Grant No. A8632. I am grateful to Henry L. Roediger III and Daniel L. Schacter for constructive comments on this chapter.

REFERENCES

Allport, A. (1988). What concept of consciousness? In *Consciousness in contemporary science* (ed. A. J. Marcel and E. Bisiach), pp. 159–82. Clarendon Press, Oxford.

Atkinson, R. C. and Shiffrin, R. M. (1971). The control of short-term memory. *Scientific American*, **225**, 82–90.

Baars, B. J. (1988). *A cognitive theory of consciousness*. Cambridge University Press.

Broadbent, D. E. (1958). *Perception and communication*. Pergamon, Oxford.

Bunge, M. and Ardila, R. (1987). *Philosophy of psychology*. Springer, New York.

Cheesman, J. and Merikle, P. M. (1986). Distinguishing conscious from unconscious perceptual processes. *Canadian Journal of Psychology*, **40**, 343–67.

Churchland, P. S. (1988). Reduction and the neurobiological basis of consciousness. In *Consciousness in contemporary science* (ed. A. J. Marcel and E. Bisiach), pp. 273–304. Clarendon Press, Oxford.

Cohen, N. J. and Squire, L. R. (1980). Preserved learning and retention of pattern analyzing skill in amnesia: dissociation of knowing how and knowing that. *Science*, **210**, 207–9.

Craik, F. I. M. and Lockhart, R. S. (1972). Levels of processing: a framework for memory research. *Journal of Verbal Learning and Verbal Behavior*, **11**, 671–84.

Eich, E. (1984). Memory for unattended events: remembering with and without awareness. *Memory and Cognition*, **12**, 105–11.

Farthing, G. W. (1992). *The psychology of consciousness*. Prentice Hall, Englewood Cliffs.

Gardiner, J. M. (1988). Functional aspects of recollective experience. *Memory and Cognition*, **16**, 309–13.

Gardiner, J. M. and Java, R. I. (1990). Recollective experience in word and nonword recognition. *Memory and Cognition*, **18**, 23–30.

Gardiner, J. M. and Parkin, A. J. (1990). Attention and recollective experience in recognition memory. *Memory and Cognition*, **18**, 579–83.

Gazzaniga, M. S. (1985). *The social brain: discovering the networks of the brain*. Basic Books, New York.

Graf, P. and Schacter, D. L. (1985). Implicit and explicit memory for new associations in normal and amnesic subjects. *Journal of Experimental Psychology: Learning, Memory, and Cognition*, **11**, 501–18.

Gregg, V. H. and Gardiner, J. M. (1991). Components of conscious awareness in a long-term modality effect. *British Journal of Psychology*, **82**, 153–62.

Holender, D. (1986). Semantic activation without conscious identification in dichotic listening, parafoveal vision, and visual masking. *Behavioral and Brain Sciences*, **9**, 1–66.

James, W. (1890). *Principles of psychology*. Holt, New York.

Jelicic, M., Wolters, G., Bonke, B., and Phaf, R. H. (1992). Implicit memory for stimuli presented during anaesthesia. *European Journal of Cognitive Psychology*, **4**, 71–80.

Keane, M. M., Gabrieli, J. D. E., Fennema, A. C., Growdon, J. H., and Corkin, S. (1991). Evidence for a dissociation between perceptual and conceptual priming in Alzheimer's disease. *Behavioral Neuroscience*, **105**, 326–42.

Kihlstrom, J. F. (1987). The cognitive unconscious. *Science*, **237**, 1445–52.

Kihlstrom, J. F. and Schacter, D. L. (1990). Anaesthesia, amnesia, and the cognitive unconscious. In *Memory and awareness in anaesthesia* (ed. B. Bonke, W. Fitch, and K. Millar), pp. 21–44. Swets & Zeitlinger, Lisse–Amsterdam.

Kinsbourne, M. (1989). The boundaries of episodic remembering: comments on the second section. In *Varieties of memory and consciousness: essays in honour of Endel Tulving* (ed. H. L. Roediger III and F. I. M. Craik), pp. 179–94. Erlbaum, Hillsdale, NJ.

Kinsbourne, M. and Wood, F. (1975). Short-term memory processes and the amnesic syndrome. In *Short-term memory* (ed. D. Deutsch and J. A. Deutsch), pp. 258–91. Academic Press, New York.

Lockhart, R. S., Craik, F. I. M., and Jacoby, L. L. (1976). Depth of processing, recognition and recall. In *Recall and recognition* (ed. J. Brown), pp. 75–102. Wiley, New York.

Mandler, G. (1975). *Mind and emotion*. Wiley, New York.

Marcel, A. J. (1983). Conscious and unconscious perception: an approach to the relation between phenomenal experience and perceptual processes. *Cognitive Psychology*, **15**, 238–300.

Marcel, A. J. (1988). Phenomenal experience and functionalism. In *Consciousness in contemporary science* (ed. A. J. Marcel and E. Bisiach), pp. 121–58. Clarendon Press, Oxford.

Marcel, A. J. and Bisiach, E. (eds) (1988). *Consciousness in contemporary science*. Clarendon Press, Oxford.

Mitchell, D. B. (1989). How many memory systems? Evidence from aging. *Journal of Experimental Psychology: Learning, Memory and Cognition*, **15**, 31–49.

Natsoulas, T. (1986). Consciousness and memory. *Journal of Mind and Behavior*, **7**, 463–502.

Nissen, M. J. (1992). Procedural and declarative learning: distinctions and interactions. In *Neuropsychology of memory* (2nd edn), (ed. L . R. Squire and N. Butters), pp. 203–10. Guilford, New York.

Olson, D. R. and Astington, J. W. (1987). Seeing and knowing: on the ascription of mental states to young children. *Canadian Journal of Psychology*, **41**, 399–411.

Perner, J. Episodic memory and autonoetic consciousness: developmental evidence and a theory of childhood amnesia. (Submitted.)

Polster, M. R., Nadel, L., and Schacter, D. L. (1991). Cognitive neuroscience analyses of memory: a historical perspective. *Journal of Cognitive Neuroscience*, **3**, 95–116.

Rajaram, S. (1991). *The components of recollective experience: remembering and knowing*. Unpublished doctoral dissertation, Rice University, Houston, Texas.

Reingold, E. and Merikle, P. M. (1988). Using direct and indirect measures to study perception without awareness. *Perception and Psychophysics*, **44**, 563–75.

Richardson-Klavehn, A. and Bjork, R. A. (1988). Measures of memory. *Annual Review of Psychology*, **39**, 475–543.

Roediger, H. L., III (1990). Implicit memory: a commentary. *Bulletin of the Psychonomic Society*, **28**, 373–80.

Roorda-Hrdlicková, V., Wolters, G., Bonke, B., and Phaf, R. H. (1990). Unconscious perception during general anaesthesia, demonstrated by an implicit memory task. In *Memory and awareness in anaesthesia* (ed. B. Bonke, W. Fitch, and K. Millar), pp. 151–5. Swets & Zeitlinger, Lisse–Amsterdam.

Schacter, D. L. (1987). Implicit memory: history and current status. *Journal of Experimental Psychology: Learning, Memory, and Cognition*, **13**, 501–18.

Schacter, D. L. (1989). On the relation between memory and consciousness: dissociable interactions and conscious experience. In *Varieties of memory and consciousness: essays in honour of Endel Tulving* (ed. H. L. Roediger III and F. I. M. Craik), pp. 355–89. Erlbaum, Hillsdale, NJ.

Schacter, D. L. (1990). Perceptual representation systems and implicit memory: toward a resolution of the multiple memory systems debate. In *Development and neural bases of higher cognitive functions* (ed. A. Diamond). Annals of the New York Academy of Sciences, Vol. **608**, pp. 543–71.

Schacter, D. L., McAndrews, M. P., and Moscovitch, M. (1988). In *Thought without language* (ed. L. Weiskrantz), pp. 242–78. Clarendon Press, Oxford.

Shallice, T. (1988). *From neuropsychology to mental structure*. Cambridge University Press.

Shallice, T. and Warrington, E. K. (1970). Independent functioning of verbal memory stores: a neuropsychological study. *Quarterly Journal of Experimental Psychology*, **22**, 261–73.

Sherry, D. F. and Schacter, D. L. (1987). The evolution of multiple memory systems. *Psychological Review*, **94**, 439–54.

Shimamura, A. P. (1986). Priming effects in amnesia: evidence for a dissociable memory function. *Quarterly Journal of Experimental Psychology*, **38A**, 619–44.

Smith, M. E. (1992). Neurophysiological manifestations of recollective memory experience during recognition memory judgements. *Journal of Cognitive Neuroscience*, **5**, 1–13.

Squire, L. R. (1987). *Memory and brain*. Oxford University Press, New York.

Squire, L. R. (1992). Declarative and nondeclarative memory: multiple brain systems supporting learning and memory. *Journal of Cognitive Neuroscience*, **4**, 232–43.

Squire, L. R. and Zola-Morgan, S. (1991). The medial temporal lobe memory system. *Science*, **253**, 1380–6.

Talland, G. (1965). *Deranged memory*. Academic Press, New York.

Tulving, E. (1983). *Elements of episodic memory*. Clarendon Press, Oxford.

Tulving, E. (1984). Multiple learning and memory systems. In *Psychology in the 1990s* (ed. K. M. J. Lagerspetz and P. Niemi), pp. 163–84. Elsevier–North Holland, Amsterdam.

Tulving, E. (1985). Memory and consciousness. *Canadian Psychology*, **26**, 1–26.

Tulving, E. (1987). Multiple memory systems and consciousness. *Human Neurobiology*, **6**, 67–80.

Tulving, E. (1992). Concepts of human memory. In *Memory: organization and locus of change* (ed. L. Squire, G. Lynch, N. M. Weinberger, and J. L. McGaugh), pp. 3–32. Oxford University Press, New York.

Tulving, E. and Schacter, D. L. (1990). Priming and human memory systems. *Science*, **247**, 301–6.

Tulving, E. and Schacter, D. L. (1992). Priming and memory systems. In *Neuroscience year: Supplement 2 to the Encyclopedia of neuroscience* (ed. G. Adelman and B. H. Smith), pp. 130–3. Birkhauser Boston, Cambridge, MA.

Tulving, E., Schacter, D. L., and Stark, H. A. (1982). Priming effects in word-fragment completion are independent of recognition memory. *Journal of Experimental Psychology: Learning, Memory and Cognition*, **8**, 352–73.

Tulving, E., Hayman, C. A. G., and Macdonald, C. A. (1991). Long-lasting perceptual priming and semantic learning in amnesia: a case experiment. *Journal of Experimental Psychology: Learning, Memory and Cognition*, **17**, 595–617.

Velmans, M. (1991). Is human information processing conscious? *Behavioral and Brain Sciences*, **14**, 651–726.

Weiskrantz, L. (1987). Neuroanatomy of memory and amnesia: a case for multiple memory systems. *Human Neurobiology*, **6**, 93–105.

Weiskrantz, L. (1990). Problem of learning and memory: one or multiple memory systems? *Philosophical Transactions of the Royal Society*, London, **B329**, 99–108.

IV. Attention, arousal, and stress

Introduction

Andrew Smith

W hen Donald Broadbent joined the Medical Research Council his first job was to carry out research on the effects of noise on performance. This research was not only of practical importance, but had a great influence on the development of his views on attention and cognitive function. The topic of noise and performance will be used to illustrate his contribution to stress research. Following this other areas will be briefly mentioned; and the list clearly shows his wide-ranging influence in this area.

One of the first things that should be pointed out about Donald Broadbent's contribution to noise research is that it has been long-lasting. It has already been mentioned that his first research was carried out in this area, and one of his last publications before retirement was also on noise (Smith and Broadbent 1991). The second point that should be made is that his research was not confined solely to the laboratory, but also involved studies in the workplace (for example Broadbent and Little 1960). His research on noise has become well known to psychologists, and has also influenced researchers from other disciplines. This has been very important, because without his contribution noise research would largely be concerned with the auditory effects of noise (effects on hearing and communication), and possible non-auditory effects on performance efficiency and safety would have been ignored.

As this book is concerned with attention, it is appropriate to outline briefly Donald Broadbent's work on noise and attention. His early studies were largely concerned with sustained attention in noise, and the type of task he used involved detection of an infrequent event, such as the movement of a pointer, or a particular position of a dial. Broadbent (1979) has summarized this work and argued that detrimental effects of noise are found in such tasks when (a) the noise level is over 95 dB, (b) the length of the task is greater than 30 minutes, (c) the signals are hard to see, and (d) the situation is not one that encourages caution. Other studies involved serial self-paced responding, and showed that noise had no effect on the average response time, but increased momentary lapses of attention (seen either as an increase in errors or gaps—occasional long responses).

Later research examined the effects of noise on selectivity in memory and attention, and Broadbent (1971) suggested that in multiple tasks, or tasks with several sub-components, noise leads to increased attention to the dominant or high-probability component at the expense of other features. All of this research used very loud noise (above 95db); but after his move to Oxford he examined the effects of moderate-intensity noise on strategies of performance. The results from these studies again influenced his views on attention, and Broadbent *et al.* (1989) have argued that the attention system is not mechanical and automatic, but is rather a flexible and adaptive system that is influenced by context. Broadbent *et al.* (1989) also suggest that selective effects of changes in state provide good evidence of whether it is important to make distinctions between different attentional mechanisms (for example filtering and pigeon-holing). Once again, this research shows the intimate links between his models of attention and the effects of abnormal states and environments.

In addition to providing a detailed profile of the effects of noise he also compared the effects of many different factors. Indeed, while he was Director of the Applied Psychology Unit research was carried out on the effects of sleep loss, time of day, alcohol, amphetamines and barbiturates, knowledge of results, and fatigue. Again, on the basis of the effects of these different variables on the five-choice serial-response task he argued that one should reject the notion of a unidimensional model of arousal, and replace it with at least a two-level model. Certain factors were assumed to influence the different levels, and the pattern of interactions between different activation states could be predicted from which level they influenced. This model was of great importance in that it led many other researchers to move away from a single arousal theory and to consider other frameworks for studying stress and performance.

Donald Broadbent's research on abnormal states and environments continued at Oxford. New areas, such as the effects of electrical fields and solvents, were studied, and issues such as 'Is a fatigue test possible?' and 'The Psychology of Risk' were addressed. Once again the research was based both in the laboratory and in the field. In the laboratory studies were carried out on anxiety and attentional bias, mood and lexical decisions, cognitive failures and aspects of attention, and the effects and after-effects of diazepam on performance. Field studies were also carried out to assess the relationship between the nature of a person's job and mental health, and on measures of vulnerability to stress.

The above account outlines Donald's personal contribution. His enthusiasm for such studies was greatly supported by his wife Margaret, who carried out a great deal of the data-collection and analysis. In addition to the topics outlined above his influence has been apparent in the research of his students, assistants and collaborators. His individual pieces of research have always been important, and collectively all his experimental studies and theoretical papers have made a massive contribution to our understanding of the effects of stress on performance.

REFERENCES

Broadbent, D. E. (1971) *Decision and stress*. Academic Press, London.

Broadbent, D. E. (1979). Human performance in noise. In *Handbook of noise control* (2nd edn, ed. C. Harris), pp. 2066–85. McGraw-Hill, New York.

Broadbent, D. E. and Little, E. A. J. (1960). Effects of noise reduction in a work situation. *Occupational Psychology*, **34**, 133–40.

Broadbent, D. E., Broadbent, M. H. P., and Jones, J. L. (1989). Time of day as an instrument for the analysis of attention. *European Journal of Cognitive Psychology*, **1**, 69–94.

Smith, A. P. and Broadbent, D. E. (1991). *Non-auditory effects of noise at work: a review of the literature*, HSE Research Report No. 30. HSE, London.

FIFTEEN

Viral illnesses and performance

Andrew Smith

INTRODUCTION

There has been considerable research on the effects of stress on human performance, and Donald Broadbent's contribution to this topic has already been described earlier in this book. The relationship between a person's psychological state and health has also been studied in some detail, and again this has been an area where the Broadbents have been active. For example, Broadbent *et al.* (1984) demonstrated that introverts show a higher degree of infection than extraverts when challenged with a cold-producing virus. In addition, they found that people with colds and high levels of obsessional symptoms produced more nasal secretion than volunteers with colds who had low scores on this scale. More recent studies (for example Cohen *et at.* 1991) have extended the work of the Broadbents and demonstrated that stress increases vulnerability to infection. Given that stress is related to susceptibility to infection, and that stress can influence performance efficiency, it is important to examine what effect infection has on performance. The main aim of the present chapter is to review some recent research on this topic. Two main lines of research will be considered. The first is concerned with the effects of upper respiratory viral infections (colds and influenza), and the second with behavioural problems associated with the post-viral fatigue syndrome.

UPPER RESPIRATORY VIRAL INFECTIONS AND PERFORMANCE

Although none of the research reported here was conducted by Donald Broadbent, it was greatly influenced by his research philosophy. One important feature of much of Donald Broadbent's research was that it originated from practical problems. Respiratory illnesses have a great socio-economic impact, and this means that it is important to conduct research in this area. Psychologists are often unaware of the impact of these diseases, and it is necessary to describe this briefly before considering the effects they have on performance, efficiency, and safety.

Socio-economic effects of respiratory illnesses

The following statistics have been produced by the Influenza Monitoring and Information Bureau, London (see Smith 1988, for more detailed coverage).

It has been estimated that respiratory diseases consume over 20 per cent of GP services. Similarly, hospital expenditure related to such illnesses amounts to over a billion pounds per year. Absenteeism figures also show that illnesses such as influenza have large economic consequences. For example, in the epidemic of 1968 it was estimated that over 26 million working days were lost in Britain due to incapacity from influenza. In economic terms it has been estimated that in the 1974–5 influenza outbreaks over £100 million was lost in productivity and in the amount paid out in sickness benefits. The impact of illnesses such as influenza can be emphasized by comparing it with other disorders. For example, influenza accounts for 10–12 per cent of all absences from work, which is similar to the volume due to musculoskeletal disorders, and about twice that produced by psychiatric disturbances. Colds and influenza are frequent and common (it has been estimated that we have one to three colds a year), and we spend over £100 million per annum on medication for them. In addition, it is possible that such illnesses also have an effect because they impair safety and reduce performance efficiency. Evidence for this last statement is reviewed in the following sections.

Anecdotal reports of the effects of colds and influenza on performance

Tye (1960) summarizes many anecdotal reports of the effects of influenza on safety. He concluded that '. . . influenza IS an invisible factor in many accidents; it DOES cost the nation millions of pounds when the judgement of individuals is "off-peak" due to an approaching influenza attack; and it CAN wipe out in one instant the safety sense in individuals which has taken years to develop'.

It is interesting that Tye's report cites cases where performance was impaired just before the illness started. It is often assumed that if an individual has influenza he or she will retire to bed, and the question of impaired efficiency will not arise. However, this is clearly not going to be the case before the onset of the illness, or in the period when the symptoms have gone. Grant (1972) states that the evidence for influenzal encephalopathy (drowsiness, confusion, etc.) is well-established. He also presents data that shows that post-influenzal effects can occur, and that these can impair the judgements of even highly-skilled professional staff. Grant presents 11 case histories which document post-influenzal impairments. The outstanding features of these case histories are (1) the individuals had been ill with influenza, but no longer had the primary symptoms; (2) the individuals made technical errors of which they were not aware; (3) there was firm rejection of advice from colleagues; and (4) the mistakes could not be attributed to poor motivational or general lack of ability.

These anecdotal reports suggest that influenza may be related to human error. This view is supported by statistics on road accidents, with accidents increasing in years when there are influenza epidemics. This point can be illustrated by considering the data shown in Table 15.1, which covers the years before the 1957 Asian influenza epidemic, 1957, and the following year.

TABLE 15.1. The number of road accidents involving illness in influenza epidemic and non-epidemic years

1954 —	742
1955 —	816
1956 —	779
*1957 —	1024
1958 —	873

* epidemic year

The evidence so far has been concerned mainly with influenza. Many would argue that the effects of the common cold are too slight or transitory to be of any practical importance. Indeed, people are often chided by colleagues for staying off work with a cold. In one of the few reports of the effects of naturally-occurring colds on performance, Heazlett and Whaley (1976) tested 120 13-year olds when they were well. Thirty pupils subsequently developed colds, and were re-tested during their illness. Thirty healthy controls were then randomly selected and re-tested. Three tasks were carried out, and the results showed that reading comprehension was unimpaired by the cold, whereas auditory and visual perception were worse when the children were ill. The tasks used in this study were very crude, yet selective impairments were demonstrated. Such results clearly require replication and extension, yet there has been little attempt to do this. Reasons for this, and the difficulties encountered in this type of study, are discussed in the next section.

Difficulties in studying the effects of upper respiratory virus illnesses

One possible reason for the lack of research in this area is that many people feel they already know about the behavioural effects of these illnesses. Another reason is that it is difficult to study such illnesses. These illnesses are hard to predict, and it is usually unclear whether a virus produced the symptoms, and, if so, which virus was the infecting agent. Indeed, the study of naturally-occurring illnesses only enables one to examine the effects of clinical illnesses. It is possible that sub-clinical infections may influence behaviour, and these can only be identified using the appropriate virological techniques. Similarly, it is also important to obtain objective measures of the symptoms, and this can often be difficult to achieve.

In order to overcome these problems researchers have examined the effects of experimentally-induced infections. Results from this type of study are now reviewed.

Studies of Alluisi and his colleagues

Warm and Alluisi (1967) stated that 'Data concerning the effects of infection on human performance are essentially non-existent.' Following this they conducted studies on the effects of experimentally-induced febrile illnesses (for example rabbit fever—characterized by headache, photophobia, myalgia, and depression) on performance efficiency (Alluisi *et al.* 1971, 1973; Thurmond *et al.* 1971). The results showed quite large performance impairments (in one study those who became ill showed an average drop in performance of about 25 per cent), and these were still observed in convalescence. There was also evidence that certain activities were more impaired than others (active tasks such as arithmetic computation showed a greater decrement than passive tasks such as watchkeeping).

Such illnesses are very severe, and one must ask whether similar effects are observed in more frequent illnesses like influenza and the common cold. This has been examined by studying the effects of experimentally-induced upper respiratory virus infections at the MRC Common Cold Unit, Salisbury.

Effects of experimentally-induced influenza on performance

The routine of the Common Cold Unit has been described in detail many times (for example Beare and Reed 1977; Smith 1990). Most of the trials examined the effects of cold-producing viruses; but a few examined the effects of influenza. Influenza can be a very dangerous illness, and even relatively mild illnesses can be unpleasant. This is one reason why only a few influenza trials were carried out at the Common Cold Unit. Another reason is that influenza vaccines are now reasonably successful, and so the search for new methods of treatment or prevention has been less urgent than in the case of the common cold.

A strong distinction between the effects of influenza and colds is made for the following reasons. First, colds and influenza are caused by different viruses and produce different symptoms. Higgins (1984) characterized a cold as 'an increase in nasal discharge often accompanied by nasal stuffiness, sore throat, coughing and sneezing, but usually lacking the constitutional symptoms of fever, headache, myalgia and malaise which are features of influenza'. In other words, colds and influenza induce different changes in state, and much of the research on stress and performance shows that different states produce different profiles of performance change (see Hockey and Hamilton 1983). Indeed, other studies of the Common Cold Unit suggest that influenza and colds differ. For example, Broadbent et al. (1984) demonstrated that introversion–extraversion was related to susceptibility to infection from cold-producing viruses. Influenza trials did not, however, show such an effect. Smith et al. (1992a) report data on the effects of experimentally-induced upper respiratory viral illnesses on mood. Influenza B illnesses were associated with a general increase in negative affect, whereas the mood changes associated with colds were more specific, and varied depending on which virus was the infecting agent.

Smith et al. (1987a) examined the effect of influenza B illnesses on three tasks. Two of the tasks required subjects to detect and respond quickly to targets appearing at irregular intervals (a variable foreperiod simple reaction-time task and a '5's' detection task—where subjects were shown single digits and had to respond as quickly as possible when they saw a 5). The other task was a pursuit-tracking task designed to test hand–eye co-ordination.

Influenza B illnesses were associated with increased reaction times in both detection tasks, and these results are shown in Fig. 15.1. Analysis of the tracking task showed no significant difference between those with influenza and those who remained healthy.

It should be pointed out that only three subjects with influenza were tested in this study. However, the effects of influenza on the simple reaction-time task were very large (a 57 per cent impairment), and the size of the effect can be emphasized by comparing the effects of known hazards such as alcohol, or having to perform at night. In both of these latter cases simple reaction time is typically impaired in the range of 5–10 per cent.

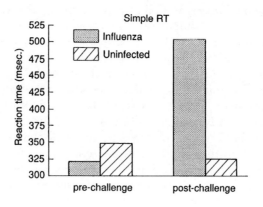

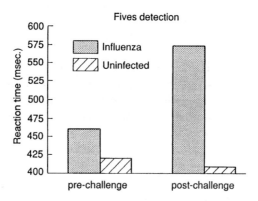

FIG. 15.1. Mean reaction time in the simple reaction-time task and fives-detection task for influenza B and uninfected groups.

Smith *et al.* (1988) used a slightly different methodology to examine the effects of influenza B on a visual-search task with a high memory-load and a pegboard task (another test of hand–eye co-ordination). Subjects carried out these tests at four times of day over the whole trial. Volunteers with influenza B illnesses were impaired on the search task but not the pegboard task. The study also demonstrated that even subclinical infections can impair performance on search tasks, and all these effects are shown in Fig. 15.2.

The results also suggested that performance impairments were present in the incubation period prior to the onset of symptoms.

Influenza is produced by either influenza A or influenza B viruses. Smith *et al.* (1989) investigated the effects of influenza A on perform-

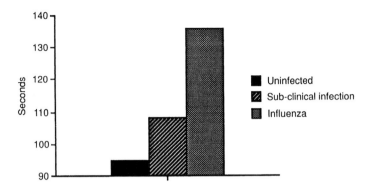

FIG. 15.2. Effects of influenza B and infection on the search and memory task.

ance of two selective attention tasks developed by Broadbent *et al.* (1986). Broadbent *et al.* (1989) have argued that a major distinction in selective attention is between tasks measuring focused attention (where the location of the target is known) and those involving categoric search. This view is supported by several pieces of evidence, one of which is that factors which change the state of the person (for example time of day, noise) have selective effects on measures from the two tasks (Broadbent *et al.* 1989; Smith 1991*a*). On the basis of the early findings on the effects of influenza one would predict that it would impair the search task. This result was obtained by Smith *et al.* (1989), and they found that influenza had no effect on the focused attention task. These effects were obtained for both speed and accuracy.

Unfortunately, no further influenza trials were carried out at the Common Cold Unit. An attempt was made, however, to examine the mechanisms underlying the effects of influenza on performance, and this study is described below.

Interferon alpha and performance

Interferon alpha is an anti-viral peptide mediator that can also have an effect on the CNS. Indeed, injections of interferon often lead to short influenza-like reactions. Smith *et al.* (1991*a*) examined whether the performance deficits observed in influenza were due to interferon or some similar molecule. Volunteers were injected with different doses of interferon or saline, and those given the highest dose (1.5 Mu) developed influenza-like symptoms (increased temperature, fever, drop in alertness, etc.). The data from the simple reaction-time tasks indicated that subjects given the 1.5 Mu injection had slower response times, just like the subjects with real influenza illnesses. This is shown in Fig. 15.3.

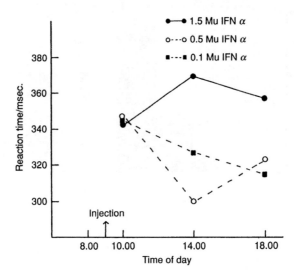

FIG. 15.3. Effects of three doses of interferon alpha on performance of the variable fore-period simple reaction-time task.

However, there were two problems in explaining the effect of influenza on performance in terms of interferon affecting the CNS. First of all, the search and memory task was not impaired by interferon, whereas influenza B infections led to slower performance on this task. Second, performance on the pegboard task was impaired by interferon, yet this was not found in the studies of influenza. These discrepant results could reflect several things. First, there are likely to be many differences between virally-induced interferon production and a single direct challenge. In order to mimic an influenza illness one would need to inject the person with varying amounts of interferon over several days. Second, other peptide mediators (for example interleukin-1) are also produced during influenza, and these could underlie certain influenza-performance effects. In other words, the interferon explanation of the effects of influenza is too simplistic, but the study clearly demonstrated that a cytokine can influence performance. Further studies are now needed to determine which behavioural effects reflect the actions of these different peptide mediators.

EXPERIMENTALLY-INDUCED INFLUENZA AND PERFORMANCE: CONCLUSIONS

These studies of the effects of experimentally-induced influenza confirm the view that has developed from anecdotal reports, namely that influenza may impair performance efficiency. The data also suggest that the effects may not be restricted to individuals who are sympto-matic, which is also consistent with the case histories described earlier. The fact that the impairments were only observed in certain tasks also fits in with recent views of changes of state and performance. However, it may be the case that the absence of more global effects reflects the small numbers of subjects tested or the level of severity of the illnesses (i.e. the methodology only picked up the biggest effects, and more general effects might be apparent in individuals with more severe illnesses).

The effects of naturally-occurring influenza are being studied in our current research programme, and this will show whether the results obtained at the Common Cold Unit generalize to real-life illnesses. By studying a range of activities and by assessing performance in different ways (for example in the laboratory; analysis of accidents; measure-ment of performance at work) we will also be able to assess the func-tional significance of any influenza-induced performance effects. As well as being of practical importance the studies of influenza suggest a new approach to examining the interaction of the brain and the im-mune system. Up to now most studies of psychoneuroimmunology have examined how a person's psychological characteristics influence the immune system and subsequent health. It is clearly also desirable to determine what effects immunological changes have on the brain and behaviour. Indeed, investigation of these processes will not only help us to understand the mechanisms by which influenza affects the CNS, but they will be relevant to many other types of infection and illness.

EXPERIMENTALLY-INDUCED COLDS AND PERFORMANCE

Smith *et al.* (1987*a*) examined the effects of colds that developed following challenge with rhinoviruses and coronaviruses on the three tasks used in the influenza trials. These results are shown in Fig. 15.4, and it can be seen that they are very different from those found with influenza.

Subjects with colds were not impaired on the two detection tasks, but they were worse at the tracking task than those who remained well. Although there was a difference between the colds and no-colds groups, the magnitude of the impairment was not related to symptom severity (amount of nasal secretion).

Smith *et al.* (1988) report data on the effects of colds following challenge with a respiratory syncytial virus on the search task and the

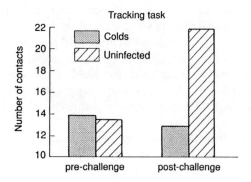

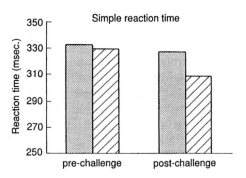

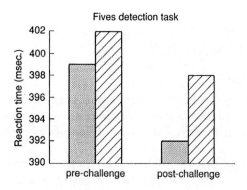

FIG. 15.4. Mean scores for volunteers with colds and uninfected subjects on three performance tasks.

pegboard task. Again, the volunteers with colds showed a different pattern of impairment from those with influenza, and in the case of colds it was the pegboard task which was impaired, not the search and memory task. This is shown in Fig. 15.5.

The direct comparison of colds and influenza involved only a small number of subjects. However, later studies involving a large number of subjects with colds (following challenge with either rhinoviruses, corona-viruses, or respiratory syncytial viruses) have shown that performance of choice reaction time tasks is impaired by colds (Smith *et al.* 1987*b*; Smith *et al.* 1989; Barrow *et al.* 1990; Smith *et al.* 1991*b*). One must now consider what underlies these effects. However, before doing this it is necessary to describe briefly other tasks which show little effect from colds.

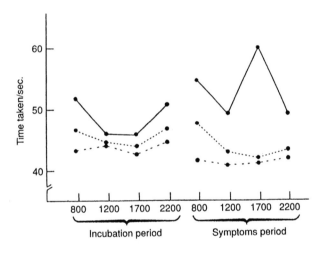

FIG. 15.5. Effects of colds on performance of the pegboard task at four times of day during the incubation and symptoms period.

Smith *et al.* (1990*a*) describes a number of studies which examined the effects of colds on memory. Many aspects of memory, such as the ability to recall a string of digits in order, or to recall a list of words, were unaffected by having a cold. Similarly, there was little evidence that colds impair the ability to reason logically or to retrieve informa-tion from semantic information. Indeed, the only evidence of impair-ments with a cold was found in a study investigating the learning and recall of information in a story. Subjects with a cold had more difficulty following the theme of the story than subjects who remained well, and they tended to focus on detail which was less relevant to the overall theme. In contrast to this, having a cold did not impair retrieval of material learnt before the cold.

Smith *et al.* (1992*b*) examined the effects of infection and illness on pattern sensitivity and contrast sensitivity. These experiments showed little effect from having a cold on the two tasks, but subclinical infections (following challenge with respiratory syncytial virus) led to increased sensitivity to a visually-disturbing figure, and contrast sensitivity improved in volunteers with subclinical coronavirus infections. These studies were also important in that they showed that pre-challenge measures can be used to predict subsequent susceptibility to infection and illness. This confirms an earlier result of Smith *et al.* (1990*b*), and suggests that not only can we look at the effects of infection and illness on performance, but performance when well may be a good indicator of an individual's vulnerability to subsequent infection.

This section has shown that the most robust effects of having a cold are observed in choice reaction time tasks and other tasks involving hand–eye co-ordination. Some of the possible mechanisms underlying these impairments are discussed in the next section.

Mechanisms underlying the effects of colds on psychomotor performance

There is considerable evidence that certain types of viruses (for example enteroviruses) have a strong affinity for muscles, and may produce muscle damage. Similarly, cytokine mediators, such as interferon and interleukin-2, have an effect on the muscles, and can lead to fatigue. Recent evidence (Mier-Jedrzejowicz *et al.* 1988) confirms that upper respiratory tract infections can influence muscle function, and this provides a plausible explanation for some of the effects on performance.

Alternatively, the impairments could reflect changes in sensory stimulation via the trigeminal nerves in the nose. Indeed, Barrow *et al.* (1990) and Smith *et al.* (1991*b*) have shown that sodium nedocromil and zinc gluconate both remove the performance impairments associated with having a cold, and one possible mode of action of these compounds is in terms of changing afferent stimulation.

The results could also reflect non-specific factors associated with having a cold. For example, subjects with a cold might be less motivated in the testing situation. This was investigated by Smith *et al.* (1987*b*), and they found little effect of having a cold on the subjects' motivation.

Finally, the results could be attributed to a 'distraction effect', produced by sneezing or other nasal irritations. The main difficulty for most of these possible explanations is in accounting for the selective performance impairments. There is also evidence that the effects of having a cold are not restricted to the time when the person is symptomatic. This can best be illustrated by considering the 'after-effects' of the common cold on performance.

After-effects of the common cold on performance

Anecdotal evidence suggests that the effects of upper respiratory tract illnesses may persist after the primary symptoms have gone. Alluisi *et al.* (1971) also found that the effects of other infectious diseases continued to convalescence; and the remainder of this chapter is concerned with the behavioural problems associated with the post-viral fatigue syndrome. Smith *et al.* (1989) examined performance during a trial where volunteers stayed at the Common Cold Unit for three weeks, and where it was possible to test them not only when they were symptomatic, but when symptoms were no longer observable. The results showed that subjects who developed a cold were still impaired even when the nasal symptoms had gone. One possible explanation of these effects is that the performance tests are sensitive to the immunological changes that occur after infection. Another possibility is that the subjects continued to perform at a lower level because they had previously performed the task when ill (a transfer effect). Further experimentation is necessary to resolve this issue.

This part of the chapter has shown that Donald Broadbent's empirical approach is of great value in helping us develop preliminary accounts of areas where there are few objective data. The next section shows that it can also clarify areas which have led to great controversy in other disciplines, and this is illustrated by considering recent research on behavioural problems associated with the post-viral fatigue syndrome.

THE POST-VIRAL FATIGUE SYNDROME

The post-viral fatigue syndrome is a chronic persistent or relapsing illness that often follows an acute viral infection, and may occur spasmodically or in epidemics. The main feature of the syndrome is overwhelming fatigue, lasting six months or more. Characteristically the fatigue reduces the patient's level of activity by 50 per cent or more, and is present despite adequate bed rest. Other symptoms such as myalgia and pain in the joints may be present, and the majority of patients also report autonomic symptoms (nocturnal sweating, inter-mittent low-grade fever, hot flushes or feeling cold, fluctuations in body weight, changes in appetite or bowel habit).

Patients with post-viral fatigue often complain of psychiatric symp-toms such as depression and anxiety. Indeed, the paucity of physical signs (as opposed to symptoms) in patients with post-viral fatigue has led some to conclude that psychiatric illness is the cause of fatigue in these patients. Disturbances of concentration and memory are often reported by patients with post-viral fatigue. Indeed, Straus (1988) reported lack of concentration in 90 per cent of his patients, and Smith *et al.* (in press) found that 68 per cent of their sample reported loss of memory.

Smith (1991*b*) and Smith *et al.* (in press) attempted to confirm the subjective reports of cognitive failures in a controlled study using a battery of tests measuring memory, attention, and psychomotor skills. This research also examined whether any impairments reflected de-pression, and compared the effects of chronic fatigue with those ob-served in acute post-viral fatigue and AIDS.

THE SUSSEX STUDY (Smith 1991*b*)

The first study of post-viral fatigue compared 18 patients with nine matched controls. The results are described in detail by Smith (1991*b*), and may be briefly summarized in the following way:

1. There was clear evidence of slower motor performance, increased visual sensitivity, and memory deficits in the post-viral fatigue patients. These results are illustrated in Fig. 15.6.
2. The performance impairments did not reflect a general decline of intellectual function.
3. There was no evidence to suggest that the performance impairments were related to the levels of depression of the patients.

The first question one must ask is whether the effects are replicable. This was examined by repeating the procedure using a sample of post-viral fatigue patients in Glasgow.

THE GLASGOW STUDY (Smith *et al.*, in press)

Fifty-seven post-viral fatigue patients were compared with 19 matched controls. Again, the performance data showed that the post-viral fatigue patients were slower on simple reaction time and five-choice

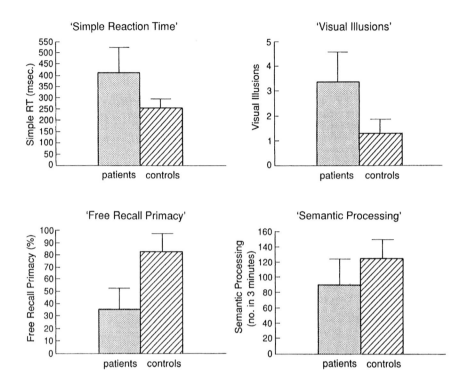

FIG. 15.6. Performance of P = FS subjects and controls on a range of tasks (after
Smith 1991*b*).

serial-response tasks. The patients were also more visually sensitive
than controls, were worse at sustained attention tasks, and were more
easily distracted by irrelevant stimuli. Semantic processing, logical
reasoning, and recognition memory were also impaired, but digit-span
and free-recall performance did not differ significantly from the
controls. In other words, the results generally replicated the findings
obtained in the initial Sussex study. Further analyses were carried out
to determine whether the performance impairments were related to
levels of depression (the post-viral fatigue patients were significantly
more depressed than the controls), but the results showed that none of
the performance impairments could be attributed to psychopathology.

Comparison with acute post-viral effects and AIDS

Smith *et al.* (in preparation, *a*) compared the performance of 25 post-
viral fatigue patients with 32 healthy controls and 10 patients with

acute post-viral fatigue following influenza. Both chronic fatigue (CFS) and influenza groups were impaired compared to the controls, and these results are illustrated in Fig. 15.7.

Smith *et al.* (in preparation, *b*) compared post-viral fatigue patients with three patients with AIDS. The results showed that the impairments were very similar in the two groups. Indeed, the post-viral fatigue patients were more impaired on the psychomotor tasks than were the AIDS patients.

Confirmation from the USA

A recent paper from the USA (Daugherty *et al.* 1991) reports data on the psychological performance of a group of post-viral fatigue patients. The results showed that the most frequent deficits were in attention-concentration, problem-solving, kinaesthetic ability, and verbal memory. These results confirm that the performance deficits observed in the

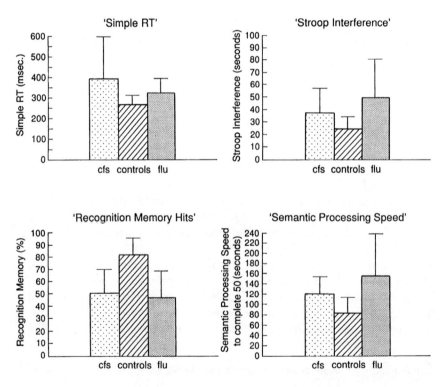

FIG. 15.7. Performance of chronic fatigue influenza, and control groups on a battery of performance tests (Smith *et al.*, in preparation, *b*). Standard deviations shown as bars.

Sussex and Glasgow studies generalize to other groups of patients, and may be detected using different tasks.

Mechanisms involved in the performance impairments seen in post-viral fatigue

While impaired function has been observed in several studies there is little evidence to suggest that it reflects depression. Other possible explanations of the impairments must now be considered. First, the impairments could reflect structural damage to the brain. MRI scans were included in the study of Daugherty *et al.* (1991), and these indicated two patterns of abnormality in the post-viral fatigue patients. The more frequent pattern showed tiny punctate foci with abnormally increased signal intensity in the upper centrum semiovale and bilaterally in the high parasagittal convolutional white-matter tracts. The second, less frequent, pattern showed multiple bilateral patchy areas of abnormally increased signal intensity in the white matter of the brain. These were located in the deep frontal white matter and peripherally in the white matter, and were not periventricular. The authors argue that the observed pattern is consistent with an atypical organic brain syndrome. It is not the same as is seen in Alzheimer's disease, focal head injuries, multiple sclerosis, systemic lupus erythematosus, personality disorders, depression, psychosis, anxiety, or stress. Indeed, the most similar effect is seen in AIDS, which fits in well with our performance data and with the clinical observation that there are marked similarities between the post-viral fatigue syndrome and the early stages of AIDS (with fatigue, myalgia, and severe night sweats being present in both groups of patients).

Alternatively, the effects could be due to an imbalance of neurotransmitter function, possibly as a result of abnormal cytokine activity. The could plausibly explain why acute post-viral effects resemble the more persistent cases. There is some evidence for this mechanism, in that results from a study measuring evoked potentials (Prasher *et al.* 1990) showed that the effects observed with post-viral fatigue patients were very similar to those produced by the cholinergic antagonist scopolamine. Other factors may be responsible for specific impairments. For example, slower motor performance may be a peripheral effect that reflects inactivity or direct damage to the muscles.

OVERALL CONCLUSIONS

The research carried out at the Common Cold Unit demonstrated that the effects of upper respiratory viral infections and illnesses depend on the type of virus and the nature of the activity being carried out. The effects were not restricted to time when the person was symptomatic, but also occurred before and after the illness. These studies, combined with anecdotal evidence and accident data, suggest that further study of the impact of these illnesses is desirable. In these future studies it will not only be essential to use the performance-assessment techniques pioneered by Donald Broadbent, but psychologists will have to collaborate with other disciplines to determine the nature of the infecting agent and to measure symptomatology objectively. It is also important to examine effects in real-life activities, and one should be aware that analogous effects will not necessarily be obtained in such situations. Naturally-occurring upper respiratory illnesses are usually more severe than those studied at the Common Cold Unit, which might lead to greater impairments. However, many real-life tasks are well-practised, and one could suggest that this will make them less vulnerable to changes in state. Other factors which influence performance will also be present, and this means that one must adopt Donald Broadbent's approach of examining combined effects.

As well as determining the functional significance of the effects and after-effects of viral illnesses on performance, it is essential to determine the underlying mechanisms linking infection, the immune system, and the brain and behaviour. In his 1971 book *Decision and stress*, Donald Broadbent discusses the relationship between psychology and physiology. The first point that he raises is that attempts to link physiology and psychology can be disastrous when they are premature. However, he also adds that it would be equally disastrous to go on treating the brain as an abstract entity with no biological reality. Indeed, he concludes that 'behavioural studies and the physiological attack upon the brain must go hand in hand'. It is hoped that the information presented in this chapter illustrates the convergence between neurology, immunology, and human performance. Donald Broadbent's approach fits into the area of psychoneuroimmunology very well, for it not only provides a methodology, but also aims to clarify the mechanisms involved, and, last but not least, stresses that one should also consider the practical significance of observed effects and the impact of these on the health, safety, and well-being of the individual. Indeed, although Donald was not involved in treating patients, I am sure that he would be pleased to know that his techniques will be of value not only in helping us to understand how viral infections influence performance, but also for diagnostic purposes and for assessing the efficacy of treatment of viral infections and of the post-viral fatigue syndrome.

REFERENCES

Alluisi, E. A., Thurmond, J. B., and Coates, G. D. (1971). Behavioral effects of infectious disease: respiratory *Pasteurella tularensis* in man. *Perceptual and Motor Skills*, **32**, 647–88.

Alluisi, E. A., Beisel, W. R., Bartelloni, P. J., and Coates, G. D. (1973). Behavioral effects of tularensis and sandfly fever in man. *Journal of Infectious Diseases*, **128**, 710–17.

Barrow, G. I., Higgins, P. G., Al-Nakib, W., Smith, A. P., Wenham, R. B. M., and Tyrrell, D. A. J. (1990). The effect of intranasal nedocromil sodium on viral upper respiratory tract infections in human volunteers. *Clinical Allergy*, **20**, 45–51.

Beare, A. S. and Reed, S. E. (1977). The study of antiviral compounds in volunteers. In *Chemoprophylaxis and virus infections*, Vol. 2, (ed. J. S. Oxford), pp. 27–55. CRC Press, Cleveland.

Broadbent, D. E. (1971). *Decision and stress*. Academic, London.

Broadbent, D. E., Broadbent, M. H. P., Phillpotts, R., and Wallace, J. (1984). Some further studies on the prediction of experimental colds in volunteers by psychological factors. *Journal of Psychosomatic Research*, **28**, 511–23.

Broadbent, D. E., Broadbent, M. H. P., and Jones, J. L. (1986). Performance correlates of self-reported cognitive failure and of obsessionality. *British Journal of Clinical Psychology*, **25**, 285–99.

Broadbent, D. E., Broadbent, M. H. P., and Jones, J. L. (1989). Time of day as an instrument for the analysis of attention. *European Journal of Cognitive Psychology*, **1**, 69–94.

Cohen, S., Tyrrell, D. A. J., and Smith, A. P. (1991). Psychological stress in humans and susceptibility to the common cold. *New England Journal of Medicine*, **325**, 606–12.

Daugherty, S. A., Henry, B. E., Peterson, D. L., Swarts, R. L., Bastien, S., and Thomas, R. S. (1991). Chronic fatigue syndrome in Northern Nevada. *Reviews of Infectious Diseases*, **13**, 39–44.

Grant, J. (1972). Post-influenzal judgement deflection among scientific personnel. *Asian Journal of Medicine*, **8**, 535–9.

Heazlett, M. and Whaley, R. F. (1976). The common cold: its effect on perceptual ability and reading comprehension among pupils of a seventh grade class. *The Journal of School Health*, **46**, 145–7.

Higgins, P. G. (1984). The common cold. *International Medicine*, **4**, 15–17.

Hockey, R. and Hamilton, P. (1983). The cognitive patterning of stress states. In *Stress and fatigue in human performance* (ed. G. R. J. Hockey), pp. 331–63. Wiley, Chichester.

Mier-Jedrzejowicz, A., Brophy, C., and Green, M. (1988). Respiratory muscle weakness during upper respiratory tract infections. *American Review of Respiratory Disease*, **138**, 5–7.

Prasher, D., Smith, A., and Findley, L. (1990). Sensory and cognitive event-related potentials in myalgic encephalomyelitis. *Journal of Neurology, Neurosurgery and Psychiatry*, **53**, 247–53.

Smith, A. P. (1988). The socioeconomic and behavioural effects of influenza. In *Influenza: strategies for prevention* (ed. C. Wood), pp. 46–52. Royal Society of Medicine, London.

Smith, A. P. (1990). Respiratory virus infection and performance. *Philosophical Transactions of the Royal Society of London*, **B327**, 519–28.

Smith, A. P. (1991*a*). Noise and aspects of attention. *British Journal of Psychology*, **82**, 313–24.

Smith, A. P. (1991*b*). Cognitive changes in myalgic encephalomyelitis. In *Post-viral fatigue syndrome (M.E.)* (ed. R. Jenkins and J. Mowbray), pp. 179–94. Wiley, Chichester.

Smith, A. P., Tyrrell, D. A. J., Coyle, K. B., and Willman, J. S. (1987*a*). Selective effects of minor illnesses on human performance. *British Journal of Psychology*, **78**, 183–8.

Smith, A. P., Tyrrell, D. A. J., Al-Nakib, W., Coyle, K. B., Donovan, C. B., Higgins, P. G., and Willman, J. S. (1987*b*). Effects of experimentally-induced respiratory virus infections on psychomotor performance. *Neuropsychobiology*, **18**, 144–8.

Smith, A. P., Tyrrell, D. A. J., Al-Nakib, W., Coyle, K. B., Donovan, C. B., Higgins, P. G., and Willman, J. S. (1988). The effects of experimentally-induced respiratory virus infections on performance. *Psychological Medicine*, **18**, 65–71.

Smith, A. P., Tyrrell, D. A. J., Al-Nakib, W., Barrow, G. I., Higgins, P. G., Leekam, S., and Trickett, S. (1989). Effects and after-effects of the common cold and influenza on human performance. *Neuropsychobiology*, **21**, 90–3.

Smith, A. P., Tyrrell, D. A. J., Barrow, G. I., Coyle, K. B., Higgins, P. G., Trickett, S., and Willman, J. S. (1990*a*). Effects of experimentally-induced colds on aspects of memory. *Perceptual and Motor Skills*, **71**, 1207–15.

Smith, A. P., Tyrrell, D. A. J., Coyle, K. B., Higgins, P. G., and Willman, J. S. (1990*b*). Individual differences in susceptibility to infection and illness following respiratory virus challenge. *Psychology and Health*, **4**, 201–11.

Smith, A. P., Tyrrell, D. A. J., Coyle, K. B., and Higgins, P. G. (1991*a*). Effects and after-effects of interferon alpha on human performance, mood and physiological function. *Journal of Psychopharmacology*, **5**, 243–50.

Smith, A. P., Tyrrell, D. A. J., Al-Nakib, W., Barrow, G. I., Higgins, P. G., and Wenham, R. (1991*b*). The effects of zinc gluconate and nedocromil sodium on performance deficits produced by the common cold. *Journal of Psychopharmacology*, **5**, 251–4.

Smith, A. P., Tyrrell, D. A. J., Barrow, G. I., Higgins, P., Willman, J. S., Bull, S., Coyle, K. B., and Trickett, S. (1992*a*). Mood and experimentally-induced respiratory virus infections. *Psychology and Health*, **6**, 205–12.

Smith, A. P., Tyrrell, D. A. J., Barrow, G. I., Higgins, P. G., Bull, S., Trickett, S., and Wilkins, A. J. (1992*b*). The common cold, pattern sensitivity and contrast sensitivity. *Psychological Medicine*, **22**, 487–94.

Smith, A. P., Behan, P. O., Bell, W., Millar, K., and Bakheit, M. (In press). Behavioural problems associated with the post-viral fatigue syndrome. *British Journal of Psychology*.

Smith, A. P., Smith, B. A., Watkins, J., and Flynn, R. Chronic fatigue syndrome, influenza and performance. (In preparation, *a*.)

Smith, A. P., Smith, B. A., Armer, L., Christmas, L., Simpson, P., and Wesnes, K. Performance deficits associated with HIV infection and the chronic fatigue syndrome. (In preparation, *b*.)

Straus, S. (1988). The chronic mononucleosis syndrome. *Journal of Infectious Diseases*, **157**, 405–12.

Thurmond, J. B., Alluisi, E. A., and Coates, G. D. (1971). An extended study of the behavioral effects of respiratory *Pasteurella tularensis* in man. *Perceptual and Motor Skills*, **33**, 439–54.

Tye, J. (1960). *The invisible factor—an inquiry into the relationship between influenza and accidents*. British Safety Council, London.

Warm, J. S. and Alluisi, E. A. (1967). Behavioral reactions to infections: review of the psychological literature. *Perceptual and Motor Skills*, **24**, 755–83.

SIXTEEN

Cognitive–energetical control mechanisms in the management of work demands and psychological health

G. Robert J. Hockey

INTRODUCTION

Concern over the impact of work on the health of employees has shifted in its primary focus over the past two decades, from the physical to the psychological environment. Recent research on occupational stress has been characterized, in particular, by the assessment of mental demands and personal control in the workplace. While it is now generally accepted that these factors play a significant role in the development of job-related ill-health, the processes through which these changes occur have rarely been examined. Apart from the appeal to relatively undisciplined concepts such as 'overload' and 'stress', it is quite unclear why exposure of normal people to moderate environmental demands (in terms of the broader biological spectrum of adaptive behaviour) should give rise to widespread organic or psychological dysfunction. In this chapter I argue that a considerable part of this problem can be accounted for in terms of a failure of regulatory processes underlying environmental management, through inappropriate emphasis on cognitively-centred work goals. The patterning of demand, and its relationship to dysfunction, are examined through a control model of the regulatory process, in which mismanagement may take several alternative forms. These are argued to result in different patterns of activation of emotional and affective reactions, as well as to changes in the relative effectiveness of cognitive and emotional goal-oriented actions.

To the extent that it has any merit, the present approach owes a great deal to the inspirational work of Donald Broadbent, in particular to his oft-stated emphasis on the importance of combining good laboratory-based technique and theoretical foundations with imaginative analysis of field-based issues and observations. Donald showed us that such an approach was not only possible, but actually necessary, if we are to make any real progress with complex problems, such as fatigue, occupational health, and job design (for example Broadbent 1979, 1985).

I would argue, along such lines, that the study of work in relation to psychological health is poorly served by the common practice of separating effects on the effectiveness of work from those concerning affective and organic outcomes. The approach adopted here takes the view that the way in which people attempt to manage their work will affect both their overt effectiveness and their well-being, by virtue of the energetic consequences of work actions.

MODELS OF THE WORK–HEALTH RELATIONSHIP

Currently accepted accounts of the work–health relationship (for example Caplan *et al.* 1975; Karasek 1979) are based largely on epidemiological analyses of the pattern of health symptoms in relation to normative features of work environments. The series of studies by Karasek and his Swedish co-workers (for example Karasek *et al.* 1988) has demonstrated the value of separating the influences of work demands and personal control (skill discretion or autonomy). This work has demonstrated considerable effects of these factors on the incidence of coronary heart disease (CHD), as well as other health indices such as satisfaction and mental health, across a range of occupations. Karasek's work has broadly supported a 'vulnerability' model of stress and disease, in which the 'protective' effects of controllability are most pronounced at high levels of demand. More recent evidence from field studies and meta-analyses has, however, argued against the implied moderating (interactive) relationship between demands and control, which may be an artefact of the use of cross-sectional data, or of the use of inappropriate tests for interaction effects in regression analyses (for example Ganster 1989; Spector 1986). A current study of our own on secretarial staff, employing both within- and between-subject analyses on longitudinal data, also finds no evidence of interactive effects, though both demands and control have marked influences on health outcome (Hockey *et al.*, in preparation).

I shall return to the question of control later, in the context of individual coping style. It is likely that the effect of control opportunities on well-being (as on performance) will depend critically on individual difference variables, such as need for control and perception of coping resources (for example Frese 1987; Parkes *et al.* 1990). The observed form of the relationship between demands and control may well differ across work contexts and personality, as well as measured ranges of the two variables in particular studies. Whatever the case, the two factors of demands and control provide a firm starting-point for an analysis of the impact of work on psychological health. The role of cognition in this relationship is, however, usually neglected, or attributed loosely to 'appraisal' (Lazarus 1966). Yet cognitive processes are central to both the action-level response to demands, and the management of demand through the planning and scheduling of tasks. Workload cannot be defined independently of individual capacity or cognitive skill (Gopher and Donchin 1986). Equally, personal control is a characteristic not only of the work environment, but of individual goal-management needs and skills and coping strategies (see for example Frese 1987). Understanding the role of individual cognition in the work–health relationship is essential to a process account of ill-health and its aetiology.

COMPENSATORY CONTROL IN PROTECTING WORK EFFECTIVENESS UNDER STRESS

One of the most remarkable aspects of the impact of work stress on human beings is how difficult it is to find examples of serious degradation in their performance. This is true in both laboratory and field studies, where impairments as high as 10 per cent are quite rare. Kahneman (1971) attributed this stability of performance to the effectiveness of attentional control in maintaining the dominance of current action plans, an insight which has been largely overlooked in later work. This notion, together with a concern for the factors which determine the level and form of control, provides the basis for a strategy-based self-regulating model of work management (Hockey 1986a; Hockey et al. 1989). Performance may be described as being 'protected' from environmental disturbance, through the maintained priority of strong work-oriented goals. As Kahneman observed, however, in his influential later monograph (Kahneman 1973), such protection is normally achieved at the expense of decreased stability in other (energetical) systems. These 'costs' are likely to be well within acceptable limits of functioning under normal circumstances, and so have no implications for health. In more extreme cases, and where control is extended for long periods, the effects of performance protection may carry over into longer-term affective states and, in some cases, into eventual organic damage.

Hockey (1979, 1986a; Hockey and Hamilton 1983) has summarized the findings from laboratory studies on performance under the influence of environmental stressors such as loud noise, heat, sleep loss, workload, and drugs. Two general conclusions emerge. First, where impairment is observed, somewhat specific kinds of change appears to be associated with different stressors (expressed in terms of patterns of decrement across different cognitive components). Second, all stressors have an additional common effect on performance, through a weakening of the effectiveness of a general-purpose attentional control system (for example, following a period of sustained work, when most effects are more pronounced).

As I have already noted, such effects are generally rather small in magnitude (though usually detectable with suitably-designed tasks). In terms of the present approach, performance may be described as being protected from (serious) disruption, at the expense of increased costs for other, currently less relevant, aspects of the human-task system. These include affective states, emotional stability, and autonomic and endocrine activation, as well as low-priority behavioural activity. This protection strategy is generally more successful, and more consistent, in operational work contexts than in laboratory tasks, since the goals and values associated with effective work activity are much stronger. One consequence of this is that there is a danger of underestimating the impact of particular work stressors on the basis of an apparent lack of disruption of work skills. The stronger operation of performance protection in real-life work contexts implies a stronger impact on affective and psychophysiological costs. In passing, it should be emphasized that a failure to find effects on well-being should not be taken as evidence that output or quality is unimpaired. Where the job allows it, reduced work goals may be adopted as a strategy for maintaining an acceptable level of well-being.

PATTERNS OF DEGRADATION UNDER STRESS AND HIGH WORKLOAD

The operation of the performance-protection strategy makes it difficult to demonstrate overt decrements in primary task performance. Several different patterns of indirect degradation may, however, be identified, in both laboratory and field studies. Table 16.1 summarizes three general patterns of indirect degradation, in addition to impairment of primary activities (Type 1). These are referred to as compensatory costs; strategic adjustments; and fatigue after-effects. Such patterns of decrement have not been systematically explored from the point of view of a single model of regulatory control, though each is well-known in more specific areas of research.

Type 1: Primary task decrement. As discussed above, decrements on primary tasks (often the only task) are rare, though they may be found under specially-designed circumstances. Broadbent recognized this problem more than thirty years ago (for example Broadbent 1957). His

TABLE 16.1. Patterns of indirect performance degradation under stress and high workload

Type	Characteristics
1 Primary decrement	direct impairment of primary task parameters
2 Compensatory costs	increases in sympathetic activation and/or negative affect during the task
3 Strategy adjustment	changes towards the use of low-effort strategies or reduced use of working memory during the task
4 Fatigue after-effects	observed preference for low-effort strategies on probe test following sustained work

insistence on the need for 'sensitive tasks' (typically vigilance or self-paced serial reaction) in the study of noise effects, was aimed at reducing the effectiveness of compensatory control and allowing decrements to be detected. Sensitive tests were long, uninterrupted, and unpredictable, and slippages of control were measured by the use of more sophisticated measures of response latency and error. Such effects have been reviewed at length elsewhere (for example Broadbent 1971; Hockey 1986a), and are not discussed further here. Such techniques are, in any case, not normally applicable in field settings, making it even more difficult to assess effects of stressors on work effectiveness. The use of primary task performance is rarely sufficient in such contexts, though it is a necessary component of the assessment process.

Type 2: Compensatory costs. The absence of impairment in primary task effectiveness may be accompanied by an increase in compensatory 'costs' (for example, sympathetic activation and/or increased reports of subjective effort or strain). This pattern of compensatory control is observed, for example, in studies by Lundberg and Frankenhaeuser (1978), and Wilkinson (1962), both using mental-arithmetic tasks. Lundberg found that decrements under noise were not accompanied by increases in catecholamines or subjective effort, while, in conditions where no decrement was found, both indices of activation were markedly increased. In Wilkinson's well-known study of sleep deprivation, decrement was least in those subjects who showed the most pronounced increase in muscle tension during the stress state. In both cases the data suggest a trade-off between control effort (with its associated costs) and the achieved level of effectiveness on the primary task.

A search through the literature makes it clear that very few studies have been analysed in this way, and almost none by design. A recent field study (Rissler and Jacobson 1987) also demonstrates this compensatory pattern of degradation. They found an increase in both adrenaline and cognitive effort in operators who managed to maintain adequate performance levels during the implementation of a new computer system, involving intense time-pressure and extensive overtime.

Type 3: Strategic adjustment. Impairment may also be detected through suitably designed performance-assessment procedures (multi-component tasks, examination of strategic shifts within the overall task goals). This may be seen to take the form of a shift towards the deployment of less effortful task strategies (rescheduling or redefining task requirements), without reducing the level of primary task goals (Bainbridge 1974). Thus effects may be observed on secondary tasks (Eysenck 1982), particularly where there are clear gradients of priority. The widespread phenomenon of attentional narrowing, or increased selectivity (Baddeley 1972; Broadbent 1971; Hockey 1979) may be seen as a general strategy for reducing attentional demands under stressful conditions or prolonged high-demand work. It has the effect of retaining performance criteria on high-priority task requirements at the expense of a reduced response to secondary elements. Narrowing is also observed in complex real-life contexts, such as the Cambridge Cockpit flying simulator (Bartlett 1943) and deep-sea diving (Weltman *et al.* 1971). As Baddeley (1972) notes, such effects may be even more common in such situations because of the state of anxiety they give rise to.

Narrowed attention is interpreted here as a strategic adjustment, rather than an automatic consequence of stress. Perhaps more obvious examples of changes of strategy are provided by studies showing changes in work patterns under increased workload. Sperandio (1971) found that air-traffic controllers changed from using multiple, individually-based routing procedures to a fixed, routinized procedure for all contacts when the number of aircraft increased beyond their normal load. Strategy changes such as these are likely to serve the goal of protecting limited general-purpose resources such as working memory or supervisory-level control.

Type 4: Fatigue after-effects of sustained work. Where information on the costs and patterning of operational performance are not available, breakdown may sometimes be detected in the form of after-effects on probe tasks administered after the work session (fatigue). Early studies of fatigue (for example Chiles 1955) failed to find any market deficit in post-work tests (typically tracking or RT) from extended periods (around 60 hours) of uninterrupted work. In addition to pointing out the various methodological shortcomings of such studies, Holding

(1983) has argued that fatigue tests need to be sensitive to a regulatory shift towards low-effort work preferences, for example by providing different (effort-related) modes of task execution. Shingledecker and Holding (1974) found marked after-effects on the COPE task, which enabled subjects to solve fault-finding problems with a choice of effort (and probability of success). Fatigued subjects made more 'risky' (low-effort) choices in the fault-finding task, as well as showing higher levels of subjective fatigue. After-effects have also been demonstrated from exposure to stressors, such as noise (Broadbent 1979). Hockey and Wiethoff have recently developed a self-paced, complex decision-making task which allows subjects to refresh information in working memory if they wish. This task has been used to assess fatigue in junior hospital doctors (Hockey and Wiethoff 1990), and has proved sensitive to effects of natural variations in workload, as well as to the sleep-based fatigue associated with extended weekend shifts (Wiethoff and Hockey, in preparation).

There are clear grounds, then, for believing that the effects of stressors are moderated through optional regulatory activity on the part of individuals. The pattern of degradation observed under difficult work conditions is, on this view, the outcome of such control activity, as manifested in the various components of the whole system. This includes both cognitive and energetic aspects of behaviour. The following section presents a model of this control process. It is meant to serve both as a framework for interpreting the effects on performance, and as a basis for developing a process account of the impact of work management on psychological well-being.

A CONTROL MODEL OF DEMAND-MANAGEMENT

The control model presented here was developed initially from a consideration of the pattern of response to stress and work demands within the human-performance literature (Hockey and Hamilton 1983; Hockey 1986a). The model follows various other treatments (Trumbell and Appley 1986; Kahneman 1973; McGrath 1976) in defining stress broadly in terms of the disruption of the equilibrium of the cognitive/environmental system by external factors. It goes further, however, in specifying the form of the mechanism underlying the regulation of stress.

The present model also builds on the foundations of Donald Broadbent's two-level model, introduced in *Decision and stress* to account for the observed complexities of interactions between stressors (Broadbent

1971, p. 441). Broadbent suggested that effects of stressors such as noise and sleep loss could be prevented by control in an upper-level mechanism '. . . monitoring and altering the parameters of the low level in order to maintain constant performance' (p. 441). Conditions which weakened this upper-level control (for example alcohol, extraversion, time on task) would allow stressor effects to be more readily observed. The two-level nature of the control mechanism had a basis in the balance of cholinergic and adrenergic activity. This was somewhat speculative at the time of *Decision and stress*, though Robbins (1986) has recently related the model successfully to current developments in psychopharmacology. This aspect of the control mechanism is undoubtedly a major growth-point in the explanation of energetical constructs such as effort, fatigue, and control costs. It is a pertinent comment on the development of theory in the stress/performance field as a whole, however, that the remarkable insights afforded by Broadbent's model have remained largely neglected in research on other aspects of stress and performance over the past twenty years.

The approach offered here differs from other control models, including Broadbent's, in its emphasis on the mechanism underlying the selection of alternative modes of coping activity. We have already seen that a stress state arising from a high level of demands may be resolved in one of a number of ways, having different consequences for performance and well-being. What cognitive and energetical processes are involved in this adaptive demand-management system?

As in all control models, behaviour is maintained at a stable level by comparison of goal-based internal reference values (targets or standards) with negative feedback from current actions. The feedback is used as the 'error signal' for modifying the behaviour until the discrepancy is resolved. A disruption of equilibrium may be brought about either by unexpected surges in external environmental sources (demands, stressors) or a fall in internal resources (for example, through fatigue or illness). The essential control elements of this model are illustrated in simplified form in Fig. 16.1.

Two main control loops are represented: A and B. Loop A may be thought of as the 'routine' control system for maintaining behavioural stability. An 'action monitor' (comparator) compares feedback from current cognitive activity with the target state, and activates familiar (automatic) adjustments which modify behaviour until it matches the target. It is assumed that the (frequent) discrepancies within the normal range are managed through the use of low-cost, routine corrections in output. In simple terms, the system changes its speed, timing, memory-use, and so on until its performance is stabilized within acceptable limits.

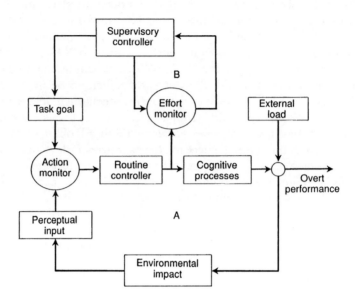

FIG. 16.1. A two-level model of control and stress regulation. See text for explanation.

In this analysis effort has two distinct roles, depending on which of two ranges is experienced. First, the detection of low-level increases in effort signals increasing failure of routine control, and results in a shift of control level (from routine to supervisory). Second, the perception of change at high levels of effort is a key element in the choice of control mode.

Shifts of control level

When the discrepancy is high, routine regulation may be inadequate to resolve the dysregulation, and a more active (high-level) controlled response is needed, as in loop (B)—a shift from automatic to controlled processing. The involvement of this supervisory controller is postulated to be activated by a sensed increase in effort requirements of the low-level regulatory mechanism. The model indicates that regulation in the main loop may proceed unless the indicated (low) level of regulatory effort exceeds the set point, when the high-level system is alerted.

The involvement of high-level control may result in various changes of regulatory activity: (1) effort levels may be overridden by the supervisory system, permitting control to proceed with an increased 'effort budget'; (2) the goal state may be modified (for example, by reducing the output requirements, or adopting different strategies demanding less effort), or disengaged completely (rare in work contexts). The system may also be left essentially unchanged, with the action discrepancy unresolved and effort high. Let us consider the implications of these various control modes.

Shifts of control mode

In Fig. 16.1 the two types of control activity in loop B are referred to as 'direct' and 'indirect' control. Direct control achieves maintenance of performance goals at the expense of increased effort (in general terms a 'trying harder' reaction). In this case the discrepancy sensed by the action monitor is resolved through a recruitment of additional (effort-sensitive) resources, without changing the configuration of the cognitive system. Such a strategy is effortful, since it involves an increased level of active cognitive work (Kahneman 1973). We have argued previously (Hamilton *et al.* 1977; Hockey 1986*b*) that direct (active) regulatory activity is based on the deployment of high-level executive (supervisory) function. Although the use of such a system is normal for many cognitive activities (see, for example, Baddeley and Hitch 1974), the sustained involvement of high-level control in the active regulation of stress may be costly in terms of affective and psychophysiological states (see below). Continued cognitive strain, through its effects on central control resources, may, in fact, be regarded as the primary source of fatigue from mental work (Hockey *et al.* 1989).

An alternative route to state resolution is through adoption of a form of 'indirect' control. In this case the discrepancy is resolved through a downwards adjustment of central motivational priorities (the target state), in order to meet available resources (in control theory terms, by a change in the reference signal or standard). As implied above, however, the selection of this low-effort regulation strategy may take several forms. In general terms a shift to indirect control may be seen in terms of a reassessment of the costs and benefits of different goal-action plans, resulting, in the extreme case, in a shift away from high-cost performance-oriented goals, in the direction of low-cost goals (for example, emphasizing personal comfort or emotional stability). Performance goals are rarely likely to be abandoned, however. Rather, they are pursued with reduced priority (Schonpflug 1983), or with modified specification requiring less use of high-cost processes such as working memory (Hamilton *et al.* 1977). This reconfiguration of the task plan, to minimize the use of high-effort operations, may only be available in particular kinds of task, though it will usually result in a reduced level of effectiveness.

In both forms of adjustment, reinstatement of equilibrium is regarded as resolving the stress state, though it may re-emerge periodically as control slips (of resource mobilization, or of goal-setting). This is particularly likely in the case of direct control, since stress may only be prevented by a maintenance of effort. The argument is not circular. A temporary reduction of effort (for example, in response to a developing state of fatigue) may result in the reappearance of the stress state. In many cases the individual may not be able to react by further direct control, yet may be unwilling to relinquish task goals. This 'steady-state error' may give rise to sustained (or chronic) stress, with a pattern of reaction that may be seen to be the worst of both worlds; reduced effectiveness of task performance, together with high effort, anxiety associated with the threat to work goals, and a perceived lack of control over external events. A further pattern of stress-regulation may involve shifting between the two extremes represented by the 'pure' types illustrated here, in response to fluctuations of both external load and internal resources (for example, phasic fatigue states, or circadian phases of alertness or sleep needs).

Effort and strain in direct control

Effort is implicated in this account through the need to account for changes in the level and mode of control when difficulties are encountered in behavioural regulation. The recent analysis by Carver and Scheier (1990) also attempts to do this, though it differs from the present approach in the mechanism underlying these changes. A 'meta-monitoring' loop is thought to signal the rate of progress towards the action goal. When progress is slower than expected this process gives rise to generalized negative affect, which causes a reassessment of cost–benefit and outcome expectancies, and a shift away from the current goal. Carver and Scheier are concerned mainly with the pursuit of complex personal and social goals over long periods of time.

The present conceptualization of an 'effort monitor' to carry out this 'control-level shift' function emphasizes the stronger involvement of energetic processes in real-time task performance, carried out over quite brief periods. Although this may be a limiting case of the more general model suggested by Carver and Scheier, it seems unlikely that subjective effort is nothing more than the output of a 'slow progress' signal. More likely is the possibility that there are various metamonitoring processes of this kind, subserving different functions in relation to long-term, medium-term, and short-term goals. The emphasis here is on control over relatively short time-periods, requiring the effective mobilization of cognitive resources to meet current task demands.

The role of effort in the selection of the mode of control (the trade-off between effectiveness and costs) is quite separate from this metamonitoring function, and may be related to individual differences in the response to strain. Cognitive strain refers to the maintenance of a high level of goal-related effort in response to increased task or environmental load, and is characterized by anxiety, distress, sympathetic activation, and increased adrenocortical activity (Frankenhaeuser 1986). High-effort regulation, by itself, may not necessarily be an aversive state, of course, so long as controllability is high (Frankenhaeuser 1986). Where options for control are limited, high-effort states may not be sustained indefinitely without significant costs: effort is widely recognized to be an aversive state. Even in purely voluntary activities, such as sport, fatigue-like after-effects of sustained effort are common, though without the negative affect associated with work-based fatigue. Controllability is clearly much lower in work than at play, and the requirement for continued executive operation much greater.

COPING AND PSYCHOLOGICAL HEALTH

The buffering effect of controllability on long-term strain consequences (ill-health, reduced well-being, impaired job satisfaction) are well-established from cross-sectional studies of work populations (for example Karasek 1979), though its role in the management of performance demands by individuals is less clear. One implication is that strain may be minimized through the availability of a greater range of information-processing options, while still allowing for the maintenance of performance goals. There is also the possibility, however, of highly controllable work environments' facilitating a relaxation of goal standards, resulting in reduced effectiveness. Some individuals may take one route, some the other.

Control modes and coping strategies

The regulatory model outlined above has direct implications for the broader study of coping strategies. Lazarus and Folkman (1984) make the important distinction between problem-focused and emotion-focused goals of coping acts. Problem-focused (PF) coping (for example, 'redoubling efforts to overcome the problem') is aimed at preserving effective orientation towards external cognitive goals (tasks, work-based demands). Emotion-focused (EF) activity, on the other hand, is concerned with the preservation of personal stability and well-being ('trying not to let it upset you'). Direct and indirect regulatory modes may, superficially at least, be seen as strategies underlying the implementation of PF and EF coping, respectively. This simple mapping is misleading, however. In Lazarus' framework PF and EF refer to the primary targets of the coping behaviour; operational effectiveness (performance) or emotional stability. The choice of direct or indirect strategy is logically independent of this distinction. We may see this more clearly if we broaden our perspective to include emotional as well as cognitive states. If the 'task' currently occupying us is 'to be happy' or 'to stay calm', any behaviour directed towards the acquisition of those goals must be considered, in Lazarus' terms, EF coping. Yet it is apparent that the same distinctions in regulatory modes apply as is the case with cognitive goals. Discrepancies resulting from social threat or perceived loss, for example, may be resolved either through direct or through indirect action. Happiness and calm may be achieved through sustained effort (in the sense of active management of internal state), as well as through attenuation of the source of the problem through reduced engagement with the frustrated goal.

The choice of coping strategy is usually attributed to situational differences (particularly in terms of the perception of control: Folkman *et al.* 1979). It may, however, also be influenced by long-term (dispositional) influences, on the one hand (coping style), and short-term energetical state, on the other.

Whether a particular strategy is appropriate (effective) in a stress situation is likely to be determined both by the individual's familiarity with its use (coping skill) and the controllability of the situation. Thus, an active, problem-focused approach to an increase in demand (work harder, for longer, to get the work completed), is appropriate only if (1) the situation is changeable, (2) increased effort will resolve the difficulty (the task is resource-limited), and (3) a further demand on energetical resources may be tolerated. Such a strategy may, nevertheless, be more likely to be adopted by individuals having an active, problem-focused style, with resulting costs when the above conditions are not met (the type A classification may be considered an example of this).

The dynamics of coping outcomes may only be understood by recognizing the intrinsic costs of coping acts (Schonpflug 1983). If these are too high for the perceived gain (of mastery of the environment), long-term preferences may be sacrificed in favour of short-term emotional stability and reduced strain. This cost–benefit aspect of coping is recognized most clearly in the concept of coping 'efficiency', developed within German action theory (for example Schonpflug 1983). On this model coping acts may be predicted on the basis of comparisons of benefit–cost comparisons, though such analyses are difficult to carry out in practice.

To return, however, to the main theme of this paper, it is clear that cognitive-based performance is but one of the goals which may be threatened by stress. Researchers interested primarily in the study of performance under stress need to be mindful of the relativity of what constitute appropriate criteria for effectiveness. The (arbitrary, temporary) goals associated with performance of a cognitive task may, in these terms, compare unfavourably with the powerful, biologically-centred goals (such as attachment, or survival) addressed by animal stress models (see, for example, Levine 1980), or the long-term, person-centred goals examined by research on personality and social stress (Carver and Scheier 1982; Lazarus 1976). Real-life work goals lie somewhere in between, though are probably closer to the latter. Maintaining performance under stress may pose more serious difficulties, in terms of the management of demands, than the maintenance of more personally-relevant activities, because of competition from stronger goals.

Implications for work and health

It is clear from what has gone before that the management of goals is assumed to be central to the development of different patterns of well-being at work. These may be expressed in terms of macro-level trade-off functions. When externally-derived work goals are protected in the face of increasing demands, work effectiveness is maintained at the expense of an increased risk to psychological health. A bias towards personal (non-work) goals, on the other hand, protects emotional stability at the expense of a reduction in effectiveness. There do not seem to be any direct data relating to this hypothesis, though elements of an appropriate research agenda are readily formulated. A particularly interesting question is whether such differences are discernible only on an inter-individual basis (i.e. as enduring coping styles), or also as variable strategies within individuals exposed to different work contexts. This would, for example, have major implications for the efficacy of alternative proposed countermeasures to occupational stress.

Two broad solutions to work stress are recognized: (1) changes in work organization, in order to reduce the incidence of stress at source; and (2) training in coping skills, in order to manage it better. Both are clearly valuable and necessary, though the current emphasis on personal stress-management may mask the central problem that work may, in many cases, be unmanageable (in the sense that it is subject to the kind of trade-off referred to above).

The large body of research on job-design (for example Wall 1980) has shown that changes in the way in which work is organized may improve job-satisfaction and well-being without sacrificing performance criteria such as output and quality-control. The central feature of these job-enhancements is an increase in controllability (autonomy, flexibility) in the flow or timing of work tasks, or in the choice and variety of possible actions. This includes the choice not to exercise control (Frese 1989), which may be an additional demand under some circumstances. Would the provision of high controllability prevent strain in the presence of high levels of demand? This would depend on the relation between demands and control, as discussed at the beginning of the paper. If they are independent, as recent studies have implied, job-design also needs to address itself to the reduction of demands, or to a philosophy where production criteria are flexible.

Direct intervention in the job may have the potential to make most work 'manageable', though individual problems will still exist. Training in the use of coping strategies has an obvious application, particularly in relation to work where different modes of control are possible (through high controllability). If trade-offs are found within individuals there are clear grounds for training at least awareness of the costs associated with continued effort, to be set against the benefits of high performance. Extreme direct or indirect coping styles may also benefit from counselling, in the context of achieving a more realistic equilibrium between work and other goals.

REFERENCES

Baddeley, A. D. (1972). Selective attention and performance in dangerous environments. *British Journal of Psychology*, **63**, 537–46.

Baddeley, A. D. and Hitch, G. J. (1974). Working memory. In *The psychology of learning and motivation*, Vol. 8, (ed. G. H. Bower). Academic Press, London.

Bainbridge, L. (1974). Problems in the assessment of mental load. *Le Travail Humaine*, **37**, 279–302.

Bartlett, F. C. (1943). Fatigue following highly-skilled work. *Proceedings of the Royal Society* (Series B), **131**, 247–57.

Broadbent, D. E. (1957). Effects of noise on behaviour. In *Handbook of noise control* (Ed. C. M. Harris). McGraw-Hill, New York.

Broadbent, D. E. (1971). *Decision and stress*. Academic Press, London.

Broadbent, D. E. (1979). Is a fatigue test now possible? *Ergonomics*, **22**, 1227–90.

Broadbent, D. E. (1985). The clinical impact of job design. *British Journal of Clinical Psychology*, **24**, 33–44.

Caplan, R. D., Cobb, S., French, J. R. P., Van Harrison, R., and Pinneau, S. R. (1975). *Job demands and worker health*, HEW Publication No. (NIOSH)75-160. US Government Office, Washington.

Carver, C. S. and Scheier, M. F. (1982). Control theory: a useful conceptual framework for personality–social, clinical and health psychology. *Psychological Bulletin*, **92**, 111–35.

Carver, C. S. and Scheier, M. F. (1990). Origin and functions of positive and negative affect: a control systems view. *Psychological Review*, **97**, 19–35.

Chiles, W. D. (1955). *Experimental studies of prolonged wakefulness*, WADC Technical Report, 55-395. WADC, Dayton, Ohio.

Eysenck, M. W. (1982). *Attention and arousal: cognition and performance*. Springer, Heidelberg.

Folkman, S., Schaefer, C., and Lazarus, R. S. (1979). Cognitive processes as mediators of stress and coping. In *Human stress and cognition: an information processing approach* (ed. V. Hamilton and D. M. Warburton), pp. 265–300. Wiley, Chichester.

Frankenhaeuser, M. (1986). A psychobiological framework for research on human stress and coping. In *Dynamics of stress: physiological, psychological and social perspectives* (ed. M. H. Appley and R. Trumbell), pp. 101–16. Plenum, New York.

Frese, M. (1987). A theory of control and complexity: implications for software design and integration of computer systems into the work place. In *Psychological issues of human–computer interaction in the work place* (ed. M. Frese, E. Ullich, and W. Dzida). North-Holland, Amsterdam.

Frese, M. (1989). Theoretical models of control and health. In *Job control and worker health* (ed. S. L. Sauter, J. L. Hurrell, and C. L. Cooper), pp. 107–28. Wiley, Chichester.

Ganster, D. C. (1989). Worker control and well-being: a review of research in the workplace. In *Job control and worker health* (ed. S. L. Sauter, J. L. Hurrell, and C. L. Cooper), pp. 3–24. Wiley, Chichester.

Gopher, D. and Donchin, E. (1986). Workload—an examination of the concept. In *Handbook of perception and human performance*, Vol. 2, (ed. K. Boff, L. Kaufman, and J. P. Thomas), Ch. 41, pp. 1–49, Ch. 44, pp. 1–49. Wiley, New York.

Hamilton, P., Hockey, G. R. J., and Rejman, M. (1977). The place of the concept of activation in human information processing theory: an integrative approach. In *Attention and performance*, Vol. 6, (ed. S. Dornic). Academic Press, New York.

Hockey, G. R. J. (1979). Stress and the cognitive components of skilled performance. In *Human stress and cognition: an information processing approach* (ed. V. Hamilton and D. M. Warburton), pp. 141–78. Wiley, Chichester.

Hockey, G. R. J. (1986a). Operator efficiency as function of effects of environmental stress, fatigue and circadian rhythm. In *Handbook of perception and human performance*, Vol. 2, (ed. K. Boff, L. Kaufman, and J. P. Thomas), Ch. 41, pp. 1–49, Ch. 44, pp. 1–49. Wiley, New York.

Hockey, G. R. J. (1986b). A state control theory of adaptation and individual differences in stress management. In *Energetics and human information processing* (ed. G. R. J. Hockey, A. W. K. Gaillard, and M. G. H. Coles), pp. 285–98. Martinus Nijhoff, Dordrecht.

Hockey, G. R. J. and Hamilton, P. (1983). The cognitive patterns of stress states. In *Stress and fatigue in human performance* (ed. G. R. J. Hockey), pp. 331–62. Wiley, Chichester.

Hockey, G. R. J. and Wiethoff, M. (1990). Assessing patterns of adjustment to the demands of work. In *Psychobiology of stress* (ed. S. Puglisi-Allegra and A. Oliverio), pp. 231–40. Kluwer, Dordrecht.

Hockey, G. R. J., Briner, R. B., Tattersall, A. J., and Wiethoff, M. (1989). Assessing the impact of computer workload on operator stress: the role of system controllability. *Ergonomics*, **32**, 1401–18.

Hockey, G. R. J., Brenner, S.-O., Briner, R. B., and Rahman, M. (in preparation). Effects of day to day variations in workload, work characteristics and hassles on mood states and health symptoms.

Holding, D. H. (1983). Fatigue. In *Stress and fatigue in human performance* (ed. G. R. J. Hockey), pp. 145–68. Wiley, Chichester.

Kahneman, D. (1971). Remarks on attentional control. In *Attention and performance*, Vol. 3, (ed. A. F. Sanders). North-Holland, Amsterdam.

Kahneman, D. (1973). *Attention and effort*. Prentice-Hall, Englewood Cliffs, NJ.

Karasek, R. A. (1979). Job demands, job decision latitude and mental strain: implications for job redesign. *Administrative Science Quarterly*, **24**, 285–308.

Karasek, R. A., Theorell, T., Schwartz, J. E., Shnall, P. L., Pieper, C. F., and Michela, J. L. (1988). Job characteristics in relation to the prevalence of myocardial infarction in the US Health Examination Survey (HES) and the Health and Nutrition Examination Survey (HANES). *American Journal of Public Health*, **78**, 910–18.

Lazarus, R. S. (1966). *Psychological stress and the coping process*. McGraw-Hill, New York.

Lazarus, R. S. and Folkman, S. (1984). *Stress, appraisal and coping*. Springer, New York.

Levine, S. (1980). A coping model of mother–infant relationships. In *Coping and health* (ed. S. Levine and H. Ursin). Plenum, New York.

Lundberg, U. and Frankenhaeuser, M. (1978). Psychophysiological reactions to noise as modified by personal control over noise intensity. *Biological Psychology*, **6**, 55–9.

McGrath, J. E. (1976). Stress and behavior in organisations. In *Social and psychological factors in stress* (ed. M. D. Dunette), pp. 1351–95. Holt, New York.

Parkes, K. R., Styles, E. A., and Broadbent, D. E. (1990). Work preferences as moderators of the effects of paced and unpaced work on mood and cognitive performance: a laboratory simulation of mechanized letter sorting. *Human Factors*, **32**, 197–216.

Rissler, A. and Jacobson, L. (1987). Cognitive efficiency during high work load in final system testing of a large computer system. In *Human–computer interaction (Interact '87)* (ed. H. J. Bullinger and B. Shackel). Elsevier–North Holland, Amsterdam.

Robbins, T. W. (1986). Psychopharmacological and neurobiological aspects of the energetics of information processing. In *Energetics and human information processing* (ed. G. R. J. Hockey, A. W. K. Gaillard, and M. G. H. Coles), pp. 71–90. Martinus Nijhoff, Dordrecht.

Schonpflug, W. (1983). Coping efficiency and situational demands. In *Stress and fatigue in human performance* (ed. G. R. J. Hockey), pp. 299–330. Wiley, Chichester.

Shingledecker, C. A. and Holding, D. H. (1974). Risk and effort measures of fatigue. *Journal of Motor Behavior*, **6**, 17–25.

Spector, P. E. (1986). Perceived control by employees: a meta-analysis of studies concerning autonomy and participation at work. *Human Relations*, **39**, 1005–16.

Sperandio, A. (1971). Variation of operators' strategies and regulatory effects on workload. *Ergonomics*, **14**, 571–7.

Trumbell, R. and Appley, M. H. (1986). A conceptual model for the examination of stress dynamics. In *Dynamics of stress: physiological, psychological and social perspectives* (ed. M. H. Appley and R. Trumbell), pp. 21–46. Plenum, New York.

Wall, T. B. (1980). Group work redesign in context: a two-phase model. In *Changes in working life* (ed. K. Duncan, M. M. Gruneberg, and D. Wallis), pp. 329–50. Wiley, Chichester.

Weltman, G., Smith, J. E., and Egstrom, G. H. (1971). Perceptual narrowing during simulated pressure chamber exposure. *Human Factors*, **13**, 99–107.

Wiethoff, M. and Hockey, G. R. J. (in preparation). A field study of patterns of workload management and cognitive strain in junior doctors.

Wilkinson, R. T. (1962). Muscle tension during mental work under sleep deprivation. *Journal of Experimental Psychology*, **64**, 565–71.

SEVENTEEN

Individual differences in personality and motivation: 'non-cognitive' determinants of cognitive performance

William Revelle

D onald Broadbent's career has been an exception to the rule that serious cognitive psychologists should treat individual differences as nuisance variables to be ignored. Donald has recognized the complexities of individual differences, has commented about the messiness of the findings relating individual differences to performance, but none the less has insisted that a proper understanding of human information-processing needs to take into account individual differences in personality and motivation. For this, as well as the many other accomplishments discussed in the chapters in this book, he is to be admired.

In this chapter I review some of the historical and current evidence showing that Donald's concern for individual differences has been well founded. I emphasize how individual differences combine with situational manipulations to affect the availability and allocation of cognitive resources. More importantly, I argue that personality effects can be understood in terms of differences in the way and in the rate at which parameters of the cognitive control system are adjusted to cope with changes in a constantly varying world. I conclude with the suggestion that an analysis of the motivational states that result from the interaction of individuals with their environment improves models of cognitive performance as well as theories of personality.*

When reviewing current research it is somewhat disheartening to realize that, although many of the questions about individual differences were first raised in *Perception and communication* (Broadbent 1958) and discussed later in *Decision and stress* (Broadbent 1971), after three

* Much of the work that I report has been done in collaboration with colleagues and students of mine. Most importantly, I want to recognize the contributions of my former colleague Michael Humphreys (now at the University of Queensland) and my former student and current colleague Kristen Anderson. In addition, the research of recent Ph.D. students Debra Loftus, Mark Puchalski, and Richard Zinbarg, and current students Kathy Nugent and Eric Rosenberg, has been very influential in my thinking. As should be obvious, many of the theoretical ideas that I will discuss have been adapted from prior work of Donald Broadbent, as well as of John Atkinson, Hans Eysenck, and Jeffrey Gray.

decades we have not made much progress on finding answers to these questions. There has been some progress, however, in determining the motivational states and individual differences most associated with efficient performance.†

Broadbent's primary observation about individual differences was that 'It has been noticed many times that some individuals show larger decrements from prolonged work than others do' (Broadbent 1958, p. 140). Who are these people and what causes these decrements were and remain important questions. A subsequent question is whether there are reliable individual differences in performance decrements associated with other stressful conditions.

In general, decrements from optimal performance may be understood in terms of motivational effects (for example Anderson 1990; Blodgett 1929; Broadhurst 1959; Hebb 1955; Hockey *et al.* 1986; Humphreys and Revelle 1984; Revelle 1987, 1989; Sanders 1983, 1986; Yerkes and Dodson 1908). Motivation is the vital link between knowing and doing, between thinking and action, between competence and performance. Theories of motivation explain why rats solve mazes faster when hungry than when well fed, why bricklayers lay more bricks when given harder goals than when given easier ones, why assistant professors write more articles just before tenure review than after, and why people choose to be fighter pilots rather than dentists. How to motivate employees to produce more widgets and how to motivate oneself to do onerous tasks are the subjects of many management and self-help courses.

Fundamental questions of motivation are concerned with the direction, intensity, and duration of behaviour. Within each of these broad categories are sub-questions such as the distinctions between quality and quantity, effort and arousal, and latency and persistence. Cutting across all these questions are the relative contributions of individual differences and situational constraints to the level of motivation and of subsequent performance.

---

† It is important to note that while Broadbent and his colleagues pointed the way, a few other cognitive psychologists have not completely ignored individual differences, for there has been some interest among experimental psychologists in individual differences in cognitive ability. Until recently, however, with the possible exception of the application of cognitive modelling techniques to the study of intelligence (e.g., Hunt 1983), the two disciplines discussed by Cronbach (1957, 1975) and Eysenck (1966) have not moved much closer together than they were 35 years ago. The thrust of this chapter is not the study of individual differences in cognitive ability, however, but rather the study of how seemingly non-cognitive or affective differences relate to cognitive performance. Examples of recent applications of cognitive theory to the study of psychopathology (M. W. Eysenck and Mathews 1987; and MacLeod and Mathews 1991) or to the study of mood represent a welcome resurgence of interest in viewing individual differences in affect as parameters that are important sources of variance in cognitive models.

Individual differences in motivation and performance may be analysed at multiple, loosely coupled, levels of generality (Fig. 17.1).
These levels reflect the time-frame over which behaviour is sampled.
Over short-time periods (for example the milliseconds of an evoked
potential study), situational constraints are extremely important. As
the sampling frame is increased (for example to the seconds of a
reaction-time study), energetic components of motivation as well as
strategic trade-offs of speed for accuracy become more important. At
somewhat longer sampling frames (for example the tens of minutes of a
typical psychology experiment) individual differences and situational
demands for sustaining performance take precedence. At even longer
intervals, differential sensitivities to positive and negative feedback
affect task persistence and choice. At much longer intervals, individual
differences in preference affect occupational choice and the allocation
of time between alternative activities. At all of these levels it is possible
to distinguish between effects related to resource-availability and to
resource-allocation. Although an adequate theory of motivation and
performance should explain behaviour at all these levels, motivational
effects at intermediate time-frames have been most frequently examined. In particular, at the focus of this chapter are those motivational
effects that can affect the link between thinking and doing within
periods of several minutes to several hours.

For psychologists concerned with linking cognition to action, it is
essential to consider how motivational variables affect the competence–
performance relationship. Ever since Blodgett's (1929) demonstration
that well-fed rats will learn mazes, but that only hungry rats will show
their knowledge by running rapidly through the maze, psychologists
have been aware that competence is a necessary but not sufficient determinant of performance. An even more important study was Yerkes
and Dodson's demonstration (1908) that motivational intensity (induced by foot shock) has a non-monotonic affect upon rates of learning
a discrimination task, and that task difficulty interacts with intensity.

Unfortunately many cognitive psychologists pay only lip-service to
the competence–performance distinction, and will report that their
subjects are well motivated, and thus it is not necessary to worry about
motivation. For such researchers, motivation is a nuisance variable
that can be ignored by increasing sample size. The possibility that
individual differences in personality might interact with situational
manipulations in ways that can completely obscure important relationships is so foreign as not even to be considered.

An exception to this rule is those who have worked with or been inspired by Donald Broadbent. The best work on the effect on cognitive
performance of non-cognitive manipulations such as noise, time of

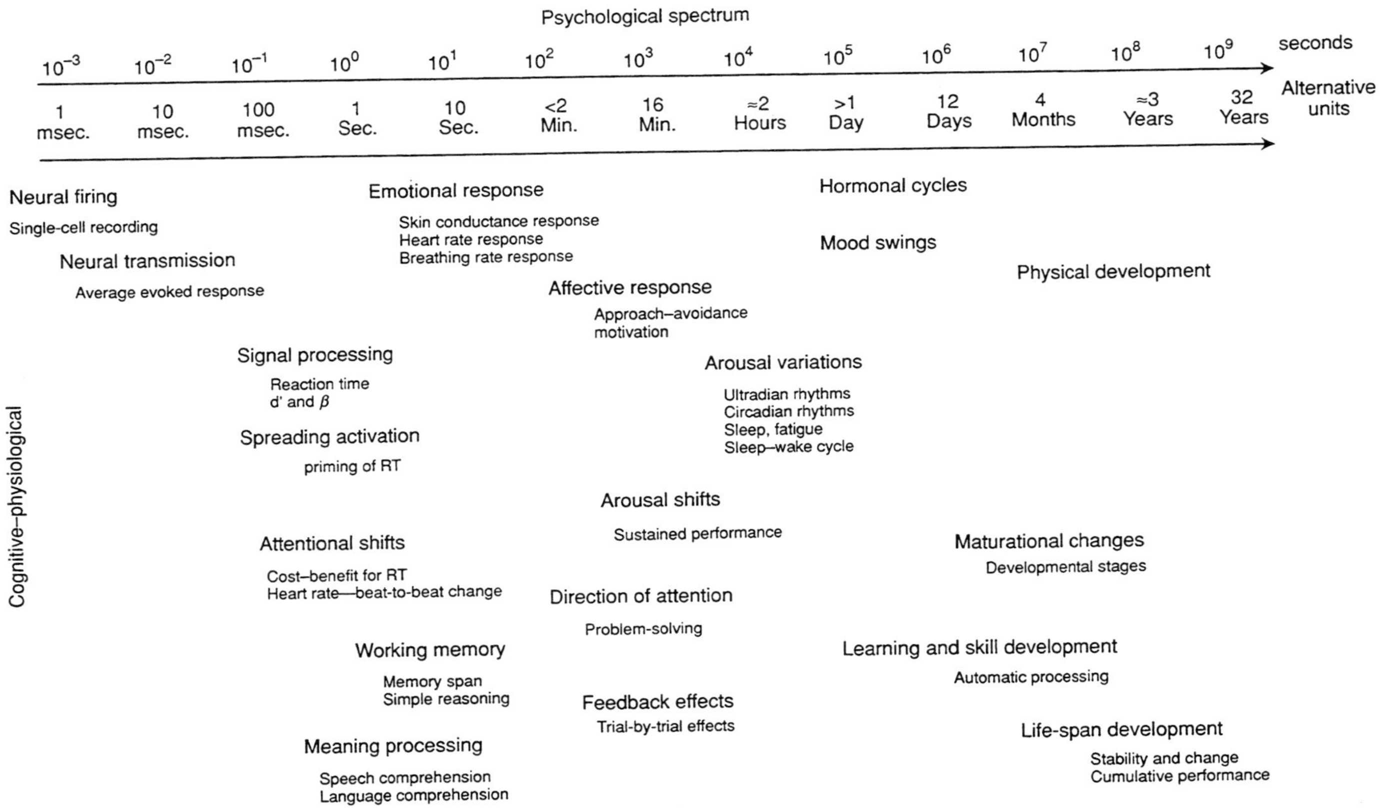

Psychological spectrum

	10^{-3}	10^{-2}	10^{-1}	10^0	10^1	10^2	10^3	10^4	10^5	10^6	10^7	10^8	10^9	seconds
	1 msec.	10 msec.	100 msec.	1 Sec.	10 Sec.	<2 Min.	16 Min.	≈2 Hours	>1 Day	12 Days	4 Months	≈3 Years	32 Years	Alternative units

Neural firing
Single-cell recording

Neural transmission
Average evoked response

Emotional response
Skin conductance response
Heart rate response
Breathing rate response

Affective response
Approach–avoidance motivation

Arousal variations
Ultradian rhythms
Circadian rhythms
Sleep, fatigue
Sleep–wake cycle

Signal processing
Reaction time
d' and β

Spreading activation
priming of RT

Arousal shifts
Sustained performance

Attentional shifts
Cost–benefit for RT
Heart rate—beat-to-beat change

Direction of attention
Problem-solving

Working memory
Memory span
Simple reasoning

Feedback effects
Trial-by-trial effects

Meaning processing
Speech comprehension
Language comprehension

Hormonal cycles

Mood swings

Physical development

Maturational changes
Developmental stages

Learning and skill development
Automatic processing

Life-span development
Stability and change
Cumulative performance

Cognitive–physiological

FIG. 17.1. Levels of analysis and the psychological spectrum. Psychological phenomena occur across at least 12 orders of temporal magnitude. Cognitive and motivational theories at each frequency make use of directional and energetic constructs. Outcome measures may be organized in terms of their temporal resolution as well as their physiological emphasis. (Adapted from Revelle 1989.)

day, distraction, and incentives has been done by those who have followed the traditions established at the Applied Psychology Unit in Cambridge and continued at Oxford. Discussing motivational and stress effects before such a group is equivalent to bringing coals to Newcastle.

The emphasis of much of the work at the APU has been on how stressors combine to affect performance.* Within this tradition, there has been great concern with the similarity and differences between the effects of different stressors. So, for example, while the effect of sleep-deprivation is to hinder certain tasks, and of noise to hinder other tasks, the combination of the two stressors can be shown to facilitate performance. An explanation that subsumes both effects is then proposed, tested, and accepted or rejected (Broadbent 1971).

This logic can equally well be applied to the combination of stressors with dimensions of individual differences. By appropriate analysis of the similarities and differences of effects due to experimental manipulations and individual differences it is possible to evaluate the construct validity of both. Certain individual differences seem to parallel certain stress manipulations, while other stressors seem to affect different individuals in different ways. Both patterns of results are of theoretical importance: parallel effects of personality and situational manipulation allow individual differences to be used to extend the effective range of experimental manipulations; different patterns for different people produce better theory by delineating the boundaries of the effects of theoretical constructs.

Parallel effects of individual differences and situational stressors can suggest that both reflect differences on the same latent construct. By appropriate combinations of subject differences and of experimental manipulations, it is then possible to achieve a much greater effective range on the underlying latent construct than would be possible by manipulation or subject selection alone.†

There are at least three possible reactions to the observation that what improves the performance of one individual hinders the performance of another: (1) ignore that particular manipulation because it does

---

* The study of stress may be divided into an examination of the effect of a variety of situational manipulations versus analyses of physiological response systems (Sanders 1983). Broadbent and his colleagues have focused on the former; Seyle (1976) and his followers on the latter.

† This concept of parallelism is the opposite view to those who apply additive-factors logic to task decompositions. In the additive-factors model, interactions are seen as suggesting effects at similar stages, additive effects as showing that different stages are affected. Parallel effects are found when two variables have similar patterns across a variety of tasks. An early example of this was the observation that extraversion had a pattern of effects that was similar to that of sleep-deprivation. More recent examples include the parallel effects of lesions to the septal-hippocampal loop and the effects of anti-anxiety drugs (Gray 1982).

not have consistent effects; (2) run more subjects in the hope that error terms will be reduced; or (3) ask what are the special characteristics of the different kinds of subjects. It is this third approach that is most useful. Understanding how manipulations differ across people leads to better theories of those manipulations, as well as to better theories of individual differences in personality.*

INDIVIDUAL DIFFERENCES IN MOTIVATION AND PERFORMANCE

Two dimensions of personality discussed by Broadbent (1958) as important sources of variation in performance were introversion–extraversion and stability–neuroticism. Extraversion was associated with decrements in performance over time, and neuroticism was associated with greater decrements following stress. Although it is tempting to propose a single model to account for these effects, what has become clear is that the effects of personality upon performance require multiple levels of explanation. The broad dimensions of personality that are consistently identified from investigator to investigator and shown to be important in different cultures and different times affect behaviour in many different ways.

Before reviewing specific effects of personality, it is necessary to consider what are the appropriate dimensions to discuss. Personality researchers can be grouped into those who study the effect of a single dimension versus those who develop taxonomic models of multiple dimensions. The first approach results in alphabetic organizations of personality traits (ranging from Type A behaviour, through Machiavellianism, to Sensation-Seeking) with numerous studies of convergent validity but few studies of discriminant validity. Within the second, multivariate–taxonomic tradition are those most concerned with description and those interested in causal (usually biological) theories. The descriptive taxonomists have agreed that a set of five dimensions can be identified consistently across methods. These 'big five' dimensions of self-report and peer-description have been labelled Surgency, Agreeableness, Emotional Stability, Conscientiousness, and

---

* This approach of studying personality variables in combination with environmental manipulations is one that has been advocated by others as well. Psychometricians such as Cronbach (1957, 1975) and Snow (1989) have long argued for the need to combine theories of individual differences with theories of the situation. Although many have proclaimed the need to study interactions of personality and situations, the best work in terms of programmatic theory-construction and testing has been done by Hans Eysenck and his associates (Eysenck 1967, 1981, 1991) and by John Atkinson and his associates (Atkinson 1957; Atkinson and Birch 1970; Atkinson and Raynor 1974; see also Brown and Veroff 1986). It is a combination of the Atkinson, Eysenck, and Broadbent traditions that has most influenced my own work.

Culture (Digman 1990; Fiske 1949; Goldberg 1982; McCrae and Costa 1987; Norman 1963; and Wiggins 1979). For the more biologically minded, the theories of Hans Eysenck (1952, 1967, 1981, 1991), Jeffrey Gray (1972, 1981, 1982, 1987), or Jan Strelau (1983, 1985) are appealing descriptions of three fundamental dimensions (Eysenck's Extraversion, Neuroticism, and Psychoticism; Gray's Impulsivity, Anxiety, and Aggression; Strelau's strength of the excitory and inhibitory processes, and balance between these processes) that fit within the five-factor model.* Whether one prefers the three-dimensional biological models or the five-dimensional semantic descriptions, it is clear that all of these dimensions have substantial genetic loadings, and that they are moderately consistent from childhood throughout the lifespan.†

Perhaps because of a greater concern for causal theory among the biologically-oriented taxonomists, there has been more research relating introversion–extraversion and stability–neuroticism to performance than there has been for the other dimensions of the 'big five'. Both of these dimensions may be associated with individual differences in motivational state. Although staying within the two-space defined by Introversion–Extraversion and Neuroticism–Stability, some of the more recent work has examined impulsivity, a component of I/E, and anxiety, a component of neuroticism.

MOTIVATIONAL STATES: AFFECTIVE VALENCE AND INTENSITY

A common assumption when studying human performance is that subjects are alert and optimally motivated. It is also assumed that the

* The 'Big 5' are thought to represent the fundamental axes of personality on the grounds that humans have developed language to describe important events and individual differences in their world. Thus, it is thought to be important to describe the dominance or energy level of a conspecific, as it is the trustworthiness and emotional stability of a potential colleague or spouse. However, it is also possible that language has developed to describe important combinations of underlying biological variability. For it is very important to describe those who are sensitive to reward *and* not sensitive to punishment *and* very aggressive (psychopathic killers), and thus it is perhaps more likely that words should be developed to describe combinations of underlying dimensions than words to describe the endpoints of the dimensions themselves.

† A synthesis of the five- and three-factor models notices that individual differences can be categorized in terms of the valence of emotional states normally experienced by individuals and in the different valence of emotional states one's behaviour produces in others. Thus Extraverts or highly Surgent individuals are more sensitive to positive mood states than Introverts or less surgent individuals (Eysenck 1952; Larsen and Kasimatis 1990); Neurotics and emotionally unstable individuals are more sensitive to negative mood states than are emotionally stable individuals (Eysenck 1952; Larsen and Kasimatis 1990); Agreeableness seems to induce positive affect in others; and finally, Psychoticism or a lack of Conscientiousness induces negative affect in others.

experimenter's task at hand is by far the most important thing the subject has to do at that time. Thus, although individual differences in cognitive ability are assumed to exist, differences in motivation are ignored. For compliant college students participating in one of only a few psychology experiments, this assumption might well be true. It is probably less true for psychiatric patients, oil-platform workers at the end of their shift, or deep-sea divers under several hundred feet of water. Indeed, for almost any subject population of interest it is difficult to believe that the specific experimental task used has an equally power-ful motivation effect upon all subjects. In fact, it is possible, even with college students, to show that variations in motivational state are im-portant sources of between-subject variation in performance.

Motivational states can be categorized in several different ways. Conventionally, it has been useful to distinguish between the *affective direction* and the *energetic intensity* of motivation (Humphreys and Revelle 1984). More recent work on affective states, however, has suggested that direction may be subdivided into positive and negative compon-ents (Watson and Tellegen 1985), and that intensity should be con-sidered in terms of energetic and tense arousal (Thayer 1989). How these four constructs interrelate is far from clear. Table 17.1 presents sample adjectives associated with each construct.

Affective states

Thayer (1967, 1978, 1989) has discussed four uni-polar dimensions that he groups into two higher-order constructs of energetic and tense arousal. He associates energetic arousal with approach behaviour and tense arousal with avoidance behaviour. Energetic arousal is increased by mild exercise and varies diurnally. Thayer (1989) adopts Gray's hypothesis that approach motivation reflects a sensitivity to cues for reward, and that avoidance behaviour reflects a sensitivity to cues for punishment (see also Fowles 1980).

Matthews *et al.* (1989) report three mood dimensions that are sensit-ive to external stressors: energetic arousal, tense arousal, and hedonic tone (positive versus negative). They show that energetic arousal is decreased by the administration of chlorpromazine, diazepam, or sleep deprivation. Tense arousal is increased by pain, or watching TV violence, but is reduced by muscle-relaxation.

Watson and Tellegen (1985) have shown that positive and negative affect are independent of each other, and can be used in combination to describe many psychopathological conditions. Clark and Watson (1991) recently proposed that differences in positive affect and somatic arousal account for the important distinction between two affective

TABLE 17.1. Adjectives associated with the measurement of affect and arousal

| Thayer's dimensions of arousal | | Watson and Tellegen dimensions of affect | |
Energetic arousal	Tense arousal	Positive affect	Negative affect
energetic	fearful	alert	nervous
full-of-pep	jittery	active	jittery
active	tense	excited	afraid
wakeful	clutched-up	enthusiastic	scared
lively	intense	attentive	guilty
vigorous	(not) quiescent	interested	hostile
wide-awake	(not) quiet	inspired	distressed
(not) sleepy	(not) placid	determined	ashamed
(not) drowsy	(not) still	proud	upset
(not) tired	(not) at rest	strong	irritable
	(not) calm		

| An alternative four-dimensional model of affect and arousal | | | |
High energetic	Low energy/tension	High depression	High tension
alert	drowsy	unhappy	nervous
full of pep	dull	gloomy	jittery
active	placid	blue	afraid
wakeful	quiet	sad	tense
lively	serene	depressed	scared
aroused	sleepy	angry	guilty
excited	calm	irritable	surprised

conditions represented by high negative affect, anxiety and depression. They suggest that while depression and anxiety share high negative affect, anxiety also reflects high somatic arousal, and depression represents lack of positive affect.

Energetic arousal   Energetic arousal is a non-directional component of motivation in all these models of affect. It is also a construct that has been found to be of great heuristic importance in theories of motivation and cognition ever since Broadbent (1958). More importantly, in that individuals seem to differ systematically in their level of energetic arousal, it is a way to link theories of individual differences to theories of behaviour.

Even though Corcoran's (1965) definition of arousal as the 'inverse probability of falling asleep' is immediately understandable, it is clear that the use of arousal as a construct is problematic. Indeed, some prefer to avoid discussing arousal and use a broader term, energetics, that subsumes many different constructs of motivational intensity and the effects of many environmental stressors (Hockey *et al.* 1986).

Most simply, arousal is a hypothetical construct used to organize the common behavioural effects of exercise, stimulant drugs, sleep-deprivation (negatively), time of day, time on task, and impulsivity (Anderson 1990). Each of these separate variables has both a common and a specific effect on behaviour. Caffeine and amphetamine both make one more alert and able to respond more rapidly and for longer periods of time. Caffeine differs from amphetamine in the locus of its action (post-synpatically versus synaptically) as well as in some peripheral effects (for instance caffeine induces hand-tremor). It is not difficult to demonstrate that different manipulations of arousal have somewhat different effects on the patterning of responses. As an example of a behavioural dissociation, simple reaction-time is facilitated by caffeine but is also faster for high impulsives (thought to be less aroused than low impulsives). High impulsives differ from low impulsives in terms of their speed–accuracy trade-off (Dickman and Meyer 1988), as well as in terms of arousal level.

Sanders (1983) discussed the multiple approaches to the study of stress. One can manipulate the antecedent conditions or examine the physiological consequences. Similarly, there are at least three ways to study the relationship of arousal to performance: (1) by varying the situational demands thought to lead to arousal; (2) by correlating psychophysiological measures to performance; and (3) by correlating self-report measures of arousal with performance.

The first approach, manipulations of arousal by the use of stressors such as stimulant drugs, noise, time on task, or time of day, is more commonly used by experimental psychologists. Broadbent's 1971 review suggested that there were common effects for some of these manipulations, but also showed that at least two levels of control processes needed to be invoked to understand all the effects. A lower level of control associated with executing well-learned responses was thought to be sensitive to noise or sleep-deprivation, and an upper-level control process responsible for monitoring the state of the lower-level process was thought to be sensitive to alcohol, extraversion, and time on task.

Hockey (1986) has proposed that each manipulation produces its own idiosyncratic state, and that it is a mistake to look for a Holy Grail of unified arousal. Several energetics theorists (Gopher 1986; Mulder

1986; Sanders 1983, 1986) have made use of Pribram and McGuinness's (1975) distinction between (phasic) arousal as affecting input processes, (tonic) activation as affecting motor outputs, and effort as an integrative resource-allocation mechanism (Fig. 17.2).

After reviewing the parallels and differences between physiological measures and psychological manipulations, Broadbent (1971) concluded that 'We have therefore no satisfactory physiological reference for the general state which we are discussing, and which we have revealed purely from behavioural studies. In some ways it might have been better therefore to avoid using the term 'arousal' for this behaviourally defined concept, but this would probably do too much violence to the common usage in the literature. The reader should remember however that we are working solely on a psychological level, and that the existence of a physiological concept of arousal is merely an interesting parallel, with no direct contact at present' (p. 413). Later he added that 'in complicating the theory of arousal we shall need to know more about the functions involved in various tasks; behavioural studies and

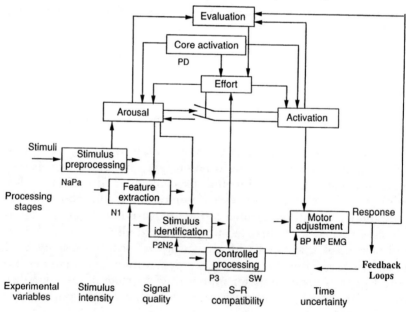

FIG. 17.2. Levels of control associated with reaction time. Different stages of information-processing are affected by different control processes. Modified from Mulder's (1986) revision of Sanders' (1983) model of reaction time.

the physiological attack upon the brain must go hand in hand' (p. 447).

The second approach, that of psychophysiological correlates, has proven to be the most difficult. Partly this is due to confusing a within-subject concept with between-subjects measurement (Venables 1984); It is also partly due to variations in the time-course of different physiological measures. Just as broad motivational constructs affect behaviour at different time-courses, so do narrow constructs of motivational intensity (for example, arousal) have different temporal parameters. EEG measures of arousal have latencies measured in milliseconds, while autonomic measures such as skin conductance have latencies measured in seconds, and body temperature reflects average levels of metabolic demands during the previous several hours. The disassociations and specific patterning of responses associated with reactions of the hand, the heart, and the head (Lacey 1967) make physiologists particularly cautious whenever they discuss a construct such as generalized arousal.

The third approach is to use self-reports of arousal. Thayer (1989) has argued that subjective estimates of energetic arousal are the most likely to be associated with performance. He has also reported that self-ratings correlate more with psychophysiological measures than the measures do themselves. This is what would expect if each psychophysiological measure had specific as well as general effects, and if subjective awareness of arousal reflected the general effects.

Matthews (1989) and his colleagues (Matthews et al. 1989) have done some of the most extensive work examining the relationship between self-reported mood and performance. They have found consistent, although complicated, relationships between self-reports of energetic arousal and performance on a variety of simple and complex detection tasks. In addition, they have found that state measures of self-reported arousal interact with trait measures of individual differences in intro-version–extraversion to affect performance on these tasks.

The use of the term 'arousal' to encompass phenomena ranging across many orders of temporal magnitude, from the milliseconds of the early stages of the evoked potential (Mulder 1986) to the effects of ten-minute brisk walks (Thayer 1989), to the tendency to seek out stimulation throughout a lifetime (Zuckerman 1991), is thought by many to be a mistake. I disagree. I believe that the concept that changes in resource-availability are associated with changes in arousal allows one to integrate the effect on cognitive performance of stable personality traits with those of a variety of environmental manipulations. This model has great heuristic value, for it allows an integration of seemingly unrelated phenomena. Such broad lumping together of disparate effects does indeed mask differences, however. Each task and each measure has its own unique variance as well as its common variance. What is important is to try to distinguish the unique from the shared variance. But this is the fundamental challenge of any theory.

PERSONALITY, MOTIVATION, AND PERFORMANCE

Over the past seventeen years, my colleagues and I have examined how personality traits combine with situational manipulations to produce motivational states that in turn affect cognitive performance. For organizational purposes, these effects can be conceived as affecting information-processing at several different, possibly overlapping, stages (Fig. 17.3).* The conceptual stage model I present is obviously derived from Broadbent's filter model (1958) and the later distinctions between filtering and pigeonholing (1971), and even more from his Maltese-cross model of memory and attention (1984), as well as Sanders' (1983) stage model of reaction time. I show it merely to distinguish between the types of demands placed upon the subject. Stimuli must first be detected, and then encoded, before this new information is able to be stored in memory. On the basis of the incoming stimuli, further information needs to be retrieved from memory, information needs to be integrated, and some response needs to be executed. This is a continuous loop, in that, as a consequence of each response, environmental feedback occurs that partly determines the next stimulus that is to be detected. Storage and retrieval processes are shown as arrows between the encoding, integrating, and memory systems.

Motivation affects each of these stages. In terms of tasks we have examined, we believe that vigilance-like tasks relate to the detection and response stages, and are affected by variations in arousal; individual differences in the learning of affectively valenced material occur at the encoding stage, and are related to differential sensitivities to rewards and punishments; memory storage and retrieval and the effect of retention interval are affected by variations in arousal; arousal facilitates storage but hinders retrieval; and the information-integration stage is curvilinearly related to arousal, because it reflects two components—a beneficial effect due to the speed of input and a detrimental effect due to the unavailability of recent events.

---

* In addition, these same personality traits affect behaviour at the different temporal levels described in Fig. 17.1. A broader discussion of how personality and motivational variables affect choice, persistence, and growth throughout the life-span is clearly beyond the scope of this chapter. The stages of processing outlined in Fig. 17.3 represent times of less than a few seconds, although effects of arousal on storage have been examined for longer periods of time.

Conceptual stages of information-processing

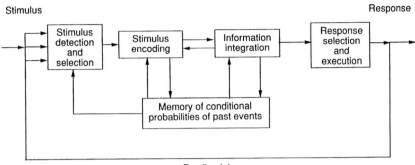

FIG. 17.3. A conceptual organization of the stages of processing that are affected by individual differences in motivation. Environmental inputs are first detected, and then encoded, stored, and integrated with prior expectancies before responses are selected and executed. Behavioural acts, through feedback, lead to new environmental input. Storage and retrieval processes are represented as arrows to and from the memory system.

On a larger time-scale, as the information-processing loop continues to be executed, resources vary in their availability and in their allocation. Knowledge structures in memory change, affective reactions to the outcomes bias expectancies of future reinforcement, and strategic decision processes are used. The encoding of environmental demands reflects differences in biological sensitivities to cues for rewards and punishment (Gray 1981), as well as the prior contents of memory. Emotional reactions to feedback reflect the interaction of expectancies and outcomes. Positive affective states result from reward following expectancies of reward, or non-punishment following expectancies of punishment. Negative affective states result from punishment following expectancies of reward and from punishment following expectancies of punishment (Rolls 1990). Positive affect facilitates approach behaviour, negative affect facilitates avoidance behaviour. Approach and avoidance tendencies are mutually inhibitory. Increased arousal facilitates the detection and storage of information, as well as the execution of the dominant response tendency. This leads to a much more complex model (Fig. 17.4), but one that is probably necessary if the interdependent effects of cognitive and affective processes are to be understood. This model is an attempt to sketch out the systems that are involved in actively processing valenced information in an ongoing system responding to environmental demands and environmental re-inforcements.*

In the following section I discuss the immediate motivational effects upon performance of various combinations of individual differences in personality and situational stressors. In the final section I suggest how an adequate theory of individual differences and cognitive performance needs to examine motivational effects on the stages of processing as well as to consider the larger temporal variations in affect, cognition, and behaviour that occur as the information-processing loop continues over time.

PERSONALITY, VIGILANCE, AND CONTINUOUS PERFORMANCE

Differences in the ability to sustain performance across time have been noticed in dogs, sonar operators, train engineers, and faculty listening to colloquia. What is particularly interesting to those interested in coherent descriptions of personality is that several of the basic dimen-sions of personality are related to performance decrements across time.

After an extensive discussion demonstrating that performance decre-ments generalize across several types of continuous-performance tasks, Broadbent (1958) presented evidence suggesting that extraverts were more likely to show such decrements than were introverts. By 1971, the evidence supporting this position was much stronger. Extravert per-formance deteriorates more rapidly in terms of detecting infrequent signals (Bakan et al. 1963; Keister and McLaughlin 1972); in terms of variability and speed of continuous reaction time (Thackray et al. 1974); and in the ability to stay awake on long-distance drives (Fager-ström and Lisper 1977).

Matthews (1989) and Matthews et al. (1990) have shown that this decrement in performance can occur very rapidly, and that self-reported high arousal is associated with the ability to maintain per-formance. They used a rapidly-paced discrimination task introduced by Neuchterlein et al. (1983), with an inter-stimulus interval (ISI) of 1 second and a priority stimulus frequency of 25 per cent (i.e. a re-sponse was required on the average every 4 seconds), with two levels of

---

* Given the elegant simplicity of the models associated with Donald Broadbent, it is problematic to present such an over-complex model. I hope that the tolerant reader will recognize that this model tries to capture the cognitive processes considered by Broadbent as well as the differential sensitivities to cues for positive and negative outcomes discussed by Gray (1981) and the general theory of emotional reactivity discussed by Rolls (1990). This figure was initially prepared to integrate the work of Clark and Watson (1991), Larsen (1991), and Thayer (1989), which has been based upon the prior theories of Broadbent (1971) and Gray (1972).

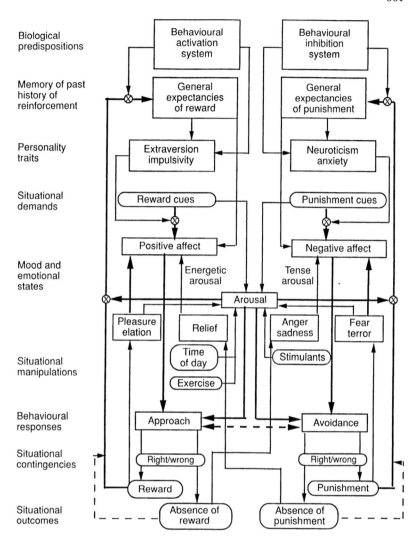

FIG. 17.4. Affective and cognitive reactions as part of an ongoing behavioural system. The encoding of environmental demands reflect differences in biological sensitivities to cues for rewards and punishment (Gray 1981), as well as the prior contents of memory. Reactions to feedback reflect the interaction of expectancies and outcomes. Positive affective states result from reward following expectancies of reward or non-punishment following expectancies of punishment. Negative affective states result from punishment following expectancies of reward and from punishment following expectancies of punishment (Rolls 1990). Positive affect facilitates approach behaviour, negative affect facilitates avoidance behaviour. Approach and avoidance tendencies are mutually inhibitory. Increased arousal facilitates the detection and storage of information as well as the execution of the dominant response. Adapted from Clark and Watson (1991), Gray (1981), Larsen (1991), Rolls (1990), and Thayer (1989).

stimulus degradation. For the degraded stimuli, performance of lowly aroused subjects deteriorated within 12 minutes, but did not for highly aroused subjects. Neither Neuchterlein *et al.* nor Matthews *et al.* found a decrement on this task with non-degraded stimuli. Neuchterlein *et al.* interpret the detection of the degraded stimuli as requiring substantial 'effortful' processing as compared to the non-degraded stimuli, which may be detected in an 'automatic fashion'. Matthews *et al.* argue that the degraded stimuli lead to the kind of resource-limited attention task that Humphreys and Revelle (1984) suggest should benefit from high arousal.

Impulsivity at the adult level has frequently been claimed to be related to the impulsivity associated with hyperactivity, or what has come to be called Attention Deficit Disorder (ADD) with (or without) Hyperactivity. ADD children are particularly susceptible to decrements on continuous-performance tasks. Sergeant and van der Meere (1990) have reviewed the application of Sanders' model of energetic effects on reaction time to the case of individual differences associated with attention-deficit disorders. Their review is an excellent example of the wealth of information that comes from combining sophisticated experimental procedures with the study of important individual differences.

Revelle *et al.* (in preparation) have recently completed three studies with an even simpler task than the Neuchterlein *et al.* task, but one that still shows pronounced decrements within a few minutes. Because of our interest in the dynamics of behaviour, we examined performance as a function of time-on-task. The task we used (variable fore-period reaction time with an inter-stimulus interval of 1–11 seconds) lasts for just a few minutes (12–15), and is typical of the demands placed upon subjects doing many monotonous real-world (or experimental) tasks. The subjects' task is to respond as rapidly as possible whenever a series of X*s* appears on the monitor of a computer. The targets remain until the subject responds. The fastest reaction times of our subjects tend to be of the order of 220–250 msec., with most responses being less than 400 msec. We discard all trials in which the subject took more than 1000 msec. to respond, although we have observed at least one subject who was taking 7–8 seconds on some trials. That is, our task succeeds in putting some subjects to sleep. More objectively, self-reports of energetic arousal decay reliably across the 12 minutes of the task.

We have done three studies with this task. The first examined the effects of impulsivity, anxiety (neuroticism), and time of day (0900 versus 1930 hours); the second added caffeine as a factor; and the third was run just in the morning, and examined the effects of an incentive (half the subjects were offered $10 if they could score in the top 33 per cent of the subjects, the other half were not told about the incentive).

Dependent measures were simple reaction time, as well as the change in reaction time as a function of trials.

When the results from all three studies are compared they clearly show a difference between the effects of (caffeine-induced or diurnally varying) arousal versus (monetary-incentive-induced) effort. Although both arousal and effort manipulations improve performance, only the arousal manipulation was able to sustain performance. The change across time clearly demonstrated the effects of arousal as well as impulsivity and neuroticism. Impulsivity was positively correlated with decay of RT in the morning, but negatively in the evening, and high neurotics were unable to maintain their performance from the first to the last part of the experiment. These results bring to mind Broadbent's (1971) two levels of control. For although effort facilitated reaction time (Broadbent's lower level), arousal facilitated the long-term maintenance of reaction time (Broadbent's higher level).

PERSONALITY AND NON-VIGILANCE INCREMENTS AND DECREMENTS

Learning valenced material. Humans as well as other animate organisms need to learn sources of reward and punishment within their environment to survive. This fundamental observation has long been ignored by many cognitive theorists concerned with memory. Although a great deal of research on human learning has been done on affectively neutral material (for example, nonsense syllables), much of the animal-learning literature has examined the effects of rewards and punishments upon learning. Jeffrey Gray (1972, 1982) has generalized from an animal model of rat learning to propose a neuropsychological basis of anxiety and to propose a revision of Hans Eysenck's theory of introversion–extraversion and neuroticism. In brief, Gray has proposed that individuals differ in their sensitivities to cues for reward and for cues for punishment. Furthermore, Gray associates the sensitivity to cues for reward with a behavioural activation system (BAS) and the sensitivity to cues for punishment with a behavioural inhibition system (BIS). He associates impulsivity with the BAS, anxiety with the BIS.

The evidence for this hypothesis is mixed. Richard Zinbarg and I have shown that when subjects learn a go–no go discrimination task to achieve rewards or to avoid punishments, impulsivity interacts with anxiety to affect rates of learning (Zinbarg and Revelle 1989). High impulsives who are low on anxiety rapidly learn to make responses to achieve rewards, but have difficulty learning to inhibit responses in order to avoid punishment. Highly anxious subjects who are also less impulsive rapidly learn to inhibit their responses in order to avoid punishment. High anxiety when combined with high impulsivity leads to poorer learning, as does low anxiety and low impulsivity. Further support for Gray's model comes from work of Fowles (1980, 1987) and Newman and his associates (Nichols and Newman 1986; Newman 1987). Failures to support Gray's hypothesis have been reported by Diaz et al. (1991) and Pickering (1991).

Kathy Nugent and I extended Gray's model and examined the effect of affective manipulations on the interpretation of stimuli and resulting effects upon memory (Nugent and Revelle 1991). We examined whether variations in affect (situationally induced by positive and negative feedback) or stable personality traits (impulsivity and neuroticism) affect the memory for neutral stimuli. The results are partly consistent with Gray's model, in that the high impulsives were more likely to remember words following reward rather than punishment, but were inconsistent in that the low impulsives remembered words better following punishment rather than reward (rather than the predicted no effect), and that there was no effect of anxiety (we had predicted that more anxious subjects would have better memory for stimuli followed by punishment).

Immediate and delayed retrieval. Honey bees as well as humans need to learn affectively important information, and cannot afford to waste cognitive resources on trivia. James McGaugh (1990) has reviewed evidence that stimulation following a particular cue enhances the long-term memory for that cue. Debra Loftus and I have reviewed twenty-five years of findings showing that a variety of arousal inductions and measures interact with retention-interval to affect memory (Revelle and Loftus 1990, 1992). Experiments using a surprising number of manipulations and measures of arousal have shown similar results: high arousal at learning inhibits immediate retrieval of the information presented, but facilitates later recall of that information. Whether this is due to different effects on different stores, or to an arousal-induced decrement at retrieval, or to some other explanation remains uncertain. What is certain, however, is that a consideration of individual differences is important. Puchalski (1988) replicated earlier work by Folkard et al. (1977) on the effects of time of day on immediate versus delayed retention, and found that the pattern reverses for high and low impulsives. Immediate memory of high impulsives was superior in the morning to the afternoon, although recall after one week was superior for information learned in the afternoon rather than the morning. This was essentially Folkard's finding. However, for low impulsives, immediate memory was better in the afternoon than in the morning, and delayed recall was equal for information learned at both times of day. Loftus (1990) found that impulsivity and self-reported arousal interacted with retention interval to affect the probability of recall. Some of the confusion relating the effects of mood to memory is probably due to ignoring these relationships between individual differences in arousal and the effect of retention interval.

Complex tasks. When information needs to be integrated and complex decisions need to be made, there seems to be an optimal level of arousal. Performance on complex reasoning tasks similar to the Graduate Record Exam is an interactive effect of impulsivity, caffeine, and time of day. Specifically, the performance of individuals thought to be less aroused (for example high impulsives in the morning, low impulsives in the evening) is facilitated by increases in arousal (for example caffeine), while that of individuals thought to be more aroused (for example low impulsives in the morning, high impulsives in the evening) is actually hindered (Revelle *et al.* 1980). This result is large and is replicable. Matthews (1985) has found a similar pattern of results for extraversion and self-reported arousal. Although Revelle *et al.* (1980) suggested that their pattern of results was consistent with an inverted-U relationship between arousal and performance, they did not have an unambiguous means of ordering the conditions in the between-subjects design they used. Gilliland (1980), in a between-groups design with three levels of caffeine did find a curvilinear (inverted-U) relationship between caffeine dose and GRE performance for low impulsives and a monotonically increasing function for the high impulsives. Stronger evidence has been reported by Anderson (1990) who, in a within-subjects design with multiple levels of caffeine, found a reliable number of subjects showing an inverted-U relationship between GRE performance and caffeine.

THEORETICAL ORGANIZATION OF RESULTS

One way to organize the results I have presented was adapted by Mike Humphreys and me from work done by Broadbent (1971), Simon Folkard (1975), Robert Hockey (1979), and others. In brief, Humphreys and I suggested that increases in both effort and arousal facilitate the ability to sustain rapid rates of information-transfer, but that arousal also inhibits some aspect of short-term or working memory (Humphreys and Revelle 1984). More recently we have proposed that, although arousal inhibits immediate availability, it facilitates longer-term availability in memory. Furthermore, we suggested that impulsivity interacts with time of day and time-on-task to affect arousal, and that achievement motivation and anxiety interact with rewards and punishments to affect task effort.

I like to explain the arousal effects on the rate of information-transfer as well as on memory by analogy to increasing the internal 'tick rate' of a computer. A faster clock-speed will lead to more samples of the environment taken per unit time, which will in turn lead to faster reaction times. However, increasing the tick rate (taking more samples of the environment) will also function to change the background context more rapidly. This will lead to greater difficulties in immediate recall, but will facilitate delayed recall.

MOTIVATION AS A CONTROL PROCESS

What complicates the relationship between stable measures of personality and performance across situations has been summarized by

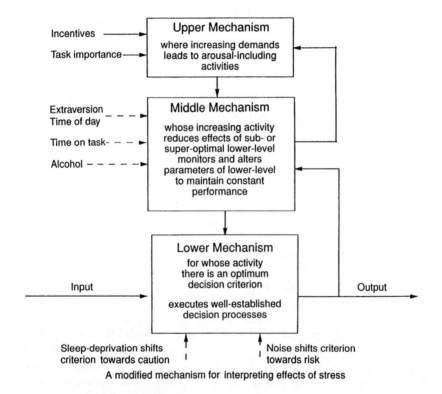

FIG. 17.5. Broadbent's two levels revisited. Higher-order controls adjust the level of arousal. Although effort cannot directly overcome the effect of inappropriate arousal without the ability to engage in behaviours that modify arousal, a high order control process can recognize inappropriate arousal levels and strategically seek out or avoid arousal-inducing behaviour. Adapted from Broadbent (1971).

Rabbitt 'the human cognitive system is designed for flexibility, and can carry out any particular task in many different ways' (Rabbitt 1986, p. 155). Indeed, not only do different people do the same task in different ways, the same people do the same task in different ways. Motivation can be seen as a control process, altering the parameters of the cognitive system so as to execute responses most efficiently. Individual differences reflect higher-order rates of change in these parameter settings (see also Sanders 1983, 1986).

Consider the results from our three reaction-time studies. All subjects could do the task most of the time. Increased incentive or caffeine-induced arousal improved performance. As the task continued, although the fastest responses remained about the same, some responses were much slower, reflecting an occasional lapse of attention. High impulsives in the morning and high neurotics throughout the day were particularly sensitive to this loss of attention. Incentives were unable to inhibit the decay across time, but caffeine was able to inhibit the decay. We interpret this result as suggesting that while effort can improve immediate performance, effort alone is unable to sustain performance. That is, in a constrained situation, one is unable to will oneself awake. But at a higher level, effort can increase alertness. As anyone knows who has struggled to overcome jetlag, drive long distances, or write an overdue paper by staying up all night, given the proper incentives one chooses activities that lead to alertness (for example stands up, takes brisk walks, or consumes large doses of caffeine). Thus, we are forced to add a higher-level control process (Fig. 17.5) to the two proposed by Broadbent (1971) or the hierarchy of resource pools proposed by Mulder (1986) and Sanders (1983, 1986).

THEORIES OF INDIVIDUAL DIFFERENCES

In 1958 Broadbent organized his discussion of individual differences around the personality and learning theories of Hans Eysenck and Kenneth Spence. Extraverts were thought at the time by Eysenck to have stronger reactive inhibition processes, and anxious individuals were thought to have higher levels of Hullian drive. Although the dimensions of introversion–extraversion and stability–neuroticism have remained important, a great deal has changed in the past 33 years in terms of our theoretical understanding of these dimensions. A particularly compelling model may be derived by integrating the neurobiology model of Jeffrey Gray (1972, 1982, 1987) with the multiple-dimensional models of affect of Watson and Tellegen (1985) and

Thayer (1989) (Fig. 17.4). An adequate model needs to integrate differences in affective reactions to feedback with differences in rates of learning and differences in performance. Such a model will certainly include the dimensions of impulsivity–extraversion–surgency and anxiety–emotionality as well as the behavioural differences observed under different stress manipulations on different types of tasks. It will also include multiple levels of control processes, and will need to account for individual differences in reactions to many different kinds of stressors. Although such a model will be more complex than the ones proposed by Broadbent (1958, 1971), an adequate model will owe a great deal to the pioneering work of Donald Broadbent. It has been his willingness to consider individual differences in models of cognitive performance that has laid the foundation upon which future theories may be built.

ACKNOWLEDGEMENTS

The research reported in this paper was partly supported by contract MDA903-90-C-0108 from the US Army Research Institute to William Revelle and Kristen Anderson. The views, opinions, and findings contained in this report are those of the author and should not be construed as an official Department of the Army position, policy, or decision, unless so designated by other official documentation.

REFERENCES

Anderson, K. J. (1990). Arousal and the inverted-U hypothesis—a critique of Neiss's reconceptualizing arousal. *Psychological Bulletin*, **107**, 96–100.

Atkinson, J. W. (1957). Motivational determinants of risk-taking behavior. *Psychological Review*, **64**, 359–72.

Atkinson, J. W. and Birch, D. (1970). *The dynamics of action.* Wiley, New York.

Atkinson, J. W. and Raynor, J. O. (eds) (1974). *Motivation and achievement.* Winston (Halsted Press/Wiley), New York.

Bakan, P., Belton, J., and Toth, J. (1963). Extraversion–introversion and decrement in an auditory vigilance task. In *Vigilance: a symposium* (ed. D. N. Buckner and J. J. McGrath), pp. 22–33. McGraw-Hill, New York.

Blodgett, H. C. (1929). The effect of the introduction of reward upon the maze performance of rats. *California University Publications in Psychology*, **4**, 113–14.

Bowyer, P., Humphreys, M. S., and Revelle, W. (1983). Arousal and recognition memory: the effects of impulsivity, caffeine, and time on task. *Personality and Individual Differences*, **3**, 41–9.

Broadbent, D. E. (1958). *Perception and communication.* Pergamon, Oxford.

Broadbent, D. E. (1971). *Decision and stress*. Academic Press, London.

Broadbent, D. E. (1984). The Maltese cross: a new simplistic model for memory. *Behavioral and Brain Sciences*, **7**, 55–68.

Broadhurst, P. L. (1959). The interaction of task difficulty and motivation: the Yerkes–Dodson Law revived. *Acta Psychologica*, **16**, 321–38.

Brown, D. R. and Veroff, J. (ed.) (1986). *Frontiers of motivational psychology: essays in honor of John W. Atkinson*. Springer, Berlin.

Clark, L. A. and Watson, D. (1991). Tripartite model of anxiety and depression: psychometric evidence and taxonomic implications. *Journal of Abnormal Psychology*, **100**(3), 316–36.

Corcoran, D. W. J. (1965). Personality and the inverted-U relation. *British Journal of Psychology*, **56**, 267–73.

Cronbach, L. J. (1957). The two disciplines of scientific psychology. *American Psychologist*, **12**, 671–84.

Cronbach, L. J. (1975). Beyond the two disciplines of scientific psychology. *American Psychologist*, **30**, 116–27.

Diaz, A., Gray, J. A., and Pickering, A. (1991). Maze learning and the anxious personality: the effects of punishment. Paper presented at the Oxford meeting of the International Society for the Study of Individual Differences, July.

Dickman, S. J. and Meyer, D. E. (1988). Impulsivity and speed–accuracy tradeoffs in information processing. *Journal of Personality and Social Psychology*, **54**, 274–90.

Digman, J. M. (1990). Personality structure—emergence of the 5-factor model. *Annual Review of Psychology*, **41**, 417–40.

Eysenck, H. J. (1952). *The scientific study of personality*. Routledge and Kegan Paul, London.

Eysenck, H. J. (1966). Personality and experimental psychology. *Bulletin of the British Psychological Society*, **19**, 1–28.

Eysenck, H. J. (1967). *The biological basis of personality*. Thomas, Springfield, Illinois.

Eysenck, H. J. (ed.) (1981). *A model for personality*. Springer-Verlag, New York.

Eysenck, H. J. (1987). The place of anxiety and impulsivity in a dimensional framework. *Journal of Research in Personality*, **21**, 489–93.

Eysenck, H. J. (1991). Dimensions of personality: 16: 5 or 3? criteria for a taxonomic paradigm. *Personality and Individual Differences*, **12**(8), 773–90.

Eysenck, H. J. and Eysenck, M. W. (1985). *Personality and individual differences: a natural science approach*. Plenum Press, New York.

Eysenck, M. W. and Mathews, A. (1987). Trait anxiety and cognition. In *Theoretical foundations of behavior therapy* (ed. H. J. Eysenck and I. Martin), pp. 197–216. Plenum, New York.

Fagerström, K. O. and Lisper, H. O. (1977). Effects of listening to car radio, experience, and personality of the driver on subsidiary reaction time and heart rate in a long-term driving task. In *Vigilance* (ed. R. R. Mackie), pp. 73–86. Plenum, New York.

Fiske, D. W. (1949). Consistency of the factorial structures of personality ratings across different sources. *Journal of Abnormal and Social Psychology*, **44**, 329–44.

Folkard, S. (1975). Diurnal variation in logical reasoning. *British Journal of Psychology*, **66**, 1–8.

Folkard, S. and Monk, T. H. (1980). Circadian rhythms in human memory. *British Journal of Psychology*, **71**, 295–307.

Folkard, S., Monk, T. H., Bradbury, R., and Rosenthal, J. (1977). Time of day effects in school children's immediate and delayed recall of meaningful material. *British Journal of Psychology*, **58**, 45–50.

Fowles, D. C. (1980). The three arousal model: implications of Gray's two factor learning theory for heart rate, electrodermal activity and psychopathy. *Psychophysiology*, **17**, 87–104.

Fowles, D. C. (1987). Application of a behavioral theory of motivation to the concepts of anxiety and impulsivity. *Journal of Research in Personality*, **21**, 417–35.

Gilliland, K. (1980). The interactive effect of introversion–extraversion with caffeine-induced arousal on verbal performance. *Journal of Research in Personality*, **14**, 482–92.

Goldberg, L. R. (1982). From ace to zombie: some explorations in the language of personality. In *Advances in personality assessment*, Vol. 1, (ed. C. D. Spielberger and J. N. Butcher), pp. 203–34. Hillsdale, New Jersey.

Gopher, D. (1986). In defense of resources: on structures, energies, pools and the allocation of attention. In *Energetics and human information processing* (ed. G. R. J. Hockey, A. W. K. Gaillard, and M. G. H. Coles), pp. 353–72. Nijhoff, Dordrecht.

Gray, J. A. (1972). The psychophysiological basis of introversion–extraversion: a modification of Eysenck's theory. In *The biological basis of individual behavior* (ed. V. D. Nebylitsyn and J. A. Gray), pp. 185–205. Academic Press, New York.

Gray, J. A. (1981). A critique of Eysenck's theory of personality. In *A model for personality* (ed. H. J. Eysenck), pp. 246–76. Springer-Verlag, Berlin.

Gray, J. A. (1982). *Neuropsychological theory of anxiety: an investigation of the septal-hippocampal system*. Cambridge University Press.

Gray, J. A. (1987). Perspectives on anxiety and impulsivity: a commentary. *Journal of research in personality*, **21**, 493–510.

Hebb, D. O. (1955). Drives and the C.N.S. (conceptual nervous system). *Psychological Review*, **62**, 243–54.

Hockey, R. (1979). Stress and cognitive components of skilled performance. In *Human stress and cognition* (ed. V. Hamilton and D. M. Warburton), pp. 141–78. Wiley, Chichester.

Hockey, G. R. J. (1986). A stress control theory of adaptation and individual differences in stress management. In *Energetics and human information processing* (ed. G. R. J. Hockey, A. W. K. Gaillard, and M. G. H. Coles), pp. 285–98. Martinus Nijhoff, Dordrecht.

Hockey, G. R. J., Gaillard, A. W. K., and Coles, M. G. H. (1986). *Energetics and human information processing*. Nijhoff, Dordrecht.

Humphreys, M. S. and Revelle, W. (1984). Personality, motivation, and performance: a theory of the relationship between individual differences and information processing. *Psychological Review*, **91**, 153–84.

Hunt, E. (1983). On the nature of intelligence. *Science*, **219**, 141–6.

Keister, E. and McLaughlin, J. (1972). Vigilance performance related to extraversion-introversion and caffeine. *Journal of Experimental Research in Personality*, **6**, 5–11.

Lacey, J. L. (1967). Somatic response patterning and stress: some revisions of activation theory. In *Psychological stress: issues in research* (ed. M. H. Appleby and R. Trumbell), pp. 14–37. Appleton-Century-Croft, New York.

Larsen, R. J. and Kasimatis, M. (1990). Individual-differences in entrainment of mood to the weekly calendar. *Journal Of Personality And Social Psychology*, **58**(1), 164–71.

Loftus, D. A. (1990). Affect and arousal in the study of mood and memory. Unpublished doctoral dissertation, Northwestern University, Evanston, Ill.

McCrae, R. R. and Costa, P. T. (1987). Validation of the 5-factor model of personality across instruments and observers. *Journal of Personality and Social Psychology*, **52**, 81–90.

McGaugh, J. L. (1990). Significance and rememberance: the role of neuromodulatory systems. *Psychological Science*, **1**, 15–25.

MacLeod, C. and Mathews, A. M. (1991). Cognitive–experimental approaches to the emotional disorders. In *Handbook of behavior therapy and psychological science: an integrative approach* (ed. P. Martin), pp. 116–50. Pergamon, New York.

Matthews, G. (1985). The effects of extraversion and arousal on intelligence test performance. *British Journal of Psychology*, **76**, 479–93.

Matthews, G. (1989). Extraversion and levels of control of sustained attention. *Acta Psychologica*, **70**(2), 129–46.

Matthews, G., Davies, D. R., and Lees, J. L. (1990). Arousal, extroversion, and individual differences in resource availability. *Journal Of Personality And Social Psychology*, **59**(1), 150–68.

Matthews, G., Jones, D. M., and Chamberlain, A. G. (1989). Interactive effects of extraversion and arousal on attentional task-performance—multiple resources or encoding processes. *Journal of Personality and Social Psychology*, **56**(4), 629–39.

Meyer, G. J. and Shack, J. R. (1989). Structural convergence of mood and personality: evidence for old and new directions. *Journal of Personality and Social Psychology*, **57**, 691–706.

Mulder, G. (1986). The concept and measurement of mental effort. In *Energetics and human information processing* (ed. G. R. J. Hockey, A. W. K. Gaillard, and M. G. H. Coles), pp. 175–98. Nijhoff, Dordrecht.

Neuchterlein, K., Parasuraman, R., and Jiang, Q. (1983). Visual sustained attention: image degradation produces rapid sensitivity decrement over time. *Science*, **220**, 327–9.

Newman, J. P. (1987). Reaction to punishment in extraverts and psychopaths: implications for the impulsive behavior of disinhibited individuals. *Journal of Research in Personality*, **21**, 464–80.

Nichols, S. L. and Newman, J. P. (1986). Effects of punishment on response latency in extraverts. *Journal of Personality and Social Psychology*, **50**, 624–30.

Norman, W. T. (1963). Toward an adequate taxonomy of personality attributes: replicated factor structure in peer nomination personality ratings. *Journal of Abnormal and Social Psychology*, **66**, 574–83.

Nugent, K. and Revelle, W. (1991). Memory biases in anxious and impulsive individuals following reward and punishment. Paper presented at the annual meeting of the Midwestern Psychological Association, Chicago, Illinois, May.

Pickering, A. (1991). Testing Gray's theory in human subjects. Paper presented at the bi-annual meeting of the International Society for the Study of Individual Differences, Oxford, July.

Pribram, K. H. and McGuinness, D. (1975). Arousal, activation and effort in the control of attention. *Psychological Review*, **82**, 116–49.

Puchalski, M. (1988). Impulsivity, time of day, and retention interval: the effect on cognitive performance. Unpublished Doctoral Dissertation, Northwestern University.

Rabbitt, P. M. A. (1986). Models and paradigms in the study of stress effects. In *Energetics and human information processing* (ed. G. R. J. Hockey, A. W. K. Gaillard, and M. G. H. Coles), pp. 155–74. Nijhoff, Dordrecht.

Revelle, W. (1986). Motivation and efficiency of cognitive performance. In *Frontiers of motivational psychology: essays in honor of John W. Atkinson* (ed. D. R. Brown and J. Veroff), pp. 107–31. Springer, Berlin.

Revelle, W. (1987). Personality and motivation: sources of inefficiency in cognitive performance. *Journal of Research in Personality*, **21**, 436–52.

Revelle, W. (1989). Personality, motivation, and cognitive performance. In *Learning and individual differences: abilities, motivation, and methodology* (ed. P. Ackerman, R. Kanfer, and R. Cudeck), pp. 297–341. Erlbaum, Hillsdale, NJ.

Revelle, W. and Loftus, D. A. (1990). Individual differences and arousal: implications for the study of mood and memory. *Cognition and Emotion*, **4**, 209–37.

Revelle, W. and Loftus, D. A. (1992). The implications of arousal effects for the study of affect and memory. In *The handbook of emotion and memory: research and theory* (ed. S.-A. Christianson). Lawrence Erlbaum Associates, Hillsdale, NJ.

Revelle, W., Amaral, P., and Turriff, S. (1976). Introversion–extraversion, time stress, and caffeine: the effect on verbal performance. *Science*, **192**, 149–50.

Revelle, W., Humphreys, M. S., Simon, L., and Gilliland, K. (1980). The interactive effect of personality, time of day, and caffeine: a test of the arousal model. *Journal of Experimental Psychology: General*, **109**, 1–31.

Revelle, W., Anderson, K. J., and Humphreys, M. S. (1987). Empirical tests and theoretical extensions of arousal based theories of personality. In *Personality dimensions and arousal* (ed. J. Strelau and H. J. Eysenck), pp. 17–36. Plenum, London.

Revelle, W., Anderson, K. J., and Rosenberg, E. (in preparation). Studies of continuous performance: the effects of personality, caffeine, incentive, time-of-day, and affect on sustained attention.

Rolls, E. T. (1990). A theory of emotion, and its application to understanding the neural basis of emotion. *Cognition and emotion*, **4**, 161–90.

Sanders, A. F. (1983). Towards a model of stress and human performance. *Acta Psychologica*, **53**, 61–97.

Sanders, A. F. (1986). Energetical states underlying task performance. In *Energetics and human information processing* (ed. G. R. J. Hockey, A. W. K. Gaillard, and M. G. H. Coles), pp. 139–54. Nijhoff, Dordrecht.

Sergeant, J. and van der Meere, J. (1990). Convergence of approaches in localizing the hyperactivity deficit. In *Advances in Clinical Child Psychology*, Vol. 13 (ed. B. B. Lahey and A. E. Kazdin), pp. 207–46.

Seyle, H. (1976). *The stress of life* (revised version). McGraw-Hill, New York.

Snow, R. E. (1989). Cognitive–conative aptitude interactions in learning. In *Abilities, motivation and methodology: the Minnesota symposium on learning and individual differences* (ed. R. Kanfer, P. L. Ackerman, and R. Cudeck), pp. 435–74. Erlbaum, Hillsdale, New Jersey.

Strelau, J. (1983). *Temperament—personality—activity*. Academic Press, London.

Strelau, J. (1985). Temperament and personality: Pavlov and beyond. In *The biological bases of personality and behavior: psychophysiology, performance, and application*, Vol. 1, (ed. J. Strelau, F. H. Farley, and A. Gale), pp. 25–43. Hemisphere Publishing, Washington, DC.

Thackray, R. I., Jones, K. N., and Touchstone, R. M. (1974). Personality and physiological correlates of performance decrement on a monotonous task requiring sustained attention. *British Journal of Psychology*, **65**, 351–8.

Thayer, R. E. (1967). Measurement of activation through self-report. *Psychological Reports*, **20**, 663–78.

Thayer, R. E. (1978). Toward a psychological theory of multidimensional activation (arousal). *Motivation and Emotion*, **2**, 1–34.

Thayer, R. E. (1989). *The biopsychology of mood and arousal*. Oxford, New York.

Toates, F. M. and Halliday, T. R. (eds) (1980). *Analysis of motivational processes*. Academic Press, London.

Venables, P. H. (1984). Arousal: an examination of its status as a concept. In *Psychophysiological perspectives: Festschrift for Beatrice and John Lacey* (ed. M. G. H. Coles, J. R. Jennings, and J. P. Stern), pp. 134–42. Van Nostrand, New York.

Watson, D. and Tellegen, A. (1985). Toward a consensual structure of mood. *Psychological Bulletin*, **98**, 219–35.

Wiggins, J. S. (1979). A psychological taxonomy of trait terms: the interpersonal domain. *Journal of Personality and Social Psychology*, **37**, 395–412.

Wilson, G. D. (1990). Personality, time of day, and arousal. *Personality and Individual Differences*, **11**, 153–68.

Yerkes, R. M. and Dodson, J. D. (1908). The relation of strength of stimuli to rapidity of habit-information. *Journal of Comparative Neurology and Psychology*, **18**, 459–82.

Zinbarg, R. and Revelle, W. (1989). Personality and conditioning: a test of four models. *Journal of Personality and Social Psychology*, **57**(2), 301–14.

Zuckerman, M. (1991). *Psychobiology of personality*. Cambridge University Press.

EIGHTEEN

Selective effects of emotion on information-processing

John D. Teasdale

In this chapter, I shall consider our current understanding of the ways in which emotions and moods selectively bias memory, perception, and judgement. Experimental studies have clearly demonstrated the existence of such effects. However, empirical findings seriously embarrass the prevailing explanatory account of these phenomena, Bower's associative network theory of mood and memory (Bower 1981). This theory also has its own inherent difficulties. The time seems ripe to consider alternative theoretical approaches. I shall describe one such approach. In contrast to Bower's model, which suggests that mood effects operate at the level of specific concepts and their relationships, this alternative proposes that effects of mood occur at a more generic level of representation, corresponding to schematic models of experience. This alternative approach provides a better explanation for existing findings. It also generates initially counter-intuitive results that are supported by the preliminary results of an empirical investigation.

THE EMPIRICAL BACKGROUND

Several reviews are available of studies investigating the biasing effects of mood on memory for hedonically valenced material (Blaney 1986; Morris 1988, Chapter 5), on evaluative judgements (Forgas and Bower 1988; Morris 1988, Chapter 5; Schwarz and Clore 1988), and on attentional and perceptual tasks (Morris 1988, Chapter 5; Williams *et al.* 1988, Chapters 4 and 10; Dalgleish and Watts 1990). The broad conclusions emerging from these studies are summarized below.

Within mood-congruent biases in memory, it is useful to distinguish between effects of mood at encoding and at retrieval. Mood-congruous retrieval occurs where material is recalled better when it is affectively congruent with retrieval mood than when it is incongruent—for example, better recall of positive as against negative material in happy as against unhappy retrieval moods. Mood-congruous retrieval has been shown for both autobiographical and experimentally presented material. For experimentally presented material, mood-congruous encoding has also been demonstrated, i.e. relatively greater recall of material when it is affectively congruent with the mood in which it is encoded then when it is incongruent. For example, positive verbal material may subsequently be better recalled in normal mood if initially encoded in happy rather than unhappy mood.

Mood-congruous memory is not shown universally for all material categorized as positive or negative in terms of its 'dictionary-defined' hedonic tone. Rather, detailed aspects of the material and the way it is encoded can powerfully influence whether or not mood-congruent memory biases occur. For example, several studies have shown mood-congruent memory when personality trait adjectives are self-referred, but not when they are referred to another person (for example Nasby 1988; Clark and Martin 1992), or when they are the object of phonetic judgements (Brown and Taylor 1986). Such observations give pointers to the boundary conditions for demonstrating mood-congruent memory. However, it has not been possible to capture those boundary conditions in terms of any simple empirical generalization. Some more theoretically oriented statement of boundary conditions seems necessary. For example, it has been suggested that mood congruence may depend on '*some ability* of the stimuli (however presented) to contact the subject's customary evaluative construct system' (Blaney 1986, p. 236, italics added).

Although mood-congruent memory biases have been widely reported in studies of depressed mood, there have been notable failures to demonstrate effects of anxious mood increasing recall of threat-related material (Williams *et al.* 1988, Chapter 10).

In perceptual and attentional tasks, mood-congruent biases are well established in anxious subjects, but have been difficult to demonstrate for depressed mood (Williams *et al.* 1988, Chapter 10). For example, anxious subjects are differentially slowed on the Stroop colour-naming task when it includes threat- rather than non-threat-related words. Anxious subjects, unlike normal subjects, are more likely to attend to locations in which threat-related rather than non-threat-related words have been presented (Mathews 1990). Comparable effects of depressed mood have been observed less often. However, there is evidence that subjects in depressed mood selectively expose themselves to negative stories or pictures longer than subjects in happy mood (Bower 1983).

Mood-congruent biases in evaluative judgements are well established. For example, subjects in unhappy moods evaluate their own personal qualities more negatively (Wright and Mischel 1982), judge future catastrophic events as more likely (Johnson and Tversky 1983), and attribute failures to their own personal inadequacies rather than to bad luck or to the difficulty of the task (Forgas *et al.* 1990).

In 1981, Bower presented an associative network theory of mood and memory which attempted to account for mood-congruent biases in memory, perception, and judgement within the same basic explanatory framework. This theory has been highly influential in guiding subsequent work in this area.

BOWER'S ASSOCIATIVE NETWORK MODEL OF MOOD AND MEMORY

(i) Mood-congruous memory

As Bower's (1981) model is well known, it will be summarized only briefly here, most attention being devoted to an assessment of its adequacy. In this model, events and meanings are represented in terms of concepts and associative links between them within a semantic network. Nodes in the network correspond to specific concepts and to events, represented as clusters of descriptive propositions. Retrieval involves the spread of activation through the network; events and concepts are recalled when the activation of related nodes and units exceeds a threshold value. Each distinct emotion has a specific node in the network. When activated above a threshold, these nodes produce their related emotions. Each emotion node is connected to nodes representing events and concepts previously activated concurrently with that emotion node, i.e. that have been activated in association with experience of the related emotion.

In a given affective state, activation of the emotion node corresponding to the prevailing emotion will be greater than that of the nodes for other emotions. It follows that more activation will spread to the nodes associatively linked to the currently active emotion node. These nodes correspond to representations of concepts and events previously activated in association with the emotion or mood, and will, for that reason, be more likely to be mood-congruent than incongruent. In this way, mood-congruent memory is explained in terms of a greater spread of activation to representations previously activated in association with the prevailing mood.

The cornerstone of the associative network account is mood-state-dependent learning: material learned in the context of one mood state is assumed to be better recalled subsequently if retrieval occurs in a mood context that is the same as that at encoding than if retrieval occurs in a different mood. Initial empirical support for this phenomenon was provided by Bower et al. (1978). They demonstrated mood-state-dependent memory using a two-list interference verbal learning paradigm. Following a number of reports of failures to replicate these findings, Bower and Mayer (1989) conducted a series of experiments to examine the replicability of the original results. The outcome was consistent failure to replicate. Bower and Mayer (1989, p. 133) concluded that the initial demonstration of mood-dependent retrieval (MDR) was 'an unreliable, chance event, possibly due to subtle experimenter demand. Given similar procedures, the MDR effect simply does not replicate.' Obviously, this conclusion is extremely damaging to the associative network theory of mood and memory within which mood-state-dependent learning is the central basic mechanism.

The network model has encountered comparably damaging problems at the theoretical level. For example, the central mechanism underlying mood-congruent biases is assumed to be the spread of activation from an emotion node to the nodes and units corresponding to events and concepts previously activated during experience of the mood. The increased activation from an emotion node will spread out divided among the links to all the nodes attached to it. As Simon (1982) pointed out, this 'fan-out' effect creates a considerable problem because there must be an enormous number of nodes corresponding to all the emotional events ever associated with each emotion node. It follows that any increment in activation from the emotion node, as a result of a change in mood state, will be divided and 'diluted' many times through these multiple connections. Consequently, the increment in activation at any one node corresponding to a specific event will be extremely small. It is difficult to see how such small increments could be sufficient to produce, for example, mood-congruous recall. Gilligan and Bower (1984) have acknowledged the fan-out problem as a formidable diffi- . culty for the network theory.

(ii) Mood-congruous perceptual and attentional effects

The associative network account predicts both reduced perceptual thresholds for and attentional biases towards mood-congruent, as opposed to mood-incongruent material. These effects are expected as a result of the greater activation flowing to the units corresponding to concepts congruent with, and previously activated in, the prevailing mood state. So: 'The spreading activation theory in my *American Psychologist* paper of 1981 predicts a perceptual effect, that a pleasant mood would prime and lower the threshold for pleasant words—or, at least, increase the response bias in their favour. And, unpleasant moods should facilitate identification of unpleasant words' (Bower 1985). In this same paper, Bower then proceeded to report four experiments that consistently failed to find any effects of happy versus unhappy mood on word perception, findings widely replicated by others (for instance

Clark *et al.* 1983). So here is another area in which effects strongly predicted by the network model have simply not been obtained.

Although perceptual and attentional effects have not generally been found with unhappy or depressed moods, they have been found with anxious mood and threat-related material, as we noted earlier. Conversely, mood-congruent memory effects have been readily demonstrated with depressed mood, but not with anxiety. This pattern of results suggests different underlying mechanisms in the biases in anxiety and depression (Williams *et al.* 1988, Chapter 10). This poses a further difficulty for the network model, which assumes that the same basic processes operate similarly in different moods.

(iii) Mood-congruous judgements

The associative network theory suggests mood-congruent memory as the basis for mood-congruent biases in judgement tasks. The theory proposes that judgements are based on retrieving relevant information from memory. Mood-congruent biases in the accessibility of memories produce a biased data-base on which judgements are based. Further, according to Tversky and Kahneman's (1973) availability heuristic, the relative ease with which material can be accessed from memory affects the weight attached to that information in the judgement process. The network theory suggests that mood-congruent memory, acting through both these mechanisms, underlies mood-congruent judgemental biases.

Three types of experimental evidence pose considerable difficulties for this account. First, dissociations between the biasing effects of mood on judgement and on recall of the memories assumed to underlie those judgements have been reported in a number of studies (for example Bower *et al.* 1981, Experiment 3; Williams *et al.* 1988, p. 139; Fiedler *et al.* 1986). Second, as was first noted by Johnson and Tversky (1983), mood effects on judgements are more global than would be expected if these effects were mediated by biased access to memories. For example, Johnson and Tversky (1983) found that unhappy moods induced by reading about someone dying of cancer had effects on judgements of risks of being struck by lightning or of becoming unemployed that were quite comparable to the effect on judgements of risk of dying of heart disease. If judgemental biases depended on biased access to related memories, some specificity of effects in relation to the topic of the mood-inducing procedures would be expected. Third, mood effects on judgements can be eliminated by providing information concerning the origins of the mood (Schwarz and Clore 1983). Schwarz and Clore (1988) have argued persuasively that such evidence is inconsistent with the view that mood-congruent judgements depend on 'automatic' mood-congruous access to relevant information.

(iv) General difficulties of the network model

In addition to the problems of the network model already noted, further inadequacies have been recognized (for example Bower and Cohen 1982). The most important of these concern the distinction between the 'hot' versus 'cold' uses of emotion concepts, and the fact that emotional experiences can be remembered either with or without emotion.

The original network model had one node for each emotion such as 'fear', and suggested that the use of that concept would turn on that node in the network. This latter is also the operation that the model identified as 'feeling afraid', leading to 'the absurd implication that people always feel afraid when they refer to the concept' (Bower and Cohen 1982, p. 308). Clearly, people can discourse coolly about emotion without feeling the emotion at all. More generally, we can use affect-related concepts (such as *loving, worthless,* or *terrifying*) without necessarily experiencing the related emotion. Within the network theory, nodes for these concepts are linked to emotion nodes by connections through which activation flows in both directions. Consequently, use of these concepts would be expected to increment the activation of related emotion nodes, and in this way to intensify emotion. Clearly, this does not inevitably occur.

A related problem is that emotional memories can be remembered either with re-experience of the original feelings ('hot') or without ('cold'). A person may be able to remember not only that an emotional event occurred, but also to remember many detailed aspects of it, without experiencing related feelings. Within the original network model only one form of representation of an event was proposed, making it difficult for this approach to handle the extremely important distinction between the 'hot' and 'cold' processing of emotional memories. Such difficulties seem inherent in an approach that (1) proposes only one form of representation of events, consisting of interconnections between nodes for the concepts encoding the event, and that (2) explains emotional effects in terms of activation flowing backwards and forwards through richly interconnected bidirectional links between emotion nodes and event and concept nodes.

The representation within semantic network models of all knowledge in a single uniform format has been noted as a general problem for network theories. Semantic network models, in general, cannot easily represent knowledge at levels of meaning beyond that of the word or sentence. The need for higher-order levels of representation is widely recognized within mainstream cognitive psychology. This need is even greater in the area of emotion, where the importance of the wider context in determining the emotional impact of an event or item of information is widely recognized (see for example Brown and Harris 1978, Chapter 5).

The associative network model of mood and memory clearly has enough problems at both the empirical and theoretical level to justify consideration of alternative proposals. In seeking alternative explanatory accounts we should remember that it is unlikely that mood effects will be satisfactorily explained by simple models with a single representational format in which mood directly primes representations of concepts and events. Rather, we are probably looking for frameworks that include qualitatively different types of representations with different functional relationships to affect (i) to accommodate the distinction between 'hot' and 'cold' memories and knowledge; (ii) to allow for multiple, functionally independent, representations in memory of related material; and (iii) to capture the need for representations at levels of abstraction higher than those of the word, concept, or sentence.

AN ALTERNATIVE APPROACH TO UNDERSTANDING AFFECTIVE INFLUENCES ON INFORMATION-PROCESSING

The Interacting Cognitive Subsystems (ICS) framework was first described by Barnard (1985). It was an attempt to fuse the more architectural and general-purpose information-processing approach, so heavily influenced and shaped by Donald Broadbent, with the more computational and representational approach of the psycholinguistic tradition. ICS aims to provide a comprehensive framework within which, in principle, accounts of all aspects of information-processing, including cognitive–affective interrelationships, can be developed. Originally presented in the context of a psycholinguistic approach to short-term memory (Barnard 1985), it has been applied to problems of human–computer interaction (Barnard 1987), and has recently been extended to the interaction of cognition and emotion (Barnard and Teasdale 1991; Teasdale and Barnard 1993).

ICS aims to be both comprehensive in its coverage and explicit in its principles of operation. Consequently, it cannot be described adequately in a short space. I shall focus here only on those aspects immediately relevant to explaining mood-related biases in information-processing.

ICS proposes nine qualitatively distinct types of information, or mental codes, each representing a different aspect of experience. Each type of information is processed by its own specialized processing subsystem. There are separate memory stores for each type of information, making nine distinct memory systems in all. Information-processing involves the transfer of information between subsystems and its transformation from one mental code to another.

To understand the biasing effects of emotion on information-processing we need to focus on mental codes related to two levels of meaning, a specific and a more generic level. Patterns of *Propositional* code represent specific meanings in terms of discrete concepts and the relationships between them, for example, the specific meaning behind the speech form 'Roger has brown hair'. Meaning at this level can be grasped relatively easily, as there is a fairly direct relationship between language and concepts at this level. The meanings represented in Propositional code are similar to those represented in semantic networks, although the means of representing them are quite different.

Patterns of *Implicational* code represent a more generic, holistic, level of meaning. Meaning at this level is difficult to convey adequately, because it does not map directly on to language. This generic level of representation encodes recurring very-high-order regularities across all other information codes, particularly patterns of Propositional code, related to specific meanings, and patterns of sensory codes. These latter are related to auditory and visual information from the external environment, and to proprioceptive information from the internal environment of the body. Three important features of Implicational level meaning have to be grasped. First, representation is at a very high level of abstraction, as an analogy may make clear. The specific meanings of sentences depend on binding together particular sequences of lower-order constituents such as letters or phonemes. In the same way, generic Implicational meanings depend on binding lower-order constituents together in particular patterns, but here the lower-order constituents are themselves patterns of specific meanings and coherent sensory patterns. The level of abstraction is comparable to that of the 'frame' (Minsky 1975).

Second, sensory features, such as tone of voice, or proprioceptive feedback from facial expression or bodily arousal, make a *direct* contribution to Implicational meanings, together with patterns of specific meanings.

Third, the implicit knowledge encoded in coherent patterns of Implicational code can be thought of as representing schematic models of experience. Just as mental models, in general, represent the interrelationships between semantic elements (Johnson-Laird 1983), so these *schematic models* represent interrelationships between *generic* features of experience.

Some 'feel' for representations at the Implicational level can be gained by considering the analogy between a sentence and a poem. A sentence conveys one or more 'specific meanings by appropriate arrangements of letters or phonemes in the appropriate sequence. A poem conveys 'holistic' meanings, that cannot be conveyed by single sentences, by arranging sentences in appropriate sequences, together, very importantly, with appropriate direct sensory contributions from the sounds of the words, and the rhythms and metres of the whole. The total meaning conveyed is qualitatively different from the sum of the separate specific meanings, just as the meaning of a sentence is qualitatively different from that of its component letters or words. Subjectively, the synthesis of the generic meaning of a poem is marked by a particular holistic 'sense' or 'feeling'. In terms of the ICS framework, this synthesis is represented in the form of a schematic model in Implicational rather than Propositional code.

The ICS approach assumes that emotional reactions originate as innate prepared biological responses to certain arrays of sensory stimuli. In a given family and culture, these prepared sensory stimuli will regularly occur concurrently with constellations of other, unprepared, sensory stimuli, and with specific-level meanings that the child derives as it develops cognitively. Features of information codes, both sensory and semantic, that regularly co-occur in situations eliciting a given emotion will be extracted and represented in patterns of Implicational code. These will capture the 'prototypical' features of emotion-eliciting situations in related schematic models. Such emotion-related Implicational patterns 'inherit' the ability to elicit emotion. In the adult, the core of emotion production is the synthesis of patterns of Implicational code extracted as prototypical of previous experiences of a given emotion. When such patterns are processed, emotion is produced.

Within ICS, the ability directly to elicit emotion is restricted to emotion-related Implicational codes; on this view, Propositional representations of emotion-related information cannot, alone, elicit emotion. Thus, processing of such specific Propositional representations would be associated with 'cold' consideration of emotion-related material. 'Hot' processing of emotion-related material depends on the synthesis of appropriate generic-level meanings in Implicational code. Within ICS, although representations at one level *can* be transformed by appropriate procedures to related representations in another information code, this does not necessarily automatically occur. It follows that different levels of representation of related material can be 'functionally insulated' from each other. Consequently, creation of a higher-level representation does not automatically produce or activate related lower-level representations (and vice versa), and different levels of representation can have functionally distinct relationships with other variables. In this way, ICS avoids the problems of the associative network theory that arise from activation spreading automatically between emotion nodes and representations of all concepts and events that have been concurrently activated in the past. So I can talk about my past failures without getting upset now, and depressed mood may affect my evaluation of myself as a failure without necessarily changing the perceptual threshold for identifying 'failure' as a word.

Within ICS, emotion production depends on the synthesis of Implicational schematic models that encode features prototypical of previous emotion-eliciting situations. Such emotion-related schematic models also play a central role in ICS explanations for emotional influences on information-processing. The specifics of these explanations differ for mood biases in memory, perception, and judgement, and are described in detail elsewhere (Barnard and Teasdale 1991; Teasdale and Barnard 1993). A core feature of all these accounts is the pivotal role played by emotion-related Implicational schematic models; it is at this, generic, level of meaning that the essential effects occur, rather than at the level of more specific, Propositional meanings.

So, for example, the ICS account of mood-congruous memory suggests that this will only occur if, at encoding, affect-related Implicational schematic models derived from the to-be-learned material have been synthesized. Words or sentences that have obviously positive or negative meanings at the Propositional level but do not lead to synthesis of affective schematic models should not show mood-congruous memory effects. In this way, the ICS account captures, within an explicit conceptual framework, the essence of the boundary conditions suggested by others, for example, Blaney's (1986, p. 236) suggestion that mood-congruence depends on 'some ability of the stimuli to contact the subjects' customary evaluative system'.

As well as suggesting different specific mechanisms for biases in different cognitive domains, ICS also suggests that different emotions will not necessarily have comparable effect across domains. So, for example, the fact that depressed mood appears to bias memory more than perception, whereas anxious mood shows the opposite effect is quite consistent with the ICS view that the two moods originate in different prepared biological responses from which different cognitive learning histories will have developed different cognitive–affective routines.

ICS VERSUS BOWER'S ASSOCIATIVE NETWORK MODEL OF MOOD AND MEMORY

The ICS approach raises the central question: what level of representation does mood primarily affect? Bower's associative network model suggests mood biases operate at the level of specific concepts and their relationships. By contrast, ICS suggests that mood has its effects at a higher level of abstraction, corresponding to the interrelationships of specific meanings and sensory elements, as captured in the notion of schematic models of experience. Let us focus on the explanations offered by these rival approaches for the negative thinking depressed patients characteristically show when depressed. Better understanding of such thinking, and of its role in the maintenance and treatment of depression, has been the applied problem motivating my interest in more basic research on the effects of mood on information-processing. Much depressive thinking is mood-dependent in that, in general, it returns to normal as depression remits.

Previously, I (Teasdale 1983) and others (Ingram 1984) developed explanations for negative depressive thinking within Bower's associative network model. These suggested that depressed patients think more negatively because their depressed mood selectively activates negative concepts, constructs, and memories, previously associated with depressed mood. This gave a plausible account, and even suggested a novel view of cognitive vulnerability to depression which generated specific predictions which experimental investigations have confirmed (Teasdale and Dent 1987; Teasdale 1988; Dent and Teasdale 1988; Williams 1988).

The ICS account of depressive thinking, by contrast, suggests that mood biases occur, not at the level of specific constructs, but at the level of schematic models of experience. Such models are more concerned with the complex interrelationships between lower-level meanings, rather than the specific meanings themselves. That is, ICS suggests that, as mood shifts, so do one's high-order mental models of self and world. The consequences predicted from a given state of affairs by the model prevailing in one mood state might be quite different from the consequences predicted from the same state of affairs by the model prevailing in another mood state.

The differences between the two explanatory approaches can be clarified by considering the findings of a study conducted by Teasdale, Taylor, Cooper, Hayhurst, and Paykel (1995, in press). The aim of this study was specifically to contrast the predictions emerging from the two accounts with respect to the increased endorsement by depressed patients of dysfunctional attitudes that are likely to perpetuate depression. As patients recover, endorsement of these attitudes decrease, so that, when they have returned to normal mood, previously depressed subjects endorse dysfunctional attitudes no more than normal controls (Teasdale 1988).

Let us consider how the two rival accounts explain endorsement of the attitude 'If a person I love does not love me it means I am unlovable' by a patient when depressed, but not when recovered. The Bower network model suggests that endorsement when depressed is primarily a reflection of a general increase in activation and accessibility of depressogenic constructs, such as 'unlovable self', associatively linked to the depression emotion node. As mood recovers, activation from the depression node is reduced and so endorsement of the dysfunctional attitude is less likely. The ICS account suggests that the shift in endorsement of the dysfunctional attitude reflects a shift in the prevailing 'schematic mental model' dominating information-processing as one moves from one mood state to another. The focus of such schematic models is the *interrelationship* between constellations of constructs, rather than simply the level of activation of *individual* constructs. On this account, change in mood is accompanied by a shift in schematic models, the implicit knowledge of what leads to what.

Dysfunctional attitudes are typically measured with Weissman and Beck's (1978) Dysfunctional Attitude Scale (DAS). By appropriate rewriting of selected DAS items it is possible to create an experimental situation in which predictions from the Bower and ICS accounts are pitted against each other. Attitude statements were rewritten so that dysfunctional models, normally associated with *depression*, would be expressed by statements which required completion by *positive* constructs. Conversely, functional models, normally associated with *happy* mood, would be expressed by statements which required completion by *negative* constructs. For example, dysfunctional completions of the stem 'Always to put other's interests before your own is a recipe for ___' would involve positive constructs such as 'happiness', whereas more functional completions would involve negative constructs such as 'disaster'.

In this way, a situation was arranged in which the ICS approach, which concentrates on the *interrelationships* between specific meanings encoded in schematic models, makes the counterintuitive prediction that *depressed* patients should make more *positive* completions than the non-depressed. With *recovery*, there should be an *increase* in the number of *negative* completions. By contrast, the associative network approach, focusing on the activation of specific constructs, predicts that *depressed* patients will be more likely to make *negative* completions, and that this tendency will *decrease* with recovery. These predictions were contrasted in a study in which patients with major depression were tested initially while depressed, and, again, three months later, when the majority were considerably less depressed. Patients were divided into those whose mood had improved over the three months, and those whose mood had stayed the same or deteriorated. Consistent with the predictions from the ICS account, patients who were less depressed showed an *increase* in *negative* completions, whereas those who were unimproved showed a *decrease* in negative completions, the changes in the two groups being significantly different. Table 18.1 gives a good illustration of the predicted changes in the case of one patient whose mood improved considerably. It does, indeed, seem that as mood shifts, so do our schematic models of self and world—in different moods we inhabit, mentally, different 'alternative realities'.

Results of this study give preliminary support to the proposal, central to the ICS approach, that affect-related biases in information-processing are better understood in terms of effects at the generic schematic level rather than at the level of the activation of specific constructs. Elsewhere (Teasdale and Barnard 1993), the ICS approach to such biases is developed in detail, and its superiority to the network approach in accommodating existing experimental findings documented more fully. The recognition, within the ICS approach, of two

TABLE 18.1. Changes in sentence completions produced by an individual patient with recovery from depressed to normal mood-state. As depression reduces, completions change from positive (dysfunctional) to negative (functional).

Example—Patient number 33

	Depressed	Recovered
Always to put other's interests before your own is a recipe for ____	success	disaster
If I could always be right then others would ____ me	like	hate
For everyone to look to me for guidance and advice would make me ____	important	frightened
To be liked by everyone is ____	very good	impossible
Always seeking the approval of other people is the road to ____	happiness	disaster

levels of meaning, with emotion-related processes directly linked only to the holistic level of meaning, overcomes the problems of Bower's associative network theory and opens up new ways of understanding a range of clinically significant phenomena (Barnard and Teasdale 1991; Teasdale 1993; Teasdale and Barnard 1993).

A PERSONAL FOOTNOTE

From my first study on mood and memory (Teasdale and Fogarty 1979) onwards, Donald Broadbent provided invaluable encouragement and guidance through an extended series of investigations of emotional influences on information-processing. I am very glad to have this opportunity to express my appreciation and thanks for this help. This line of research has now reached the point where the Interacting Cognitive Subsystems conceptual framework provides valuable new insights into the nature of cognition–emotion relationships. It is wholly appropriate that this framework, in its origins, was heavily influenced by the Broadbent tradition (Barnard 1985), although this might not have been fully appreciated by Donald himself.

REFERENCES

Barnard, P. (1985). Interacting cognitive subsystems: a psycholinguistic approach to short-term memory. In *Progress in the psychology of language*, Vol. 2, (ed. A. Ellis), pp. 197–258. Erlbaum, London.

Barnard, P. (1987). Cognitive resources and the learning of human–computer dialogs. In *Interfacing thought: cognitive aspects of human–computer interaction* (ed. J. M. Carroll), pp. 112–58. MIT Press, Cambridge, Mass.

Barnard, P. J. and Teasdale, J. D. (1991). Interacting cognitive subsystems: a systemic approach to cognitive–affective interaction and change. *Cognition and Emotion*, **5**, 1–39.

Blaney, P. H. (1986). Affect and memory: a review. *Psychological Bulletin*, **99**, 229–46.

Bower, G. H. (1981). Mood and memory. *The American Psychologist*, **36**, 129–48.

Bower, G. H. (1983). Affect and cognition. In *Functional aspects of human memory* (ed. D. E. Broadbent), pp. 387–402. The Royal Society, London.

Bower, G. H. (1985). *Review of research on mood and memory*, presented at the Symposium on Affect and Cognition, British Psychological Society Cognitive Psychology Section, Oxford, England.

Bower, G. H. and Cohen, P. R. (1982). Emotional influences in memory and thinking: data and theory. In *Affect and cognition* (ed. M. S. Clark and S. T. Fiske), pp. 291–331, Erlbaum, Hillsdale, NJ.

Bower, G. H. and Mayer, J. D. (1989). In search of mood-dependent retrieval. *Journal of Social Behaviour and Personality*, **4**, 121–56.

Bower, G. H., Monteiro, K. P., and Gilligan, S. G. (1978). Emotional mood as a context for learning and recall. *Journal of Verbal Learning and Verbal Behaviour*, **17**, 573–8.

Bower, G. H., Gilligan, S. G., and Monteiro, K. P. (1981). Selectivity of learning caused by affective states. *Journal of Experimental Psychology: General*, **110**, 451–73.

Brown, G. W. and Harris, T. (1978). *Social origins of depression*. Tavistock, London.

Brown, J. and Taylor, S. E. (1986). Affect and the processing of personal information: evidence for mood-activated self-schemata. *Journal of Experimental Social Psychology*, **22**, 436–52.

Clark, D. M. and Martin, M. (1992). *Effects of induced mood on recall of adjectives encoded by self- or other- reference*. Unpublished manuscript, University of Oxford Department of Psychiatry.

Clark, D. M., Teasdale, J. D., Broadbent, D. E., and Martin, M. (1983). Effect of mood on lexical decisions. *Bulletin of the Psychonomic Society*, **21**, 175–8.

Dalgleish, T. and Watts, F. N. (1990). Biases of attention and memory in disorders of anxiety and depression. *Clinical Psychology Review*, **10**, 589–604.

Dent, J. and Teasdale, J. D. (1988). Negative cognition and the persistence of depression. *Journal of Abnormal Psychology*, **97**, 29–34.

Fiedler, K., Pampe, H., and Scherf, U. (1986). Mood and memory for tightly organised social information. *European Journal of Social Psychology*, **16**, 149–64.

Forgas, J. P. and Bower, G. H. (1988). Affect in social and personal judgements. In *Affect, cognition and social behaviour* (ed. K. Fiedler and J. P. Forgas), pp. 183–208. Hogrefe, Toronto.

Forgas, J. P., Bower, G. H., and Moylan, S. (1990). Praise or blame? Affective influences on attributions for achievement. *Journal of Personality and Social Psychology*, **59**, 809–19.

Gilligan, S. G. and Bower, G. H. (1984). Cognitive consequences of emotional arousal. In *Emotion, cognition and behaviour* (ed. C. E. Izard, J. Kagan, and R. Zajonc), pp. 547–88. Cambridge University Press, New York.

Ingram, R. E. (1984). Toward an information-processing analysis of depression. *Cognitive Therapy and Research*, **8**, 443–78.

Johnson, E. J. and Tversky, A. (1983). Affect, generalisation, and the perception of risk. *Journal of Personality and Social Psychology*, **45**, 20–31.

Johnson-Laird, P. N. (1983). *Mental models*. Cambridge University Press.

Mathews, A. M. (1990). Why worry? The cognitive function of anxiety. *Behaviour Research and Therapy*, **28**, 455–68.

Minsky, M. (1975). A framework for representing knowledge. In *The psychology of computer vision* (ed. P. Winston), pp. 211–77. McGraw-Hill, New York.

Morris, W. N. (1988). *Mood. The frame of mind*. Springer, New York.

Nasby, W. (1988). Induced moods and selective encoding of personal information about the self. Unpublished manuscript, Boston College.

Schwarz, N. and Clore, G. L. (1983). Mood, misattribution, and judgements of well-being: informative and directive functions of affective states. *Journal of Personality and Social Psychology*, **45**, 513–23.

Schwarz, N. and Clore, G. L. (1988). How do I feel about it? The informative function of affective states. In *Affect, cognition and social behaviour* (ed. K. Fiedler and J. P. Forgas). Hogrefe, Toronto.

Simon, H. A. (1982). Comments. In *Affect and cognition* (ed. M. S. Clarke and S. T. Fiske), p. 339. Erlbaum, Hillsdale, NJ.

Teasdale, J. D. (1983). Negative thinking in depression: cause, effect or reciprocal relationship? *Advances in Behaviour Research and Therapy*, **5**, 3–25.

Teasdale, J. D. (1988). Cognitive vulnerability to persistent depression. *Cognition and Emotion*, **2**, 247–74.

Teasdale, J. D. (1993). Emotion and two kinds of meaning: cognitive therapy and applied cognitive science. *Behaviour Research and Therapy*, **31**, 339–54.

Teasdale, J. D. and Barnard, P. J. (1993). *Affect, cognition and change: remodelling depressive thought*. Erlbaum, Hove and London.

Teasdale, J. D. and Dent, J. (1987). Cognitive vulnerability to depression: an investigation of two hypotheses. *British Journal of Clinical Psychology*, **26**, 113–26.

Teasdale, J. D. and Fogarty, S. J. (1979). Differential effects of induced mood on retrieval of pleasant and unpleasant events from episodic memory. *Journal of Abnormal Psychology*, **88**, 248–57.

Teasdale, J. D., Taylor, M. J., Cooper, Z., Hayhurst, H., and Paykel, E. S. (1995). Depressive thinking: shifts in construct accessibility or in schematic mental models? *Journal of Abnormal Psychology*. (In press.)

Tversky, A. and Kahneman, D. (1973). Availability: a heuristic for judging frequency and probability. *Cognitive Psychology*, **5**, 207–32.

Weissman, A. and Beck, A. T. (1978). *The dysfunctional attitudes scale*. Paper presented at the meeting of the Association for the Advancement of Behaviour Therapy, Chicago.

Williams, R. M. (1988). Individual differences in the effects of mood on cognition. Unpublished D.Phil. thesis, University of Oxford.

Williams, J. M. G., Watts, F. N., MacLeod, C., and Mathews, A. M. (1988). *Cognitive psychology and emotional disorders*. Wiley, Chichester.

Wright, J. and Mischel, W. (1982). Influence of affect on cognitive social learning person variables. *Journal of Personality and Social Psychology*, **43**, 901–14.

NINETEEN

Interaction of arousal and selection in the posterior attention network

Michael I. Posner

INTRODUCTION

In his book *Decision and stress* (1971), Donald Broadbent speculates about the future of the field. In discussing the role of psychology and physiology he says:

The attempt to link physiology and psychology can be disastrous when it is premature; as for example we have regarded attempts to treat as criteria measures of arousal indices such as skin conductance or percentage alpha in the EEG. But it would be equally disastrous to go on forever treating the brain as an abstract and ideal construct having no biological reality . . . in complicating the theory of arousal we shall need to know more about the functions involved in various tasks; behavioural studies and the physiological attack upon the brain must go hand in hand (p. 447).

In the same chapter Broadbent also speculates that arousal could be viewed as involving two control mechanisms. One is mainly reactive to stimuli, and the other mainly a control system modulating the reactive arousal. He also suggests that these levels may relate to separate neuro-transmitter systems (see Robbins and Everitt 1987 for a discussion of studies related to Broadbent's idea).

Much has happened in the twenty years since the book appeared. One major advance came, not from the behavoural studies of animals upon which Broadbent relied in the final chapter of *Decision and stress*, but from cellular recording in alert monkeys. These studies indicated that a few areas of the brain appeared to be devoted to selective atten-tion (Mountcastle 1978; Wurtz *et al.* 1980). Moreover, the cellular activity of these areas was influenced in important ways by transmitter substances from the brain-stem reticular formation (Foote *et al.* 1980). This seems to be the relevant level of physiology (now neuroscience) which was needed to provide detailed links between the levels of physio-logical and cognitive analysis.

Another change was also required, and this change took the form of the behavioural or task analysis that Broadbent advocated. In his first book Broadbent (1958) developed a view of behavioural tasks that has been of primary importance in this enterprise. The flow diagram (boxes and arrows) was an effort to picture a functional analysis of the human nervous system that could complement blueprints (anatomy) and wiring diagrams (physiology). Broadbent's 1958 model was austere, and general to a wide variety of human tasks; but a more differentiated task analysis was needed to develop a psychology that could fit well with the emerging neuroscience. The overall mental architecture emerged from cognitive neuropsychology. On the basis of human patient data, it was possible to parcel the mind into rough cognitive systems, including language, object recognition, motor control, and selective attention, which could be selectively injured or preserved according to the logic of double dissociation (Shallice 1989).

If the insights from cognitive neuropsychology were to be pursued it was important to design tasks that fit within divisions emerging from neuropsychological analysis. In these 'model tasks' one attempts to study the simplest tasks that can define the operations of a particular cognitive system. The term 'model task' has a metaphorical relation to the use of model systems in neurobiology, where one studies the simplest nervous system that exhibits the desired property. Even so, no model task will consist of a single operation. Careful experimental investigation of the model task within each cognitive system is needed to provide the level of cognitive analysis that is most likely to make serious contact with neuroscience. Several generations of such experiments allow analysis of a number of tasks, such as search of active memory (Sternberg 1966); visual search (Treisman and Gormican 1988); lexical access (LaBerge and Samuels 1974); selective attention to sensory events (Posner 1980); construction of images (Kosslyn 1980, 1988); timing (Wing and Kristoferson 1973); and some others.

When new neuroimaging methods began to be widely used (Raichle 1987) it was possible to ask how the mental operations of cognition could be related to brain anatomy. The resultant evidence for rather exquisite localization of component operations (Posner 1988; Posner and Petersen 1990) forms the background for the current effort to realize some aspects of Broadbent's 1971 goal of analysing arousal. This review will be confined to one form of arousal × cognitive interaction, but it is hoped that the principles will prove to be more general. The specific instance chosen is the innervation of the posterior attention system by more general modulatory systems such as the norepinephrine system arising in the locus coeruleus.

To develop this review the chapter first defines a model task for the study of one aspect of the arousal. Second, it considers how arousal influences the model task. Third comes a review of two different forms of deficit that can be produced in the posterior attention system, the one resulting directly from lesions of the posterior parietal lobe, and the second, indirectly, from blocking modulatory input into this system. Next, new studies are described that manipulate arousal in the selected model task in normal subjects when they are required to sustain attention for ten seconds or more. These new results are used to understand the effect of sustained performance in normal adults, and to consider deficits in some forms of attentional pathology. Finally, a current programme of research designed to understand these arousal × cognitive interactions at the cellular level is outlined. The chapter is both far narrower and somewhat broader than the goals set by Broadbent. By examining only a single instance of the influence of arousal on cognitive computations we follow the neurobiological method of in-depth analysis of a single model, rather than the often more sweeping approach often characteristic of cognitive theory (Easterbrook 1959). However, there is the hope that the fundamental principles of arousal × cognitive interaction may extend widely to other transmitter systems and to other tasks and cognitive systems.

A COGNITIVE THEORY OF PHASIC AROUSAL

In Posner (1978) I reviewed the literature on the effect of warning signals on performance in reaction-time tasks. This review led to a rather surprising interpretation. The warning signal seemed to improve the speed at which subjects responded to signals, but often produced an increase in errors. At the time, speed–accuracy relations were very popular topics in reaction-time studies, and in general it had been found that many task manipulations caused a co-variation which improved speed and also tended to improve accuracy. There were occasions, however, when these two indices of performance were dissociated; and the use of warning signals appeared to be one of them.

   These data suggested that the warning signal did not improve the rate at which input evidence accumulated from the stimulus, but improved instead the rate at which it reached a criterial state or threshold for attention. If attention occurs early in the build-up of information the evidence upon which selection is made must be of lower overall quality, and this resulted in the increase in error-rate. In Broadbent's 1971 book this process of selection is called pigeonholing. In terms of internal processes it could be viewed as an attentional system enhancing information build-up in a sensory memory system (Posner 1978).

   The idea of a separation of data-processing (sensory-memory systems) from attentional systems was implicit in this viewpoint. It suggested that the human nervous system can be divided into mechanisms that operate automatically and those control systems that form the basis of attention. At the time this theory was purely cognitive. There was little basis for making the connection to the underlying neurology. For that goal it was necessary to have ideas of the anatomy of selective attention and of visual information accrual.

In order to relate attention to the underlying anatomy it was important to begin with a model task that might be used in normal humans, patients, and alert monkeys. The model task we adopted consisted of using a cue which directed the subjects' attention toward the most likely target location. The presence of the cue signalled the start of a trial and acted as a general warning signal, as well as telling the subjects where the target was most likely to occur. Two forms of cue were used: a peripheral cue was one close to the target, and tended to summon the subjects' attention; the central clue was at fixation, and indicated where the subjects should orient (Posner 1980). The simplicity of this model task allowed it to be studied with a wide variety of patient populations, monkeys, and other animals, as well as with normal humans.

On the basis of earlier work with monkeys (Ungerleider and Mishkin 1982) there is reason to separate the visual system into two major information streams: the ventral pathway from V1 to TEO, involved in object recognition; and the more dorsal pathway, including the inferior parietal lobe involved in location. Studies in the human brain confirm this. PET studies have shown the ventral pathway active for the analysis of colour, form, motion, and visual words (Corbetta et al. 1991; Haxby et al. 1991; Petersen et al. 1990). When subjects are required to attend to a location or a shift from location to location, as in the model task, PET studies show activation in the parietal and lateral frontal lobe (Corbetta et al. 1993); when selection is by colour, form, or speed more anterior activation occurs in the anterior cingulate or basal ganglia (Corbetta et al. 1990). We (Posner and Petersen 1990) have summarized this evidence by outlining two vertically organized attention networks, one involved in orienting to visual location (posterior system) and one to detecting targets (anterior system).

LESION EFFECTS ON AROUSAL
AND COMPUTATION

Elsewhere the computations of the parietal lobe, pulvinar, and colliculus that constitute the posterior visual spatial attention system have been reviewed (Posner 1988; Posner and Petersen 1990). From work in monkeys (Morrison and Foote 1986) it is known that each of these areas receives a very heavy input of norepinephrine from the locus coeruleus. NE input to these areas is much greater than to the classical geniculo-striate pathway or to the areas along the ventral pathway from primary cortex to the inferior temporal lobe visual areas. This anatomy corresponds well to the cognitive idea that a separate attention system serves to amplify and give priority to the output of a visual pattern-recognition (sensory-memory system).

By far the most common lesion site to produce contralateral neglect of visual stimuli is the posterior parietal lobe. It is well documented that damage to this area produces neglect which, among other things, involves a specific abnormality in dealing with visual stimuli contra-lateral to the lesion. Shortly after the lesion there is widespread dys-regulation of metabolic activity, which may extend over the whole hemisphere; but after about six months this has usually cleared (Duell and Collins 1984). While neglect as a clinical syndrome has many features, the lasting deficit appears to be primarily attentional. Subjects may appear to be normal, but if they are tested on their ability to deal with a contralateral target when already attending to visual information, the impairment is revealed in terms of a greatly magnified cost in reaction time. These basic results have been replicated with many parietal patients, and the time-course of recovery has also been thoroughly traced (Morrow and Ratcliff 1988; Posner et al. 1984; Posner 1988).

It has been known for many years that neglect as a clinical syndrome is more prevalent with right- than with left-hemisphere damage (Heilman and Van Den Abell 1980; Mesulam 1981). This has led some to suppose that the right hemisphere controls attention to both sides of space. Recent PET work has confirmed this idea by showing that shifting attention in the left or right visual field activates specific areas of the right superior parietal cortex, but the left superior parietal cortex is only active during shifts in the right visual field (Corbetta et al. 1993).

A second factor also differs between left and right parietal patients. In the attention-shifting task described above the cue to draw attention also serves as a warning signal for the upcoming target. Patients with right parietal lesions are extremely slow to targets in the left visual field after omission of the cue, while patients with left parietal lesions are not affected more strongly than normal subjects by the omission of a warning. Although it is difficult to make direct comparisons between groups of subjects in most of our data and in Ladavas' work with the same model task (Ladavas et al. 1989), the right parietal patients are generally quite slow in comparison to those with left parietal lesions. The warning signal appears to interact with the efficiency of the visual spatial attention system.

The reason for the strong effects of warning signals on right parietal patients may rest with the apparent specialization of the right cerebral hemisphere for maintaining the alert state (Posner and Petersen 1990). There is abundant evidence that patients with right-sided lesions have reduced ability to stay alert during vigilance tasks, and that the right hemisphere in split-brain preparations maintains effective vigilance, but the left does not. Studies with neuroimaging techniques indicate right frontal and parietal activation during vigilance tasks (Pardo et al. 1990).

These findings have led us to the hypothesis that the NE system operates to modulate the activity of the posterior attention system, and that it does so more effectively in the right hemisphere than in the left. This hypothesis is based on the strong anatomical connections of the NE system for the posterior attention system and on the idea that arousal acts to modulate attention.

It might seem parsimonious to suppose that the arousal system is itself involved in the computations of the posterior attention system, rather than serving as a modulator of its efficiency. Indeed, this is just the link between arousal and attention proposed by Heilman (Heilman and Van Den Abell 1980). However, two recent results suggest that the modulatory system operates in quite a different way. Recall that patients with parietal damage show greatly exaggerated costs when attention is cued to their good side and the target goes to the bad side. This increase in cost due to parietal lesions contrasts markedly with the reduction in cost that occurs from blocking NE. In one study the NE system was reduced in efficiency by administration of the drug clonodine (Clark et al. 1989). The results showed a very specific effect on attention-shifting; but it was the opposite of that found with parietal lesions. Subjects showed a reduction in cost. While a reduction in cost might, at first, be thought of as improved performance, it also has a strong disadvantage. What we call cost in this attention-shifting paradigm is a measure of how well one can restrict attention to the locus of the target. Difficulty in doing so may well be what in normal life we would call abnormal distractability.

A second situation in which modulation of orienting seems to be dissociated from a deficit in parietal function arises in dementia. A subset of Alzheimer's disease patients with reduced metabolism of the parietal lobe consequent to their degenerative process were studied (Parasuraman et al. 1992). These patients showed the same type of increase in cost that is observed for stroke patients, and the degree of this deficit was correlated with the reduction of metabolism in the superior parietal lobe. On the other hand when a different subset of Alzheimer patients were selected by the fact that they showed reduced metabolites of NE

(MHPG 3-methoxy, 4-hydroxyphenol glycol), and thus were assumed to have degeneration of the locus coeruleus, a reduced validity effect (cost plus benefit) was found in comparison to normal subjects (Freed *et al.* 1988).

Unfortunately, there are many difficulties in putting together the present literature. First, they are not specific for any particular transmitter. It was shown that blocking dopamine may affect attention-shifting in a similar way as was found with NE, and also that Parkinson's disease patients whose major deficiency is in dopamine show reductions in cost (Wright *et al.* 1990). The Alzheimer's studies use quite different methods of subject-selection, and different although related tasks. None the less, the results do suggest that whatever transmitter(s) are involved in modulating the posterior attention system operate in a way quite different from the intrinsic computations of the parietal lobe, since lesions and blocking transmitters have opposite effects upon the costs found in the model task. In order to pursue these issues it is important to study the interaction between modulation and cortical computation in a more detailed way.

ASYMMETRIES IN SUSTAINED ATTENTION

While there have been scattered reports of asymmetries in information-processing tasks related to preparing for target stimuli (Heilman and Van Den Abell 1980), they have been neither strong nor replicable. It seems important to develop a model task that could be related both to arousal or sustained attention and to shifts of spatial attention. Recently, it has been possible to demonstrate systematic arousal affects in normal persons (Whitehead 1991) that appear to interact with the operation of the posterior attention system. In these studies subjects received a warning interval followed by delays of from 3 to 30 seconds, arranged so that the length of the delay does not affect the likelihood of a signal (non-ageing foreperiods). The striking effect found in four studies is that, for delay intervals of 12 seconds and longer, stimuli presented to the left visual field are responded to significantly faster than those presented in the right visual field. For intervals of three seconds or less there was a tendency for right visual field stimuli to be faster.

The asymmetry produced by longer delay intervals appears to be due to the facility with which the subject can orient attention to the target event. This was shown by two converging operations. In one study a non-informative auditory signal sometimes accompanied the target. It had been shown previously such a signal produces a change in phasic alertness (Posner *et al.* 1977). The presence of the auditory signal completely eliminated the asymmetry. The auditory signal also increased errors. In addition, the asymmetry was shown to interact with central cues presented at the start of the trials, suggesting that the asymmetry involved some of the same mechanisms as are involved in the cueing effect (posterior attention system).

Easterbrook had proposed that as arousal is increased there is a reduced tendency to use irrelevant or peripheral cues. Thus the range of cue utilization is reduced in stressful states. This view is also supported by studies of rat behaviour following lesions that affect NE and DA systems. Robbins and Everitt (1987) conclude that:

we do not see the locus coeruleus as mediating cortical arousal, rather its noradrenergic projections become active under conditions of cortical arousal and this action helps to preserve discriminative selectivity of responding. In simple terms, it may be part of a mechanism which helps us to maintain concentration and efficient cognitive function under stress and which may have its experimental counterpart in the data reviewed by Easterbrook (1959) . . . suggesting that high levels of arousal normally narrow the focus of attention (p. 155).

In the model task developed in this chapter, increasing the level of arousal is assumed to involve increasing the activation of the posterior attention system from the NE system. As we have seen, blocking NE input reduces cost; and it seems reasonable that more NE would increase cost, and thus produce better concentration at the selected location. If the selected location is appropriate for the target we should find improved performance and reduced distractability from irrelevant locations. Moreover, the relative dominance of the right cerebral hemisphere under these conditions would also mean that more global aspects of the task might control behaviour. Whether or not this would be advantageous for performance would depend upon the importance of local and global cues to the task.

One way to interpret these results is as follows. The right hemisphere maintains its alert state by innervations of the posterior attention system of the right hemisphere from the locus coeruleus. Initial activation also influences the posterior attention system of the left hemisphere. However, over time the left hemisphere shows less sustained activation. This view supposes that there are two separate mechanisms controlling the shift of attention. The first, involving the actual operations of the posterior attention system, is used to shift attention; and the second involves modulation of the relative efficiency of this first mechanism. Tests of this idea require the development of more refined analysis of the NE-attention interaction within the posterior parietal lobe. Efforts to push these ideas further are examined in the final section of this chapter; but first it is necessary to consider potential pathological consequences of deficits in the arousal–attention interaction.

PATHOLOGY OF SUSTAINED ATTENTION

Attention-deficit disorder has been studied from many viewpoints, but work from a cognitive–neuroscience perspective has not been extensive. As has been noted, blocking norepinephrine in normal subjects can produce a pattern of reduced cost in spatial orienting that could also be described as increased distractability, since non-attended locations would be more effective in attracting attention. Because of the common descriptions of attention-deficit disorder (ADD) as involving increases in distractability, and because the symptoms of ADD are often improved by drugs that are agonists of dopamine and NE (Zametkin and Rapoport 1987), it is reasonable to suppose that cognitive tasks would show reduced costs, perhaps primarily to right-hemisphere stimuli.

Two studies have been guided by this hypothesis. The first used manual responses to visual stimuli, and the second eye-movement responses to visual stimuli (Rothlind et al. 1991; Swanson et al. 1991). The results of the first study showed a very specific abnormality in ADD children. At the longer (800 msec.) delay interval they showed little difference between valid and invalid trials compared to normal age-matched controls. This reduction in the normal advantage for valid trials was most apparent for left visual field stimuli. The result confirmed our expectation of a lack of cost, as would be expected if there was reduced norepinephrine. The normal children at both delay intervals showed the usual effects that we have found for adults. The fact that this effect was found only for the long delay interval (800 msec.) suggests that it is due to sustaining attention at the cued location rather than merely to a shift of attention. However, the time-intervals used in this study were very different from those employed by Whitehead in his study of sustained attention, and more research using these longer intervals is obviously needed.

Rothlind et al. also found evidence of a difference between ADD and normal children in eye-movements toward visual events. Under condition of no warning, leftward eye-movements, controlled by the right cerebral hemisphere, were faster than rightward eye-movements in normal children, but not in ADD children.

These two findings taken together give some support to the idea of a specific deficit in ADD children in the operations of the right hemisphere in maintaining the alert state. The deficit might operate through a reduction in right-hemisphere availability of NE, and by this mechanism a reduction in the ability to restrict information to a selected location. This view would be supported by evidence in neuroimaging studies of some deficiency of right-hemisphere activation during vigilance. The most thorough PET study to date of this hypothesis (Zametkin *et al.* 1990), conducted with adults who had ADD when children, showed a large number of areas activated, which were mainly left frontal and did not correspond to the arousal system in normals.

CELLULAR MECHANISMS

This chapter so far has been concerned primarily with the documentation of arousal and selection interactions at the cognitive and neurosystems levels. In the course of doing this we have developed some constraints upon the underlying mechanisms; however, the details of these mechanisms have not been specified. Such specifications require computational and/or cellular analysis. These levels of analysis are currently under way as part of the work of our Center for the Cognitive Neuroscience of Attention. Let me describe our current three-pronged attack on these issues.

Regional EEG analysis. We have developed a system for recording scalp electrical responses from arrays of 64 electrodes (Compton *et al.* 1991; Osgood 1990, 1991), and are attempting to relate the electrical scalp distributions recorded from these arrays to specific generators found in studies using PET. Our goal is to validate the use of scalp distributions by comparison with PET, and to test algorithms for locating the sources of the scalp distribution (Scherg *et al.* 1989).

So far we have been successful in relating two areas found in PET studies (Petersen *et al.* 1989; Petersen *et al.* 1990) of visual word-reading with what appear to be scalp-electrical signs of the same two generators. PET studies of passive reading of words, regular non-words, consonant strings, and nonsense forms all show a very strong right-posterior occipito-temporal area of increased blood-flow. We (Compton *et al.* 1991) found a similar asymmetry in our scalp electrodes over several posterior temporo-parietal sites at about 100 msec. after input. PET studies show a ventral occipital activation for words and orthographically regular non-words that is not present for consonant strings. Our ERP experiment also showed this difference at about 200–250 msec. after input, and provided some support for the idea of a posterior left lateralized generator.

PET studies (Pardo *et al.* 1991) have shown high levels of activity in right frontal and parietal sites in sustained attention tasks. We are now applying our EEG technology to recording of electrical activity following warning signals and ERPs to subsequent targets. We are using the 3- and 12-second foreperiods found by Whitehead (1991) to produce asymmetries in RT favouring the left visual field. We have found so far evidence of differences between the two visual fields in the P300 component of the ERP in those subjects who showed the RT pattern Whitehead previously reported (Whitehead and Liotti 1991). This finding would fit with recent results indicating that lesions of the locus coeruleus produce changes in the P300 in the monkey (Foote *et al.*, in press).

Cellular recording. The ERP studies are a prelude to efforts to further our understanding of the cellular basis of interactions between NE and the posterior attention system. This effort builds upon previous work which has sought to monitor NE release within the primary visual areas of the anesthetized monkey (Marrocco *et al.* 1987). These studies have relied upon the use of special electrodes that respond specifically to the presence of small amounts of NE and DA. The method has difficulty in discriminating between NE and DA, however. The studies of primary visual cortex indicated that NE release was regulated at the terminal field by local neurones without mandatory activation of the LC cell bodies. A given striate area would only release NE when the appropriate visual stimulus for that cell is presented. It is not yet known how general this finding is beyond the primary visual areas of the monkey.

In our project we intend to study the release of NE in alert monkeys following warning signals and cues to shift attention in a visual field. We will be looking for changes in NE in the left and right parietal lobe following a cue to prepare for a visual target. The review outlined in this paper provides some specific hypotheses about what will be found. If NE release is related to the attention-shift, we would expect it to accumulate in the interval during which the monkey maintains covert expectation at a contralateral location.

Because of the opposite effects of parietal lesions from what is found with reduction of modulator input we do not expect NE to be the basis for an attention-shift. However, we do expect its presence to serve as a modulator of the attention-shift. It has already been possible to show in one monkey that global reductions of NE by the drugs clonodine and guanfacine reduce or eliminate the effects of a warning signal on reaction time (Witte *et al.* 1992). One important issue is how evidence of local control can be reconciled with the idea arising from cognitive studies of general alerting effect from warning signals. One possible fact that might lead to reconciliation between local release and more global arousal is that the receptive fields of neurones in the parietal lobe are quite large. Thus the modulation, even if controlled locally, might extend over quite a range. This could be consistent with the well-known gradients that surround the facilitated areas in cognitive studies (LaBerge and Brown 1989). Warning signals may have their effects within a few hundred milliseconds. The Whitehead data suggest that these effects are symmetric or nearly symmetric in the two hemispheres. The warning signal may potentiate local release of NE in the region of the following target. In this way a global effect of the warning signal may relate to local release of NE. This local release would occur in equivalent fashion in the two hemispheres. If attention had to be sustained over a long interval modulation would require control from the locus coeruleus, which might produce the asymmetry observed at longer intervals. Since cells in the locus are phasic in operation it seems likely that its sustained activity might require input from another source.

Neural modelling. The results of our ERP and cellular studies of NE release should be useful in supplying the needed constraint to support more exact models of how the posterior attention system interacts with accumulating data related to the content of visual information. Several connectionist models of this interaction already exist (LaBerge and Brown 1989; Mozer and Behrman 1990; Sandon 1990). They make specific predictions about such tasks as searching letter strings, perceiving words, and feature and conjunction search. They generally model the posterior attention system as a network of interacting nodes that respond to cues or features in a second network that simulates the ventral pathway. However, they do not include the idea of an arousal system that might modulate the activity of the posterior attention network in a particular way.

Recently, an effort has been made to simulate the effect of dopamine in the forebrain by assuming its presence changes the gain parameter in a network designed to carry out the Stroop task (Servan-Schreiver *et al.* 1990). An extension of this idea to the study of spatial attention has recently been made in a model of the role of the basal ganglia in mediating visual orienting (Jackson and Houghton 1992). This model attempts to predict a number of known cognitive phenomena including the validity effect produced by peripheral cues. Models of the NE system might be assumed to involve an increase in relative signal strength (signal to noise ratio), and predictions might be made for things such as slope of the cueing gradient around the selected location.

CONCLUSION

The approach outlined in this chapter involves a programme of research designed to specify in some detail interactions between levels clearly related to neuroscience (nature of transmitters involved, anatomy) and those at the heart of cognitive psychology (how arousal mediates selectivity). These issues were at the heart of the goals that Broadbent laid down in the final chapter of *Decision and stress* to which we referred at the start of this chapter. There are differences. Methods are now available to investigate the issues at each level, and to combine the results into detailed simulations that capture the results and allow new predictions. This is an advance, but there is also a cost. *Decision and stress* laid out very general mechanisms that were thought to hold generally irrespective of the domain involved. We have shrunk the inquiry to the interaction between some forms of arousal (following warning signals) and some types of attention (orienting of visual attention). Hopefully this level of detail will produce general principles that will illuminate other issues; but there is no guarantee that they will emerge. None the less, it seems possible that this level of detail may produce the convergence between the neural and the performance levels for which Broadbent hoped.

ACKNOWLEDGEMENTS

The research presented here was supported by ONR contract N0014-89-J3013 and by the James McDonnell Foundation and the Pew Memorial Trust grant to the Center for the Cognitive Neuroscience of Attention. The author is grateful to Richard Marrocco and Mary K. Rothbart for their help on this manuscript.

REFERENCES

Broadbent, D. E. (1958). *Perception and communication*. Pergamon Press, Oxford.
Broadbent, D. E. (1971). *Decision and stress*. Academic Press, London.
Clark, C. R., Geffen, G. M., and Geffen, L. B. (1989). Catecholamines and the covert orientation of attention in humans. *Neuropsychologia*, **27**(2), 131–9.
Compton, P., Grossenbacher, P., Posner, M. I., and Tucker, D. (1991). A cognitive-anatomical approach to attention in lexical access. *Journal of Cognitive Neuroscience*, 3(4), 304–12.
Corbetta, M., Miezin, F. M., Dobmeyer, S., Shulman, G. L., and Petersen, S. E. (1990). Attentional modulation of neural processing of shape, color, and velocity in humans. *Science*, **248**, 1556–9.

Corbetta, M., Miezin, F. M., Dobmeyer, S., Shulman, G. L., and Petersen, S. E. (1991). Selective and divided attention during visual discrimination of shape, color and speed: functional anatomy by Positron Emission Tomography. *Journal of Neuroscience*, **11**, 2382–402.

Corbetta, M., Meizin, F. M., Schulman, G. L., and Petersen, S. E. (1993). A PET study of visual spatial attention. *Journal of Neuroscience*, **13**, 12020–6.

Duell, R. M. and Collins, R. C. (1984). The functional anatomy of frontal lobe neglect in the monkey: behavioral and quantitative 2 DG studies. *Annals of Neurology*, **15**, 521–9.

Easterbrook, J. A. (1959). The effect of emotion on cue utilization and the organization of behavior. *Psychological Review*, **66**, 183–201.

Foote, S. L., Aston-Jones, G., and Boom, F. E. (1980). Impulse activity of locus coeruleus neurons in awake rats and monkeys is a function of sensory stimulation and arousal. *Proceedings of the National Academy of Science of the USA*, **77**, 3033–7.

Foote, S. L., Berridge, C. W., Adams, L. M., and Pineda, J. A. Electrophysiological evidence for the involvement of the locus coeruleus in alerting, orienting and attending. *Progress in Brain Research*. (In press.)

Freed, D. M., Corkin, S., Growdon, J. H., and Nissen, M. J. (1988). Selective attention in Alzheimer's disease: CSF correlates of behavioral impairments. *Neuropsychologia*, **27**, 895–902.

Haxby, J. V., Grady, C. L., Ungerleider, L. G., and Hurwitz, A. B. (1991). Mapping and functional neuroanatomy of the intact human brain with brain work imaging. *Neuropsychologia*, **29**, 517–38.

Heilman, K. M. and Van Den Abell, T. (1980). Right hemisphere dominance of attention: the mechanisms underlying hemispheric asymmetries in inattention (neglect). *Neurology*, **30**, 327–30.

Jackson, S. and Houghton, G. (1992). *Basal ganglia function in the control of visuospatial attention: a neural network model*. Technical Report No. 92-6. University of Oregon, Eugene, Oregon.

Kosslyn, S. M. (1980). *Image and mind*. Harvard University Press, Cambridge, Mass.

Kosslyn, S. M. (1988). Aspects of a cognitive neuroscience of mental imagery. *Science*, **240**, 1621–6.

LaBerge, D. and Brown, V. (1989). Theory of operations in shape identification. *Psychological Review*, **96**, 101–24.

LaBerge, D. and Samuels, J. (1974). Toward a theory of automatic processing in reading. *Cognitive Psychology*, **6**, 6293–323.

Ladavas, E., Pesce, M. D., and Provinciali, L. (1989). Unilateral attention deficits and hemispheric asymmetries in the control of visual attention. *Neuropsychologia*, **27**, 353–66.

Marrocco, R. T., Lane, R. F., McClurkin, J. W., Blaha, C. D., and Alkire, M. F. (1987). Release of cortical catecholamines by visual stimulation requires activity in thalamocortical afferents of monkey and cat. *Journal of Neuroscience*, **7**(9), 2756–67.

Mesulam, M. M. (1981). A cortical network for directed attention and unilateral neglect. *Annals of Neurology*, **10**, 309–25.

Morrison, J. H. and Foote, S. L. (1986). Noradrenergic and serotoninergic innervation of cortical, thalamic and tectal visual structures in old and new world monkeys. *Journal of Comparative Neurology*, **243**, 117–28.

Morrow, L. A. and Ratcliff, G. (1988). The disengagement of covert attention and the neglect syndrome. *Psychobiology*, **16**, 261–9.

Mountcastle, V. B. (1978). Brain mechanisms for directed attention. *Journal of the Royal Society of Medicine*, **71**, 14–27.

Mozer, M. C. and Behrman, M. (1990). On the interaction of selective attention and lexical knowledge: a connectionist account of neglect dyslexia. *Cognitive Neuroscience*, **2**, 96–123.

Osgood, G. (1990). *The electrophysiological graphical imaging system: Part I*, Technical Report No. 90-9. University of Oregon, Eugene, Oregon.

Osgood, G. (1991). *The electrophysiological graphical imaging system: Part II*, Technical Report No. 91-11. University of Oregon, Eugene, Oregon.

Parasuraman, R., Greenwood, P. M., Haxby, J. V., and Grady, C. L. (1992). Visuospatial attention in dementia of the Alzheimer type. *Brain*, **115**, 711–33.

Pardo, J. V., Pardo, P. J., Janer, K. W., and Raichle, M. E. (1990). The anterior cingulate cortex mediates processing selection in the Stroop attentional conflict paradigm. *Proceedings of the National Academy of Science of the USA*, **87**, 256–9.

Pardo, J. V., T, F. P., and Raichle, M. E. (1991). Localization of a human system for sustained attention by positron emission tomography. *Nature*, **349**, 61–3.

Petersen, S. E., Fox, P. T., Posner, M. I., Mintun, M., and Raichle, M. E. (1989). Positron emission tomographic studies of the processing of single words. *Journal of Cognitive Neuroscience*, **1**, 153–70.

Petersen, S. E., Fox, P. T., Snyder, A. Z., and Raichle, M. E. (1990). Activation of extrastriate and frontal cortical areas by visual words and word-like stimuli. *Science*, **249**, 1041–4.

Posner, M. I. (1978). *Chronometric explorations of mind*. Erlbaum, Hillsdale, NJ.

Posner, M. I. (1980). Orienting of attention. *Quarterly Journal of Experimental Psychology*, **32**, 3–25.

Posner, M. I. (1988). Structures and functions of selective attention. In *Master lectures in clinical neuropsychology and brain function: research, measurement and practice* (ed. T. Boll and B. Bryant), pp. 171–202. American Psychological Association, Washington DC.

Posner, M. I. and Petersen, S. E. (1990). The attention system of the human brain. *Annual Review of Neuroscience*, **13**, 25–42.

Posner, M. I., Nissen, M. J., and Ogden, W. C. (1977). Attended and unattended processing modes: the role of set from spatial location. In *Modes of perception* (ed. H .J. Pick), pp. 137–57. Erlbaum, Hillsdale, NJ.

Posner, M. I., Walker, J. A., Friedrich, F. J., and Rafal, R. D. (1984). Effects of parietal lobe injury on covert orienting of visual attention. *Journal of Neuroscience*, **4**, 1863–74.

Raichle, M. E. (1987). Circulatory and metabolic correlates of brain function in normal humans. In *Handbook of physiology, Section I–V, Part 2* (ed. V. B. Mountcastle and F. Plum), pp. 643–74. American Physiological Society, Bethesda, MD.

Robbins, T. W. and Everitt, B. J. (1987). Psychopharmacological studies of arousal and attention. In *Cognitive neurochemistry* (ed. S. M. Stahl, S. D. Iversen, and E. C. Goodman), pp. 135–70. Oxford University Press.

Rothlind, J., Posner, M. I., and Schaughency, E. (1991). Lateralized control of eye movements in attention deficit hyperactivity disorder. *Journal of Cognitive Neuroscience*, **3**(4), 377–81.

Sandon, P. A. (1990). Simulating visual attention. *Journal of Cognitive Neuroscience*, **2**(3), 213–31.

Scherg, M., Vajsar, J., and Picton, T. W. (1989). A source analysis of the human auditory evoked potentials. *Journal of Cognitive Neuroscience*, **14**, 336–355.

Servan-Schreiver, D., Printz, H., and Cohen, J. D. (1990). A network model of catecholamine effects: gain, signal-to-noise ratio, and behavior. *Science*, **249**, 892–5.

Shallice, T. (1989). *From neuropsychology to mental structure*. Cambridge University Press.

Sternberg, S. (1966). High speed scanning and memory. *Science*, **153**, 652–4.

Swanson, J. M., Posner, M., Potkin, S., Bonforte, S., Youpa, D., Fiore, C., Cantwell, D., and Crinella, F. (1991). Activating tasks for the study of visual-spatial attention in ADHD children: a cognitive anatomic approach. *Journal of Child Neurology*, **6**, S119–S127.

Treisman, A. M. and Gormican, S. (1988). Feature analysis in early vision: evidence from search asymmetries. *Psychological Review*, **95**, 15–18.

Ungerleider, L. G. and Mishkin, M. (1982). Two cortical visual systems. In *Analysis of visual behavior* (ed. D. J. Ingle, M. A. Goodale, and R. J. W. Mansfield), pp. 540–80. MIT Press, Cambridge, Mass.

Whitehead, R. (1991). Right hemisphere processing superiority during sustained visual attention. *Journal of Cognitive Neuroscience*, **3**(4), 329–37.

Whitehead, R. and Liotti, M. (1991). Right hemisphere lateralization for arousal? A high density ERP study. Poster presented at the Annual Meeting of the Psychonomic Society, San Francisco, CA.

Wing, A. and Kristoferson, A. (1973). Response delays and the timing of discrete motor responses. *Perception and Psychophysics*, **14**, 5–12.

Witte, E. A., Gordon-Lickey, M. E., and Marrocco, R. T. (1992). Pharmacological depletion of catecholamines modifies covert orienting in rhesus monkey. *Society of Neuroscience*, Abstract, **226**, 11.

Wright, M. J., Burns, R. J., Geffen, G. M., and Geffen, L. B. (1990). Covert orientation of visual attention in Parkinson's disease: an impairment of the maintenance of attention. *Neuropsychologia*, **28**, 151–60.

Wurtz, R. H., Goldberg, M. E., and Robinson, E. L. (1980). Behavioral modulation of visual responses in the monkey: stimulus selection for attention and movement. *Progress in Psychobiology and Physiological Psychology*, **9**, 43–83.

Zametkin, A. J. and Rapoport, J. L. (1987). Neurobiology of attention deficit disorder with hyperactivity: where have we come in 50 years? *Journal of American Child and Adolescent Psychiatry*, **26**, 676–86.

Zametkin, A. J., Nordahl, T. E., Gross, M., King, A. C., Semple, W. E., Rumsey, J., Hamburger, S., and Cohen, R. M. (1990). Cerebral glucose metabolism in adults with hyperactivity of childhood onset. *The New England Journal of Medicine*, **323**(20), 1361–415.

TWENTY

Self-report questionnaires in cognitive psychology: have they delivered the goods?

James Reason

INTRODUCTION

Throughout his long and exceptionally distinguished research career, Donald Broadbent has employed a wide range of techniques to investigate the ways in which people manage their cognitive affairs. This paper is concerned with only one of them: the use of self-report questionnaires (SRQs) to obtain subjective estimates of individual proneness to everyday slips, lapses, and minor blunders.

Since the mid-1970s a variety of cognitive questionnaires have been employed by different research groups. This work has already been extensively reviewed and evaluated elsewhere (Herrmann 1982, 1984; Martin and Jones 1984; Morris 1984; Reason 1989; Rabbitt 1990). Similarly, the results obtained by the Oxford group's Cognitive Failures Questionnaire (CFQ) are well known (Broadbent et al. 1982; Broadbent et al. 1986). Rather than covering old ground, I will take a rather parochial approach to the question posed in the title, and summarize some eight years of research with a Manchester cousin of the CFQ, the Short Inventory of Minor Lapses (SIML).

What are the 'goods' mentioned in the title? There are at least three criteria that might be applied. Can self-report questionnaires produce robust and consistent findings? Have they told us anything that is new and interesting? Do they have any practical utility? I will try to show that the answers to all three questions are in the affirmative, though in sometimes unexpected and unusual ways.

THE SHORT INVENTORY OF MINOR LAPSES

The SIML is a 15-item questionnaire, comprising general descriptions of 12 of the most frequently occurring slips and lapses (Reason 1984). These relate to both action slips and memory lapses. There are also three further questions concerning failures of voluntary attentional control. Like the CFQ, the SIML instructions require the respondent to rate approximately how often each type of cognitive failure has been experienced, but over the past year rather than 6 months. Correlations between the CFQ and the SIML total scores have been found to be of the order of 0.6 and 0.7 on several occasions (Reason and Lucas 1984).

Five response categories are offered for each item: hardly ever, sometimes, quite often, frequently, nearly all the time. These are scored on a 1–5 scale and summed to give a total score. The individual questions are listed below in the order in which they appear in the SIML.

1. How often do you forget to say something you were going to mention?

2. How often do you have the feeling that you should be doing something, either now or later, but you can't remember what it is?

3. How often do you find your mind continuing to dwell upon something that you would prefer not to think about?

4. How often do you find you can't remember what you have just done or where you have just been (e.g., when walking or driving)?

5. How often do you leave some necessary step out of a task (e.g., forgetting to put tea in the teapot)?

6. How often do you find that you cannot immediately recall the name of a familiar person, place or object?

7. How often do you think you're paying attention to something when you're actually not (e.g., when reading a book or watching TV)?

8. How often do you have the 'what-am-I-here-for?' feeling when you find you have forgotten what it was you came to do?

9. How often do you find yourself repeating something you've already done or carrying out some unnecessary action (e.g., flicking on the light when you're leaving the room in daylight)?

10. How often do you find you've forgotten to do something you intended to do?

11. How often do you decide to do something and then find yourself side-tracked into doing something different?

12. How often do you find yourself searching for something that you've just put down or are still carrying around with you?

13. How often do you forget to do something that you were going to do after dealing with an unexpected interruption?

14. How often do you find your mind wandering when you're doing something that needs your concentration?

15. How often do you make mistakes in which you do the right actions but with the wrong objects (or people) (e.g., unwrapping a sweet, throwing the sweet away and putting the paper in your mouth)?

NORMATIVE DATA

The SIML norms have been obtained from two independent samples:

Sample A was made up of 543 people, comprising 112 male and female undergraduates (mean age, 20 years, range, 18–45); 88 female patients undergoing treatment for breast cancer (mean age, 52 years, range, 24–85); 225 elderly females (mean age, 65, range, 50–90); and 118 elderly males (mean age, 67, range 50–93). The last two groups were members of the Age and Cognitive Performance Research Centre's (ACPRC) subject panel.

Sample B was made up of 1656 car-drivers, comprising 847 males and 809 females. The age-range was from 17 to 69 years.

The mean scores for the two samples are shown in Table 20.1. Standard deviations are given in parentheses. The close similarities between the means and standard deviations for both the individual items and the total scores for these two independent samples would appear to satisfy the criterion of robustness. Whatever the SIML is measuring, it is evidently doing so consistently across the 15-item profile. The correlation between the two sets of item means is 0.879. There were no sex differences, but there were some unexpected age differences.

TABLE 20.1. Summarizing the normative data

SIML item	Sample A ($n = 543$)	Sample B ($n = 1656$)
1. Forget to say	2.4 (0.83)	2.3 (0.79)
2. Should be doing	1.9 (1.00)	2.0 (0.78)
3. Mind-dwelling	2.2 (1.10)	2.5 (0.97)
4. Forget past actions	1.4 (0.82)	1.5 (0.71)
5. Omit planned step	1.4 (0.61)	1.5 (0.64)
6. Can't recall name	2.6 (1.00)	2.4 (0.92)
7. Not paying attention	2.2 (0.91)	2.2 (0.82)
8. Why-am-I-here?	2.1 (0.86)	2.1 (0.82)
9. Repetition, etc.	1.6 (0.89)	1.6 (0.73)
10. Forget intention	2.2 (0.95)	2.0 (0.77)
11. Sidetracking	2.3 (0.97)	2.4 (0.89)
12. Searching/carrying	2.1 (1.10)	2.1 (0.92)
13. Omit/interruption	2.1 (0.86)	2.2 (0.83)
14. Mind-wandering	2.2 (0.97)	1.9 (0.86)
15. Transpositions	1.3 (0.53)	1.3 (0.56)
Totals	30 (7.2)	30 (7.1)

AGE DIFFERENCES

Another robust though counter-intuitive finding is that the self-reported incidence of minor slips and lapses declines with age. These age differences are highly significant in both Samples A and B, as shown in Figs. 20.1 (Sample A) and 20.2 (Sample B).

In Sample A, the reduction of reported slips and lapses with age is significantly reversed on Item 6 (difficulty in recalling names). If one accepts these data at their face value, then this finding is consistent with William James's observation that 'when memory begins to decay, proper names are what go first . . .' (James, 1890, p. 683), and with Cohen and Faulkner's (1984) experimental results. Exactly the same reversal is evident in Sample B. This difference is highly significant ($p < .0001$). With the exception of Items 5 (omitting necessary task steps) and 12 (searching for something being carried or just put down), all the other items show a highly significant decline with age ($p < .0001$).

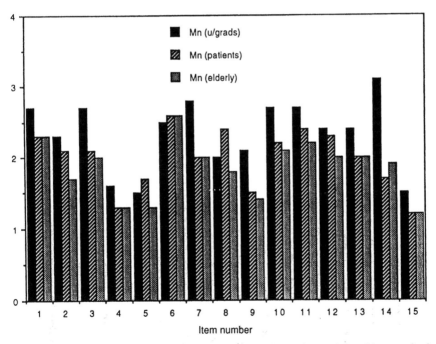

FIG. 20.1. Age comparisons for Sample A. The undergraduates (u/grads) comprised 112 males and females (mean age 20 yrs, range 18–45 yrs); the patients were 88 females undergoing investigation for suspected breast cancer (mean age 52 yrs, 24–85); and the group labelled 'elderly' was made up of 225 females (mean age 65, 50–90) and 118 males (mean age 67, 50–93).

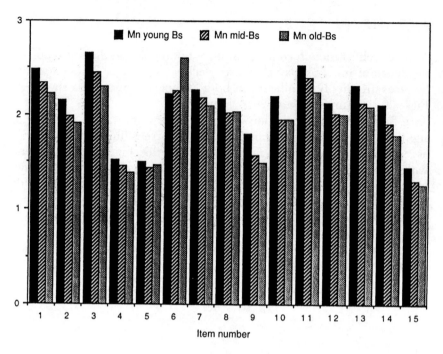

FIG. 20.2. Age comparisons for Sample B. There were 522 young subjects (mean age 22 yrs, range 17–29 yrs, standard deviation 3.6), 546 middle-aged subjects (mean 39 yrs, range 30–49, standard deviation 5.7), and 578 older subjects (mean 59 yrs, range 50–69 yrs, standard deviation 5.7). The total sample comprised 847 males and 809 females.

This paradoxical negative correlation between age and the reported frequency of cognitive failures is in close agreement with other results obtained with the CFQ. In one study, Rabbitt and Abson (1990) found that 50-year-olds reported significantly more slips and lapses than either 60-year-olds or 70-year-olds (who did not differ significantly). In a second study (Rabbitt and Abson 1991) they found significant differences between all three age-groups. The mean CFQ score for 50-year-olds was 40.6 (SD = 12.5); for 60-year-olds, 37.4 (SD = 11.5); and for 70-year-olds, 34.5 (SD = 12.3).

Though exceedingly difficult to interpret, these findings cannot easily be dismissed. There would seem to be at least two ways of treating them. One can either accept these self-report data as reflecting the behavioural reality, or one can challenge the validity of the instruments by which they were collected, as Rabbit and Abson (1990, 1991) have done. But neither is an easy path to take for the reasons set out below.

If one assumes that these self-report judgements correspond to actual cognitive performance, then there are at least two candidate hypotheses to consider initially, one relating to age differences in activity (and hence opportunity to make errors) and the other to various forms of age-related compensation.

The *activity hypothesis* states that older people have 'less taxing life-styles' (Rabbitt and Abson 1991) and engage in fewer tasks requiring the sharing of limited resources between different informational demands. As a result, they encounter fewer opportunities for making the kinds of error sampled by either the CFQ or the SIML.

The *compensation hypothesis* takes various forms. One variant is that older people, being aware of their diminished cognitive capabilities, rely more heavily on external memory aids and hence suffer fewer lapses. Another is that, whereas younger people take the slips and lapses of everyday life as a matter of course, older people may see them as the harbingers of cognitive decline and feel far more anxious about them. As a result, they invest a greater degree of custodial attention (Reason and Lucas 1984) in the performance of routine activities, and, in consequence, make fewer absent-minded errors.

Unfortunately, neither of these hypotheses explains the large differences between the young (mean age 22 years, 17–29) and the middle-aged (mean age 39 years, 30–49) in Sample B. No significant loss of cognitive competence is found before the age of 50 (Rabbit and Abson 1990), nor are there likely to be major differences in the level of activity between these younger groups. Moreover, on the one occasion in which we sought to test the anxiety variant of the compensation hypothesis, we found no significant differences between younger and older subjects in the degree of anxiety likely to be associated with each of the 15 SIML items.

So what of the other alternative, namely that these self-reported differences are an artefact of the measuring instrument? Rabbitt and Abson (1990, 1991) offered several reasons why the use of SQRs is problematic, particularly when making age comparisons. They argue, for example, that the domain-specificity of everyday memory skills is masked by reliance upon total scores. But this cannot apply to the data from Samples A and B, since the comparisons were made with regard to specific kinds of cognitive failure.

They also raise the possibility that old people are more likely to 'forget that they forget' and so under-report their lapses. This may be so, but the force of this criticism would be stronger if respondents were asked to gauge actual numbers of cognitive failures. But the SIML and many other SRQs require them to make only very approximate ordinal judgements of relative incidence. For this kind of assessment, memory distortions may work either way: lapses may be underestimated, as Rabbit and Abson suggest, because they are forgotten, or their reported occurrence may be inflated owing to the vividness (Nisbett and Ross 1980) or availability (Tversky and Kahneman 1974) of particular experiences.

A further possibility (not raised by Rabbitt and Abson) is that there may be systematic age differences in the way people perceive the response scale. Viewed against the perspective of a long life, categories such as 'quite often' and 'frequently' may have a different significance than they do for those with shorter personal histories. However, there are two reasons to doubt this. First, the SIML-item differences between the young (excluding undergraduates*) and the middle-aged were, in many instances, greater than those between the middle-aged and the elderly. Second, all SIML respondents are asked to judge the frequency of their slips and lapses over the past six months rather than over an entire lifetime.

The large differences observed between the young and the middle-aged also cast doubt on the idea that the age-related decline in SRQ scores reflect life-span variations in confidence and self-regard (Rabbitt and Abson 1990, 1991) rather than actual changes in error-rates. This argument could apply to 50-year-olds, but hardly to 20-year-olds.

Rabbitt and Abson (1990) assert that people are incapable of making absolute judgements about their cognitive efficiency. This may be true, but the SIML is not asking for such judgements. Its respondents are required to make 5-category ratings of the frequency with which 15 well-defined cognitive events occurred during the course of their daily lives over the preceding six months. Although not free from bias, there is considerable evidence to show that people are exceedingly sensitive to event frequency (see Zechmeister and Nyberg 1982). In some instances, these frequency judgements are almost perfectly calibrated. Brown (1990), for instance, had her subjects rate the frequency of appearance of characters in the TV serial, *The Forsyte saga*. The correlation between their subjective frequency ratings and actual time-on-screen was 0.905.

At several points in their critique of SRQs, Rabbitt and Abson (1990) equate the occurrence of minor slips and lapses with diminished cognitive competence. But is this necessarily the case? It has been argued that absent-mindedness is the penalty we pay for the essential ability to automatize our routine actions (Reason 1979). This permits the withdrawal of conscious attention from some highly-practised tasks

---

* It is interesting to note that, for undergraduates, the high-scoring items are 'attending but not taking in' and 'mind-wandering'. Both of these may have more to do with the occupational hazards of being a student than with age.

so that we may perform other more resource-intensive mental activities, such as analytical reasoning or future planning, with greater efficiency. In some individuals (i.e., the depressed or brain-damaged) and in highly stressful situations, this withdrawal is largely involuntary; but, for many people, it is a matter of personal style, influenced by occupation, perceptions of hazard, and local circumstances. Archimedes, Montaigne, Coleridge, and G. K. Chesterton, for example, were notoriously prone to periods of lapse-prone abstraction; but they were hardly incompetent.

Rabbitt and Abson (1990) concluded their critique by enjoining us to 'compare older and younger individuals' self-assessments with their actual performance on specific tasks that they very clearly understand'. Driving a car seems to fit this bill. In addition to the SIML, the Sample B subjects completed a range of paper-and-pencil measures of driving performance (Reason *et al.* 1991). One of these, the Driver Behaviour Questionnaire (DBQ), asked respondents to rate the frequency with which they committed 8 potentially dangerous errors (for

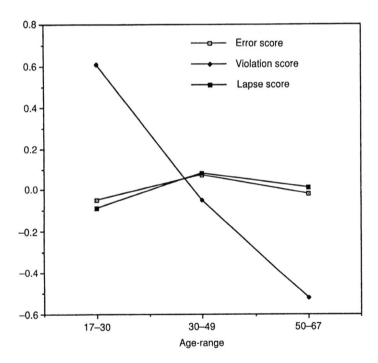

FIG. 20.3. Comparing factor scores on the Driver Behaviour Questionnaire in Sample B. The values shown are mean deviations in each group from the whole-sample mean. Their possible values run from −3 to +3.

example, not attending to the vehicle ahead, failing to see a cyclist), 8 dangerous violations (for example, not stopping at red lights, overtaking on the inside), and 8 relatively harmless lapses (forgetting where the car is parked, being on one's usual rather than one's intended route). The mean factor scores for the three age-groups are shown in Fig. 20.3.

These results do not exactly clarify the picture. Neither of the error factor scores showed a linear decline with age and, of these, only the lapse score differed significantly between the three groups. Here, younger drivers reported significantly fewer harmless lapses than did older drivers. Thus, task-specific instruments can produce age relationships that differ from those obtained by more global SRQs, such as the CFQ and the SIML. The negative correlation between age and violation scores was highly significant. This accords with several studies of driver behaviour and with demographic accident trends. The variables that correlated significantly with personal accident histories (having controlled for annual mileage) were age, sex, and violation score.

At present, neither the possible explanations for a genuine age-related decline in cognitive failures, nor the arguments against the validity of SQRs are especially convincing. The only solid thing we are left with is the finding itself. This is not new, but it is perhaps more difficult to explain, or even to explain away, than earlier results in view of the wider age-span. It is likely that this uncomfortable result, real or otherwise, will continue to trouble age researchers for some time to come.

THE STRESS-VULNERABILITY HYPOTHESIS

One of the most interesting and important findings to emerge from SRQ studies is the relationship between a high level of reported cognitive failures, assessed retrospectively over a period of months, and the number and degree of self-reported psychiatric symptoms, experienced during or immediately following a period of real-life stress (Broadbent et al. 1982). Donald Broadbent has expressed this in the form of a hypothesis: namely, that characteristically high rates of cognitive failure are related to increased vulnerability to externally-imposed stress. We have made a number of independent tests of this hypothesis in Manchester, using the SIML.

(a) *Examination stress*: Kane (1987) administered the SIML and Goldberg's (1972) General Health Questionnaire (GHQ) to groups of sixth-formers and undergraduates just before ($n = 245$) and just after ($n = 173$) sitting a major examination. The sample was split into stressed and non-stressed groups on the basis of their GHQ scores. In keeping with the predictions of the stress-vulnerability hypothesis, positive and significant correlations were found in the stressed groups between psychiatric symptomatology and typical rates of cognitive failure over the preceding twelve months. No such relationship was obtained for the non-stressed groups.

(b) *Stresses associated with breast surgery*: In a three-year study at the University Hospital of South Manchester (Lucas *et al.* 1985; Lucas 1986), 100 women were interviewed and tested around the period of their surgery. Sixty-seven of these patients had breast cancer and 33 had benign breast disease. Sixty of the patients with breast cancer and 29 with benign disorders were interviewed again four months after the surgery. Both sets of interviews included the administration of a variety of paper-and-pencil measures, including the SIML (see Reason 1989).

At first interview, SIML scores correlated significantly with the number of psychiatric symptoms reported at that time (0.395; $p < .01$). There was also a significant point-biserial correlation between the SIML total score and the presence of depression. Depressed subjects had higher SIML scores. There was no relationship between the SIML score and the number of negative life events occurring during the 12 months prior to surgery. In addition to supporting the findings of the Oxford group, these results further highlight the relationship between general absent-mindedness and depression (Broadbent *et al.* 1982).

Analysis of the data obtained at the 4-month interview focused on possible predictors of psychiatric morbidity. The dependent measure was the number of psychiatric symptoms yielded by the Present State Questionnaire (Wing *et al.* 1974).

Nine factors accounted for over 35 per cent of the variance in the multiple regression analysis. The following ranking of predictors was obtained using the method of elimination (figures in parentheses indicate the percentage reduction in the R-squared value as each factor is removed): upset by scar (24.2); SIML score (18.6); radiotherapy (14.9); pain in scar (8.0); no confiding tie (7.9); previous psychiatric problems (1.6); children under 14 (0.7); mastectomy (0.5); and difficulty in moving arm (0.3). Thus a marked degree of absent-mindedness (in the year previous to surgery) was a better predictor of psychiatric morbidity than a number of more obviously relevant medical and social factors. The retest reliability of the SIML scores between the first and second interviews was 0.69. This accords with other reliability assessments.

These findings provide strong support for the stress-vulnerability hypothesis, as do those obtained by the Dundee homesickness studies (Fisher and Hood 1987). What are the underlying mechanisms?

One tenable assumption is that people differ characteristically in the way they deploy their limited attentional resources in the face of competing demands. This, in turn, appears to influence the selection of coping strategies (Broadbent *et al.* 1986; Kane 1987). High-error individuals appear to select more resource-intensive strategies and are less able to adjust them to the discretionary aspects of the situation than low-error individuals.

It is not so much that stress induces a high rate of cognitive failure (though that may indeed be so); rather it is that a certain style of cognitive resource-management can lead to both absent-mindedness and to the inappropriate matching of coping measures to stressful situations.

DAILY ERROR-RATINGS AND MOOD

The stress-vulnerability work supports the idea that individual error-proneness is determined by some relatively enduring trait. However, we have now accumulated a reasonable amount of evidence to show that error-rates are also susceptible to state-dependent variations. The research paradigm involves two stages. First, the standard SIML is used to obtain a baseline assessment of previous error-liability. Second, the basic 15 items are assessed on a daily basis to reveal the extent to which each type of cognitive failure is judged as occurring more or less frequently than the typical rate as a consequence of mood changes, feelings of well-being, and point in the menstrual cycle (Lucas *et al.* 1985; Kane 1987; Reason 1989; Wyatt 1991).

One highly reliable result from these studies was that days in which a negative mood state predominates are associated with increased error-rates, and conversely. No comparable variations were found with transition through the menstrual cycle (Wyatt 1991).

Among female patients awaiting admission for a biopsy to establish whether a breast lump was benign or malignant, it was found that certain SIML items were more responsive to stress than others. Those items most sensitive were mind-dwelling, difficulty in concentration, and 'attending but not taking in'. Other SIML items, particularly memory lapses, were reported as increasing by between 7 and 20 per cent during this highly stressful pre-operative period (Lucas *et al.* 1985).

A FORENSIC USE OF THE SIML

Evidence has been presented to show that SRQs, like the CFQ and the SIML, can produce robust and important findings, even if they are sometimes hard to interpret. But what of their practical utility? Have these instruments been of any real use outside the mainly academic sphere?

In this penultimate section, I will discuss a recent trial in which the SIML played an important role in obtaining a 'not guilty' verdict for a man charged with double shop-theft. This episode is also of interest because it involved a technique for convincing a jury of the veracity of the person's responses.

The accused, let us call him Mr X, was charged with leaving a supermarket on two occasions (separated by a week) with goods that had not been paid for at the checkout. Although he was charged with the two offences, Mr X was not stopped on the first occasion, but items apparently observed in a separate front compartment of the trolley did not appear on the till audit. On the second occasion (at which he was arrested) the disputed items were again in the front section of the trolley. Both times, however, a large number of items contained in the body of the trolley had been checked through. On being stopped by the security staff, Mr X apologized, said that he had absentmindedly overlooked the items in the front compartment, and offered to pay for them. This offer was not accepted.

Mr X readily admitted the act, but vehemently denied any intention to steal the goods. There were many circumstantial reasons for believing him; but what is of more relevance here is that Mrs X claimed that her husband was an exceedingly absent-minded man, and wrote a detailed account of his recent slips and lapses.

Retained by the defence solicitors, I interviewed Mr X some months after these events. One of the main purposes was to assess his level of absent-mindedness using the SIML. The SIML was completed twice, once by Mr X in regard to himself and once by Mrs X, who was asked to rate her husband's proneness to each of the 15 cognitive failures. Both tests were carried out in isolation, with each unaware of the other's responses, either then or later. Neither had encountered tests of this kind before, nor knew of their existence. Neither was forewarned of the test, though both readily consented to it. The procedure was modelled upon Donald Broadbent's practice of using 'close others' to check upon the validity of an individual's ratings (Broadbent et al. 1982).

Mr X's SIML result supported his wife's contention that he was an exceedingly absent-minded man. He obtained a total score of 42, placing him on the 95th centile for both sets of normative data (Samples A and B). Mrs X's assessment of his liability (a total score of 47) put him slightly higher than this. There was also a close correspondence between Mr and Mrs X in their judgements of Mr X's

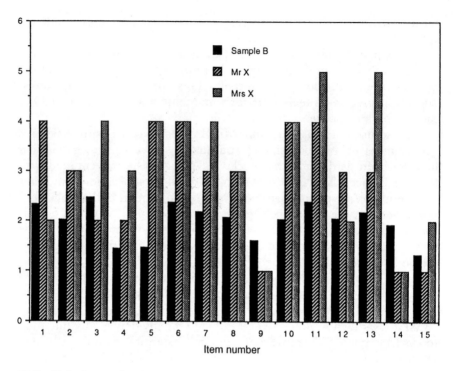

FIG. 20.4. Comparing Short Inventory of Minor Lapses scores for Mr and Mrs X with the Sample B norms. Mrs X's responses related to her husband's perceived absent-mindedness.

proneness to specific forms of cognitive failure, and both profiles reveal a rather unusual pattern, as shown in Fig. 20.4.

The idiosyncratic pattern of Mr X's responses and its close correspondence with his wife's ratings ($r = 0.64$) indicated that both sets of judgements related to the same person; and this, in turn, suggested that both respondents were being truthful. But would this be enough to satisfy a jury? Given the subjective nature of these ratings and the fact that a high absent-mindedness score would be to Mr X's obvious advantage, it was almost certain that prosecuting counsel would direct his cross-examination at challenging the credibility of this evidence.

One way of answering this challenge was to discover what people (of comparable age and intelligence to Mr X) did when they were directly instructed to fake their responses. Twenty-six management students completed the SIML after being told to imagine that they had been accused of shop-lifting and were, in fact, guilty of the offence, but had offered absent-mindedness as a defence. They were then asked to fake

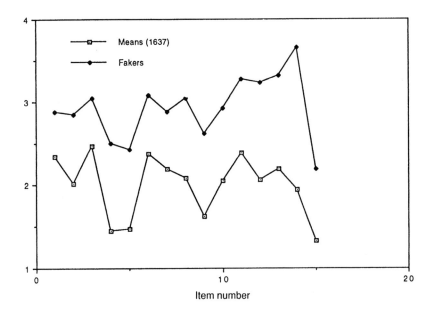

FIG. 20.5. Comparing the mean SIML item scores for the fakers ($n = 26$) with the Sample B norms ($n = 1637$).

their responses, knowing that it was to their advantge to obtain a high score. The results of this exercise are shown in Fig. 20.5.

The first thing to note about these data is that the fakers' profile corresponds very closely to the normative one ($r = 0.77$), but is elevated over the whole range of items. This suggests that the fakers approached their task by first asking themselves how they would normally respond to the item, and then adding a fairly constant 'faking factor'. The one point where this 'faking factor' is unusually large is on Item 14 (mind-wandering when trying to concentrate on something important).

From Fig. 20.6 (see below) it is clear that Mr X did not fit the faking pattern of responses. The correlation between these profiles was only 0.11. On items 9, 14, and 15, Mr X's scores were approaching 1 standard deviation below those of the normative samples.

Clearly, no one of these pieces of evidence was sufficient to establish Mr X's innocence; but (together with other circumstantial factors) they added up to a 'reasonable doubt' that his actions might, in fact, be commensurate with a high degree of absent-mindedness, rather than with a deliberate intent to steal.

The picture that emerged of Mr X was of someone acutely aware of his natural proneness to distraction, but who had worked hard to improve his powers of concentration for professional purposes. The resulting almost cat-like ability to sustain a narrow attentional focus, while essential in his work, very nearly proved to be his undoing in the supermarket.

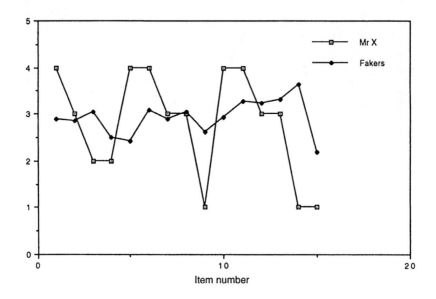

FIG. 20.6. Comparing Mr X's SIML profile with that for the fakers.

CONCLUSIONS

No technique that, of necessity, collects its target data via the distorting media of memory and impressionistic judgement is ever going to be more than a blunt instrument. But SRQs share this difficulty with a wide variety of workable psychological methods. One of the methodological problems of cognitive psychology is that reasonably accurate and well-controlled measurements of highly specific processes often lack ecological validity, while the more global or stylistic features of cognition, pervading many aspects of mental life, are rarely amenable to precise assessment. The answer, as Donald Broadbent's work has amply demonstrated, is to use a well-stocked toolbag and to employ a variety of methods in concert.

In this paper, I have examined one particular member of the SRQ family in some detail. The principal findings of these SIML studies are summarized below.

1. Judgements of the relative frequency of 15 slips, lapses, and attentional problems are highly consistent over two large normative samples. The characteristic shape of the 15-item profile remains relatively stable even when subjects are asked to fake their responses so as to exaggerate their normal level of absent-mindedness.

2. While there are no clear differences between the sexes, there is a highly significantly decline with age in the reported frequency of most slips and lapses. The one recurring exception is that older people report significantly more occasions when they have difficulty in recalling names. The bases of these age differences, whether real or artefactual, are not well understood.

3. Two Manchester studies, involving severe real-life stresses, have produced clear support for Broadbent's stress-vulnerability hypothesis. High-scoring SIML subjects show significantly greater evidence of psychiatric symptoms on exposure to externally-imposed stresses such as examinations and breast-cancer surgery. These and other findings suggest that instruments like the CFQ and the SIML are tapping the characteristic ways in which people deploy their limited attentional resources in the face of competing informational demands. These individual differences in 'cognitive management' appear to affect the way people select strategies for coping with stress. Those people with a typically high level of everyday slips and lapses tend to employ maladaptive, resource-intensive strategies.

4. Several studies involving daily error-ratings in relation to a SIML-established baseline indicate that the incidence of everyday slips and lapses is influenced by state-dependent as well as trait-like factors. Days in which a negative mood state predominates are associated with relatively increased rates of minor slips and lapses, though these rates were not affected by position within the menstrual cycle.

5. The paper concluded with an account of an idiographic application of the SIML in defence of a man accused of shop theft. This individual scored on the 95th centile for the SIML, and a number of methods were used to convince the jury of the truthfulness of his responses. Deliberate fakers appear, first, to judge their own normal liability to each SIML item, and then to add a fairly constant 'faking factor'. The resulting profile, though elevated across the 15-item range, mirrors the normative profile quite closely. The accused man's profile was widely discrepant from that of the fakers.

ACKNOWLEDGEMENTS

I gratefully acknowledge the work of Professor Patrick Rabbitt and his colleagues in the Age and Cognitive Performance Research Centre at the University of Manchester. They administered and scored the SIMLs for the 343 elderly subjects, described in Sample A. I am also greatly indebted to Dr Deborah Lucas, the senior research associate on the Withington Hospital breast-cancer project, and to Mrs Dianne Parker, senior research associate of the Manchester Driver Behaviour Group, who collected and analysed the Sample B data. Finally, I must thank Professors Willem Wagenaar and Patrick Hudson, of Leiden University, for their invaluable help and advice in the matter of Mr X's defence.

REFERENCES

Broadbent, D. E., Cooper, P. J., Fitzgerald, P. F., and Parkes, K. R. (1982). The Cognitive Failures Questionnaire (CFQ) and its correlates. *British Journal of Clinical Psychology*, **21**, 1–16.

Broadbent, D. E., Broadbent, M. H. P., and Jones, J. L. (1986). Correlates of cognitive failure. *British Journal of Clinical Psychology*, **25**, 285–99.

Brown, G. M. (1990). Knowledge retrieval and frequency maps. Ph.D. Thesis, University of Manchester.

Cohen, G. and Faulkner, D. (1984). Everyday memory in the over-sixties. *New Scientist*, October.

Fisher, S. and Hood, B. (1987). *Mobility history and psychological disturbance following transition to university.* Department of Psychology, University of Dundee.

Goldberg, D. P. (1972). *The detection of psychiatric illness by questionnaire.* Oxford University Press.

Herrmann, D. J. (1982). Know thy memory: the use of questionnaires to assess and study memory. *Psychological Bulletin*, **92**, 434–52.

Herrmann, D. J. (1984). Questionnaires about memory. In *Everyday memory, actions and absent-mindedness* (ed. J. Harris and P. Morris), pp. 133–51. Academic Press, New York.

James, W. (1890). *The principles of psychology.* Henry Holt & Co., New York.

Kane, G. (1987). Studies of coping in stressed populations. Unpublished Ph.D. thesis, University of Manchester.

Lucas, D. A. (1986). Predicting psychiatric morbidity in women treated surgically for breast cancer. Paper given to the Annual Conference of the British Psychological Society.

Lucas, D. A., Reason, J. T., Maguire, G. P., Goldberg, D., Sellwood, R., and Bawako, L. (1985). *Absent-mindedness and stress in breast cancer patients*, Report to North West Regional Health Authority. The Authority, Manchester.

Martin, M. and Jones, G. V. (1984). Cognitive failues in everyday life. In *Everyday memory, actions and absent-mindedness* (ed. J. Harris and P. Morris), pp. 173–90. Academic Press, New York.

Morris, P. E. (1984). The validity of subjective reports. In *Everyday memory, actions and absent-mindedness* (ed. J. Harris and P. Morris), pp. 153–72. Academic Press, New York.

Nisbett, R. and Ross, L. (1980). *Human inference: strategies and shortcomings of social judgment*. Prentice-Hall, Englewood Cliffs, NJ.

Rabbitt, P. and Abson, V. (1990). 'Lost and found': some logical and methodological limitations of self-report questionnaires as tools to study cognitive ageing. *British Journal of Psychology*, **81**, 1–16.

Rabbitt, P. and Abson, V. (1991). Do older people know how good they are? *British Journal of Psychology*, **82**, 137–51.

Reason, J. T. (1979). Actions not as planned: the price of automatization. In *Aspects of consciousness, Vol. I: Psychological issues* (ed. G. Underwood and R. Stevens), pp. 67–90. Academic Press, London.

Reason, J. T. (1984). Lapses of attention. In *Varieties of attention* (ed. R Parasuraman and R. Davies), pp. 515–49. Academic Press, New York.

Reason, J. T. (1989). Stress and cognitive failure. In *Handbook of life stress, cognition and health* (ed. S. Fisher and J. Reason), pp. 405–21. Wiley, Chichester.

Reason, J. T. and Lucas, D. (1984). Absent-mindedness in shops: its correlates and consequences. *British Journal of Clinical Psychology*, **23**, 121–31.

Reason, J. T., Manstead, A. S. R., Stradling, S. G., Parker, D., and Baxter, J. S. (1991). *The social and cognitive determinants of aberrant driving behaviour*, Contractor Report 253. Transport and Road Research Laboratory, Crowthorne, Berks.

Tversky, A. and Kahneman, D. (1974). Judgment under uncertainty: heuristics and bias. *Science*, **185**, 1124–31.

Wing, J. K., Cooper, J. E., and Sartorius, N. (1974). *The measurement and classification of psychiatric symptoms*. Cambridge University Press.

Wyatt, C. (1991). Variations in daily error rates with mood and menstrual cycle. Final year project, University of Manchester.

Zechmeister, E. B. and Nyberg, S. E. (1982). *Human memory: an introduction to research and theory*. Brooks/Cole Publishing Company, Monterey, California.

Name Index

Subject Index

accidents, road, influenza and 309
Acoustical Society of America xiv
action
  control of 155–6, 171–84
  see also motivation
Advisory Committee on the Safety of
    Nuclear Installations xv
age 188–228
  automaticity and 265, 267, 269, 278
  self-report questionnaires and 408–14
agnosia 255–6
AH4 IQ test 189, 194, 207–11
AIDS 321–2, 323
aircraft cockpits 120, 129, 333
air-traffic control 116–17, 121, 122, 124,
  125–9, 333
alarms (warning signals) 392–3, 394–5,
  396–7, 400–1
  design of 130–1
alcohol 225
alexia 255–6
Alzheimer's disease 161–5, 396
American Psychological Association xiv
amnesia
  anterograde 293
  childhood 293
  implicit processing and 244, 255–6, 261,
    265, 277, 293
amphetamine 355
anaesthesia 265, 291–3
anoetic awareness 287, 291, 293
anxiety 352, 354, 362–4, 375, 383
aphasia 255–6
Applied Psychology Unit (MRC) xii–xiv,
  36, 152, 304, 350
arousal 304, 353–67, 390–402
articulatory (phonological) loop 154–5, 166,
  167, 223–4, 226
artificial-grammar learning 246–57 *passim*
artificial intelligence 173, 175
associative network model 376–80, 384–7
attentional template(s) 58–61, 62
Attention Deficit Disorder 362, 398–9
auditory distraction 88–98
automaticity 261–79
autonoetic awareness 287, 289, 291, 292,
  293
awareness 263, 287–94
  consciousness and 290–1
  levels of 287, 291–4

basoventral region 182, 184
blindsight 235–45, 255–6, 261
boats and ships 116–17, 122–3
brain 54–5, 59–61, 72–3
  age and 191, 197–8, 199
  blindsight and 236, 243
  damage 61–2, 64–7, 79–80, 174–84,
    235–45, 394–6, 397
    post-viral fatigue syndrome and 323
  immune system and 315, 324
  posterior attention network 390–402
  prefrontal regions of 181–2, 184
British Association for the Advancement of
    Science xiii
British Broadcasting Corporation (BBC) xiii
British Psychological Society xiii, xiv, 111
Brixton Spatial Anticipation test 178–81,
  184

caffeine 355, 362–3, 365, 367
Cambridge, University of xi–xii, xiv
central executive 154, 155–7, 167–8
  Alzheimer's disease and 161–5
  chess and 157–61
chess 157–61
Cognitive Failures Questionnaire 406
'cognitive tunnel vision' 122–3
colds 307–8, 309, 311, 315–19
Common Cold Unit (MRC) 310–14, 319,
  323–4
Confidence Accuracy Slope model 257
conjunctions 17, 19–21
  filtering by movement and 74–7, 81, 82–5
  of parts 21, 26–7
  within-dimension 7–8
consciousness 283–95
  awareness and 290–1
  forms of 287, 291–4
  memory and 287–94
  process-dissociation procedure and
    265–70, 276–9
  unitary 283–4
contention scheduling 172–84
contrast, direction of 10–12
control systems (workplace)
  air-traffic 116–17, 121, 122, 124, 125–9,
    333
  implicit learning and 247–55 *passim*
  industrial 116–17, 122, 124–5, 129
    automatic 123